Property of
Briarcliff Manor U.F.S.D.
Superintendent's Office
45 Ingham Road
Briarcliff Manor, NY 10510

P9-CEO-036

THE OVERACHIEVERS

ALSO BY ALEXANDRA ROBBINS

Pledged: The Secret Life of Sororities

*Secrets of the Tomb: Skull and Bones, the Ivy League,
and the Hidden Paths of Power*

*Conquering Your Quarterlife Crisis: Advice from Twentysomethings
Who Have Been There and Survived*

THE
OVERAC

HIEVERS

The Secret Lives of Driven Kids

ALEXANDRA ROBBINS

New York

Copyright © 2006 Alexandra Robbins

All rights reserved. No part of this book may be used or reproduced in any manner whatsoever without the written permission of the Publisher. Printed in the United States of America. For information address Hyperion, 77 West 66th Street, New York, New York 10023-6298.

Library of Congress Cataloging-in-Publication Data

Robbins, Alexandra
  The overachievers : the secret lives of driven kids / Alexandra Robbins.— 1st ed.
    p. cm.
  ISBN 1-4013-0201-7
    1. Overachievement.   2. Overachievement—Case studies.   I. Title.
  BF637.O94R625 2006
  305.2350973—dc22   2006041244

Hyperion books are available for special promotions and premiums. For details contact Michael Rentas, Assistant Director, Inventory Operations, Hyperion, 77 West 66th Street, 12th floor, New York, New York 10023, or call 212-456-0133.

Design by Renato Stanisic

FIRST EDITION

10 9 8 7 6 5 4 3 2 1

DEDICATED WITH LOVE TO
MISSY, ANDREW, IRA, JO, IRVING, RACHEL, MARTY, SEENA,
AND DAVE

Chapter 1

July 20–September 1

MEET THE OVERACHIEVERS

JULIE, SENIOR | PERCEIVED AS: THE SUPERSTAR

On the surface, Julie seemed to have it all. A straight-A student without exception since sixth grade, she took a rigorous high school curriculum that had included eight Advanced Placement classes thus far. Walt Whitman High School's most talented female distance runner since her freshman year, Julie had co-captained the varsity cross-country, indoor track, and outdoor track teams as a junior. School and local newspapers constantly heralded her athletic accomplishments. An aspiring triathlete, Julie was president and co-founder of the Hiking Vikings Club (named for Whitman's mascot), a yoga fanatic, a member of the Spanish Honors Society, and a big buddy to a child at a homeless shelter.

As a freshman and sophomore, Julie was one of three elected class officers and, as a junior, co–sports editor and co–student life editor of the yearbook before she quit. To top it off, she was a naturally pretty sixteen-year-old with a bright, mesmerizing smile, cascading dark blond ringlets, and a slender figure that she was known for dressing stylishly. Her friends constantly told her that boys had crushes on her, though she rarely picked up on those things. She was currently dating her first real boyfriend, a family friend headed to college in the fall. There were students at Whitman who revered her.

Julie had earned her summer vacation. Junior year had been stressful, both academically and socially. She took eight academic classes the first semester, skipping lunch to squeeze in an extra course. Socially, she began to question whether she belonged in her tight-knit clique of fourteen girls, a group other students knew as the River Falls crew, even though only a handful of the girls lived in that suburban Maryland neighborhood. Though Julie had known many of them since elementary school, she didn't feel comfortable opening up to them. Even in that large group of girls, she still felt alone.

Throughout her junior year, Julie's hair gradually had begun to thin. In June her concerned mother took her to the doctor. After the blood tests returned normal results, the doctor informed her that thinning hair was "not unheard of among junior girls, as stress can cause hair loss." Julie told no one at school about her ordeal. She was able to bulldoze through junior year with the hope that, if she pushed herself for just a little while longer, she would have a good shot at getting into her dream school. She had wanted to go to Stanford ever since she fell in love with the campus during a middle school visit. It seemed natural to her to aim high.

One summer evening, Julie was buying a striped T-shirt at J. Crew when she heard a squeal. A Whitman student who had graduated in May was bounding toward her. The graduate didn't even bother with small talk before firing off college questions: "So where are you applying early?" Julie demurely dodged the question with a polite smile and a wave of her hand.

The graduate wasn't deterred. "Well, where are you applying to college?"

"I don't know," Julie said, keeping her mouth upturned.

"Where have you visited?"

"Some New England schools," Julie said, and changed the subject. *So this is what the year will be like,* Julie thought. *Endless questions and judgments based entirely on the name of a school.* Julie hadn't decided where she would apply. She wondered if the pressure simply to *know* was going to be as intense as the pressure to get in.

Julie's parents had hired a private college counselor to help her work through these decisions. Julie was excited for her first serious meeting with the counselor, who worked mostly with students in a competitive Virginia school district. Julie had been waiting for years to reap the benefits of her years of diligence. At last she felt like she could speak openly about her college aspirations without fear of sounding cocky.

Normally not one to saunter, Julie glided into Vera von Helsinger's office, relaxed and self-assured. She crossed her long, tanned legs and politely folded her hands in her lap. After mundane small talk with Julie and her mother, Vera asked for Julie's statistics and activities. Julie listed them proudly: a 4.0 unweighted GPA, a combined score of 1410 out of 1600 on the SAT, good SAT II scores, a 5 on the Advanced Placement Chemistry and English Language exams, and a 4 on the Government exam. When Julie told her college counselor about her extracurricular load, triathleticism, and interest in science, Vera proclaimed her "mildly interesting."

Julie handed Vera a list she had taken the initiative to compile from *Outside* magazine's annual ranking of top forty schools based on their outdoor opportunities. Julie's list began with Stanford, Dartmouth, Williams, Middlebury, the University of Virginia, UC Santa Cruz, and the University of Miami. Vera asked, "Is there anyone else at Whitman who has the same personality as you?"

"No," Julie said in her typically breathy voice. "I consider myself an individual."

"Well, Taylor is kind of a do-er," Julie's mother pointed out.

Julie nodded. "Taylor is an athlete who wants to apply early to Stanford," she said. Julie's friend Taylor also was active in school and a good student, especially in math and science. "I guess you can also say Derek." Rumor was that Julie's friend Derek, widely considered Whitman's resident genius, scored his perfect 1600 on the SAT without studying until the night before the test. He had mentioned that Stanford might be his first choice.

Vera said she considered herself a "brutally honest" person, but Julie was nonetheless taken aback when the counselor told her not to bother applying early to Stanford because she was unlikely to get in. Applying early to that kind of a reach school, Vera said, was not a strategic move to make in the game of college applications.

Julie was crushed. She hadn't been dreaming of the California campus for so many years only to be told that even sending in an application was a waste of time. Applying early to a school she wasn't in love with didn't make sense to her. "What . . . what would it take for me to get into Stanford?" she stammered.

"You would have to have lived in Mongolia for two years or have been in a civil war," Vera replied.

Julie looked at her mother and rolled her eyes. *I've done everything*

3

within my power that I can do, Julie thought. *It's not my fault I live a normal life!* Vera caught the glance. It was so difficult to get into college these days, she told Julie, that if she didn't have her lineup of interesting extracurriculars, the best school she could consider was George Washington University. *I don't have a chance at my dream school when I've done everything right,* Julie thought, feeling helpless. If Taylor and Derek got into Stanford and she didn't apply because of a counselor's strategy, she would be angry, because she was just as qualified.

After the meeting, Julie channeled her frustration into a journal entry:

The mix of schools on my list must have been bewildering to Vera because she asked how much prestige mattered to me. Evaluating the importance of prestige reminded me of shopping. Some people only like clothes once they find out they are designer—Seven jeans, Juicy Couture shirts, North Face fleeces—but I get much more satisfaction out of getting the same look (or, in my humble opinion, a better look) from no-name brands. The label matters to a lot of people, but not to me. Unfortunately, I don't feel the same way about college. I wish I could have said that it doesn't matter and that I know I can be successful anywhere, but I grew up in Potomac and go to Whitman, so obviously prestige is important to me. As an example, Vera asked me to choose between UC Santa Cruz and Cornell. I deliberated for quite a while, trying to will myself to say Santa Cruz. Santa Cruz is beautiful on the outside, but I hear Cornell is, too. Also, I always hear about the people who commit suicide at Cornell, while everyone is supposedly happy and totally chill at Santa Cruz. However, Cornell is in the Ivy League, which would make it attractive to many people. "They both have their pros and cons," I said diplomatically.

Vera is also really into the whole early-decision craze. I can't see myself applying to any school early except Stanford, because how do I know that school is perfect for me? I love all those New England schools except for one thing: the cold. I don't even know that Stanford is perfect, but there is something about that location that screams perfection. But it's all a game of odds. I could settle to apply early somewhere else and then be rejected. Or, I could "waste" my early decision on Stanford when I could have gotten into Williams early (especially since I have been in contact with the coach). It is a lot to think about.

**After shaking Vera's hand, I walked out of the office. I felt like I
was leaving something behind, but then realized it was only my
confidence that she had stolen from me.**

Julie had no idea what her college counselor really thought of her.
But I did.

I was not supposed to be a part of this story. As a journalist, I view my
role as that of an observer, not a participant. As a storyteller, I like the
novelesque quality of scenes in which readers forget that a reporter
buffers them from the "characters." For the rest of this book, my perspective will be absent from the students' stories. In this case, however,
it's important to share how I got in the way.

When Julie and her mother invited me to accompany them on their
second official visit to the college counselor, I readily agreed. I was interested to see whether Julie would stand by her personal preferences or
decide the "expert" knew best. We agreed that Julie's mother would tell
the college counselor I would join them. The day before the meeting, I
learned that Vera wanted to speak with me.

The college counselor informed me that she had a "near-perfect
record" of getting her students into elite universities. Julie, she said, was
far behind the rest of her clients in the application process. "All my
other students are almost done. Julie hasn't even started her essays," she
said. (Julie, who was itching to write her essays, had told me that Vera
instructed her not to start them.) Then Vera hit me with something unexpected. She said, "She's not a great student. She's not going to get
into a top college." And if I, as a reporter, happened to follow one of
her clients who didn't end up getting into such a school, Vera told me,
her reputation would be "slammed."

Brutally honest, indeed. It was hard to believe we were discussing
the same girl: straight-A, Advanced Placement student, three-sport
varsity captain, triathlete, excellent writer, a girl with a passion for
science . . . At first I assured Vera that she could be anonymous in this
book, with no identifying details disclosed. "Oh, anonymity isn't the issue. I wouldn't mind my name in there. It's publicity," she said. She told
me she would love to be interviewed, she could introduce me to people,

she had so much to say. "I can be helpful in other ways!" she said eagerly. I was perplexed. The conversation ended unresolved.

The next morning Vera left a message on my voice mail: "Julie and I have decided to postpone our meeting."

Now that the afternoon was free, I called Julie to see if she wanted to get lunch instead. While on the phone, I asked her why she and Vera had postponed the meeting. "Oh, wow," she breathed in an even more halting voice than usual. "Um . . . Well, Vera told my father that she wouldn't work with me if I worked with you."

I was mortified. Julie's family had barely gotten to know me, and already my presence in their lives, which was supposed to be as a sideline spectator, was an obstacle in the very process through which I hoped to follow Julie. I called Vera to tell her that I wouldn't attend her meetings, I wouldn't mention anything about her if she kept Julie on as a client, and it wasn't worth dropping Julie because of me. But I was too late. Vera had delivered her ultimatum. She maintained that if a reporter shadowed one of the few clients she had who she believed wouldn't be accepted into an elite school, then Vera's record would be ruined. It was either Vera or me.

I backed off. For days I waited on pins and needles for the situation to be settled one way or the other. Then one afternoon I got a call from Julie. "This is going to make a great college essay!" she said. "My college counselor fired me!"

AUDREY, JUNIOR | PERCEIVED AS: THE PERFECTIONIST

Audrey's alarm rang at 6:10 A.M., but she didn't awaken until 6:40. For the first time since she could remember, she didn't get up early on the first day of school. In prior years, she had beaten her alarm, excited to get the year started, her outfit chosen well in advance. But this year, junior year, would be different. She could feel it already. She had spent much of the previous night rereading her assigned summer books. She had finished the reading days ago, even annotating every page of the optional book, but didn't realize until the night before school started that she was also supposed to define vocabulary words from the literature. Until 2:30 A.M. Audrey pored through the hundreds of pages of all four books again in order to get the assignment done perfectly.

Audrey could pinpoint the beginning of her perfectionism to the moment. At age six, she was in a two-year combination class for first- and second-graders. Midway through the year, Audrey's teacher persuaded her parents to make her officially a second-grader instead of a first-grader. That year Audrey had a homework assignment to decorate a rock as an animal. Other kids spent forty-five minutes on the project and were satisfied. Audrey spent all day gluing pipe cleaners and googly eyes to the rock, hysterically crying when she couldn't get the pink construction-paper nose exactly as she wanted, desperately trying to prove herself worthy of second grade by producing the perfect rock puppy.

Now, in high school, when Audrey's teachers assigned reading, she wouldn't just read; she would type several pages of single-spaced notes about the material. When studying for exams, she would then rewrite, in neat longhand, every word of her typed notes. She couldn't help it. Audrey couldn't do work that was merely good enough. It had to be the best.

Worried she would be late for carpool, Audrey grabbed a denim skirt out of her closet, fretting briefly about its length—Whitman's dress code mandated that it fall below her fingertips. She yanked on a polo and a cotton long-sleeved sweater over her wavy golden hair, because the school's air-conditioning made her small frame shiver. She wolfed down some of the eggs her Puerto Rican father had cooked for her, hefted her bulging backpack, and bolted out the door.

The carpool driver must have noticed that the juniors in his car were particularly unhappy to be returning to school. "How do you feel about waking up early?" he asked. Audrey laughed from the backseat, her braces gleaming. Audrey and C.J., her best friend until recently, had spent the summer lifeguarding the first shift at the neighborhood pool, so they were used to waking up early. But Audrey privately wondered why she had so much trouble getting out of bed that morning. For the first time on a school day, she didn't even have time to finish her breakfast. She wondered if her already shifting schedule was an ominous sign. She had heard rumors about how junior year, the most important year for a college résumé, could wallop even the most accomplished student.

The car pulled into the school driveway with minutes to spare before first period began at 7:25. Before Walt Whitman High School was renovated in 1992, it had been a nondescript building except for its gym, a magnificent enclosed dome. When the new building was erected, the beloved dome was torn down. Now the school's green-trimmed brick facade resembled a Nordstrom department store.

Audrey followed the throng of students trying to squeeze through the green double doors of the main entrance. Even though it wasn't yet 70 degrees, the 96 percent humidity, typical for August in Bethesda, Maryland, left a heaviness in the air. The new principal, Dr. Goodwin, stood inside, amiably chatting with students who clustered in the halls, scanning the lists of alphabetical homeroom assignments posted on sheets of paper taped to the walls. Audrey was relieved to see that among the girls in jeans and capris, there were plenty with skirts much shorter than hers. She found her homeroom on a sheet posted next to the main office, not far from a framed *Newsweek* cover and a plaque commemorating Whitman as one of America's best high schools.

Audrey took advantage of much of what Whitman had to offer. She was particularly devoted to the school's award-winning newspaper, the *Black & White,* which arguably took more time and energy on a daily basis than any other extracurricular activity at Whitman. The student-run paper, with a staff of about 115, was printed about every two weeks as a sixteen-page issue along with *The Spectator,* an eight-page sports and arts supplement. The paper's professionalism rivaled that of many college newspapers. The harder Audrey worked this year as a reporter, the better the editorial position she would get in May, when the seniors who ran the paper announced the following year's appointments. She had her eye on the top three positions.

Audrey walked into her second-period Advanced Placement English class and stopped short, surprised to see the seats full of seniors. She looked again at her schedule. She was in the right room at the right period. "Audrey!" said a senior she knew, "you're in the wrong room!"

Confused, Audrey returned to the hallway. She knew she had read her schedule correctly. *If I go in again, they're going to laugh at me because I'm a junior and I can't find my classroom,* she thought. Known for being assertive, she walked back into the room. "Excuse me," she stammered to the teacher, her hands flapping as she tried to explain. "My name is Audrey. I'm a junior, and I think they—they put me in your class." She tried to ignore the seniors, who were now laughing at her, and handed her schedule to the teacher.

"You're right, they enrolled you in the wrong class," the teacher said.

"What should I do?"

"Go down to guidance."

Her face beet red, Audrey went downstairs to the guidance office, thinking that anything that could possibly go wrong with her schedule usually did, like on her first day in middle school, when the school didn't even have her name down as an enrolled student. The line to speak to a guidance counselor was half an hour long. If Audrey had any work to do, she would have started on it right away, but she didn't, which meant the waiting period was a major waste of time. Good grades were important to her, as they were to her parents.

By the time her counselor fixed her schedule, Audrey had missed the entire period. At lunch, Audrey slid into an empty seat at a table where friends were talking about junior Advanced Placement English, the class Audrey had missed. "We already have all this work!" they complained. *Great,* Audrey thought. *It's only the first day, and I'm already behind.* That instant was when it hit her that she might never catch up.

AP FRANK, COLLEGE FRESHMAN | PERCEIVED AS: THE WORKHORSE

His hand tucked sheepishly in a pocket, AP Frank, he of Whitman lore, ducked through the main doors into the school building just after second lunch began. Immediately, he was surrounded. "AP Frank!" squealed a girl who launched herself into a bear hug that widened his shy grin into a full-on beam. He greeted his younger brother, a Whitman junior, as he continued down the hall to the lunchtime hot spots in search of Sam, a senior friend he had come back to visit.

On his way to the music hallway, where he thought he might find Sam, AP Frank was stopped repeatedly by students he didn't know. "Hey, AP Frank, what are you doing here?" they asked.

"I'm bored, so I'm coming here to see some people," he replied.

"What do you want to major in at college?" they pressed.

AP Frank shrugged and moved on.

A tall kid in an orange shirt stopped directly in front of him. AP Frank had never seen this person before.

"Legendary AP Frank! What are you doing here?" the kid asked.

AP Frank smiled uncertainly. "School hasn't started yet, and I'm really bored."

The kid nodded. "What's your major going to be?"

"I don't know."

The kid smirked. "Come on, man, *you* really don't know?"

"I don't know, man." AP Frank wouldn't even be a college freshman for another ten days.

"You're AP Frank," the kid insisted. "You don't want to be a doctor or a politician or something?"

AP Frank still found it strange that so many students at his old high school knew who he was, or thought they did—a far cry from when he first arrived as a timid sophomore transfer. He grew accustomed to his reputation as a lovable geek, though he was embarrassed when, at the graduation ceremony in June, then-principal Jerome Marco—himself a Whitman legend—praised him in front of everyone. What weighed on AP Frank most heavily were the expectations.

Whitman students—many of whom wanted to be him, many of whose parents pushed them to emulate him—didn't know AP Frank as well as they thought. Expectations from strangers probably wouldn't have bothered him if they hadn't suffocated his home life for as long as he could remember. By the time AP Frank and his brother Richard arrived at Whitman, the pressure had become routine. Each afternoon, as soon as the brothers got home from school, they were expected to sit at their desks in their adjacent bedrooms and study, backs to the hallway, doors open. From an office chair stationed in the hall, positioned precisely so that she could see every move the boys made, their mother peered at them over her newspaper. And she watched them. From 2:30 in the afternoon until they went to sleep, with only a quick break for a dinner of Hot Pockets, gyoza, kimchee, or a microwaved meal, and a half-hour time-out to watch either NBC or ABC News, she watched them.

If the brothers so much as looked up from their homework for more than a passing glance, she snapped at them to return to their studies. Even when they stood up to go to the bathroom or to grab a glass of orange juice from the kitchen, if they were out of range for longer than five or ten minutes, she reeled them back in. They could not chat on the phone; she screened their calls. They could not watch non-news television; she deemed it "junk." They could not go out with friends; she did not approve of social activities. In Mrs. AP Frank's household, which was small and cluttered—perhaps only twenty-four square inches of the dining room table were visible—there was no idle computer time, no athletics. Mrs. AP Frank was "against extracurriculars," including sports, that "won't get you into medicine or law."

Sometimes during the school year, AP Frank would peek into the hallway to see that his mother had dozed off behind her newspaper. The moment her eyes closed, he scampered to the computer in her bedroom, where he would sign on to instant messenger and gab with friends. His brother would wait five more minutes to make sure their mother truly was out, then tiptoe either to the other computer in the hall or downstairs to watch TV. Inevitably, Mrs. AP Frank would wake up, see that her boys weren't at their desks, and quietly, very quietly, sneak up behind them to catch them in the act of non-studying.

For years AP Frank thought he had some sort of sixth sense about her; although he couldn't hear her, he would somehow know when she was approaching him in time to minimize the windows on the computer seconds before she appeared. "I'm just looking up something in the encyclopedia," he would say. She would smack him on the head and tell him to get back to his room. The last time this had happened, soon before he finished his senior year, AP Frank realized he didn't have that sixth sense after all. It turned out that light reflected off the periphery of his wire-rimmed glasses so that, just beneath his floppy black bangs, he could glimpse his mother's shadow looming ever larger behind him.

Lately, when AP Frank was in the shower, letting the water run over him, lost in his thoughts until he forgot where he was, he would suddenly realize he was only days away from college, days away from moving out. He was ready to go. He would miss his friends, most of whom had already left for school, which was why he was visiting Whitman. But it seemed that wherever he went in Bethesda, he couldn't escape the expectations.

Orange Shirt Kid's interrogation echoed the arguments AP Frank was already having at home about his major. His mother demanded that he be certain, before he arrived on campus, that he was going to major in biology as a pre-med student or political science as a pre-law student. AP Frank wasn't interested in either of those supposedly pre-programmed paths. Classes were still weeks away, and he would have advisers—real advisers—to help him choose. The other day he had mentioned to his mother that he might like to take an environmental science class.

"No," she replied.

"But there's this website that rated the environmental science professors really well. And the class isn't too hard, so I could get an A," he lobbied.

"Are you crazy?" she said in her thick Korean accent. Her tone was a mixture of indignation, anger, and disgust that filled AP Frank with loathing. She used it with her sons and her quiet Caucasian husband, whom she met on a military base in Korea, where AP Frank was born. "If major in biology, you take these classes freshman year"—she ticked off the usual suspects—"and these sophomore year." She harped on AP Frank until he told her he would consider biology. But the idea of her assigning his college course load, as she had done throughout high school, mortified him. He couldn't let her guilt him into fulfilling a path she had predetermined.

It could be argued, however, that her strategy had worked, and now AP Frank feared she would do the same to his younger brother. In AP Frank's junior year, she signed him up for an eight-period day consisting only of Advanced Placement courses. The fact that he had no lunch because he was taking eight classes during Whitman's seven-period day wasn't rare among Whitman's top students (he didn't have a lunch period at Whitman until second semester senior year), but his Advanced Placement course load was. Senior year, his mother signed AP Frank up for seven classes plus a two-hour daily internship at the National Institutes of Health, which translated to a nine-period school day. AP Frank came home, studied until 2:00 A.M. or later, and then woke up for school at 6:30. He routinely fell asleep in class.

Despite the physical and mental tolls of his mother's whip, all of her efforts had landed AP Frank the ultimate perfectionist student's holy grails. (As he saw it, he had "taken everything she threw" at him.) She demanded he earn a 4.0 unweighted GPA—straight As—throughout high school, despite the brutal class schedule. He complied. She ordered 800s on all of his SAT II subject tests. He delivered. She would not accept anything less than a perfect 1600 score on the SAT; when his 1570 horrified her, he retook the test and got the 1600. All of these stepping-stones, she told him, were necessary to get into the college of her choice. And he did. Early. If he had been left to manage his studies on his own, he wouldn't have chosen to be the Perfect Student. He would have focused more on making friends and allowed himself to get a B once in a while.

Instead, he did everything she asked so that she would leave him alone, so that she would realize she didn't need to control him because he was capable on his own. Only now, when he could see himself through the eyes of complete strangers who cornered him at Whitman, did he understand that by proving he could handle her demands, he managed to confirm for his mother that the way she raised him had worked. "I'm scared," he told a friend. "I don't want to be a stress freak for the rest of my life. I'm becoming someone I don't think I can be. These expectations aren't mine, and I don't see why I should live up to them. I'm eventually going to have to break out."

AP Frank longed to emerge from the shell of his mother's influence, but it was so overbearing that it had become a part of his identity. It was the reason why two of his buddies had come up with his nickname in the spring of sophomore year, and the reason the nickname stuck. It was the reason that the principal, who thought the world of AP Frank, had him stand up in front of thousands during graduation. "This is such a smart class," Dr. Marco said to the audience, "that we even have an Advanced Placement Presidential Scholar. [Mrs. AP Frank] wanted her son to take every AP class there was. She even wanted us to give him an AP PE," he joked. And AP Frank was embarrassed, because of his mother, because of himself, and because of his achievement: A typical gung-ho overachiever would take perhaps seven AP classes and exams during his high school career. AP Frank took seventeen.

He would find out only later that the principal hadn't been joking. At some point during the school year, his mother had indeed called up Dr. Marco, infuriated, demanding to know why there wasn't an AP gym class so that AP Frank could have a perfect weighted GPA of 5.0.

✑

This is not just a book about overachievers. It is not just a book about students like AP Frank, who grapples with parental pressure; Audrey, whose perfectionism overshadows her life; and Julie, who struggles with finding her place. Although all of the main characters begin the book at Whitman, this is not just a book about high school. This is a book about how a culture of overachieverism has changed the school experience so drastically in even the last ten years that it has startlingly altered what it means to be a student today.

I should know. I didn't choose to follow students for three semesters at Walt Whitman High School because it is one of the best public schools in the United States or because it is located in Bethesda, which has been called "the smartest city" in the country. I selected Whitman because in the mid-1990s, in many ways I was these students, rushing through the same hallways, cramming anxiously for tests in the same classrooms, battling rivals on the same varsity fields. Walt Whitman, my alma mater, was where I became an overachiever, and during the year of my ten-year reunion, I went back to discover firsthand what had changed.

In present-day America, school for many students has become a competitive frenzy. The high school environment is no longer about a student's pre-adult exploration with the goal of narrowing down likes and dislikes so that he or she ultimately can choose a college curriculum, vocational school, or career path that fits. Instead, it has become a hotbed for Machiavellian strategy in which students (and parents) pile on AP after AP, activity after activity, acclaim after acclaim, with the goal of tailoring high school résumés for what they often feel will be the defining moment of their lives: the college admissions process. Never mind if students don't care about the prestige level of their post–high school tracks; never mind if college is not for them. Sometimes from as early as their toddler years, millions of students are raised to believe that there is nothing more important than success, and nothing that reflects that success more than admittance to a top-tier college.

Decades ago, college was a privilege. When I was in high school, to get into one of the "good" colleges, well-roundedness was enough. Today even perfect grades and SAT scores won't necessarily guarantee entrance into "HYP" (Harvard-Yale-Princeton), the acronym that has become the ultimate overachiever crown. Our perfectionist society is fueled partly by the competition: While in 1975, only 50 percent of high school graduates nationwide went to college, 86 percent attend today. In the fall of 2005, a record 16.7 million students enrolled in college, 1.2 million more than only five years before. That figure is expected to increase another 2.1 million by 2013. But while the number of college applicants has increased, the number of available slots at prestigious universities has not, leading students to overwork themselves sick while attempting to squeeze into ever-narrowing funnels they vehemently hope will drop them onto the campus of their dreams.

This is a book about pressure—about how the pressure on students, parents, teachers, and graduates has whirled out of control and will continue to do so exponentially unless there is a massive change of attitudes and educational policies. The intensifying pressures to succeed and the drive of the overachiever culture have consequences that reach far beyond the damaged psyches of teenage college applicants, though that effect alone should be enough for us to take notice. Overachiever culture affects not only overachievers and the college application process, but also the U.S. education system as a whole, non-overachieving students, the booming college counseling and test-prep industries, the tendency to cheat and use cutthroat tactics to get ahead, the way parents raise children, and campus drug culture. It contributes directly to young adults' paralyzing fear of failure. It has diminished leisure time for all ages. It is believed to be a major factor in the 114 percent spike in suicide rates among fifteen-to-nineteen-year-olds between 1980 and 2002.

There were other reasons I wanted to base my research at Whitman. First, I knew that the administrators cared about the problems I would outline, and worked hard to combat them. Alan Goodwin, the man who stepped in as principal the summer I began this project, instantly became a popular figure in the school community. Like his predecessor, Jerome Marco, Goodwin is a congenial, compassionate principal with whom students are friendly and comfortable. At almost all of the school events I attended as a reporter, from athletic games to musicals to Welcome to Whitman Night, Goodwin was also there to support his school.

I want to make clear that Whitman is not this book's target; it is simply the setting. Indeed, while the school is excellent, it is not extreme. Whitman is not the most decorated or the most difficult high school in the greater Washington, D.C., metropolitan area. For the purposes of this book, Whitman could be any competitive school, public or private, almost anywhere in the country. I chose to follow students from a single school in order to observe how different people acted in the same environment.

Whitman is not an underprivileged school, and some of the students I followed were fortunate enough to choose among colleges without regard for tuition costs. I hope that readers don't trivialize what often become gut-wrenching dilemmas for students. By no means is the panic over appearing successful and navigating the admissions process limited to families near the top of the socioeconomic chain. To make sure the views in this book represented as broad a range of students as possible, I contacted hundreds of other teens at high schools in many regions of the country, including group interviews in states as varied as Kentucky, Vermont, New Mexico, Washington State, North Carolina, Illinois, and Texas. I visited with educators in Hawaii and young people in China. Although I did not have room to quote all of those individuals, several of them appear in this book, and their perspectives informed the points in these pages.

By the end of *The Overachievers,* you will have become well acquainted with Julie, Audrey, and AP Frank. You'll also meet Taylor, a "hottie" whose academics conflict with her social status; Sam, who worries that his years of overachieving will be wasted if they go unrecognized; Pete, who is determined not to get caught up in the frenzy; C.J., who feels second-tier compared to Whitman's overachievers; the Stealth Overachiever, a mystery junior who flies under the radar; and Ryland, for whom college pressure becomes his downfall. (Some but not all of the students asked for a pseudonym; one student requested that two identifying characteristics be changed.[1] All conversations for which I was not present are written as relayed to me; Mrs. AP Frank's broken English, for example, is as her sons conveyed.)

You'll notice that at the beginning of their sections, I distinguish the students not only by their name and grade but also by the way they were perceived, rightly or not, by certain circles at Whitman. I did this

---

[1] The subject of one of the main characters' teachers was changed to protect the teacher. Outside of the main characters, some other characters' names have been changed; in two cases, two additional details were altered.

because a good deal of the high school experience can stem from the brief label that peers thrust upon one another, whether it's the Jock, the Brain, or the Pothead. Students often struggle with how their identities match up to those labels, even when the label has no factual basis. The way other students—and, subsequently, adults—see them can blur the borders of how they see themselves.

That's one of the issues at the core of overachieverism: how overachievers are seen by others (or how they believe others see them, judge them, and make assumptions about them) and how they perceive themselves. This is a book about students' struggles with comparisons, with the way aspects of their lives are magnified, overanalyzed, and refashioned in desperate steps to measure up to the competition. It is a book about how lives, leisure, and learning are shoved aside in favor of strategy and statistics, obscuring what should be a developmental experience beneath the frenzy of "getting in."

Overachiever culture is disturbing not because it exists but because it has become a way of life. Nationwide, the relentless pursuit of perceived perfectionism has spiraled into a perpetual cycle of increasing intensity and narrowing ideals. When teenagers inevitably look at themselves through the prism of our overachiever culture, they often come to the conclusion that no matter how much they achieve, it will never be enough. And the pressure steadily mounts.

TAYLOR, SENIOR | PERCEIVED AS: THE POPULAR GIRL

Taylor expertly covered the windows of her good friend's house with trash bags so that outsiders couldn't see in. She laid down a tarp on the main floor and secured the sides with electrical tape. Her friend's parents, who were upstairs, had agreed to let their daughter host a party with alcohol as long as she kept the crowd small.

Less than an hour later, nearly two dozen students were crammed into the main level of the house, many of them drinking beer or doing shots of vodka from water bottles. Taylor was on her third game of beer pong when one of the boys in the room heard a knock, opened the front door with a beer in his hand, closed it abruptly, and said, "Oh, shit, sorry you guys. There are cops here."

The partygoers looked up to see red and blue flashes pulsating faintly through the trash bags. Chaos ensued as the students scattered. One boy opened the back door, hoping to make a run for it. He quickly shut it, yelling, "There are cops there, too!" The mass of students hurtled upstairs. An adrenaline rush shot through Taylor as she scrambled. She and a few others who were familiar with the house sprinted to the second-floor bathroom, where a window faced the side yard. They opened it, hoping to jump, but the glass didn't tilt all the way. They heard a door open downstairs. An authoritative voice boomed, "Everyone come down here! Sit down! Be quiet!" Police officers stormed through the house.

Taylor slinked to an upstairs living room, where she squeezed into a narrow space between the chimney and the wall. She heard an officer say to the hostess's mother, "Find all the kids." The officer searching through the upstairs level pulled students out from their hiding places, one by one, and sent them downstairs. As he walked by the chimney, brandishing his flashlight, Taylor held her breath. When the light dimmed, she exhaled. She could hear the policemen downstairs asking, "Is everybody here?" Taylor shifted her feet nervously, wondering if they would find her. Again an officer walked by the chimney. Taylor could see his flashlight beam shining on the brick wall in front of her before it disappeared.

The students present that night were, like Taylor, considered many of Whitman's popular seniors. Even the Nastys had put their stamp of approval on the party; more than half of them were present and accounted for. It was in vogue among Whitman girls to name their circles of friends. The juniors had various named cliques—the Bitches & Hos, the Dolls, the Eight—while the seniors were dominated by one group of thirteen attractive students: the Nasty Girls, or the Nastys. The Nastys often wore skimpy clothes and struck sexy poses in their Webshots (photos posted on the Web). The ringleader was the senior class president. Some seniors dismissed the Nastys' "popular group" designation as self-proclaimed, calling them social climbers who competed to get the good-looking guys to go to their parties. Other students idolized them.

The Nastys respected Taylor, probably because she had been voted sophomore homecoming princess and, as a junior, had gone to prom with the chiseled winner of the Senior Superlative "Senior Sex Symbol." Taylor's group, though nameless, was also popular—perhaps more so than the Nastys—but classmates had no inkling that Taylor wasn't sure she belonged with the popular crowd. At another party, one of the Nastys' favorite boys had turned to Taylor and asked out of the blue, "Have you retaken the SAT yet?"

"No, not till October," she said.

"What did you get?" The rest of the room quieted.

Taylor wasn't thrilled to be asked in front of everyone. "If I say, you can't get mad at me for retaking them." When he nodded, she said, "I got a 1490." The others in the room murmured words of surprise. They knew Taylor only as a popular babe, as one of them.

"But you're just studying verbal again, right?" he asked.

"Yeah, that's the only thing I care about," Taylor replied, sheepish.

"Wait, what about math?" another guy asked.

Taylor lowered her voice. "I got an 800." The silence in the room felt awkward.

Taylor didn't actively hide her intelligence from her popular friends, but when she was around them, she tried not to "act smart," as she put it. The popular students treated her differently whenever her academics came up. Taylor believed they didn't like her as much as they would otherwise, because she made an effort to hang out with smart kids, too. She sometimes sensed the popular students' resentment, not necessarily because she was intelligent but because she was motivated. She had been student government treasurer, oversaw the annual Mr. Whitman pageant (a student-run show that raised thousands of dollars for the Muscular Dystrophy Association), and had founded an annual book drive for underprivileged elementary school children.

Taylor's popular friends seemed more interested in parties and hookups (teenspeak for making out). But as her friends paired and broke up in a kaleidoscopic tango, Taylor stayed unattached and didn't care much about it. She didn't have time. With the exception of a hookup here and there, Taylor was focused on college applications, classes, and sports. Between Whitman's soccer team, which few people expected to do well this season, and her club lacrosse team, Taylor practiced or played in games seven days a week. On varsity game days, she often couldn't start her homework until eleven P.M.

The police officer returned, this time peering around the corner of the chimney and shining his flashlight in Taylor's face. She grinned. "Hi!" she said.

"I found another one!" the officer called. He turned to Taylor and smirked. "What is this, a hiding party?"

"Um, no!" Taylor answered, and half skulked, half strutted downstairs, proud to have hidden for that long. When she reached the sitting room, her friends snickered. "Nice try, Taylor," one said.

"Is that everyone?" asked an officer. The group nodded, although one of the Nastys still hadn't been found. "Is anybody over eighteen?" They shook their heads.

"My parents don't know," a student moaned. "I'm going to be in so much trouble." A Nasty was petrified about the prospect of adding another citation to her collection. "Oh my God, ohmyGod, ohmyGodohmyGod," she kept repeating.

The officers asked the group to divide so that those who had consumed alcohol were on one side of the room and those who hadn't were on the other. The officers administered a Breathalyzer test to each self-proclaimed non-drinker. When one of them blew a .01, the officers ushered her to the drinking side of the room. The students who blew a zero were told they could go home. About half a dozen left.

Taylor sat on the drinking side, where most of the students were on their cell phones. Two girls were freaking out in the background. "We're not going to get into college!" one shrieked.

Taylor called her mother, who didn't know she drank. "Mom, you're going to be a little unhappy with me. I'm at a party that got busted. I think you need to come here and pick me up."

"I'm glad you called," her mother replied.

The police officers approached the drinkers. "Everyone spit out your gum," one said. Taylor watched as the officers tested the first two students, who blew low numbers that were nonetheless enough to get them cited. Taylor tried to conjure up any facts she could remember from her science classes. She believed she had drunk enough that she would test high unless she could somehow trick the Breathalyzer. *The alcohol is mostly in my digestive system by now,* she thought. *There might be some residue in my mouth, but if I can breathe from my nasal passage, the air won't come from my mouth or my diaphragm.*

The officer who found Taylor behind the chimney held out the Breathalyzer, a small black box with a digital readout and a clear tube. *Fuck,* Taylor thought. She exhaled only the air in her throat, careful not to bring up any from her diaphragm. She blew a zero. "You can just stand over there," the officer said, gesturing to the non-drinking side of the room. "You're not going to get in any trouble."

Taylor stood next to a Nasty, who muttered, "How'd you do that?" Taylor tried to explain through whispers and gestures when she thought the police weren't watching. An officer standing on the drinking side glared at her sharply and walked over to her. At five-nine, Taylor could look him in the eye. "I saw you telling your friend how to get out of it," the officer said, scowling. "You didn't give me a sample the first time. You need to blow again." He inserted a new tube in the Breathalyzer and held it out to her.

"You have to blow again, haha," laughed one of her friends. Taylor concentrated on her breathing. She tried to block off her windpipe with her tongue, breathing only through her nasal passage. She blew a zero.

"You had a method. Do it again," the officer said.

As Taylor took her third test, she realized she wasn't getting enough air. Feeling faint, she was leaning over precariously when the test ended, again resulting in a zero. The officer looked disgusted. "You know I could cite you just for being here," he sneered. He told her to leave.

Outside, Taylor hopped into her mother's car. "Mom, we can leave! I blew a zero, let's go!" She wasn't lying, she reasoned; she just wasn't telling her mother that she had blown a zero despite having played three games of beer pong in an hour.

SAM, SENIOR | PERCEIVED AS: THE TEACHER'S PET

At two A.M., Sam couldn't believe he was still doing homework. On the second day of school, he had already studied seven hours at home, significantly more than the five and a half hours he spent in his academic classes. Clearly, there was something wrong with this picture.

Although summer had unofficially ended two days ago, it seemed to Sam as if it had been months. On his bedroom desk, next to his computer, Sam's last souvenir of the season taunted him: a rock he found on his last day at the beach in Martha's Vineyard. On it someone had scrawled a saying, reminding him of what he assumed was his close friend Julie's philosophy, an attitude Sam hoped to emulate. Sam's hardest working friend, Julie meant more to him than she realized. "Life just is," read the ink on the rock. "Go with it. Grow with it. Live and let live." Yeah, well, easy for the rock to say. The rock wasn't stuck with seven hours of homework.

Sam had spent the summer chasing that philosophy—the idea that he could live free from worry, letting the usual daily stresses slip from his mind like the tide slid off the rock. In June and July, he taught English to teenagers in China, one of the most rewarding experiences of his life. He raised $2,500 from family friends by writing a journal for them about his trip, and he donated the money to various Chinese schools, charity projects, and a Chinese boy who needed surgery.

In August he spent several days relaxing at the beach with his parents and younger brother. He enjoyed spending time with his family and he thoroughly respected his parents. His father was a professor at Georgetown, and his mother recently had left a powerful legal career in order to devote time to her sons. Sam was proud of both parents and grateful for the support and opportunities they provided. In eighth grade, after a field trip to the Supreme Court during the *Bush* v. *Gore* hearings that had piqued Sam's interest, his father had encouraged him to write the marshal. "Do you have internships?" Sam wrote. "Would you like an eighth-grader?" The Supreme Court of the United States agreed to take Sam on for a few weeks, an unpaid job to which Sam returned, awestruck, every summer.

Sam knew, too, that his parents presented him with privileges and connections that other students didn't have. His parents had friends who could put in good words for him at several schools, including Harvard and Yale. Sam's Whitman guidance counselor had told him that Georgetown admitted qualified children of faculty most generously. But while it was humbling to have a great university practically as a safety school, Sam had learned in China that sometimes you could learn more about yourself and others if you went farther from home. Besides, his parents had raised him not to take the easy way out but to work hard and aim high. His mother often told him, "Do your best, because the only one you're doing it for is you."

Tired of gazing at the computer, Sam glanced around his bedroom. There was the keyboard that he wouldn't have time to play often, despite his commitment to his twelfth year of weekly piano lessons. Among various sports trophies was one for Student Congress—as captain, he would spend autumn preparing younger teammates for tournaments, as well as putting in hours of practice on his own. Slung over the doorknob of the closet was his Whitman tennis sweatshirt, a frustrating reminder of the stress fracture in his elbow that would have him rehabbing until the spring season. The varsity letter and pins on his bulletin board were now dwarfed by senior-year logistics: his SAT course schedule, a reminder of the transcript request deadline, a list of college application deadlines, and a letter recognizing his accomplishments as a top Maryland student.

Sam believed that at other high schools, or in other areas of the country, he would have been set. With his voluminous list of unusual and time-consuming extracurriculars—his position as co–news director of the *Black & White* took up more hours than would a part-time job—his parents' connections, high GPA, AP classes, writing talent, unique summer activities, and evident gusto for learning, he knew he would be an attractive applicant to most college campuses. But Sam didn't go to other high schools. Sam went to Whitman.

A few days before school started, he had explained to a rising junior how strenuous her year would be, particularly with college pressure hanging over her head. "It's a crazy little game, and anything you can do to get an advantage might help," he told her. (She had responded, "That's what my father said!") Well, game on. The pressure to get into college—no, the pressure to get into a *top* college—was what made Sam dread school. It didn't have to be this way, he thought. Classes could be interesting, and he usually didn't mind a reasonable amount of work. But the competitive mentality could be oppressive.

Many of his classmates were obsessed with college rankings (which Sam referred to as the "U.S. News & Bogus Report" but still took note of) and focused almost exclusively on elite schools. By Sam's count, between forty and sixty Whitman students had been accepted to Ivy League schools the previous year. There was a pattern of perception. A friend with a perfect SAT score was rejected from Stanford and went to Rice. Rice, Sam knew, was a top-tier school, but because at Whitman it didn't have other universities' prestige factor, students assumed the only reason she didn't go Ivy was that she was offered a free ride (she wasn't). On another occasion, Sam mentioned the University of Chicago to a junior who replied, "That's not an Ivy. Isn't it a safety school?"

One of Sam's favorite potential colleges was Middlebury. While he knew he shouldn't let other people's opinions sway him, he couldn't help it. Students were already gabbing about the rankings, which, if they hadn't read about in the usual magazines, they had seen in the colleges' slick marketing literature. If he were smart, Sam thought, he would apply to Middlebury early, probably get in, and be done with it. Yet Stanford was his dream school. If he could boost his SAT scores just fifty more points, he would be within range. And how could he overlook his family's connections at Harvard and Yale?

As much as Sam knew he should ignore the rankings and follow his gut, it bothered him that the college admissions process seemed like such a crapshoot. He could work extremely hard throughout high school, find a college he loved, and get in, while other students who didn't work as hard, who didn't regularly stay awake studying until three in the morning like Sam was tonight, might get into more prestigious schools. Then, in other people's eyes, those students would be perceived as more academically inclined than Sam, while in his eyes, as superficial as he knew it was, all of his hard work would have been for nothing.

"Live and let live," the rock said. Sam typed an email to a friend. "School beats other options, but the disturbing mentality that surrounds school is destructive to our conscience. School takes over. Everyone is searching for that summer feeling again; the ability to live without worry. But everything not related to school right now seems so small and unimportant. School does not let a kid live. School has its bright moments, its entertainment, and its long-lasting value, but the overbearing competitiveness and work combine to create one of the most stressful environments I can imagine." Sam turned the rock over and went back to work.

PETE, JUNIOR | PERCEIVED AS: THE MEATHEAD

Pete looked forward to his early-morning journalism class, but not because of the journalism. By that time, the junior was already wide awake, thanks to a first-period weight-lifting class. Thus he was in fine form to banter with one of the most amusing guys in school: Cliff, a shaggy 255-pound senior offensive lineman who made no secret of his apathy toward classes. Cliff wasn't at school to learn. He was there to play football, hang out with friends, and meet girls.

A skinny kid approached the table where Pete and Cliff sat. "Hey, Cliff, where's my hug?" the kid said.

Cliff ambled over to him, engulfed him in a warm hug, clapped him on the back, and said, "Hey, I missed you, man."

As the skinny kid, smiling, walked across the room, an onlooker asked Cliff "Do you do a lot of hugging?"

"Oh, yeah," Cliff said. "I like hugs, long walks in the park, romantic dinners . . ."

Pete cracked up. He knew Cliff from the football team; Pete, a stocky lineman, had played both ways on junior varsity for two years but was taking this year off rather than moving up to varsity. He admired how Cliff could simply not care about classes. Cliff's outlook on Whitman, in his own words, was "I try to do as little work as possible and have as much fun as I can. That's the way to do high school." Cliff never seemed to let anything get to him. His nonchalance could have been related to his plans not to apply to college as a senior because he was in a talented band that had the potential for success. Cliff was not unintelligent, but in Pete's opinion, if you hung around him for long enough, he made you want to be blissfully ignorant.

Pete was doing his best to adopt a similar attitude. It repulsed him to watch the overachievers in his classes grub for grades and stress out about getting into colleges with impressive names. Ever since an incident in the spring of his freshman year, he had promised himself that he wouldn't panic about his grades like his classmates did. A straight-A student back then, he once left finishing a research paper until the night before it was due. By two A.M. he was exhausted, but the paper wasn't close to complete.

Pete had gone upstairs to his kitchen and rummaged around for something with a high dose of caffeine. Far back in one of the cabinets, he came upon a stash of diet pills. He read the ingredients: Each pill contained hundreds of milligrams of caffeine. He took two. Back in the basement computer room, he detected butterflies in his stomach, which felt full. Suddenly, he was awake and could concentrate. Less distracted than usual, Pete plowed ahead, working steadily on the paper until he finished at 6:30. He raced to his bus stop in time for the 6:40 pickup and popped two pills on the ride to get him through the morning. At lunch he took two more pills to last the afternoon.

At football practice after school that day, Pete began running laps with the rest of the team. Midway through the first lap, he started to feel dizzy. He kept running and was one of the first players to finish the lap. Then he crashed. He felt like a sledgehammer was hitting his chest, and he couldn't catch his breath. His knees buckled, but he righted himself. He tried to get going on the second lap, then noticed that all of his teammates were far ahead of him. His heart raced. His usually pale skin drained of color, his already heavy-lidded eyes glazed.

"Pete! Why are you on your knees?" barked the senior captain supervising the practice.

"I pulled an all-nighter and took diet pills to stay awake," Pete said.

"That was stupid," the senior said. "Go get a drink." Pete walked to the gym, took a long drink of water, sat down, and waited for his head to stop spinning. He concluded that taking the pills was one of the dumbest things he had ever done, and there had been some doozies. Then and there, Pete decided he would never again let himself care about classes or grades to the point where he would feel the need to consume strange substances to stay awake.

Eighteen months later, Pete had stuck to that promise, determined to enjoy high school as a healthy developmental experience without worrying about college consequences. At Whitman, where the students considered smart were often the same ones who constantly talked about their grades, Pete was more comfortable talking about his Ds than his As. He preferred to do high school the way Cliff did it. He preferred to appear carefree.

Just before the bell rang, Pete and Cliff fell into a conversation about a topic not exactly related to their journalism studies.

"I like goats! Goats have fur!" Cliff said.

"Goats don't have fur," someone else interjected.

"Yes, they do," Cliff insisted. "How do you think they make cotton?"

Pete laughed at him. "That's sheep, idiot!"

Chapter 2

September 2–September 26

PRESSURE

JULIE, SENIOR | PERCEIVED AS: THE SUPERSTAR

A few days into the school year, Julie had already fallen into her routine. Her class schedule consisted of five AP classes followed by an hour-long thrice-weekly environmental education internship at a natural science museum. At 2:30 each day, she returned to school for cross-country practice. After dinner, she descended into the basement—she called it her "homework cave"—to start her work, which took up most of the rest of the night. During breaks, she either studied her SAT book or made herself feel guilty for not doing so.

The difference between this week and the week before was stark. All summer she swam and biked several days a week because the activities made her feel simultaneously sharper and more relaxed. This week she didn't have time to do either. She had lost the summer's clearheadedness and the mental and physical edge. When she was training hard, she had more energy and got more done. Now that school took up most of her time, her energy lagged.

Her lethargy caught up with her late one night. She chatted online with friends, who were already talking about homecoming, which would come early this year. They reminded her that with the dance only a month away, they had three weeks to organize dinner reservations, limousines, and other plans. It annoyed Julie that they were already discussing possible dates. The night before school began, Julie and her boyfriend had broken up. She told him she couldn't bear to tie him down to a girlfriend back home when he was heading off to college. He told her he loved her. They said goodbye. Julie had put so much effort into having a boyfriend, and abruptly, he was gone. Now she was back where she started, and completely uninterested in thinking about someone new, not with all she had to do for college applications. Julie had heard about a triathlon during homecoming weekend, which would give her a good excuse to skip the dance.

She was about to go offline when her mother, an upbeat, good-humored woman, came into the computer room and sat next to her to chat. One of Julie's biggest pet peeves was when her mother sat next to her or stood over her when she was instant-messaging, though her mother insisted she couldn't see what Julie was typing. When her mom did this, Julie referred to her as "the hovercraft." Tonight, noticing that Julie was dispirited, her mother kept prodding, "Come on, Julie, let's do yoga." Julie usually loved yoga and did it often with her mother, an instructor. Tonight, though, yoga was just one more thing to think about.

Julie's inner voice reminded her she should be working on her SAT practice book, but she couldn't bring herself to do it. Before dropping her as a client, her college counselor had told her not to bother taking the SAT again, apparently believing that Julie's 1410 was reflective of her abilities. When Julie's then-boyfriend had insisted she give it one more shot, she agreed to take the SAT for the third and final time on October 9. *One more month,* she tried to tell herself. *It's one more thing you need for college. I know you want to be done, but you don't want the SAT to be the one factor that keeps you out of your college choice, whatever that is.* It was the first week of school, and she was already exhausted. She groused about her workload to her mother.

"Julie, last year you complained when you had too much work. I let you do that junior year, but this year you have to be nice," her mother said. "How about we do yoga?"

Julie started to cry. She was tired, overwhelmed, and angry. Yoga would make her feel better, but she didn't want to give her mother the satisfaction. She knew her wild emotions weren't her mother's fault. Her parents rarely pressured her about anything. They trusted her to get her work done, and during freshman year, she had trained them not to bother her about running, either, because she wanted to keep her athletics on her own shoulders, too.

Concerned, her mother tried to guess what was wrong. Julie wanted to tell her everything, but she couldn't. Already the year seemed to be too much. She wanted to tell her mom that she missed swimming, for example, but then her mother's response would be "Then get in the pool." With what time? Ignoring her mother until she gave up and left the room, Julie curled up on the floor in despair, fixated on the pressure to find the right place for her future when she hadn't yet been able to find herself.

SAM, SENIOR | PERCEIVED AS: THE TEACHER'S PET

As Sam backed out of his driveway in his parents' Camry, his mind raced with reminders about everything he had to do that night. In addition to homework and editing article drafts for the newspaper, he had four tests the next day and a newly assigned major research paper. Now he was on his way to spend three full hours in an SAT class, as he would every Thursday for the next month. He had scored well on the test in the spring, but when he heard about other Whitman students' higher scores—students he believed weren't as smart as he was—he resolved to take the test again.

There was also the matter of the fifty extra points Sam assumed he needed to be Stanford material. At the same time, he fell into his usual debate with himself: *I'd love to go to a school like Stanford, Harvard, or Yale, but Middlebury doesn't even care about SAT scores. It's almost a guarantee to get in, and then I don't have to worry about it. Why bother to take SAT classes if Middlebury doesn't care about the SAT? Because, wait a minute, I have a shot at Stanford. At any moment, though, I could say I'm not taking the SAT. If I just decide now to apply to Middlebury early, then I don't have to waste three hours on a Thursday night.* Angrily, he pressed the gas pedal. The car shot backward out of his driveway and crunched into a parked car. Sam froze.

In a panic, he shifted into drive, nudged the Camry slightly forward, and glanced back. He had seriously dented his neighbor's car. Sam drove to the end of his street and stopped the car, vacillating. *I have to tell my neighbor,* he thought. *No, I have to go! He won't know it was me. No, no, I can't do that.* For five minutes, Sam sat there, glancing nervously in his rearview mirror. Then he turned the car around and went home to tell his father.

Sam's father inspected the neighbor's car. "Yeah, this is some real damage. This isn't something you can fix easily." The two of them knocked on the neighbor's door.

When Sam finally arrived at SAT class, held at a private school not far from Whitman, he couldn't concentrate. The mostly private school crowd was joking around, giddy because it was practically the weekend. The teacher was droning on about how he had gotten drunk with students. Sam didn't find this unusual; a previous SAT teacher had attempted to teach ratios by explaining how to make a Sex on the Beach cocktail. But with tests the next day in all four of his AP classes, Sam couldn't think of a reason to stay in SAT class until it ended. When the teacher called for a break halfway through, Sam slipped out of the classroom, gave a flimsy excuse to another teacher who stopped him in the hall, and went home to study.

AP FRANK, COLLEGE FRESHMAN | PERCEIVED AS: THE WORKHORSE

As the Washington, D.C., area's notorious humidity waned, so did summer and, with it, perhaps the last time AP Frank would ever be free of responsibilities. At a party in Georgetown, he and a few friends toasted summer's last hurrah and said their final goodbyes. AP Frank didn't drink the alcohol—he never really did—but he held a plastic cup in his hand to blend in with the crowd.

Socially, AP Frank had come a long way. In middle school, he had fallen into the "nerd" category, which he didn't necessarily mind; he was happy being known as the outgoing guy who did slightly bizarre things, like the time he and a friend blew up a melon. In his freshman year, AP Frank had attended a magnet program consisting of many Asian students—students whose values, interests, and family life matched his own. AP Frank thrived alongside eighty students he considered his best friends. But his mother, dissatisfied with the administration's unwillingness to let AP Frank take more advanced courses as an underclassman, pulled him from the school and enrolled him at Whitman his sophomore year.

At Whitman, AP Frank knew nobody and nobody knew him, until word spread that the new transfer student was taking three AP classes as a sophomore. By junior year, when the newly christened AP Frank finally was meeting a slew of potential friends, he was taking the eight-period, seven-AP course load that had him studying every afternoon, sleeping during class, and going lunchless. His Whitman fame granted him access to the close friends he craved, but he lacked the time to get to know them.

Now, at the party, he looked gratefully at the friends who had made the extra effort to socialize with him during school and, though they might not have known it, helped to keep him alive. They had stuck by him. He would miss them terribly. It was one last glorious night.

The next day his mother called him names. "You want spend time with friends?" she screamed. "You are social whore! If you hang out with everyone, you be everyone's tool." She castigated him for going out with them at night rather than during the afternoon. When AP Frank protested that his friends had afternoon jobs and family activities, she moved his curfew from one A.M. to ten P.M. "You falling into habit of seeing people instead of staying home and studying," she said.

"But I don't have anything to study," AP Frank replied.

"You have four-hundred-page booklet of [college] courses and requirements. You read that."

AP Frank sighed. He didn't have to declare a major until sophomore year, but he knew what he had to say to get his mother to stop talking. "It's okay," he told her, resigned. "I'll consider the biology major." He knew better than to push her. The "social whore" argument bore echoes of an earlier, more disturbing encounter that he had no desire to repeat. In January of his senior year, AP Frank had assumed, because he had been admitted early into his mother's only acceptable college, that he would be able to see his friends. When a good friend invited him to go to a lake house in Canada, AP Frank was ecstatic about his first chance to spend time with friends away from home.

His mother said he couldn't go. "You only hang out with worthless kids, no futures, spoiled, stupid brats," she said. AP Frank had had it. She'd gone too far. He was accustomed to her degrading him, but when she insulted the people who were closest to him, the people who kept him from succumbing to his darkest thoughts, he flipped out.

Rage shot through him. "Don't you dare attack my friends. Who are you to talk about friends? You have no friends!"

"Ohh, shuuut up." Her voice dripped with scorn.

AP Frank ran downstairs to the living room and picked up the phone. Most of his Whitman friends knew about his situation with his mother, and many had offered to let him stay with them.

As he dialed, AP Frank heard a noise on the stairs. His mother rushed into the room, and just as his friend's voice mail picked up, Mrs. AP Frank hauled back and punched her son in the face. For the first time in AP Frank's life, he could not control the fury and frustration that welled up inside. In an instant, it was as if his leg acted on its own. His foot planted into his mother's stomach and shoved with such force that she staggered backward about five feet before falling down.

AP Frank watched the chain reaction as if it were a movie, someone else's mother, someone else's life. His mother called the police and asked them if physical punishment was legal for a disobedient child. Satisfied with the answer, she hung up the phone and taunted him, "What you gonna do? You gonna kill me?" AP Frank stared off into space. When she could elicit no reaction from her son, Mrs. AP Frank turned on her husband, who was trying to calm her down. "What kind of father you? Stupid son-of-a-bitch kid can do whatever he wants without fearing his father?"

To AP Frank, it felt like the pieces of his life were crashing down around him while he stood still in the middle of the avalanche, withdrawing inside himself. He had never felt so strongly that he should not have been born to these two people. He wished he could somehow block this night from his mind so that he would never remember it. He desperately wanted to belong to another set of parents, in a home where his life would be so blissfully mundane that his biggest worries in high school would be a chemistry test and whether that nice redhead in English liked him back.

When he could, AP Frank sneaked upstairs and went online, begging his friends for help of any kind. As he instant-messaged a close friend, he heard a noise on the stairs and abruptly logged off before his mother saw him. Immediately, the phone rang. AP Frank ran to the phone, where his mother waited with a snarl that dared him to take the call. He glanced at the caller I.D. It was his friend. All AP Frank could do was wait for the message and pray that his friend remembered that Mrs. AP Frank screened calls. "Uh . . . I'm calling for Frank. I just wanted to talk about the physics homework. Call me back whenever you can." AP Frank sighed in relief. His friend knew the drill. When his parents left the room, AP Frank called his friend, who answered just as AP Frank's mother crept up behind him and punched him in the back of the neck. AP Frank gasped.

"Frank? Are you okay? Frank?"

AP Frank could hardly say anything, not with his mother standing over him, threatening months of terror ahead. "No," he wheezed.

"You can't talk because your parents are there?"

"Yeah," AP Frank whispered.

"Are you going to be at school tomorrow?"

"Yeah."

"Are you going to be okay?"

No! AP Frank wanted to shout, *I'm not okay! Nothing in my life is even remotely close to "okay" right now. What did I do to deserve this?* "Yeah," he whispered.

His friend paused. ". . . Talk to me before school, Frank."

"Okay, 'bye." And his mother erupted again.

The next morning, as he was about to walk into class, AP Frank saw the friend with the lake house. His friend's face lit up. "You're coming with us to Canada, right?"

Memories of the previous night flooded AP Frank. "Um," he managed to choke out, "I don't think I'll be going to Canada."

The boy's friendly smile fell. "But why?"

AP Frank wiped his eyes with his sleeve. "I can't take my life anymore," he managed between breaths. "I can't take it, I can't take it."

His friend's voice filled with concern. "Do you want to go to a counselor, Frank?"

"Yeah. Could you . . . could you . . . could you just tell the teacher where I'll be?"

"Okay, Frank. I'll do that."

"Thanks," said AP Frank, who stumbled downstairs to the guidance department to see his counselor, Mr. Murphy, a balding man whose wide-rimmed square black glasses made him look like a teacher from a bygone era.

"Mr. Murphy, I need to talk to you."

"Sure, Frank. Sit down," Mr. Murphy said, motioning to a chair.

AP Frank slumped into a chair, took a breath, broke into sobs, and poured out his feelings. He wasn't allowed to do anything. His mother didn't want him to have friends, she didn't want him to have a will of his own, she didn't want a son, she wanted a puppet. He had thought that getting into the college she demanded of him would solve all of his problems with her, but it had merely raised the bar.

Mr. Murphy called AP Frank's father, speaking sternly and nodding while AP Frank sat quietly and wondered, *Is this going to change things? Is my life going to get better because of this?* Mr. Murphy hung up the phone and put his hand to his forehead. He looked at AP Frank gravely. "How serious do you think this is?" he asked. "Because if this is child abuse, then I'm going to have to call in a social worker."

AP Frank paused to think. It seemed strange to debate with himself whether he had been a victim of child abuse. After several minutes, he responded, "Tentatively, I think so, but I'm not sure."

Mr. Murphy sighed. He thought for a few moments, choosing his words carefully. "Frank, your mother just wants the best for you. She's terribly misguided, and you need some personal freedom, but she loves you, and you have to realize that."

AP Frank wanted to laugh a loud, bitter laugh. The idea that his mother loved him seemed absurd. He nodded and blew his nose as Mr. Murphy left the room to speak with someone else about the situation. When he came back, he handed AP Frank the letter of recommendation he had written for his college applications, which AP Frank read, his tears subsiding. Mr. Murphy had written a flattering note about how he was an exceptionally personable, wonderful kid who could deal with excessive amounts of stress. AP Frank put down the piece of paper, feeling much better but at the same time more forlorn.

"Six more months," Mr. Murphy said. "Can you just be brave for six more months, Frank?" Then the counselor was there in front of him, holding out his large hairy arms, enveloping AP Frank in a hug, and AP Frank thought with relief that although he didn't know what his life was going to come to, he finally believed he had at least one adult on his side.

❧

To better understand Mrs. AP Frank's perspective, it's important to note where she came from. In many countries, parents begin plotting to get their children into the top high schools, which lead to prestigious colleges, as soon as they get to kindergarten, if not before. The small percentage of students admitted to top universities are rewarded with desirable jobs. The rest are often considered failures—outcasts who could be doomed to a life of menial labor because of a disappointing performance on a single test.

East Asian educational systems have come to be known for two things: first, what *Time* magazine has called "an almost fanatical belief in the value of education"; and second, the unyielding emphasis on grades and test scores, largely blamed for the soaring suicide rates among teens. In 2001 in Hong Kong, where one in three teenagers have suicidal thoughts, a student who failed a Chinese dictation exam leaped to his death from his high-rise apartment. He was seven.

In Korea, Mrs. AP Frank's birthplace, a popular saying is "Four in, five out," a reference to how many hours of sleep students can allow themselves nightly if they want to get into an elite university. Three-year-olds must display skills on a musical instrument before being admitted into some preschools. In a typical Korean schedule, students work straight through their waking hours, from classes to homework to "cram school"—costly private lessons to supplement classwork. Competition for grades can be cutthroat, as some students steal classmates' notes to sabotage their test performance.

The college tiers are so crucial that a Korean's career, life, marriage, and family pride may depend largely on where he attended school. Even into middle age, an employee's salary, position, and reputation can be based less on his job performance than on how he did on the college entrance exam he took as a teen. On exam days, mothers pray at houses of worship, the Korean Air Force and U.S. Army suspend flights so the city is quiet for testing, workers delay their commute to keep the roads clear, and police and other emergency vehicles are available to drive students who are running late. More than eight out of every hundred thousand students between the ages of fifteen and nineteen committed suicide in 2003.

In 2005 South Korea changed its university admissions standards, beginning with the class of 2008, to place less emphasis on national entrance exams and more on high school grades. The problem? Grades are curved, and classes ranked. Reliance on cram schools and tutors has increased, and many students now panic over every test. In a two-month period during midterm season in 2005, more than ten South Korean junior high and high school students committed suicide because of academic stress or discouraging grades. The new system pits students against one another; as a sixteen-year-old girl said in a speech at a rally to protest the sharpened focus on grades, "Schools are driving us to endless competition, teaching us to step on our friends to succeed. We are not studying machines. We are teenagers."

Other Asian countries admit similar woes. In China a young woman told me that many six-year-olds stay up until midnight finishing homework before waking up at 6:30 for school. Doing poorly on the entrance examination for college "brings shame to family," she said. In China and Taiwan, a recent uptick in the number of student suicides was attributed to the intense pressure to succeed in school. Indian officials report increased student suicides as well as traumatic disorders and hysterical psychoses due to fear of exams. An Indian psychiatrist told *India Today* magazine, "In the past ten years, pressure on students has increased by 50 percent." The doctor also noted that she has hospitalized parents who suffered breakdowns during their children's board exams, and she had a young patient who staged his own kidnapping to avoid a test.

In Japan, as in Korea, a student's worth is often tied to exam scores, which distribute children into hierarchical levels of schooling based solely on their test-taking abilities. If a student as young as fourteen doesn't score well enough on a high school entrance exam, he could be diverted instantly to a track toward vocational school.

A Japanese mother plays a crucial role in her child's education. It is up to her, not her child's preschool teacher, to teach basic letters and numbers. On a daily basis, many mothers exchange notes with teachers about the student's progress. The *kyoiku mama,* or "education-obsessed mother," will even go to school when her child is sick and sit at a desk in his classes taking notes on the teacher's lessons for the day. In 1999 Mitsuko Yamada strangled her neighbor's two-year-old daughter, who beat out her own daughter for a spot at a prestigious preschool. The community blamed the murder on the country's "high degree of exam fever."

Until 2002, Japan's 240-day school year included half days on Saturdays and only a forty-day summer break, during which students were given copious amounts of homework. In 2002 some Asian countries realized the disadvantages of a school system in which success was based on rote memorization rather than on a joy of learning. Surveys revealed that, although Asian students placed first in international academic tests, they retained the information for the least amount of time, because they could not apply what they had learned. In a poll of nearly two dozen countries, Asian students ranked first in math and science competitions but scored second to last in enjoyment of those subjects. The factory-like academic settings were churning out adults who couldn't think independently or creatively. A former minister of education in Thailand told *Time*, "Students can't really read or write. All they know how to do is tick a box next to a multiple-choice question." As a result, in the spring of 2002, Japan stopped mandating school on Saturdays, and Taiwan eradicated its practice of basing college admissions only on entrance exams.

In 2004, however, two new international surveys convinced Japan's Education, Science, and Technology Ministry that Japanese students no longer led the world in academic ability. Subsequently, Japan vowed to restore some of its traditional educational practices, including thicker, more challenging course books, longer school days, and, at some schools, Saturday classes.

Like AP Frank, Asian-American students in the United States often speak of relentless pressure and expectations placed on them by their immigrant parents. Some of the students are immigrants themselves; rising numbers of Korean schoolchildren are leaving their country—Koreans call them *kirogi,* or wild geese—to escape that country's rigorous education system. But in many cases, the culture follows them. A Korean student in Kentucky told me, "From when you're first growing up, there's so much pressure, because the Asian community is really competitive. All of our friends' parents were comparing their children, what schools they got into."

Is the United States headed toward that test-driven, stressed-out Asian educational culture? It might not be a coincidence that U.S. students' high school experiences—the exams, the stress, the tunnel-vision hurtle toward a top university—seem to be trending toward those in Asia. In 1983, President Reagan's Department of Education commissioned a landmark report called *A Nation at Risk*. In a nutshell, the study censured the American educational system for its supposedly poor performances on international standardized tests, warned about its "rising tide of mediocrity," and directly blamed U.S. schools for the alleged loss of America's edge as a global superpower. As education expert Gerald W. Bracey retorted twenty years later, "The members of the National Commission tightly yoked the nation's global competitiveness to how well our 13-year-olds bubbled in test answer sheets. The theory was, to be kind, without merit."

Nevertheless, the response to the report, which recommended more homework, tougher classes, longer school days, and additional days in the school year, was immediate. Within a year, forty-four states increased graduation requirements, and twenty-seven lengthened the school day. *A Nation at Risk* triggered what has been called the longest sustained period of education reform in U.S. history. Most important, it raised expectations among parents, schools, and government officials, possibly the spark that first ignited the overachiever frenzy as a counter to the mediocrity label.

Parents and educators insisted to students that their success as adults now would depend largely on their teenage grades, test scores, and single-minded devotion to school rather than to life—much like the educational system in a certain foreign country. A Department of Education report hailed that country's education system, which was so grueling that students didn't have time to date, drive, hold jobs, or do chores. It was a country where 137 primary and middle school students committed suicide during the 2003 school year. The country that government officials wanted the U.S. education system to emulate? Japan.

AP FRANK, COLLEGE FRESHMAN | PERCEIVED AS: THE WORKHORSE

A few days before AP Frank was to leave for college, he had another argument with his mother about his major. She tried to shove her law or medicine ultimatum down his throat again—his parents were paying for college, so he had to play by her rules—and he protested loudly. Because of AP Frank's objection, his mother yelled at his father to take away his car keys.

AP Frank's father sighed. "Give me your car keys," he said.

AP Frank handed him the keys and went to his room, where he stewed for a few hours. He had worked at the esteemed National Institutes of Health for two summers and had used this past summer's wages to pay for his laptop. Because his parents never gave him the $2,000 he had earned the previous summer, he assumed that they had used the money to help pay for their old 1990 Corolla, which he drove.

A couple of days later, AP Frank's father drove him to the store to buy towels and an alarm clock. AP Frank was happy to have some rare quality time with him. He loved his father and considered him a kind-hearted person who, unfortunately, didn't have a say in how the boys were raised. But AP Frank was still upset with him for rarely standing up to his wife for his sons; his father didn't seem to agree with his mother but followed her orders to avoid conflict. During the car ride, AP Frank tried to express his disappointment. "Dad," he said, "are you going to defend me when I'm deciding my major instead of just sitting there and letting her control me? And before I know it, I'll be in med school, pushing myself to be a doctor when I don't want to be one, just so you don't get yelled at?"

His father said nothing. AP Frank looked out the window, dejected.

Back at home, AP Frank packed for school. As much as he wanted to get out of his house, he had mixed feelings about leaving. He worried that when he was gone, his mother would focus all of her attention on his younger brother, who would be taking six AP courses as a junior. Per their mother's instructions, Richard spent the summer studying for the SAT II subject tests, as AP Frank had done before his junior year. But Richard was different from AP Frank; he was more carefree, more popular. While AP Frank received an A in every class he took at Whitman, Richard received one B as a first-semester freshman, which, as AP Frank saw it, took the pressure off.

AP Frank didn't consider himself the genius that everyone seemed to think he was. In his opinion, a person either had natural talent or worked hard. AP Frank believed he lacked talent in most areas and had achieved his accomplishments because of his diligence. He certainly wasn't Derek, a Whitman senior he considered a true genius, who scored the elusive six out of six at math team events, whereas AP Frank had scored only threes or fours.

AP Frank initially had believed his college acceptance letter would be the end of it; throughout his time at Whitman, his mother had told him repeatedly, "You have to get 4.0 to get in." But now that he was in, she expected him to get a perfect 4.0 in college. AP Frank didn't think that was possible. He had heard a rumor that T. S. Eliot had received a B-plus in English at the same college, so how could AP Frank score an A? One of these days, AP Frank expected it to happen: He would get a B-plus, and his mother would have to accept it. He wasn't sure what his own reaction would be.

Recently, he had been trying to sort out his personal hopes from the expectations his mother had been drilling into him since childhood. He liked to think that he would be satisfied with himself if he tried his hardest. If he got a B-plus because he didn't do his work or because he got drunk the night before an exam, then he would be upset. But AP Frank was almost convinced that he didn't need a 4.0 GPA to validate his existence. Instead, he craved a social life. He had batted .000 in his attempts to have a girlfriend in high school, which gnawed at him partly because, as he put it, "When you're bogged down by seven APs, it gets lonely." AP Frank's plan was to give his mother as little information as possible, so she would have less control. She couldn't tell him not to do something if she didn't know he was doing it.

AP Frank took photographs of friends down from his wall and placed them in a duffel bag. He picked up a license plate that a friend had brought him from a city in India where license plates began with the letters AP; his friend had paid someone to make a license plate that said AP FI2 ANK. He didn't think he wanted people in college to call him AP Frank. It was fine for people he knew to call him that, but he disliked the "Oh, you're that kid" reaction he got from strangers at Whitman. He was half hoping to shed the AP prefix so his college peers would take the time to get to know him without any preconceived notions. But he would probably hang the license plate on his wall anyway, as a memento of good times in high school.

AP Frank smiled as he decided not to pack the banner that he kept next to the pillow on his bed. In the spring, he had participated in Mr. Whitman, Whitman's male pageant, in which he had been a finalist. (Though his mother disapproved of the time that dance rehearsals took away from homework, she allowed participation in that extracurricular activity because it was a competition, and her sons were born to win competitions.) He didn't care when he didn't win, despite his awesome talent performance: making balloon animals to loud techno music. But he loved the enormous banner that his friends made for him, a large white bedsheet on which they had written in enormous letters AP FRANK. AP Frank had asked his mother not to wash the banner, but a month later, she did. The washing machine had bled the banner pink, yellow, and purple—and blurred away the P. Now, according to the bedsheet, he was just A FRANK.

TAYLOR, SENIOR | PERCEIVED AS: THE POPULAR GIRL

Taylor was procrastinating. She needed to study for an AP BC Calculus test and to work on her college essays but instead had played several games of computer solitaire, engaged in lengthy IM conversations, and examined her friends' Webshots. Even after the distractions, she couldn't bring herself to work. She had three essay drafts written: one about September 11, 2001, another about her parents' divorce, and another about philosophy, but she hated them all because none characterized her. She just wasn't a dramatic person, she wasn't dark, complex, or moody. Yet it seemed the best essays were those that dramatically revealed some Great Truth behind the surface of the applicant.

For Stanford, her first-choice school, Taylor felt pressured to distinguish herself. Stanford inexplicably was this year's hot college for Whitman seniors. Even though relatively few students had applied early from Whitman in past years, many of the top seniors had declared their intentions to do so, including Derek. Taylor never felt badly when Derek "beat" her at something, because he was Derek. He deserved the acclaim; he had a gift, not to mention that he was cute and funny without trying to be.

While she believed they were technically competing for the same (Whitman) spots at Stanford, their credentials were different. Derek was the straight-A SAT-whiz math team/chess team guy. Taylor had received three Bs (all in English; at least she was consistent in her weaknesses, she figured). Because she listed on her résumé her junior-year position as student government treasurer, her leadership activities, her title as co-captain of the varsity soccer and lacrosse teams, and her avid participation on a club lacrosse team, which had garnered her recruitment letters from some small colleges, she hoped admissions officers would at least see that she kept busy with activities outside of class.

When she told her college counselor, who was also Derek's college counselor, that she wanted to apply early to Stanford, he had urged her to visit Duke. "Duke is similar to Stanford. You'd have a much stronger chance at Duke because your mom went there," he said.

"Do I even have a chance of getting into Stanford?" Taylor had asked him.

"Yes, but a very small one," he answered. "The people who go to Stanford are either the most intellectual people you will ever meet or Olympians."

"Sweet." She agreed to visit Duke before the end of September.

Unable to concentrate on work, Taylor pattered downstairs in her usual sportswear to the family room, where her stepfather was watching TV. She stared at herself in the mirror: Her long, straight dark hair was loose, her lips full, her lanky limbs tan, her large eyes lightly rimmed in mascara, the only makeup she wore during the day. She decided her hair was boring.

"I want to cut bangs," she said to her stepfather. Taylor considered her stepfather the coolest of her parents and the easiest to talk to.

"Why don't you make a hair appointment?" he said.

"I'm going to cut them," she resolved.

"Do whatever you want. It's your hair."

Taylor went to the downstairs bathroom. She gathered the hair that fell in front of her face and snipped it just above the eyebrows, aiming for the sideswept look that was the current Hollywood craze. She analyzed her work. Oops. On one side of her part, her bangs were the right length, but on the other side, they fell high above her eyebrow. She tried to trim the longer side down to even out the line and ended up with short fringe that somehow reminded her of Pee-wee Herman. Then she remembered she was scheduled to take her senior portrait in the morning.

The next school day, as bad as Taylor thought her bangs looked, she received compliments from popular girls, smart girls, underclassmen, and teammates. Soon afterward, several other girls showed up at school with similar newly shorn bangs.

SAM, SENIOR | PERCEIVED AS: THE TEACHER'S PET

Sam was riding home from a night out in Baltimore with his good friend Brad and a Whitman senior girl. As Brad and the girl discussed homecoming, Sam mulled over his prospects. While it would be nice to go with a girl who had the potential to be more than friends on one of the biggest date nights of the year, he didn't want a rerun of last year's homecoming. As a junior, he had taken a popular girl who was a friend of a friend. Sam had spent the days leading up to the dance, and the early hours of the dance itself, enjoying the anticipation of possible romance. Except for perhaps two dances, his date avoided him most of the night, and at an afterparty at a classmate's house, she spent two hours in the basement with friends, leaving Sam upstairs angrily speculating where he went wrong.

At the other end of the spectrum was Debate Girl. A year older than Sam, Debate Girl was a student from another state who had been on the same tournament circuit as Whitman. At various tournaments around the country, she and Sam had hooked up in hotel rooms. He kept her a secret from his friends, whom he assumed were too innocent to approve of a purely physical relationship. At least he kept that secret until the annual Harvard tournament in February, when she booty-called him and came over to his room. On his bed, as they got increasingly intimate, Sam turned down her request for sex—he didn't want it to happen that way, that soon, with her, but he didn't tell her that—so they did other things instead. In the middle of a compromising position, someone banged on the door. Sam ignored the pounding until he and Debate Girl had finished. Then Sam walked out of the room with a wide grin and Debate Girl in tow to see ten teammates staring at them. Sam's close female friends at home, even Julie, didn't know about Debate Girl. Although Debate Girl was now a freshman at a local university, Sam planned to keep his secret. Despite her frequent IMs asking to resume their physical relationship, Sam hadn't seen her since a Student Congress tournament in May, and he wasn't sure he wanted to.

Then again, there was no one else on the horizon. Sam's one serious relationship had been a summer-camp romance that ended with the season. There had been rumors that Audrey, the cute blond junior who wrote for Sam's news section on the *Black & White,* had a crush on him. Sam considered Audrey "the biggest overachiever in the junior class" because she was such a hard worker, but at the same time, she had a busy social life. Sam suspected her alleged crush on him was only a rumor. Anyway, as much as he liked her intelligence and feistiness, it didn't seem proper to consider an editor-writer relationship.

The girl dropped Brad off at his house and drove toward Sam's. Sam glanced at her. She was attractive. He wanted to have fun at homecoming. He wanted to go with a friend, but not as close a friend as Julie, because he wouldn't want her to think he intended anything more-than-friends to happen. With this girl, he could have the comfort of going with a friend and maybe, just maybe, the potential for something more. *Why the hell not,* Sam thought. When he got out of the car, he calmed his nerves and leaned through the open window. "Quick question," he said to her. "Do you think you would go with me to homecoming?"

Sam interpreted the girl's smile as a revealing one. *Hey, maybe she expected me to ask her!* he thought. "Sure!" she answered.

AP FRANK, COLLEGE FRESHMAN | PERCEIVED AS: THE WORKHORSE

The night before he left for college, AP Frank posted the following on his blog for his Whitman friends:

Weighted GPA: 4.83
SAT: 1570, 1600
SAT II Physics: 790, 800
SAT II Writing: 800
SAT II Math IIC: 800
Number of APs taken: 17
Number of 5s received: 16

Number of times I wish that my parents would see me as a
person, not as a résumé: 4 years = 365 days + 1 day for the leap
year = 1461
Number of times I have skipped class: 1
Number of school dances I have been to: 2
Number of times I have been drunk: 0
Number of times I have slept over at a friend's house: 2
Number of times I have hooked up: 0
Number of times I have fallen for a girl: 3
Number of times I have been turned down by a girl: 3
Number of sports I have come to actually love playing: 1
Number of times I have wanted to break out of the cage: 1461 – the 7
days of Beach Week = 1454
Number of times my friends—who are my family—have saved me,
rescued me, brought me back from the horror and terror of being
alone: 1461
Number of times I have realized that with every beginning comes an
end, that in hatching, the chick destroys the egg, that in leaving, I
leave the people who are closest to me, who have shaped me, who
have made me who I am today, and that when we all return to the
starting point (for we all do, inevitably), nothing will be the same: 1

AP Frank's and his brother's eyes widened as they looked out the windows of the rental van their parents were driving at dusk from the airport to their hotel. Gorgeous women sauntered past them, followed by a throng of people in Hawaiian shirts. AP Frank thrilled at the sight of a group of men wearing giant stuffed crabs on their heads. He didn't know what kind of town this was, but it seemed to be the right place for a dude who blew up a melon.

It turned out that the crowd was filtering out of a baseball stadium, and AP Frank's parents were lost. As they navigated their way to campus, AP Frank's mother lectured him about how he should never consider majors like environmental science and public policy, one of his interests. Some options were simply "crap majors," she explained, that didn't hold a future for AP Frank because he wouldn't be able to get a job. AP Frank had heard this from her before. Mesmerized by the lights of the city, he quietly put on his iPod earbuds and turned on a lulling set of Led Zeppelin songs, making sure to say "uh–huh" and "okay" every once in a while so his mother wouldn't know he wasn't listening.

Soon there they were. Harvard. The Xanadu of his mother's dreams, the ticket to a life free of failure. Growing up, AP Frank had never fantasized about this place. In fact, he had been repelled by the prospect of attending Harvard, which was for the kind of person strangers assumed him to be, not for the person he actually was.

AP Frank and his family lugged duffels and suitcases into the single room he was assigned in the dorm. His first college residence would be the smallest, quietest dorm at Harvard. He never would have chosen to live in Massachusetts Hall, which he envisioned as being full of "the goody-goodies of Harvard who don't know what a keg is." But he didn't seem to have a choice. Harvard had sent a questionnaire to students that asked them to indicate, by circling a number from one through five, items such as how clean they were and whether they preferred a quiet or sociable dorm. AP Frank wanted to put down a four for sociable; this was finally his chance to start over and do school the way he truly wanted to do it. But not a single Harvard form came into the house without his mother reviewing it, telling AP Frank what to write on it, and, in some cases, editing it. She forced AP Frank to circle the one on the social scale because Harvard was supposed to be for studying. He had a sneaking suspicion that his mother had specifically requested Mass Hall.

If he was going to be surrounded by nerds, at least AP Frank hoped to be the "party guy in the goody-goody dorm." As he walked inside his new home, he wondered, *Wouldn't it be interesting if I'm playing my guitar at night and someone tells me to be quiet?* Yes, AP Frank's image would definitely be different than in high school. As he saw it, he didn't have to be AP Frank at Harvard. For all he knew, he could meet other Harvard students who had AP nicknames, too.

SAM, SENIOR | PERCEIVED AS: THE TEACHER'S PET

Sam hunkered down at his desk on a beautiful Saturday afternoon to write his college essays and work on his common application. He turned on his computer and went to the TCCi Family Connection Web page. TCCi (the College Counselor Internet edition) was a college-planning website that tracked the last few years of Whitman students' acceptance, rejection, and wait-list histories at the schools where they applied. Students obsessed over this feature, for which scattergrams plotted their chances based on their GPA and SAT scores. This was Sam's first visit to TCCi, and he was curious how he stacked up against Whitman peers.

He held his breath, opened the Stanford scattergrams, and gaped at the screen in shock. His GPA put him close enough horizontally to the cluster of green dots representing past Whitman acceptances, but his SAT scores distanced him from that cluster, which bunched near the 1560s. The extra fifty points he thought he needed on the SAT, he realized with dismay, wouldn't put him in the Stanford pool. As a Whitman student, he needed something on the order of a 130-point improvement. Not only was Sam stuck in a school where admissions officers practically expected 1600s, he also happened to be a member of a class that was smart even by Whitman standards, with eighteen National Merit semifinalists. According to Sam's calculations, there were nine Whitman seniors applying early to Stanford, and from what he heard, he had the lowest SAT scores of any of them.

His heart sinking, Sam clicked on the scattergrams for his safety schools to find that the colleges he previously had considered safeties weren't safeties for a Whitman student. If he looked slightly lower down the rankings, he found only schools that he would prioritize below Georgetown, his one top-ranked safety. Aghast, he opened his dog-eared copy of a nearly 800-page Princeton Review guidebook. According to the Princeton Review, to get into Columbia, he might need about a 700 verbal score. He turned back to TCCi and looked up the Columbia scattergram. From Whitman, by contrast, he would need a 760. There was a reason, Sam decided, that SAT was part of the word "Satan." He couldn't bring himself to look up the pages for Harvard and Yale.

"Dad!" Sam called, and went downstairs to commiserate with his unofficial college counselor, who was managing Sam's application process because as a professor, he said, he could tell Sam the same things a college counselor could, for free.

"Sam, you are ninety-five percent more interesting than those other kids applying. When you do your application, you just have to push

'Supreme Court, Supreme Court, Supreme Court, China,'" his father said. "These kids come from the upper crust in society. You are the first and you are the only one to have the Supreme Court. That's the one thing you've done that no other kid will have done."

Before going back upstairs, Sam went outside to get the mail. Sticking out among college literature was a local magazine with a cover story about top high schools. Of the six cheerleaders on the cover, two of them were Whitman Vikings. Sam immediately leafed through the article. Whitman was ranked the fourth best school in the state for athletics, third in Maryland on state achievement tests, and second in the metropolitan area (first in the county) for highest SAT average. Of all the days to receive yet another reminder of Whitman's dominance.

Sam scooped up the college mail and took it to his room. Against the wall, his mother had stacked a tower of ten plastic crates from floor to ceiling. He flicked that day's mail in the top crate, which was for mail from colleges he wasn't interested in. Compared to the top crate, the Brown, Yale, Williams, Middlebury, Stanford, Harvard, Bowdoin, and Amherst crates were relatively empty. Sam flipped on an old OutKast CD and stared at his computer screen, ready to tackle the short-answer question on the common application. *Please describe which of your activities (extracurricular and personal activities or work experience) has been most meaningful and why.* He had 150 words to explain himself. Piece of cake. He could write about how he loved the hectic journalistic atmosphere of the *Black & White* while simultaneously getting across his passion for writing and his leadership capabilities as co–news director.

Sam brought his finished essay downstairs to his parents to trim. It was 172 words, 22 words over the limit, and he was sure that admissions officers would cut it off at word 151 rather than read further. Meanwhile, Sam moved on to the next essay question: the personal statement. This one wouldn't be so easy. He shoved aside the books on his desk: SAT guides, a French textbook, *Webster's Dictionary*. He knew he had to write this essay about the Supreme Court, but he also understood that the subject didn't matter as much as what he was able to reveal to admissions officers about his character. He could write about witnessing the decision of *Lawrence* v. *Texas* (a landmark decision extending the right to privacy to gays and lesbians), where he had watched citizens in the public arena with tears of joy streaming down their faces, one of the most powerful images in his life. For a brief moment, Sam considered writing the essay as if he were gay—that would make him stand out from other Whitman applicants. Rejecting that plan, Sam turned off the music and huddled over the keyboard.

∽

Several Whitman students were convinced that their heavy stress loads and intense competition were a "Whitman thing" or an "East Coast thing." I knew the scope wasn't so narrow—there are Whitmans all over the country—but I was curious to know whether students' stress levels decreased in less urban, less privileged areas.

Portales is a small rural college town with a population of 11,000, occupying about seven square miles of the high, flat plains of eastern New Mexico. The easiest way to get there is to fly into Lubbock, Texas, drive about a hundred miles down a two-lane road, and turn left at the livestock yard. On an autumn afternoon three days before the ACT was administered, I met with four of Portales High School's overachievers: Charles, who was president of the student body and the district student council; Adriana, a star varsity athlete for Portales since the eighth grade; Keri, a president of three societies, with a 4.0 GPA; and Falan, a musician and the vice president of both the student body and the senior class. All but Keri were Hispanic.

First I gave them each a piece of paper and asked them to write down their schedules, awards, and extracurricular activities. All four started writing feverishly. "This could take a while!" one of them exclaimed. "I'm not sure I can remember everything, but I can give you my résumé," Charles offered. (He later sent me the six-page document.)

I began the conversation by asking them, "How do you define overachievers?"

"Us!" they said in unison, laughing.

"Overachievers are the well-rounded kids who don't just stick to one small section, kids who actually do stuff like sports as well as drama and student council," said Charles, a debate and drama standout.

"There are kids who just get their classes done and over with, then go home and stay there. Then you have kids with the full schedule who don't have time to do all the extra stuff but do it anyway," said Falan.

I told the students that East Coast overachievers were convinced that outside of their geographic areas, student attitudes were laid-back and much less stressed. "Do you get stressed often?" I asked.

"YES!" all of them shrieked at once.

"*More* stressed than them!" Charles said.

The students talked about the pressure to be perfect; they worried about disappointing their parents and measuring up to others' standards. "We have to keep up with the expectations that have already been set. To get anything less than an A would disappoint me. I have maybe too high goals for myself at times," Keri said.

"That's what pushes me. I push myself," Charles said. "I love this town, but all of us here are so talented that we want to prove ourselves to our community, for everyone's expectations: our parents, society, peers, people who look up to us—"

"And ourselves," Falan broke in.

Charles nodded. "All these expectations build up, and after so long, it's like that's all you're living. Everyone is stressed for the simple fact that we're not sure if we're working for our own passion and dreams or for other people's expectations." I pictured AP Frank.

"My family has high expectations because they know what I'm capable of," said Adriana. "To let them down, to say, 'I didn't do that well'—to see that on their face sometimes . . ." She sighed.

"So you push yourself," Charles said.

Falan spoke up: "Since a lot of people look up to us and we don't want to show our emotion, we always make ourselves out to be happy. We don't want them to know it's affecting us. It's pressure."

Charles, a talented vocalist, and his best friend, the valedictorian of their junior high school class, had dreamed of attending Juilliard together. When they got to high school, Charles said, "The stress of this town was so much that she dropped out." Charles regularly took NoDoz to stay awake during his freshman and sophomore years. Keri said she once had a kidney infection because she overdosed on caffeine, drinking a six-pack of Red Bulls in a two-hour period to get through a test and a softball game. At one point during the week, she was so stressed about applying to college that she wept. "I was crying because I've worked so hard and I'm not going to have anything to show for it because I'm not going to get accepted. I'm going to feel like I was gypped. The stress for me is having so many goals for myself and I'm not going to achieve them," she said. "I was so sick yesterday, and my mom didn't want me to go to school. I said, 'no, I have meetings today' and this and that, and even when I'm sick, I have to go, because I'm going to miss so much just from one day."

"When you miss one day in AP classes, you fall so far behind," Adriana agreed.

"And the reason we get so far behind," Charles said, "is because we have to do all that other stuff."

The Portales students struggled with their philosophies about college. While they spoke wistfully of the prestige of going to a private out-of-state university, the reality was they mostly couldn't afford those schools. So their current strategy was to go to a university they could afford for their undergraduate courses, which they called their "basics." Then they believed they had a better shot at scholarships and fellowships at a more elite level—Charles and Keri were gunning for Ivies—of graduate schools. "My parents don't put me into all these organizations," Keri said. "These are things I want to do myself, because I know if I'm not involved, I'm not getting scholarships. My mom's still paying off college, and she raised three kids by herself."

Although the four weren't chasing top-ranked universities, the competition among top students at Portales High School was intense. They talked about students who grubbed for extra credit by grading papers for teachers, and several classmates who were battling Charles for salutatorian because, he said, they were pressured to. Some of those students, he said, were taking only four classes so that, with an all-AP course load, their weighted GPAs could nudge 5.0. Falan, meanwhile, took a "zero hour" seven A.M. marching band class that preceded first period, stayed in school until four P.M. after another extra class on speech and debate, had teen court or student council meetings through the early evening, did her homework, then went to bed at one A.M. for a whopping four hours of sleep. The other students didn't find this unusual; Keri said she usually slept only from three to six A.M.

"That's why we're all stressed. We have no time to rest," Charles said.

"I think that's what we live for: time to sleep," Adriana muttered.

"Stress is something you always have," Keri said. "I always thought I have to do so well in high school so I can get into college, and then I can get a B without freaking out. But then I think I still have to make those As to get into grad school. I still have to be good so I can pay off school. It's, whew."

"And then to get a good job," Adriana said. "It always feels like it's wrong if you're not doing something somewhere right now."

Charles looked down. "There are times when it's too much and you just want to drop everything," he said. "I came home one day and told my mom, 'I quit.' My mom said, 'Quit what?' I said, 'Life.'"

JULIE, SENIOR | PERCEIVED AS: THE SUPERSTAR

Julie wasn't nearly as self-confident about going to homecoming by herself as she pretended in front of the River Falls girls, who had convinced her to go to the dance instead of the triathlon. She dreaded the moment when the group would take pictures on her porch, because most of the other girls had dates. Julie tried to persuade herself that she didn't care. She had never been the kind of girl who needed a boyfriend to validate her self-worth, but now that she'd had one and lost him, it was somehow difficult to go back to being the independent person she was before. In past years, she had a date for any school dance she wanted to attend, and turned down several other offers. But when she was with her boyfriend over the spring and the summer, she cut off contact with other guys.

She supposed she could have made more of an effort to find a date, but why bother? She wasn't interested in anyone, except perhaps her friend Derek, a deep crush she had kept quiet for years. It was funny, she thought, that people like her would rather be alone than put themselves in a potentially awkward situation, even though the risk could turn out to be rewarding. There were reasons she and some of her friends referred to her as "the Queen of Awkward." It was her own fault she didn't have a date. She was too worried about awkwardness to be more forward with guys.

When Julie came home after a particularly stressful cross-country practice during which her teammates talked endlessly about homecoming, she noticed something odd on her front porch—a rock on top of a note. "Life just is," read the ink on the rock. "Go with it. Grow with it. Live and let live." Julie didn't even have to look at the note to know who it was from. She took the rock inside and opened the note.

"Julie—here's to telling you that you are awesome and that despite the fact everything is hectic beyond belief, we *will* make it in the end. Always, Sam."

Julie admitted the note was cute. Sam was such a thoughtful friend; it was no wonder her parents hoped she would date him. He was a nice-looking guy, with olive skin and sincere, narrow eyes that crinkled when he smiled. Who else would take the time to gauge her level of stress and give her an object of inspiration?

The next day, at a Sunday brunch with the River Falls crew, one subject eclipsed homecoming to dominate the conversation: college stress. As the thirteen seniors discussed where they and other students were applying early, Julie sat to the side of the group, quietly eating, trying not to let on how much the conversation annoyed her. Some of the girls had already finished all of their college applications. Everyone else had figured out where they wanted to go to college and had chosen schools that seemed right for them. Why couldn't Julie find her niche, too? Then again, as much as she wanted the college application process over with, she had an intense fear that if she applied early somewhere, she would get in, regret her decision, and be stuck with it.

Julie couldn't think of a school that would be "perfect" for her, except maybe Stanford. As much as she liked certain schools, she could already spot disadvantages. If she went to a small school, it would be nice to have close relationships with professors, but she might not encounter as wide a variety of students as she would have liked. Did she prioritize the outdoors? In that case, Dartmouth might be ideal, except for the cold; she thought she might have seasonal affective disorder. Was it important to her to avoid the cold? If so, she could apply to several California schools, but was year-round warmth reason enough to apply to a college? Sometimes at cross-country practice, she ran around and around the track, pretending she was running for a college and trying to picture which school that would be. Julie knew that all students headed for college worried about picking the right campus, but she also knew that the same internal drive she could muster to outperform peers in school and athletics caused her to cycle more obsessively over what might seem to others to be common concerns.

As the conversation shifted from colleges to the SAT, which was two weeks away, Julie wanted to bang her head against the wall. Most of the girls would be taking the exam for the second or third time, assuming that even the tiniest bump in points would help. Julie daydreamed. If she could surpass 1500, she could apply anywhere she wanted and, she was certain, she would be the happiest person in the world. Her SAT score, in her opinion, was the one factor holding her back from a stellar application. Beginning in the summer before her junior year, she had seen two sets of SAT tutors who improved her score by only forty points. Now she was relying on herself and an SAT prep book for "advanced students." She couldn't believe, after more than a year, she was *still* studying for the SAT. *I've put so much time into those stupid tests; this is how sick I am. Think of all that I could have been doing instead,* Julie thought. *Every time I look at that book, a little bit of me dies.*

Julie looked around the room at her friends. She spent more time with the River Falls crew than she did with closer friends like Sam and Derek, but she still felt out of place with them. The Queen of Awkward kept her inner turmoil to herself.

AP FRANK, COLLEGE FRESHMAN | PERCEIVED AS: THE WORKHORSE

AP Frank's friends had told him that the first few weeks of college were like summer camp. Having never been allowed to go to summer camp, he took their word. Harvard, though, wasn't your typical camp. AP Frank now lived a few campus buildings away from a beauty-pageant winner. Harvard's freshman talent show featured students ranging from one of the top-ranked DJs in the country to a guy who played AC/DC on the bagpipes.

AP Frank immersed himself in activities that he had always wanted to try. He played his guitar and kicked around a Hacky Sack. At the Harvard activities fair, he signed up for the college's Ultimate Frisbee team and wushu club. Wushu, the contemporary martial art that was an acrobatic descendant of kung fu and the national sport of China, intrigued him because he could learn mental strength, discipline, and self-defense, all while getting into shape. Between wushu practices on Mondays, Wednesdays, and Saturdays, and Frisbee practices on Tuesdays and Thursdays, AP Frank hoped that for once in his life he would be physically fit. Meanwhile, he was quickly getting to know his Massachusetts Hall dormmates. He spent most of his time downstairs in the common room of B31, a five-man suite that included Mike, one of the funniest guys he had ever met, and Andrew, who was the nicest guy he had ever met. He found that Frisbee was an easy way to break the ice. He convinced Andrew to come to practices with him.

Just before the first freshman intramural meeting, the Mass Hall proctor sent an email asking for a third intramural representative to help coordinate the Mass Hall teams. AP Frank volunteered. At the meeting, Mass Hall chose its team captains. "I nominate Frank because he's on the Frisbee team and he's really hard-core," Andrew said. AP Frank grinned at the thought of being identified by something other than academics. Now all he needed was to find a "real" party and a girl who was interested in him, both of which had eluded him thus far.

At AP Frank's first meeting with his academic adviser, he chose his words carefully, conveying a vague idea of his parental control without sharing unnecessary details. He told the adviser how he didn't want to "fall into the trap" of confirming every set of expectations that others had for him. Not only did he want to defy the stereotype of the Asian Harvard perfectionist, but he also wanted to study subjects he was interested in, so that he would eventually find a career that he enjoyed for its merits, not its prestige.

When AP Frank had finished, the professor leaned back in his chair and placed his hands behind his head. AP Frank noticed that the man wasn't wearing a shoe on his right foot. The room was silent as the adviser reflected for a few minutes. "You need to think about what else is interesting to you," the adviser said. He picked up the hefty Harvard course book and leafed through it. "I'm going to tell you about some of these courses here, and you tell me how much you like them, with 'one' being completely uninterested and 'three' being very interested." He read dozens of course descriptions, asking AP Frank how he would rate each course, taking notes, and making recommendations for courses and professors. When they finished, AP Frank had a schedule through which he could pursue a biology concentration, as his mother wanted him to, with an extensive list of backup classes to investigate in case he decided to shift directions.

"Now, I want you to put next week's shopping period to good use," the adviser said, referring to the period when students could check out various classes before setting their schedule, "and email me next Thursday about what you're feeling. Take it easy, Frank."

AP Frank stood up, unable to contain his smile, the product of both nervousness and relief. He shook the adviser's hand, again noticed the shoeless right foot, and left.

More than two weeks into college, AP Frank hadn't yet managed to succeed in his quest for parties and hot girls. He was playing the guitar when Kristen, a dormmate, came in. He had already grown close to her. Kristen, whose quarter-Asian background AP Frank recognized in her tanned skin and long black hair, was quiet, thoughtful, and happy to listen to AP Frank when he needed someone to talk to. When Kristen asked him to go to a party with her and her roommate at a nearby dorm, AP Frank enthusiastically rounded up other Mass Hall students.

The small dorm room was dimly lit, but AP Frank and his friends could make out about twenty dancing people dressed in 1980s fashion. AP Frank took to the dance floor, dancing wildly, jubilantly, as if he had never danced before. (He had, but only about three times.) For an hour, AP Frank was buoyed by the hope of experiencing a true college party. Then he realized it sucked—and it was dry. Dejected, he and his friends returned to Mass Hall. AP Frank went to his room alone, logged online, and asked Whitman friends at other colleges for "insane partying and hookup" stories through which he could at least live vicariously.

At midnight, a Harvard junior who had been in AP Frank's multivariable calculus class at Whitman IMed him. "HEY I'm drunk," he wrote.

"HEY I'm sober, you bastard," AP Frank replied.

The junior invited him to his dorm to share a bottle of wine with him and his roommate. AP Frank didn't think twice. He practically sprinted to the room, where the junior greeted him at the door with a hug and a glass. When AP Frank, who had never tried wine before, poured himself a good five inches, the junior's eyes bugged out.

An hour and a half later, AP Frank was wearing the junior's olive-green noise-canceling pilot headphones and mike set, sending prank IMs, and joking about things like the junior's fake ID, which bore a photo of a Mexican man. (The junior was Indian.) AP Frank discovered that he couldn't juggle balls like he used to. He wondered when the wine might take effect. Hungry, he spotted an unopened box of doughnut holes on the fireplace mantel. "Mind if I take some of these?" he asked the junior.

"Go for it."

An hour later, the junior reached into the doughnut-hole box and hit cardboard. "Frank," he said, laughing, "we gotta talk about this addiction you have."

"What are you talking about?"

He lifted the lid of the box so AP Frank could see that there were only three left.

"I did *that?*" AP Frank was stunned. He didn't remember eating that many.

"Hell, yeah, you did. What the heck? You got the munchies or something?"

"No, man, no."

So this was what it was like to be tipsy. AP Frank remembered that one of his friends had asked him to call her the first time he got a buzz. He fumbled through his pockets for his cell phone, dialed his friend's number, and put the phone to his ear. *Thwack.* The sound of plastic bumping against plastic startled him. He tried again, putting the phone to his ear. *Thwack.* He couldn't do it. What kind of alternate universe was this? Alcohol had trippier effects than he had anticipated. He tried again. *Thwack. Thwack. Thwack.* Oh. AP Frank took off the headphones and left his friend a message.

Chapter 3

September 29–October 6

FINDING A PLACE

RYLAND, JUNIOR | PERCEIVED AS: THE SLACKER

I n the back of the first-period Modern World classroom, darkened for a movie the substitute teacher was showing, Ryland sat quietly, shaking, hyperventilating, and desperately trying to hold back his sobs. Since freshman year, Ryland had become adept at concealing his emotions so that no one would see him cry. Now a junior, he knew to sit in the back of the classroom, and that a sudden rush of tears could be hidden in a well-timed fake yawn behind his shoulder-length reddish-brown hair. His cold sweat, however, was more difficult to address while he was surrounded by classmates. He tried to map out a plan to leave the classroom, complete with excuses in case anyone asked him what was wrong.

Ryland had a lot going on in his life. He spent most of his time outside of school doing community service activities. Every Sunday at lunchtime, he helped run a project for which students made food—usually pasta, beans, and vegetables—and served it to homeless people in downtown Washington. He helped run the county student environmental activists' group as well as a club that worked to conserve energy at Whitman, and he was an avid participant in a school humanitarian group. Two days a month, he sat on the jury for the county teen court to help decide verdicts for minor juvenile crimes. On top of that, he took most of the photos for the *Black & White,* which meant he had to attend varsity and junior varsity games two or three times a week, in addition to covering other events.

Ryland's on-and-off girlfriend couldn't understand why he spent so much time doing community service and accused him of avoiding her. He wasn't intentionally avoiding her; he was swamped with all of the activities he had taken on, and she knew it. He had tried to persuade her to volunteer with him—he thought all teenagers should be enthusiastic about helping less fortunate people. She wasn't interested. She wasn't involved in anything Whitman-related and didn't participate in any extracurricular activities. That turned Ryland off. He liked a girl to have what he called "real commitments" to things, which showed she had spirit and drive. All his girlfriend did was chat online with her friends, then tell Ryland that he was "too busy" and that his activities were making him stressed out and unpleasant to be around. Ryland agreed but would get defensive because he couldn't imagine which activity he could possibly drop in order to free up some time.

Ryland's classmates weren't aware of any of this. Except for the students he met through his various activities, he generally kept within his and his girlfriend's tight circle of friends and avoided drinking, smoking, and out-of-control parties. So if his Modern World classmates had spotted him weeping in the back of the room, they wouldn't have known to guess that he was having girlfriend trouble or that he was overwhelmed by his activity load. Either way, they would have been wrong.

When the bell finally rang, Ryland realized he couldn't endure another period. He skipped his next class to go to the guidance department, where, still shaking and sweating, his heart racing, he feverishly attempted to cram for the source of his misery: his physics test.

During freshman year, Ryland's test anxiety had been so severe that before tests, he would hide in the bathroom, where he sat on the floor, crying, shivering, and wishing he could disappear. By sophomore year, the anxiety and pressure had subsided. But he had been told that junior year was the most stressful in high school. This was the year he had to start thinking about colleges. It was the year Montgomery County had begun to implement a new grading and reporting policy that devalued class participation, extra credit, and certain types of homework in favor of tests and papers. The county policy confused and/or outraged several communities and schools, including Whitman, which decided to accept only some of the changes for the time being. Adherence to the county's requirements and recommendations, however, varied by the teacher. Ryland's physics teacher was a no-nonsense man who was following the policy to the letter: Ryland's only grades would be based on tests, quizzes, labs, and the Physics Olympics project.

Every time he had a test in physics or with a similarly strict teacher in classes that required formula recall, Ryland had an anxiety attack. (English essays and non-science-or-math tests didn't faze him as much.) He had discussed with his guidance counselor the possibility of having extended time to work on tests, either during class or after school, but his counselor told him that his teachers would never allow it as long as he continued to get As and Bs. So far, the only way he had learned to avoid the attacks was to not study. That way he went into a test knowing that he would fail and escaped feeling any pressure at all.

AP FRANK, COLLEGE FRESHMAN | PERCEIVED AS: THE WORKHORSE

Another Friday night, another night of no parties. Alone in his room as usual on a weekend night, AP Frank reflected on his first three weeks at college. He loved his dormmates, but when his Whitman friends talked about college, they said things like "I'm having the best time of my life!" When they asked AP Frank how he liked school, he could muster only "It's very nice."

He was trying to act the way a college student should, but he somehow felt removed from himself as a college student. His friends from home spoke of parties, multiple hookups, attractive girls, and wild adventures, while AP Frank's wildest night involved an Indian guy with a Mexican ID and a box of doughnut holes. AP Frank spent most of his evenings studying or playing video games in B31 with Mike and Andrew, whom he already knew would be lifetime friends. The next four years didn't seem like they would be the summer camp that his friends had assured him it would be. AP Frank felt as if he were missing out on something. He felt inadequate. Maybe, he thought, Harvard had been the wrong choice.

Granted, life at college was better than life at home. His mother reminded him of that with phone calls every other day. Sometimes the calls began harmlessly: "Frank! Remember to wash color clothes and white clothes separately!" she would say.

"Yeah, I know, Mom. You know, I got into Harvard. You're not giving me much credit for intelligence here."

Then the conversation would go where it always went: "And you must always study hard and get 4.0!"

This would be the point where AP Frank would hold the phone away from his ear until his mother's voice was a faint, unintelligible buzz. A 4.0 seemed impossible. AP Frank would wait until the buzz stopped and then say, "Yeah," into the mouthpiece. The buzz would start up again. When it slowed down, he would say, "I gotta go do homework now." After several more minutes of buzzing, AP Frank would say, "I really gotta do homework. Okay, 'bye," and hang up. Two days later, the conversation would repeat.

AP Frank's first semester included classes in French, multivariable calculus, expository writing, and classical music history, which fulfilled a core graduation requirement, so his mother couldn't protest. She didn't know, however, that AP Frank didn't like the idea of being a biology major. He detested memorizing what he called "endless facts of useless information"—hadn't he wasted high school doing exactly that? Instead, he was considering switching to an environmental science and public policy major, a shift that he fully expected his mother would view as cataclysmic should he choose to make it.

JULIE, SENIOR | PERCEIVED AS: THE SUPERSTAR

When Julie visited Brown for an autumn weekend, she liked that it seemed to be a relatively laid-back Ivy. Julie tried to compare some of the colleges she was considering. Dartmouth was a jock school where Julie didn't think she was fast enough to run. At Williams, students seemed intelligent and athletic. At Brown, she decided, the student body was so diverse that she couldn't place it under any umbrella terms. She could see herself in Providence, she thought. But she was waiting for a vision.

After lunch, Julie met with Brown's cross-country coach, who was friendly but forward. "What are your times?" he asked. She listed them, ending with her best 5K time, 19:36.

"To be a walk-on on my team, you'll need to be under 19:30," he said. "I don't want a big team, so I wouldn't be able to take you otherwise."

Julie thought she could hit that time. What the coach said next, however, gave her pause. He told her that he expected his athletes to keep up their academics and their running, and all other activities should be limited to one to two hours per week. Julie's heart sank. She loved running and wasn't sure if she wanted to stop being an athlete. But why bother going to a university that had so much to offer if she couldn't take advantage of the range of opportunities?

While other students could determine during a college visit whether they loved or hated the school, for Julie it took days of pondering before reaching her conclusion. Several days after her visit, Julie decided she didn't think Brown was right for her. Not long afterward, she wrote the following in a journal:

I'm waiting for an epiphany. I just know there will be some unmistakable sign that will tell me where to apply early for college. Early decision applications are due in exactly one month and I am so confused. I just hope that the epiphany comes before it's too late. I think my epiphany got stuck in traffic. I wonder if he's the kind to get stressed out and honk his horn or the kind to turn up the music and relax. I just hope he realizes that this is EARLY decision and he is way late.

So here I am waiting and hoping and translating my thoughts into Spanish (which I have the tendency to do, especially in the shower) when I realize that to wait and to hope is the same word in Spanish—esperar. I thought that this was merely coincidental until now. Are to wait and to hope really the same thing? I mean, as long as you are waiting, you still have hope, right? This realization about hoping and waiting must be good for something. Could I turn it into a college essay? Or perhaps I could sell it to Carrie Bradshaw as an idea for her Sex and the City article. I can just imagine her saying, "Women of New York: When you wait for love, are you really hoping it will come?"

TAYLOR, SENIOR | PERCEIVED AS: THE POPULAR GIRL

As Taylor walked in front of the bleachers at Whitman's homecoming football game, she looked around. She stood directly in front of the senior section, where Nastys were planted in the front rows, their faces painted blue, white, and black (Whitman colors) and their bodies squeezed into cutoff shorts and flip-flops, despite the early-October chill. They stood with guys who had their shirts off and successive letters—W, H, I, M, N— painted on their torsos in blue. The smart kids were gathered a few rows back. Taylor wasn't sure with which group she belonged.

She was stopped by a teacher who knew her through her student government activities. "So where are you going to college?" he grilled her. "What are you going to study?"

"Um . . ." Taylor hesitated. She had recently visited Duke, as her college counselor had instructed. On the rainy day she and her mother toured campus, the school failed to impress her, perhaps because the only reason for her trip was to compare it to Stanford. Taylor didn't rule out the state of North Carolina entirely. If she didn't get in early to Stanford, she would apply to Duke regular admission. In addition, Whitman administrators had chosen Taylor to be the school's nominee for the Morehead Scholarship at the University of North Carolina at Chapel Hill, a merit award for a four-year scholarship to UNC, including tuition, books, room and board, a laptop, and a semesterly stipend. She doubted her chances but agreed to fill out the application. "I'm applying to Stanford," Taylor finished.

"Oh, you can apply as an engineer and switch," the teacher said, implying that she should back-door her way into college with the intent of switching undergraduate programs once she got in.

"I have good math scores," Taylor said, too distracted to point out that she actually wanted to be an engineer.

"What's your GPA?" he asked.

"I don't know unweighted, but weighted, it's 4.71."

"What's your SAT?"

"1490."

"Smart."

Taylor was saved by a loud "Go Whitman!" cheer that lasted for thirty seconds, drowning out the conversation. The head Nasty came over and painted a white W on Taylor's cheek. Taylor had been close friends with the Nastys as a freshman and sophomore, when she hung out exclusively with the popular crowd, but had drifted from them junior year, when she focused on her studies more than they did. She still counted some Nastys as friends. When she heard the smart kids talking trash about the Nastys and other popular students, she stuck up for them, particularly the head Nasty, who was one of the sweetest people she knew.

By the waning minutes of the homecoming game, Taylor was standing with the Nastys in front of the bleachers, trying to rouse the fans. "Come on, parents!" Taylor and the Nastys yelled, hopping up and down. "Let's go, defense!" Taylor blended in seamlessly.

JULIE, SENIOR | PERCEIVED AS: THE SUPERSTAR

Midafternoon on the day of the homecoming dance, Julie and her mother went to the hair salon. Julie was sitting in the stylist's chair, trying to sort out her ambivalent feelings about homecoming as the stylist blew her ringlets straight, when she heard a gasp. The stylist called Julie's mother over and loudly pointed out the area where Julie's ponytail bump usually rested, where the hair had thinned so much that there was a noticeable spot. The Queen of Awkward said nothing while the stylist fussed in his thick French accent. Was it really necessary to call attention to it in front of the salon? As far as she knew, her stress had thinned her hair, and other than continuing to get doctors' opinions, there was nothing more she could do.

Back at home, Julie got ready by herself. Her bedroom had a soothing feel to it, with dark-and-light-blue-striped walls and a door covered in her race numbers from triathlons, road races, and state championships. Julie put on a little bit of makeup, then sat on her bedroom floor, painting her toenails light green to match her dress. Two weeks ago, she had bought an '80s-style dress to wear on Whitman Spirit Week's Decade Day, when students dressed in costume. She ultimately decided not to dress up; she didn't want to do something just because everyone else was doing it. Instead, she would wear the getup to homecoming, rationalizing that at least other students would assume she didn't take the dance seriously. Maybe they would even think she didn't care about not bringing a date. She kept her expectations low.

She slipped on the dress, which was patterned with hundreds of tiny light green, orange, black, and purple flowers. Slim-fitting with a short, pleated skirt, it flattered her trim runner's body. She ducked through a necklace of layered pearls, fitted neon fabric bracelets on her wrists, and put on large green hoop earrings and the big green plastic ring that had come with the nail polish. She dug a black leather Steve Madden purse out of her closet and, at her mother's insistence, wore black strappy heels instead of flip-flops. She looked down at herself. "I'm such a joke," she laughed, shaking her head. "I'm a living joke."

Julie sat with her mother at the kitchen table, babbling nervously as she waited for the doorbell to ring. The group would convene at Julie's house for pictures, get picked up by two Hummer stretch limos, go to a hotel for dinner, then arrive at the dance. Julie jabbered about her crush: "Derek was taking five APs, but he dropped one," she said. She looked at the clock. People were supposed to start arriving fifteen minutes ago. "I hate when the first person comes and you don't know the person very well."

As Julie drummed her fingers on the table, her mother went to look out the window. "Everyone's already outside, Julie!"

"Oh." Julie reluctantly followed her mother toward the mass of people.

About forty high school students in formalwear were gathered in the street in front of Julie's house. Julie found two of her closer River Falls friends and stood in a tight circle with them. The other River Falls girls joined them. Parents and little sisters dotted the curb, watching the students mingle and divide. The mother of a junior sighed to another spectator. "She's not in the alpha group," she said of her daughter, pointing to the River Falls crew, who were now posing in various permutations for pictures. "No more, no more! We can do this later!" the students insisted to their parents.

Julie was overwhelmed, lost within the crowd. Because she was dateless, she didn't have someone she could stand next to in the midst of the pandemonium. The sky was so heavy with the humidity of the coming rain that her straightened hair already was starting to frizz. She escaped from the mob scene back into the refuge of her bedroom. She gave her hair a disgusted grimace and tugged it into a high side ponytail that matched her '80s look. *There,* she thought, immediately feeling better about visually distancing herself from the group. *Now I look as ridiculous as I feel.* When she went back outside, she was surprised to find herself surrounded by girls who complimented her funky style.

At the sound of thunder, the parents shooed the group toward the

Hummers, trying to shield their children with umbrellas. "Load 'em up!" yelled a parent. The students filed inside the Hummers. Julie was the last one in.

❧

If Julie's thinning hair was a physical manifestation of stress, she wasn't alone. The rise of overachiever culture in recent years has led an alarming number of students to become overwhelmed by the pressure to succeed. A 2004 Mediamark survey found that more than half of American teenagers reported they were "stressed out all of the time or sometimes." More than two thirds of teens said that their biggest cause of stress was schoolwork, which beat out every other category listed, including money, body image, appearance, and relationships with friends, boyfriends/girlfriends, parents, and siblings. In 2000 a national teen newsmagazine attributed the rise in teen stress to "America's upwardly mobile, ultra-goal-oriented mindset." As one teen in that article said, "I even compete with my parents about who's stressing more. My dad's a lawyer, so I'm sure he's more stressed than I am. But there are days when I wonder."

There are some who say that stress can be a motivator and that the subsequent adrenaline rush can turn achievers into high achievers. Three quarters of honors and AP students report that homework- or activity-related stress is a serious problem among friends, as opposed to 57 percent of non-honors students. If for no other reason, student stress levels should be a cause for concern because of the dramatic effects stress can have on students' health. Mentally, overachiever stress can lead to events like Julie's September crying episode and Sam's fender bender, or, on a larger scale, depressive thoughts and behaviors, like those that a few Whitman students revealed to me later in the year (mental health is discussed in more detail in Chapter Fifteen). Physically, stress boosts levels of adrenaline and cortisol, which can suppress the immune system. If a child is stressed for a long enough period of time, the sustained high levels of those chemicals can cause changes in the body that could make it harder to learn as he or she grows older.

Beyond common stress-induced problems such as nausea, stomachaches, and headaches, high school students across the country report a number of other disturbing ways that school-related stress affects their health. A Colorado junior told me, "When I'm nervous, I run my fingers through my hair, and my hair has been thinning. It's horrible. And—this is really weird—when I'm worried, I peel the skin off my fingers around the nails and pick scabs and stuff. I'm constantly fretting about my future. It's not so much the grades or the tests. It's just . . . the pressure itself."

Caitlin, a Minnesota junior, described the symptoms that caused a doctor to diagnose her with a digestive disorder due to stress. She was so caught up in overachieving in classes and extracurriculars that she didn't even give herself enough relaxation time to use the bathroom. On one Saturday, after a week's worth of her usual severe constipation and stomach pains, Caitlin had both a speech tournament and a school basketball game. She woke up at five A.M. and advanced through the rounds to get second place in the tournament. After the awards ceremony, she had twenty minutes to change from her business suit to her basketball uniform. Already feeling queasy, she was warming up on the court when she realized she should have made time to go to the bathroom. Throughout the game and until late that night when she got home, the constipation pains were so sharp in her chest and stomach that she vowed to take basketball off her plate the following year. Though she did drop the sport, she was still taking doctor-prescribed medications a year later. "I have very physical reactions to stress, and I take on way too much by myself," Caitlin said.

Eating disorders are another pervasive health problem that can be caused by stress, particularly, doctors say, when students are perfectionists. "The girls with anorexia are primarily straight-A students," said Douglas Gray, University of Utah child and adolescent psychiatry training director.

Alyssa was in the top 10 percent of her 2,500-student Kentucky school, taking several APs, regularly winning school awards, and earning first place in a state art competition. But she felt she couldn't match up to her parents' standards or her own. She told me, "Perfection is something I constantly try to attain, even though I know deeply that it is impossible to achieve." Alyssa worked so hard that she couldn't remember the last time she "did anything that was normal teenage fun." By the end of junior year, her parents were pressuring her to work harder for colleges and to add more clubs to her list of eight, she was pulling a B in one of her classes, and her friends were falling by the wayside because she couldn't make time for them. That was when the panic attacks started. Her chest would close up, and her breathing would quicken as she was consumed by a feeling of being overwhelmed, thanks to "major school stress."

As a result, Alyssa turned to what she called her coping device: anorexia and bulimia, over which the overachiever in her could have full control. Her eating disorders were a "relief," she said, because she was able to cross at least one item—her weight—off the list of things she had to worry about. "If I wasn't eating, I wouldn't have to worry about it at all. I'd just work, work, work, fall asleep," she said. "Bulimia made me think it helped, because after you purge, it's like a relief, like it's all out, thank God. Like when you finish a big project and you're so relieved. It was a way to get that relief even though I hadn't finished the project yet."

While at one point she was purging five times a day and binging on 6,000-calorie meals, when we spoke, Alyssa was trying to battle the temptations to starve herself—but it was difficult for her to stop. "There's only so much you can push on someone. There's only so much you can do in school, classes you can take, hours you can put in before you start losing it. It makes you a wreck," she said. "There's only so much you can take before you just start breaking down."

SAM, SENIOR | PERCEIVED AS: THE TEACHER'S PET

Sam spent the afternoon of the homecoming dance getting a haircut, shopping with his mother for a shimmery purple shirt and bright purple tie, and playing basketball with his younger brother. He was both excited to attend his first big dance as a senior and anxious about whether the dance would be a repeat of last year's fiasco.

Sam's date was friendly enough at her house, while her parents and Sam's mother took pictures. She didn't flinch when Sam put his arm around her for the typical "cute couple" shot. When they walked into the gym, Sam's date immediately wanted to "find people," so they searched for her friends. They connected with the group and spent some time dancing in a circle and in twos. Surrounded by couples freaking (the twenty-first-century version of dirty dancing) and hooking up on the dance floor, Sam freaked his date briefly before backing off because he didn't want to make her feel uncomfortable. The second Sam stepped away, another senior freaked her from behind. She seemed to enjoy the attention. When she said she had to go to the bathroom, Sam didn't think much of it, until he realized she had been gone for half an hour. As the next slow song came over the speakers, Sam stood awkwardly in the middle of hundreds of swaying twosomes until a friend who didn't have a date spotted him and took pity.

When his date returned, Sam was irritated. "You missed a slow dance," he told her.

"Really, I couldn't give a shit," she responded.

"Oh . . . well, that's too bad," Sam said.

"Yeah, I guess so."

Sam was peeved. Why would you go to homecoming with someone you didn't want to slow-dance with? "You know what? I'll be back later," Sam said, and left to find Julie and her friends. He happily danced with them as they reveled in their seniorhood. He caught Ellie, another senior, looking at him from midway across the room. Ellie was a talented artist who was rumored to have a crush on Sam during sophomore and junior years. In June, they had gone on an unremarkable date. Afterward, Sam brushed her off and told other students that she was interested in him but the feeling wasn't mutual. Furious, Ellie had barely talked to him since. Tonight, he noticed, she looked beautiful.

When homecoming came to a close, Sam returned to his date for the final slow song. She seemed to consider the dance an obligation; there was perfunctory swaying, no eye contact, and complete silence between them. She spent the dance looking around the room at everyone but Sam.

At the after-party house, Sam and his date changed out of their formalwear for a sleepover. Immediately, she went upstairs, where she remained for the next hour with friends. At about one A.M., Sam went into the backyard, lay down on the lawn, looked up at the stars, and, alternating between anger and anguish, puzzled over where he had gone wrong. There was only one person who had the ability to make Sam feel better when he was this dejected.

JULIE, SENIOR | PERCEIVED AS: THE SUPERSTAR

After homecoming, Julie was sitting at a table of fifteen students, next to Derek and a few other guys talking about molecules at the Tastee Diner, a twenty-four-hour popular down-home diner. Most of the group was trying to figure out where to go next; cell phones rang every few minutes as calls came in from students either offering an after-dance option or asking if there were any parties with alcohol. A boy sitting near Julie asked another one if he drank. "No," the second boy said, and turned to the next guy. "Do you drink?" "No," said the next guy, who asked Julie. "No," she said.

Julie's phone rang. "What's up?" she answered.

"Well, I'm lying on the grass looking up at the stars outside the house," Sam said.

"Why?"

"I can't believe it. The exact same thing happened last year. My date's inside. She ditched me." He sounded glum.

"I'm sorry. You'd think you would have learned."

"Yeah. I hope you're having fun at Tastee's, and we definitely need to figure out what went wrong here."

"Okay," she said. With everyone else's phones ringing repeatedly, Julie felt cool getting a phone call, too, even if it was only Sam.

In the end, Julie enjoyed homecoming. The girls at her table had revealed their own awkward moments. All of them had something go wrong with their dresses: One girl's strap broke, another admitted she wore the same dress sophomore year, another got butter on her dress, and a third overheard a girl saying she didn't like her dress. Julie had such a good time dancing that she forgot she didn't have a date. When the last song of the night came on, a slow, cheesy song, Julie and about ten friends wrapped their arms around one another's waists and swayed in a circle together. It was their last song of their last homecoming. Thank God they wouldn't have to do it again.

TAYLOR, SENIOR | PERCEIVED AS: THE POPULAR GIRL

Welcome to Whitman Night was like overachiever heaven. The annual event, held in the cafeteria, showcased about a hundred extracurricular activities, mostly to give freshmen the opportunity to sign up for clubs. Student leaders vied for attention behind their assigned tables, from the Ping-Pong Club to the Juice Enthusiasts. The *Black & White* sold subscriptions, the Russian Club and Anime Club offered Russian and Japanese candy, the Spooky Movie Club showed *Freddy vs. Jason* on a small TV, and Whitman techies advertised with a poster: JOIN WHITMAN TECH: USE POWER TOOLS! BUILD SETS! PLUS, BLACK IS VERY SLIMMING! A huge crowd hovered around the DDR Club's attraction: Dance Dance Revolution, the interactive dance video game that was its namesake, in which two students at a time competed, jumping on the floor-pad footprints. Off to the side, girls practiced sock-footed on the tile, following the moves on the screen.

Not far from the Robotics team, Taylor played chess with Derek. Taylor liked hanging out with Derek, with whom she usually had substantive conversations. She also liked flirting with him; it was safe, because he already had a girlfriend, which was why she didn't let herself think of him as more than a friend. She often joked to her popular friends that if she and Derek both went to Stanford, she could end up marrying him.

Taylor surveyed the room. Some of her friends stood behind the tables, like Julie, who was advertising an Election Day hike, and Sam, who manned the debate table a row away. Taylor's popular friends were mostly in the courtyard, where student bands were playing a few sets. Tonight Taylor was at Welcome to Whitman to represent her Aid for AIDS club, which promoted AIDS awareness, though she had also participated in other groups.

An older gentleman watched Taylor and Derek for a few minutes before speaking. "You know, you can win in two moves," he said to Taylor.

"Umm, how?" she asked. He reached across the board and made the next two moves for her so that she had the chess club president in checkmate. Derek, always mellow, took it well. The few times Taylor had beaten him, she felt like she did when she was little and playing games against her parents, because, like them, Derek seemed genuinely happy for her when she won.

As Taylor and Derek set up the board for another game, they made fun of their private college counselor. Taylor liked the counselor because he thought she was funny, but she wasn't sure how helpful he was. When she got a C on a math test—the test she was studying for when she cut her bangs—her counselor told her to switch out of her AP BC Calculus class and drop down to the AB-level so she wouldn't get a B for the quarter. Taylor wasn't too upset about the C because the test was the hardest one she had taken in her life and she heard only two students got As. Plus, the night before, she had a soccer game at 5:15, a lacrosse meeting at 7:15, and then homework to do. Taylor ignored her counselor. She liked calculus and wanted to learn more about it, no matter how challenging it was. Quitting wasn't for her.

Taylor's counselor also had told her that none of her three college essays were good. He asked her to try a humorous essay and then said her attempt wasn't "intellectual enough." Yet when he edited the essays for her, his contributions included changing one sentence to a grammatically incorrect fragment, another into passive voice, and a third to include the phrase "during my freshmen year." Taylor didn't make any of the changes.

Taylor happened to mention her counselor's opinions to AP Frank during an online chat. She had met him in a biology class and gotten to know him better when he was a contestant in the Mr. Whitman pageant. Over the last few weeks, she had emailed him some of her essays to critique. When she told him that her counselor had pronounced one of the essays unsalvageable, AP Frank got angry. He despised the concept of a college counselor because he couldn't fathom, in his words, "the idea of anyone actually making a living telling kids what to say and what not to say for getting into college, for blowing the college application out of proportion, for stressing everyone out."

"Tell him AP Frank says to pack it in his rear," he typed. Those words of wisdom graced Taylor's IM profile for several days.

◦◦◦

M any people share AP Frank's opinion of private college counselors. In some circles, college counselors have acquired a reputation as overpriced status symbols who don't accomplish anything more than what parents could do on their own with a little time and thought. Parents pay anywhere from the low three figures to upward of $30,000 to individuals who may or may not be qualified to help them navigate the process.

Certainly, the experience depends on the counselor. As previously mentioned, Julie's college coach, Vera von Helsinger, was so fixated on her own reputation and so preoccupied with elite colleges that she dropped Julie rather than let a reporter follow a student whom she didn't expect to get in anywhere "good." Clearly, Vera had a narrow-minded interpretation of what a good college is. One would hope that most college counselors wouldn't be so obsessed with prestige—in this case, personal as well as institutional—that they would sacrifice their clients' best interests. But even the names of some college counseling companies illustrate where some advisers' attentions are focused; for starters, there's IvyWise, IvySuccess, PlayIvy, and the Ivy Guaranteed Admissions Program.

The Independent Educational Consultants Association (IECA), a national nonprofit professional association for private-practice "educational placement counselors," states that the consultant's job is to "find the best college 'fit.' " One IECA brochure explains, "By learning as much as they can about the student and family, the consultant can help identify the most suitable learning environments. . . . [Consultants] spend 20% of their time on the road, meeting with admissions officers, touring campuses, and exploring the campus environment. This personal insight provides a student with a much deeper understanding of a college than a catalog or website can convey. Because consultants are familiar with a multitude of colleges, they can present students with a wider selection of possibilities."

Another pamphlet states (emphasis theirs), "*Educational consultants are first and foremost advocates of the student.* Consultants help the family identify the learning environment that best suits the students." Unfortunately, the appeal of using a consultant who spends time visiting campuses to introduce students to a broader selection of possibilities is squelched when the consultant wants to focus only on the top twenty schools with which families are already familiar.

On several college counselors' websites, paragraphs are devoted to lists of clients who got into a specific pool of elite schools. IvySuccess crowed in 2005, "Last year, we've had students admitted to Brown with 1260 SAT; Harvard, Stanford, Yale, Princeton with 1360 SATs, just to name a few." Leaving aside the questionable decision to give your child's college application to a company that advertises itself with such a grammatically awkward sentence, one notices that the emphasis is only on names and numbers. The company doesn't say, for example, "We helped 95 percent of our clients find schools they love." Instead, many consultants base their reputation on the number of students they've helped place at prestigious universities, regardless of whether the students were actually happy there.

It's disconcerting enough that an entire industry treats the college application process like a business, but worse, in many cases, private college counselors' aim appears to have shifted from finding a school that matches a student to retooling a student to match a school. Some of today's college counselors tell parents that they should begin to sign up for services when their children are in middle school. That way the counselors can start molding students early, choosing classes and extracurriculars, lining up internships and community service opportunities, and selecting a unique activity to make a student stand out among competitors in the application process several years away. Counselors can go from helpful guides to Dr. Frankensteins, re-creating lives and rewiring identities to have the teenage monsters perfected in time for their admissions debuts.

New Jersey IvySuccess consultant Robert Shaw had an Asian client who was in the top fifth of her class at Holmdel High, a school where Asian-Americans comprise 22 percent of the student body. In order to make the student better resemble Ivy League material, Shaw told her to move. She and her family moved ten miles north to a school district with few Asians and an SAT average that was 300 points lower than in her old district. The consultant also told her to enter the Miss New Jersey Teen pageant because it would set her apart from other top students. At her new school, the girl was class valedictorian; in the pageant, she won the talent competition with a piano performance. She was accepted to Yale and MIT.

Maybe more startling than the consultant's suggestion to move was the parents' willingness to do so. College counselors report that they receive increasing numbers of panicked phone calls about students at younger and younger ages. Massachusetts educational consultant Mary Mansfield said, "We're trying not to be bulldozed by the pressure from the media and the families. Our job is to make the best match. I actually had an inquiry come to me within the last couple of weeks: 'How can you get my child into the best possible college?' I answered, 'We try to make the best possible match for *your student,* and I want you to understand that's what we do.'"

Others don't. The founder of IvyWise, which charges up to $33,000 for two years of her services, told the *Wall Street Journal* that if a student's résumé needs a boost, "I might put you in an art program in Mexico for 10 weeks in a little town where you can do pottery and learn Spanish [or suggest a trip to Asia] where you study with Tibetan monks." Some college counselors seem to have forgotten that there's a monumental difference between college search and college prep. Ivy-Success advertises (caps theirs) that "getting into the right college is a matter of INSIDE KNOWLEDGE, EARLY PLANNING, and STRATEGIC POSITIONING." The company bills itself as "an admissions strategy firm" and declares, "We are STRATEGISTS." That's precisely the problem.

Some companies run college application camps, two-week programs on university campuses during which students are coached through the application and essay-writing process. For a few thousand dollars, parents can send their children to be counseled on where to apply, how to handle interviews and take standardized tests, and what to include in their essays. The essay coaching highlights another questionable issue with the college consultant industry: Instead of merely helping students present themselves in the best light, companies are fiddling with their content, and some consultants actually write the essays themselves.

EssayEdge, the self-proclaimed biggest online essay service, provides a college applicant with a "Harvard-educated editor" who, for $299.95, helps select an essay topic, then edits the essay until it is perfected. Its website boasts, "Our 200+ Harvard-educated editors do not merely offer critiques and proofing; they also provide superior editing and admissions consulting, giving you an edge over hundreds of applicants with comparable academic credentials." If a professional vaults a student's essay to the "superior" level, how does that essay truly reflect the student? Letting a "Harvard-educated editor" perfect a student's essay seems akin to hiring a NASCAR driver to steer a kid through his driver's test. Admissions officers detest essay consulting, for the most part, and sometimes can tell when an essay has been professionally polished.

In fact, if an applicant has relied too much on outside help, his chances of acceptance could drop. A former Dartmouth admissions officer remembered "fantastically packaged applications with names of Such-and-Such Associates on the cover and with the applicant's name in the window." He said, "That gave you a bad feeling right from the outset. Here you are, making a case that you're ready for the nation's finest schools, and you can't even do your own application." Swarthmore dean of admissions Jim Bock said that professionally polished applications in plastic or binders "can leave a bitter taste."

The IECA doesn't encourage this kind of packaging; one consultant who sent applications to colleges packaged with cover sheets advertising her services is no longer a member. The IECA requires members to have three years of industry experience, visits to at least a hundred college campuses, at least seventy-five prior clients, references from clients and colleges, and a master's degree in a related field. But it has seen the industry tainted as unqualified individuals have rushed to take advantage of the admissions hype. Between 2002 and 2005, the number of private counselors jumped from 1,000 to 3,000. Subsequently, the IECA, which has about 500 approved consultants, recently began reviewing the marketing materials of prospective members. "If a person spends too much of their marketing talking about getting a kid in, or emphasizes putting together the student's application, we deny them membership," IECA executive director Mark Sklarow told me. "Packaging the kid won't give colleges an accurate view of the applicant right from the beginning."

Many of these new, uncredentialed consultants don't have the necessary training or qualifications, but because there's no central governing board, anyone can call herself a private college counselor. About ten years ago, 1.5 percent of parents with college-bound students hired one of the 400 or so private college counselors in the United States. Today 6 percent of parents hire counselors—the number leaps to 20 percent in the Northeast—and 10 percent of high school seniors pay for some sort of professional assistance with their applications or essays. Even test prep services are jumping onto the bandwagon. Several parents have complained that their children's SAT tutors badger them to sign on with their company's college counseling services.

There are, however, hundreds of counselors who genuinely have their clients' best interests in mind, including companies that offer free services to help low-income students navigate the admissions process and financial aid applications. In another effort to help level the playing field, some corporations—among them IBM, Johnson & Johnson, PepsiCo, and Goldman Sachs—contract with College Coach to offer admissions assistance as an employee benefit.

In 2000 a Massachusetts high school also contracted with College Coach. It was reportedly the first public high school to outsource college counseling to a private company, to the dismay of guidance counselors statewide. The high school claimed it chose to privatize because of a sudden shortage of experienced guidance counselors. That concern is one of the justifications that private college counselors cite. While the American School Counselor Association recommends a ratio of one school counselor for every 250 students, the reality is that the national average is about one for every 500; California's average is closer to one for every 1,000.

There are plenty of school counselors who can handle the workload on their own. In Hawaii, I visited Earle Hotta, the post–high school counselor for Maui High School, at the home where he hosts college directors of admissions who come to the island on recruiting trips. When Hotta, a past president of the Hawaii Association for College Admission Counseling, realized several years ago that college admissions officials ignored the Hawaiian representatives at national conferences, he changed his game plan. He began offering college officials his own home as a free place to stay, and persuaded his mother, "Grandma Doris," to sew hundreds of Hawaiian-style welcome bags, which Hotta fills with jams, tea leaves, and fruit from his own backyard garden. Hotta and his secretary make leis for the guests, and Hotta and his wife host home-cooked meals. Hotta pays for all of this himself but said the benefits have been "tremendous"; on an island where Hotta knew of only one private college counselor, admissions offices now pay attention to Maui.

But most counselors don't have the time to be Earle Hotta, so the brunt of the college search often falls on parents, many of whom find the process complex and overwhelming. That's where private college counselors can come in handy. For every college counselor who is blinded by prestige, there are others who are determined to do the right thing.

In 2004 I attended the IECA's fall conference in New Orleans, where I sat in on a discussion entitled "Selective College Admissions: 2005 Outlook." (Disclosure: I was a keynote speaker at this conference.) The consultants began by talking about an issue with which many of them were clearly struggling: the increasingly complicated admissions pool options of early action, early decision, and early decision 2, a second-round option with a later deadline. The counselors had seen a marked rise in the number of students applying early. "I don't think it's a good thing," one counselor said. "However, if you're going to have a strategy for these kids, they may lose out, and it may be your fault."

The counselors discussed the difficulty of catering to parents who couldn't understand how quickly the college admissions landscape had changed. "Parents say, 'Fifteen years ago, you only had to be barely breathing to get in there,'" said Mary Mansfield, the moderator.

"Or 'Two years ago, when my other child applied, that was on his safety list, and he wasn't as good a student,'" an audience member added.

The counselors debated the merits of early-decision programs. "We, as educational consultants, have to understand that colleges are doing this from a marketing perspective. The more supply and demand they can create, the more frenzy they can create," said a counselor with a twang. "At what point do we let their marketing propaganda influence us? Colleges just want to fill seats. I don't think we should get into that frenzy."

"It's about the rankings, frankly," said a Maryland consultant. "They want the yield." (The yield is the percentage of admitted students who accept an offer to enroll.)

The discussion moved on to address the growing level of competition for college spots. "Everyone has become more competitive. We know that it is overall a shift, a seismic shift," the Maryland consultant said.

"[Financial] aid is leveraged in so many schools," another consultant added. "You really need to drop the selectivity down."

"And they're still—hello!—going to get a great education," Mansfield said. "They are going to get a great education."

AP FRANK, COLLEGE FRESHMAN | PERCEIVED AS: THE WORKHORSE

AP Frank was still in his slump. His weekdays were all right; most of his classes were engaging, and he loved his dorm friends, especially Kristen, Mike, and Andrew. Between his thrice-weekly wushu practices, which enthralled him, and biweekly Ultimate Frisbee practices, he had gained ten pounds of muscle. Ultimate practices exhausted him, but he was willing to work through the exhaustion and pain in order to improve, and because he was happy to be playing outside regularly, which he hadn't done in years. As a Mass Hall intramural representative, AP Frank also played several other intramural sports. For their team name, Mass Hall had chosen the Silencers, because of its reputation as the quietest freshman dorm.

Weekend nights were another story. AP Frank had yet to attend what he considered "an actual party." He didn't know many Harvard students outside of his dormmates and was wary of calling people too many times a week because he didn't want to seem needy. He knew he wasn't the only one who was slumping. Even Mike, who was usually a riot, seemed subdued. A group of Silencers were walking back to their dorm on the notoriously cracked pavement along Massachusetts Avenue, when AP Frank tripped so hard he almost face-planted. Embarrassed, he looked around. It seemed that nobody had noticed. But back at the dorm, Mike said to him, "Shit, man. I'm feeling so down lately. Like, when you tripped back there, any other day I totally would have laughed my ass off and made fun of you, but today I'm just not feeling it."

AP Frank had spent his first month of weekends at college mostly wandering around the campus, searching unsuccessfully for parties, and returning to his room alone, dejected, bored, and feeling "like a freshman." At this rate, Harvard wasn't going to give him the chance to shed his self-described "skinny, nerdy kid who's never had a girl" aspect. Harvard, considered the most desirable school for many overachievers worldwide, didn't seem to be the school for him, a notion he found depressing.

AP Frank shared some information about his activities with his father but told his mother nothing. As far as she knew, all he did was study, which was the way she would want it. Her calls had gradually waned to once or twice a week, and he was slowly beginning to separate her dreams from his. A 4.0 in college was different from a 4.0 in high school, because in high school, a 90 percent was an A, or a 4.0; in college, a 90 percent was an A-minus, or a 3.7. In high school, he had gunned for the 4.0 to get his mother off his back, but now he wanted to be good enough only for himself. He was consciously doing his best, but if it didn't amount to a 4.0 in the end, then that was fine with him.

When it came to study habits, that attitude and other factors took some of the pressure off. He had half the classes he did in high school, it was easier to find ways to waste time in college, and he realized he didn't have to be so hard-core about studying. At Whitman, if a teacher assigned a chapter and said there would be a test on it in two weeks, AP Frank memorized every piece of information in the textbook until he could cite precisely on which page each fact appeared. At Harvard, by contrast, he would read a chapter, underline the information he deemed important, and study only that. To him, these new habits seemed lazy, but he was a happier person for them. He told a Whitman friend, "I have very little pressure to overachieve—nobody's judging me now. The 4.0 and the job at NIH and all that bull was to get into college. Now I do what I like. I'm not going to take more advanced classes if I don't like the subject or if they cut into my social life, and I'm not going to do clubs that I don't enjoy. I only have to satisfy my own ambition now, and no one else's."

The friend told AP Frank he might use that philosophy to address his perception of his social life, too. She told him to organize social activities with his Frisbee and wushu teammates and to get out of his room more often. "You know," she said, "nothing sucks as much as sitting alone in your room, *thinking* that everything sucks."

AP Frank considered this. She was right. Just as he didn't have to live his academic life by someone else's standards anymore, he didn't have to live his social life by other people's rules. "Yes, a lot of my friends are getting drunk as hell. Yes, a lot of my friends are getting incomprehensible amounts of ass. Yes, a lot of my friends aren't freaking out about their work like I sometimes do. Or people may be getting drunk, but not everyone is getting ass. But I think that that's just the type of people they are," he said.

AP Frank realized he wasn't alone in feeling that college wasn't all he had envisioned it to be. He resolved to try to take his social life as it came instead of worrying about it—and to try not to think about the lack of girls who were interested in him. If he could bide his time, something would come eventually. "Harvard isn't the issue," he concluded. "It's just me. Which is okay."

Chapter 4

October 7–October 23

NUMBERS

THE STEALTH OVERACHIEVER, JUNIOR | PERCEIVED AS: ?

The Stealth Overachiever, a Whitman junior, was sitting in PSAT prep class, waiting for the teacher from the company running the class to hand out the latest round of diagnostic test scores. "Pretty good," the teacher said as he handed Stealth the score breakdowns: a 2380 out of 2400. Stealth was pleased but guardedly so. What if the company made the diagnostics easier so students would think the class was working? Stealth carefully slipped the paper into a binder before anyone could see.

The Stealth Overachiever was perhaps a Whitman anomaly, the type of student who racked up an impressive college résumé while flying beneath the radar. Students and teachers alike didn't know that Stealth was an overachiever. They didn't know Stealth spent part of each summer at debate camp or that often, when Stealth was "going out of town for the weekend," there happened to be a debate tournament. Most students didn't pay attention to the debate team. They didn't keep track of Stealth's long list of extracurricular activities, and Stealth didn't talk about standardized test scores or other achievements. Others in the Whitman community simply assumed that because, to their knowledge, the junior wasn't a standout, Stealth must have been no better than average. Once, when Stealth had done well on an English paper, a friend happened to spot Stealth's grade and remarked, astonished, "I can't believe you did well on this! I'm a slacker, but I get it done. You're a slacker, but you don't get it done." Stealth was amused by the grade discrepancy that had the friend so nonplussed: Stealth scored a high A. The friend got a low A. Classmates wouldn't have been surprised to know that, the night before an AP BC Calculus test, Stealth went to a Metallica concert. They wouldn't have guessed, however, that Stealth brought the calculus textbook and some homework along to the concert to study during the opening act.

AUDREY, JUNIOR | PERCEIVED AS: THE PERFECTIONIST

By October, Audrey's routine was a wreck. She had to set two or three alarms to jolt her out of bed by 6:50. Breakfast now consisted of grabbing a plastic bag of cereal that a parent left for her on the kitchen counter, then running out the door. It was no mystery why Audrey had been sleep-deprived since the first week of school. Her long list of activities—*Black & White,* varsity swim team, weekly mass, Young Democrats, Model United Nations, Spanish Honors Society, Art Honors Society, a Native American youth outreach program, and recreational soccer—sapped her time and energy. Audrey and a friend also ran a catering service, creating menus, cooking, serving, and cleaning for everything from a bat mitzvah to a dinner party for forty people. Yet Audrey knew a handful of students involved in even more activities. She was most jealous of their ability to get by on less sleep.

When Audrey's Honors Physics teacher announced in class that he was handing out packets outlining the requirements for this year's Physics Olympics competition, Audrey perked up. Physics Olympics was an engineering/design competition for which students had three days to choose a partner and a project, due in a month. The top project in each category would move on to the county-level competition. Her heart racing, Audrey was tantalized by the idea of an academic contest, especially in Whitman's ultra-competitive atmosphere. She knew that she worked harder and spent more time on long-term assignments than most of her peers, and with this project, her perfectionism could bring an additional payoff. She was determined to make it to the county Physics Olympics.

Audrey wanted to prove herself to her physics teacher, because she hadn't been doing wonderfully in the class thus far. Because of the county's new grading policy, her B grade was based mostly on tests, which was unfortunate because test scores rarely reflected her knowledge of a subject. Teachers seemed to be confused about how to implement the new grading policy, and the students were paying the price. But Audrey had heard from older friends that if a student qualified for the Physics Olympics, the physics teachers were so besotted with the competition that they would be more lenient when it came to report card time, bumping, say, an 86 up to an A. Of course, there was also the college résumé. Winning a science competition indisputably would look good to colleges.

As soon as the teacher finished explaining the rules, a friend of Audrey's asked to partner with her for the first group project of the year. Usually, Audrey ended up doing all of the work on a group project, often hosting meetings at her house, spending hours preparing for the meetings, and later, redoing other students' work. Sometimes her redos would upset groupmates who felt that Audrey considered their work inferior, but most loved working with her because they knew they would get the A without having to work too hard for it.

Audrey and her partner decided to take on a bridge project. The bridge was to be built with only toothpicks and glue (though it was against the rules to coat the bridge in glue), and it had to hold one brick for ten seconds in two places, on its center and toward its side. That night Audrey spent hours online, looking up toothpick projects from high schools across the country to collect tips and ideas. By the time her partner came over for the first weekend of work, Audrey already had pages of research organized and was busy at her calculator, working out the lengths the toothpicks needed to be in order for the bridge to stand solidly between the two supports.

SAM, SENIOR | PERCEIVED AS: THE TEACHER'S PET

It was the Friday before Whitman's Senior Stress Week, which couldn't have come at a better time for Sam. Senior Stress Week was a time chosen by the administration when teachers weren't supposed to give major assignments or tests so that seniors could focus on college applications. Not only was it the day before the SAT, but Sam also had to complete his personal statement essay and an AP English research paper, edit the next *Black & White* issue, train the Student Congress team for the upcoming tournaments, and rehearse for hours on *Les Mis*, Whitman's fall musical, for which he was playing keyboard. Like the other seniors, Sam was relying on Senior Stress Week to allow him to catch his breath. His teachers, however, had other ideas.

In AP Calculus, when the teacher announced that there would be a test the following week, the students were silent. "Um"—Sam raised his hand—"isn't there any way we can get a tiiiny break?"

"This is an AP class. We don't have time to slow down," the teacher said. "I'm sorry, but that's just the way it works."

When the AP Physics teacher, too, announced a test, no one else had the courage to complain. Sam looked around the room in disgust. Did people not realize it was Senior Stress Week? Sam saw his classmates as "humorless robots" who sucked in the information thrown at them, divided it into folders on their mental computers, and then processed it without protest. Again Sam was the lone voice of dissent: "Isn't it supposed to be Senior Stress Week?"

The AP Physics teacher adopted his usual patronizing tone. "This is AP. This is Whitman. You guys are more than capable." That was practically his catchphrase, in various permutations: "This is physics. This is AP. This is Whitman." Actually, this was hell.

In AP French, Sam halfheartedly tried again to postpone the next week's test. "You, as students, are at a complete disadvantage," the teacher responded. "This is one of the most difficult AP exams, and we can't take a break. I need to teach you five years of French so that you know it as well as you know counting to ten." Sam didn't argue her point; he agreed that this was the one class in which students who needed to do well on the AP exam couldn't afford to fall behind.

In Honors Modern World History, yet another teacher announced an upcoming test. This time Sam heard murmurs around the room. Sam again spoke up for the seniors, presuming that this teacher, at least, couldn't use the AP excuse, because the class was only honors level.

"I'm sorry, no," the teacher said. "This is effectively an AP class."

∽

Sam's Senior Stress Week experience underscores a larger issue that many students grapple with, particularly in AP classes: Increasingly, classes are taught to a test. Teachers are pressured to ignore students' workload concerns and interest in perspectives that deviate from the schedule's steady, unrelenting march toward a state or AP exam. Some schools require that any student who takes an AP class must take the national test. For these reasons, over the past few years, many elite private schools have dropped AP courses.

Obsessed with the perceived prestige of AP classes, certain school districts do whatever they can to persuade students to take an AP test (even if students haven't taken the class). Some AP teachers automatically boost students' grades if they do well on an AP exam. Several schools offer incentive programs providing AP tutoring, teacher training, and the $82 test fee, not to mention cash, cars, and computers.

Top students need little arm-twisting to load up their schedules with AP classes. Where AP and International Baccalaureate classes used to be marks of an overachiever, now students view them as necessities to get a high class rank (some schools' GPA calculations give students one or two bonus points for AP and IB classes) and to be accepted into a selective college. In a 2002 survey, 83 percent of high school seniors who were awarded a three or higher on certain AP exams said they took AP courses because they wanted to be a more attractive applicant to the colleges of their choice. Students fear that if they don't pack their schedules with the available AP classes, they won't be seen as good students. As a parent told *The Washington Post,* "We're turning into a two-tiered system. You're either advanced or you're remedial. There's no room for anyone in between."

Indeed, some parents judge high schools based on the number of AP classes offered, pressuring schools to offer AP courses for which they may have neither the resources nor properly trained teachers, and pushing students into these advanced classes. Meanwhile, a 2004 Berkeley study found that, "controlling for other academic and socioeconomic factors, the number of AP and honors courses taken in high school bears little or no relationship to students' later performance in college."

The high-stakes testing culture shifted into overdrive in 2002, when George W. Bush's No Child Left Behind Act (NCLB) was signed into law. The act requires all schools to test every student on reading and math each year in the third through eighth grades and at least once from the tenth through the twelfth grades. Schools that don't demonstrate acceptable progress in each of their student subgroups (including racial and economic groups, non–native English speakers, and children with disabilities) are penalized with sanctions, including withdrawal of federal funds and being forced to allow students to transfer to higher-scoring schools. Beginning in 2008, three grades will also be tested on science knowledge. By the 2013–2014 academic year, all children must score at grade level on the annual state tests that track their achievement. (Under NCLB, which comes up for reauthorization in 2007, schools that don't release student information to military recruiters also lose federal funds.)

No Child Left Behind has already changed the face of the United States classroom, and the results are disturbing. The exclusive emphasis on tests has left students sick with stress in even the youngest grades; some schools reported that on testing days, up to two dozen children vomit on their test booklets. In Florida, when a seventeen-year-old honor roll student failed the state test and was told she wouldn't graduate with her class, she attempted to kill herself. A 2005 *Psychological Science* study found that heightened test pressure decreases test results for strong students more so than for mediocre students; the performance of top students, therefore, could drop in an intense testing atmosphere.

Most notably, because schools are held accountable for their students' scores and punished if all scores aren't up to par, they have shifted their curricula to teach to the test. Because of time and budgets, subjects not covered by NCLB are often eliminated, including art, music, gym, foreign languages, and even social studies and science. Certain elementary schools prohibit teachers from teaching some of these subjects until after the tests are administered in the spring.

Teachers spend classroom hours not only on the tested subjects but also on how to mark answer bubbles on a score sheet. In 2003, four out of five elementary school teachers surveyed by the National Board on Educational Testing and Public Policy said that they had little time to teach students material not included on state tests. Almost 70 percent of teachers report feeling test stress, and veteran teachers are leaving public schools for private schools, which aren't forced to give NCLB exams. School counselors, too, are affected: Researchers have found that when counselors take on increased administrative and test proctoring tasks, the number of students at their school who go on to college decreases.

President Bush has said that No Child Left Behind "makes sense, frankly, if you're an innovative teacher." In truth, the unwavering spotlight on tests has sent innovation out the window. There's no time for it. When children have personal observations or questions about current events, or when they are eager to explore a new subject, many teachers aren't afforded the flexibility to carry that enthusiasm and curiosity into a classroom lesson. Unless a topic can be drilled into students, memorized, and tested on a state exam, in the government's eyes, it's apparently not worth teaching. Neither teachers nor students are encouraged to think creatively and independently. They are taught to be good test takers. They are taught there is only one answer per question (and a corresponding test bubble). They are taught that they are numbers, they are scores, they are cogs in a wheel.

In what's been called a "rebellion" and an "unprecedented bipartisan revolt" against the White House's education centerpiece, at the time of this writing, forty-seven states were considering action against NCLB mandates. In August 2005 Connecticut was the first state to sue the federal government over NCLB, charging the Bush administration with being "rigid, arbitrary and capricious" in enforcing annual testing that was "unsupported by significant scientific research" and wouldn't help its students.

The same year, nine school districts and ten chapters of the National Education Association (NEA)—the country's largest teachers' union—sued the Department of Education over NCLB. By law, the government can't require states to spend their own money to enforce federal policies, but the NEA estimated NCLB funding was at least $27 billion short of what was needed to prepare, test, and score students. In response, former education secretary Rod Paige, who had worked with the White House to draft the NCLB law, called the 2.7 million–member union a "terrorist organization."

There are signs that No Child Left Behind was flawed from the start. In his 2000 campaign, Bush hailed what he called the "Texas Miracle," a sharp turnaround in dropout rates and test scores that accompanied new policies holding principals and teachers directly accountable for their students' test scores—particularly in Houston, the largest school district in Texas. Under then–Houston school superintendent Rod Paige, principals had yearly contracts. Those who achieved low dropout rates and high test scores were rewarded with bonuses up to $5,000; those who didn't could be transferred or demoted. With its nationally recognized increase in test scores and staggeringly low dropout rates, Houston became both the impetus and the model for NCLB, and Bush appointed Paige to his cabinet as his education secretary.

But the Texas Miracle has since been exposed as something more resembling the Texas Fraud. While Houston reported a dropout rate of 1.5 percent in 2001–2002, an investigation revealed that the actual figure was closer to between 25 and 50 percent; citywide, nearly 3,000 dropouts were hidden in other categories to keep the recorded rate low. Investigators also discovered that Houston's test scores were suspect. Under pressure to raise scores or leave the school system, principals cheated on the tests by making sure low-scoring students didn't sit for the exams, holding students back, forcing the students out of school before testing years, or skipping them over the tested grade. One Houston high school allegedly held back almost two thirds of its freshmen so they wouldn't take the tenth-grade state assessment test.

Teachers and local officials contend that NCLB may actually reverse the positive inroads states were making before the law went into effect because of the way it has changed classroom learning. In Washington State, most principals and three quarters of teachers surveyed said that their test score gains were attributable to improved student test prep, not improved student knowledge.

There's also the issue of the tests, which are created and scored under increasing time pressure. In 2004, 120,000 Connecticut students' state tests had to be reevaluated after state officials noticed a glitch in the scoring. In Massachusetts, 1,115 students failed state math tests because a question had more than one correct answer; when the tests were rescored, the students passed. In Minnesota, when a girl flunked the state math test by one answer, her father had to threaten a lawsuit to get state officials to show him the answers; he discovered that six of the sixty-eight answers on the test were incorrectly keyed. Incorrect answer keys were also discovered in Arizona, Michigan, and Washington.

Because of NCLB, one researcher said, "It's just really happening that schools are sacrificing kids to make schools appear to look better." At some schools, students who do well on NCLB state tests are rewarded with exemptions from final exams. Those who don't, however, face grave consequences. In 2003 approximately 12,800 high school seniors in Florida—most of whom had fulfilled their school's graduation requirements—were refused diplomas because they hadn't passed their state's assessment test, some by only a point. In Massachusetts, special education students were refused test waivers, meaning that a student with Down syndrome who had been accepted to culinary school could not attend, and a special-needs student who failed the state math test for the fifth time was denied a diploma. Within a year, the latter student died of an OxyContin overdose. "I listen to these politicians talk about No Child Left Behind," this student's father told the *Boston Herald*. "What a sham, a fraud. The children who need their help the most, like my daughter, are the very ones they're leaving behind."

Instead, they've been sucked into the dreary tedium of a hypertesting culture that affects all students, a culture that compromises the quality of education in the United States—stressing out students, draining passion from learning, and siphoning money from classrooms to private testing and tutoring companies. It is a culture that teaches us to judge and divide schools and students exclusively by test scores, although even the companies that create the tests have warned that this is not a prudent way to make important decisions about students' learning. Little wonder that one critic refers to the law as "No Child Left."

JULIE, SENIOR | PERCEIVED AS: THE SUPERSTAR

The night before the SAT, Julie IMed Derek: "So what should I do to prepare to get 1600 like you?"

"You should cram a thousand vocabulary words the night before, like I did." Evidently, the legend was true: One last-minute cram session was all Derek had done to study for the biggest test of most students' lives. Julie went to a football game instead.

The morning of the SAT, she woke up grumpy and with a stomachache. On the way to Whitman, she remembered that Derek had taken caffeine pills before the test. *Gotta be like Derek,* she thought, and stopped at Starbucks for tea. The test seemed to go all right, and afterward she felt as if a weight that had been on her shoulders for so long that she had forgotten about it was finally gone.

Unfortunately, when she should have been out celebrating with friends, Julie had to go home, inhale a quick lunch, and run in a tough cross-country meet in Virginia. Because the team bus left during the SAT, Julie had to make the long drive with her mother. It was just as well—Julie was still crabby. If she had been on the bus with her teammates, however, she was sure they wouldn't have been talking about the race. Julie's mother kept bringing it up. "You have to beat those C. Milton Wright girls!"

Julie chafed. C. Milton Wright was a rural Maryland school that was famous for its championship running program. Julie was tired of talking about running, weary of running itself. "Stop! I don't want race strategy from you. I don't want to be here," she said. "I don't want to do cross country anymore."

Her mother didn't seem fazed. "All right, if you don't like it, there's no reason you have to do it."

"I hate this. I'm so done with this," Julie affirmed. "I'm ready to move on. And my shoulder hurts."

"Maybe that's your epiphany," said her mother.

When they got to the meet, Julie's mother helped her do some yoga to stretch her shoulder and to calm down. By the time Julie joined her team on the sidelines, she was feeling slightly better but still not fired up to run. At the starting line, she set her feet, leaned forward, and tried to focus on the race, though she cared less about this meet than about any other she could remember. The gun went off. Three hundred girls started exceptionally fast across the field. Julie usually began races too quickly and had hoped to pace herself, but she was immediately boxed in, with no choice except to keep up with the pack. She looked around her. Most of the girls up front were from Virginia schools she didn't recognize. Then she spotted a girl from her county who often ran at Julie's speed. *Stick to her,* Julie told herself. *Do whatever she does.* For the first mile, Julie concentrated on staying with her. At the mile mark, a coach called out her time: 5:52, the fastest mile she had ever run in a 5K. *That's too fast!* Julie thought. Frustrated with herself for not following her own pace, Julie let the county girl slip away.

The pattern of the course was called a "lollipop loop," up and around an enormous field. As Julie passed the team tent, she heard cheers and glanced toward the sidelines. She saw her mother pumping her fists. Her coach was smiling at her, the boys' team was cheering for her, and even a few Whitman alumni home for fall break were clapping for her. *I have to show them I'm good,* Julie thought. Running, according to experts Julie had read, was supposed to be a 95 percent mental sport. Julie disagreed with this assessment. She tended to think too much during races (as she did when she wasn't racing); when she just stopped thinking, she was "on." Julie was convinced that running was a 100 percent mental sport in that successful runners could clear their heads of distractions.

During the second mile, Julie's thoughts of the SAT, colleges, stresses, epiphanies—all of the issues that had been dogging her—dissolved. She heard only the cheers. Every time she heard spectators yell another name, she pretended they were screaming for her.

Julie zeroed in on the girl from her county and passed her. She saw four girls from a highly respected Virginia school racing in a pack and told herself to pretend she was part of their circle. She stuck to them throughout the second mile, after which her time was 12:15, a more reasonable pace for a 5K but still faster than Julie had gone in the past without burning out. Normally, when Julie raced, she did the math in her head to calculate how she could finish with a good time. Today she was too focused to care. But as she approached the last section of the course, a gradual uphill three-quarter-mile, she held back. *I'm going to die on that hill because I went out way too fast.*

The girl in front of Julie turned her head to listen to her coach's instructions from the sidelines: "Use your miler's kick! Take it in!" *Hey, I'm a miler. I can take it in, too,* Julie thought. She sped up and passed the girl. She heard a spectator goading another girl, "That girl in front of you has your medal! Go get your medal!" *I can do that,* Julie thought, and sprinted harder than she had run a final leg the entire season. Racing so quickly she was afraid she would trip, she homed in on the girls ahead of her in the open field and picked off two of them. Gunning for the one last girl between her and the end, Julie blew by just before she whipped across the finish line.

Julie looked at the time board: 19:20. She did a double take. She had run a full ten seconds faster than she needed to in order to make the

Brown varsity team. She had just completed the fastest race of her life. The girl Julie had passed in the final seconds approached her. "Good race," she said.

"You, too," Julie said. "What school are you from?"

"C. Milton Wright."

A volunteer handed Julie her place card: 14/300. Members of the Whitman boys' team crowded around to congratulate her. Her mother gave her a hug. "And you thought you never wanted to run again!" she said. "By the way, I was talking to the C. Milton Wright coach, who told me a girl who finished twentieth today and runs a five-minute mile is probably going to run at Yale."

This got Julie thinking. She had given up on too many things in high school that she had been good at, among them student government and yearbook. *I keep on starting over,* she thought. *Maybe I should stick with running. If I don't run in college, I might regret it and then spend the rest of my life going around saying, "I could've run in college. I was good enough. I just decided not to."*

AP FRANK, COLLEGE FRESHMAN | PERCEIVED AS: THE WORKHORSE

AP Frank was hanging out in his friend Lydia's room one evening when they got to talking about classes. An even more disciplined student than AP Frank, Lydia asked him about the kind of GPA he was willing to work for. "Certainly not a 4.0," he said. "It's simply not worth the required effort."

"Well, you know, it's pretty much impossible to get a 4.0 at Harvard, anyway. My professor said the last person to get a 4.0 did so in like 1979 or something," Lydia said.

"Wait . . . what?!" AP Frank asked, figuring he misheard her.

"Yeah, 1979! Isn't that insane?"

AP Frank could have kissed her. He was overcome with a mix of relief and utter euphoria. It was *okay* not to aim for a 4.0. He suddenly had a rational justification to not push himself at Harvard. He no longer had to be nervous about what his mother would do if he wasn't able to achieve her goal. He had known that it would be difficult to earn a 4.0

at Harvard, but his biggest fear had been that it was possible. Now that he knew it wasn't, his nervousness evaporated.

The next day he called home. At first he asked to speak to Richard, who gave him the usual Whitman news about classes, friends, and teachers. Then he asked to speak to his mother. "Hey, Mom, you know how you said you wanted me get a 4.0?" he asked. "That's simply not happening."

"What? Did you get bad grade or something?" she responded.

"Nooo. You know when the last person to get a 4.0 at Harvard did so? More than twenty years ago! It's impossible!" AP Frank was unable to suppress his triumphant smile.

"No, Frank, you must have heard wrong," she said. "Ninety-nine percent of Harvard kids get 4.0! The only person who *didn't* get 4.0 was twenty years ago. That is what is true."

AP Frank started laughing. "No, don't be dumb, Mom."

"No! Is true! You *must* get 4.0!"

"No, Mom, that's not happening."

Eventually, AP Frank hung up to take a nap. It was one of the most stress-free slumbers he could remember having in years.

SAM, SENIOR | PERCEIVED AS: THE TEACHER'S PET

On the day before Senior Stress Week, Sam was as stressed as—if not more than—he had ever been. He had two tests and an interview with a Muslim due Monday, one test and a rough draft of his AP English research paper due Tuesday, and tests on Wednesday and Thursday. Senior Stress Week was supposed to be the least stressful week of the year, yet the only comparably difficult time Sam could remember had been a few weeks before, when he had four tests on one day and two tests the day after. Stress, for Sam, didn't build gradually. It popped up when he stopped to think for a moment, and once he recognized everything he had to do, it multiplied exponentially, leading him to a meltdown.

Sam sat at his bedroom desk, cursing his luck. On a beautiful Sunday afternoon in October, he should have been outside strumming his guitar or playing tennis with Julie. Instead, he was sitting in what felt like a prison, growing increasingly agitated as he realized there was no way he could finish everything he had due in the next few days. His parents, who weren't home, had already called him three times in the past two hours to remind him to work on his college essays. Sam disconnected his computer cable so he wouldn't be tempted by the distractions of instant messenger.

Sam acknowledged that it was his own fault for not yet completing the Muslim assignment. His Modern World teacher had assigned the project a month ago: Find a Muslim and interview him or her. Sam reflected that he might have put off the interview because he didn't like the idea of sauntering into downtown Bethesda and approaching the first Muslim he spotted. What if the Muslim thought he was a CIA agent? Or maybe he just hadn't found the time to come up for air, what with all of his other assignments and activities. Either way, now he had only twelve hours to produce a Muslim. So he made one up.

The words came quickly. "Interviewee: Raheem Azzam Labib. Time: 7:25 P.M. Raheem, 50, is a friend of my dad's from Harvard Law School. He is a practicing Sunni Muslim, a former resident of Iran and now teaches at the University of Stanford's law school as a full-time tenured professor. He lived in Iran until the age of 16, when he be-friended a Harvard professor named George Brandle who offered to take Raheem from his home and get him out of the country to the United States. He managed to half-sneak out of the country and went to Harvard undergraduate and law school. In the 1990s he was able to move what was left of his family here and now he currently resides . . . in Palo Alto."

Sam reviewed his introduction with satisfaction. As he put it, he was the "best bullshitter in the entire school." He didn't care that a two-second Internet search would reveal that Raheem Labib didn't exist and certainly didn't teach at Stanford. The teacher seemed to love him, he had a 98.7 percent average in the class, and he was convinced he wouldn't get caught. Sam began concocting the transcription of a fake interview with Raheem.

Fourteen hundred words later, Sam had finished one assignment, at least, but his stress hadn't diminished. He hadn't studied for any of his tests, and his research paper still loomed. He had made zero progress on the remainder of his college essays, which weighed on him because he had no idea how he had fared on the SAT. A few hours into his research paper, Sam was at the breaking point. He was tired of focusing on English when he had four other tests coming up, he hated being alone in the house, he wondered why his friends in the neighborhood weren't calling, and he was getting such a bad cold that he had gone through almost a box of tissues in a day.

He felt badly about fabricating his Modern World assignment. He didn't consider it cheating, per se, but his project was a lie. What he had done, he reasoned, wasn't as bad as the scene during breaks in the SAT the day before, when students were milling in the hallways, asking one another the answers to the math questions and then going back into the classroom to change their answers.

Nevertheless, he didn't have time to deal with it. There was still the research paper, and now his ear was hurting—really hurting—and he wondered if he had an ear infection. And he was starving. And his computer kept freezing. And he couldn't take it anymore; he needed someone to listen to him, to help him.

"Dad!" he yelled, remembering afterward that the house was empty. Disgruntled, he stormed downstairs; at least hunger was one problem he could address easily. But the only interesting item he could find in the refrigerator was leftover chicken. Sam slammed the refrigerator door shut, thinking about how he had no interest in school because it had all become too much, and he didn't want to go on Monday. Before he stomped back upstairs to study, he yelled, "FUCK!" and, as hard as he could, he hurled a bunch of bananas at the couch.

Later that night, Sam reconnected his computer cable to discover an important development: In trolling his Modern World classmates' IM away messages, Sam estimated that approximately two thirds of his classmates had invented their own Raheems. As one away message read, "I need a name for my fake muslim and FAST!"

✺

Sam's profile doesn't fit the stereotypical image of a student who would resort to cheating. He is a good-hearted, genuine guy, smart and talented, and generally concerned about doing the right thing. But Sam has plenty of company nationwide. Cheating is on the rise as a standard modus operandi for high school students today. In 2004 the Carnegie Foundation reported that 90 percent of high school students cheat on homework, and two thirds cheat on tests. The same year, a Josephson Institute of Ethics survey of 25,000 high school students found that 62 percent had lied to a teacher about something significant, and 23 percent had cheated to win in a sport.

In the past, these numbers might have been dismissed as the survival tactics of floundering students desperate to get into college. But these measures are perhaps even more likely to be taken by superb students desperate to get into a *top* college. In a 1998 survey of high achievers chosen from the *Who's Who Among American High School Students'* "honor roll," four out of five confessed they had cheated to improve their grades. That figure was the highest percentage in the thirty years the survey had been administered.

With rising numbers have come a variety of creative new methods. The familiar standbys remain popular: looking at classmates' tests or asking friends for help; using cheat sheets smuggled into class, positioned precisely on the floor, hidden in the bathroom, or condensed onto a gum wrapper; and writing notes on shoes or skin, like the thigh beneath a skirt, which teachers are unlikely to see. Some students signal test answers to one another with gestures or with different-colored M&M's. They put a clear cover on their notebooks or folders and read the notes beneath. They peel labels off water bottles, print notes on the labels, and refasten the labels, which are then magnified by the water. Some West Coast students call East Coast students to get standardized test questions, taking advantage of the time difference.

The increase in cheating could be fueled partly by technological advances. The old store-the-formulas-in-the-calculator trick is still a favorite among students nationwide, and as handheld devices have evolved, their storage space has grown to the point where entire libraries, including digital CliffsNotes, can be housed on them. Even some digital watches can now store many pages of text and display graphics. Students plug notes into PDAs and cell phones, and use phones to take photos of tests to share with friends. They record formulas on iPods or other MP3 players, which they listen to through earphones during exams. In wireless schools, some students use handheld Internet-capable devices to look up answers on the Web. On Mathnerds.com, students doing math homework can get instant, free help from experts online, where replies can be tantamount to outright answers.

The Internet has spawned a lucrative cheating industry: paper mills through which students can purchase pre-written or custom-made papers of varying quality for up to $250 apiece. "Cybercheating" has become commonplace, especially in high school. Students who don't download a complete paper might cobble one together by pasting verbatim lines from various Internet documents without citing the sources.

During a group interview in Kentucky, high-achieving students told me that adults have no idea how widespread cheating is in high school. One boy said, "You can cheat your way through a whole class."

"People do that all the time," a girl agreed. "Last year one of our history teachers had us write a movie review and caught many people in the top rank for plagiarizing."

"I've cheated!" another boy volunteered. "I've copied papers, but I'm really against cheating. I was lazy and stressed out. I didn't even know I was plagiarizing."

"People steal tests all the time," the girl said.

"People take answer keys from the teacher's desk and use it on the test," the first boy said. "You realize you can get away with it."

"Sophomore year—this is really embarrassing—there was this one class where we had the test answers passed to us every week. One of my friends put the answers into his watch. He'd just scroll through the letters."

"People do a lot of text-messaging answers in class."

"The whole reason cheating is popular is because it's busywork, for the most part, and you don't feel you need to learn the material because it's not important," one of the boys said. "For teachers I respect, if they make the effort to teach me something useful, I'm not going to cheat."

"Has everybody here cheated?" I asked.

The group of top students answered with a resounding yes. With all that they had to do in school, they viewed cheating as a necessary—sometimes the only—way to get everything done. "If it's busywork," one said, "I'm not going to waste my time doing it for real."

College students continue the habit. At the University of Maryland, several students brought cell phones into an accounting exam and text-messaged with friends outside the room; the friends looked up the answers on an answer key the professor posted on the Web after the exam began. A UC Santa Barbara student was charged with identity theft and illegal access into a computer system after resetting two professors' passwords to change one of her grades from a B to an A.

To catch students who submit other people's work as their own, many high schools, including Whitman, use a company called Turnitin. Students email their papers to Turnitin.com, which scans its database, previously submitted student papers, and the Web for matching text strings. Within forty-eight hours, Turnitin.com delivers a paper's "originality report" to the teachers. Turnitin founder John Barrie has said that, of the papers scanned from hundreds of high schools, about 30 percent of them have "significant levels of plagiarism." Whitman began using turnitin.com in 2003.

High school cheating scandals are constantly in the news. In 2003 New Hampshire's Salem High School suspended a student for scanning report cards into a computer and charging $25 to $50 to change grades. In 2004 a senior at Glenbard North High School in Illinois was expelled for stealing an AP calculus midterm from a teacher's computer. Also in 2004, at California's Saratoga High School, school officials learned that several students had used a device to record teachers' passwords, then retrieved tests and answers from English department computers. Another student at that school allegedly changed his math grades on his teacher's computer, and two other students stole a test.

The series of incidents at Saratoga, where a third of students had GPAs higher than 4.0, led to debates over whether the pressure to succeed was too intense. "They're under tremendous stress, these kids," a Saratoga parent said publicly. "They come home with a 4.0 and the parents are disappointed." Staples High School, in Westport, Connecticut, held similar discussions after a student was caught using the water-bottle trick a few months after an essay in the school newspaper described "epidemic cheating" as "part of the routine: Wake up, come to school, cheat." (The day after the essay appeared, two students were spotted cheating on an AP History test.)

When the principal at Staples, a pressure-cooker environment like Saratoga, decided to crack down on cheating, he was surprised to learn that students were relieved. *The New York Times* reported the students were "eager to help him stamp out behavior that they said was driven by a frenzied competition to get into an Ivy League school." Topics at the subsequent meetings included: "Are parents' expectations unreasonably high and thus a goad to dishonesty? Are the students overscheduled with a full load of Advanced Placement classes, extracurricular activities, and community service? What about a Board of Education that wants more and more Advanced Placement offerings and posts schoolwide SAT scores on its Internet home page? Or a student newspaper that lists graduating seniors and the colleges they attend?"

All of those factors help to explain cheating by students who could ace the work honestly. A Staples student told the *Times*, "Expectations are set here, externally and internally. In Westport, getting a B is like getting an F. So if you don't feel you can achieve it on your own, you find another way." As a sophomore honors student told the Carnegie Foundation in 2004, "If you already have straight A's, then why cheat? But yet we still seem to do it. It's kind of like insurance, like you feel better, you feel safer. . . . Then I will have that 95 instead of like the 90 because that's almost like a B." She explained, "People have morals, they don't always go by them. . . . Even if you [cheat], it doesn't lessen the grade. It says an A on the paper and you don't go, 'Oh, but I cheated.' You're just kind of like, 'Hey, I got that A.' So it doesn't really matter necessarily, if it has to do with your morals or anything. You just kind of do it."

SAM, SENIOR | PERCEIVED AS: THE TEACHER'S PET

One day in mid-October, Sam was in class, reviewing a paper due that afternoon, when he discovered a minor error and panicked. He had typed "America" instead of "American." Any other year, for any other assignment, he would have made the change by hand. But not for this essay. This was the paper he had selected as the graded paper he would send to colleges that requested it. During journalism class, Sam raced home to add the letter to his paper.

Now that Sam's sights were set on Stanford, pending the SAT scores he would receive in six days, he supposed he needed all the help he could get. Sam's strength was the interview, which he believed was the only part of the application process that he excelled at. Get him in front of an admissions officer, and he could charm his way in. But Stanford, which didn't have applicant interviews, would meet Sam only on paper. This was why Sam was agonizing so intensely over his essays; it was why he had become so overwhelmed with pent-up anxiety that he had launched projectile bananas at the couch. (Later, he had returned the mashed fruit to the kitchen counter.)

When Sam came home from school that afternoon, he was still wound up. Senior Stress Week had been one of the worst academic weeks he could remember. Also, he was anxious to find precisely the right present for Julie's seventeenth birthday, which was in a week. Sam dropped his backpack on the floor and went into the kitchen, suddenly recognizing a familiar aroma. There on the counter was a magnificent loaf of warm banana bread. Before attacking, Sam cocked his head and smiled, remembering where the smashed bananas had been. He loved his mother's banana bread. Maybe he had been focusing too much on college, putting too much pressure on himself to reveal the essence of Sam in one measly 500-word personal statement. For a brief moment, Sam reminded himself that "life is goofy." He grabbed a slice of bread, went upstairs, and, more relaxed, got to work on his essay.

JULIE, SENIOR | PERCEIVED AS: THE SUPERSTAR

While eating lunch with Derek and another student applying early to Stanford, Julie told them she had narrowed down her early-application schools to Williams and Dartmouth, even though she wasn't head over heels for either of them. "You should apply to Stanford," one student said. As much as she loved Stanford, Julie felt that too many classmates were selling out to the same four schools: Harvard, Stanford, Yale, and Princeton. She didn't want to be a part of that. At the same time, she was conflicted over the way other students who weren't smarter than her, and who didn't have better grades and activities, were applying. If they got into Stanford, she would be happy for them, of course, but also jealous.

A few days later, Julie visited Williams, where she spent most of her time with a cross-country runner who had been her first Whitman crush. They put whipped cream in the ice bag of one of his teammates, danced around to a children's CD, and took photos of themselves in funny poses. The campus was beautiful. Seduced by the New England autumn, Julie stared at the rows of brightly colored leaves on her way to the Williams cross-country coach's office. New England was too beautiful to pass up, she decided. The cold weather would be outweighed by the variety of winter activities. *I don't like how everyone's going to Stanford. I'm kind of different. I'm going to do my own thing,* Julie thought. *I don't think I'm even going to apply to Stanford.*

The Williams coach told her he was highly impressed by her most recent race, and he wanted to know her new SAT scores when she received them. "If someone's on the border, good enough to get in but not for sure, if I mention she'll be on the cross-country team, I have some pull," he told her. "In some cases, I can take someone and say [to admissions], 'I really want this person.' I'm not sure I would need to do that for you, but I'm willing to pull strings to get you. I hope to see you running for the Purple Cows."

He was the second coach at a prestigious school who had reached out to Julie that week. Before she left for Williams, the Haverford coach had called her out of the blue to ask if she would be applying, because, he said, "I can help you with your application." Haverford wasn't on Julie's list, but Williams was tempting. She loved spending time with her former crush, who told her, "I was thinking I might not run cross country next year, but if you're on the team at Williams, I will."

Julie was cheered by the fact that if she went to Williams, she would be a second-varsity runner—in the top fourteen—as a freshman. The students she met also told her that Williams was a flexible school where she could probably swim as a walk-on in the winter. But the school's small size—2,000 students—was also a detriment. She was afraid that she would know everyone there too quickly.

By the time Julie got home from her visit, she had no idea which way to lean. Dartmouth was twice the size of Williams, which appealed to her. She could envision having a fantastic two years at Williams but getting fed up once she knew all of the people and the campus seemed to close in on her. Then again, her first high school crush was waiting for her at Williams. Running with him again would add a giddy element to her college life. *Or,* she thought, *would I just feel stupid knowing that I chose to go to college for a boy?*

SAM, SENIOR | PERCEIVED AS: THE TEACHER'S PET

Finally, the night arrived when Sam would learn his SAT scores. At six P.M., he closed his bedroom door and fired up the computer. It seemed like the scores meant everything; his whole future could be reduced to a four-digit number. If he went up by just a few more correct answers, then tomorrow—the deadline for transcript requests—he could tell Whitman to send Stanford his transcript. If his scores didn't improve, he had only tonight to rethink his strategy and decide on another school to which to apply early.

Sam typed the College Board website address into his browser and waited. Nothing. "Collegeboard.com cannot process your request at this time." He tried a different browser. Again nothing. Over and over again, Sam tried to load the College Board website, to no avail. Distraught, he IMed a friend who told him that the website had been unavailable since four P.M. Sam tried to simmer down as he reloaded the broken page.

Two hours later, he was still at it. Every Whitman student he knew who was waiting for scores was panicked. Without the scores, the seniors couldn't make the decision due the next day. Maybe, Sam thought, all 465,000 SAT takers were checking their scores now and the site was overloaded. But why wasn't the College Board prepared for the traffic? While Sam waited for each reload, he scanned other students' away messages. "College Board sucks." "College Board blows." "College Board is ruining my life." "BASTARD FUCKING ASSHOLE BITCH College Board website is down." "I'm going to be sweet for a few more hours." (That last one was Julie, the soon-to-be-birthday girl for whom Sam had gone to an artsy store and purchased a soapstone box and a pair of earrings.) Sam pounded on his guitar.

At eleven, Sam was still at his computer, his eyes glazed over, as he clicked and reclicked his mouse. "Nooo! Timed out!" he said to a friend on the phone, his voice rising. "It's all some big joke to them, isn't it. All I see is an ad for the TestMaker flashing in my fucking face. The longer I sit here and do nothing, the worse I think my scores are going to be." Finally, at around 11:30, five and a half hours after he had sat down in front of the computer, the site loaded. Sam scrolled down the page. *Oh, crap,* he thought. His verbal had dropped thirty points. Then he saw the math: He had jumped from a 710 to an 800. Sam opted to take his chances in the Stanford pool, but first he had to rewrite his essays, which focused on his writing skills. Because the SAT was the barometer colleges used, he would have to flip his application to decrease the emphasis on the verbal skills that his score didn't reflect.

Later that night, the College Board put up the following message on its website: "Due to exceptionally high traffic, collegeboard.com is experiencing technical problems. We apologize for any inconvenience and recommend returning to view your SAT scores later."

The next night Sam was home alone, embarrassed to have no social plans on a Friday night. Somehow he had expected to IM Julie that he wanted to take her out to celebrate her birthday. But he hadn't seen her online, which typically meant she was busy, and because it was her birthday, he didn't want to bother her with a phone call. He didn't know what else was going on that night because his closer friends probably thought he was with Julie. Now it was nine P.M., and the only person Sam had talked to was the pizza delivery guy.

That was one of the problems with being a floater in high school: Sam had plenty of friends but no one to carry him along. Friends in various circles constantly assumed he was out with other groups, and he was tired of taking the initiative. Tonight he didn't want to call them because he knew they must be out doing fun, life-changing things, and he didn't want them to think he was a loser for not having weekend plans. Sam was a social guy who thrived on being with other people. He often wondered what his social life would be like if he weren't such a high achiever, stretched across so many activities. If he had more time for his friends, would he really be home alone on a Friday night without knowing what everyone was doing? Sam had made that trade-off, sacrificing play for work. For success.

For about two hours, Sam wallowed in self-pity. Then he decided that senior year was too short for wallowing, and he should take advantage of it while he could. Everyone else he knew was probably out having the time of their lives—why shouldn't he? Sam called a friend who was with several people gathered at a girl's house. "I just got up from a nap," Sam lied. "Maybe I'll drop by to come see you guys." He grabbed his car keys and took off.

At the house, more than a dozen kids lounged around, some playing foosball, some parked in front of a sixty-inch television set. Sam took a seat on the floor and chatted with a few students about baseball and school gossip. He was surprised to learn that two girls who hadn't been on his competition radar screen were applying to Harvard and Duke. As the group discussed colleges, Sam realized that all of the students present were convinced they would get into top-tier schools.

When pizza arrived, the conversation shifted. After complaining about the College Board website, the seniors talked about their scores. "How'd you do?" they asked one another. "Did your scores go up?" Sam stayed quiet, hoping that if he avoided eye contact, no one would ask him. In other circles, a 1460 would be considered outstanding, but not here, not among Whitman's so-called best and brightest.

The party hostess mused aloud, "If I added up my SAT score and my three SAT IIs, I wonder what I have out of 4,000." (A 4,000 would mean a perfect score on all of the tests.) The other seniors perked up. The hostess grabbed a piece of paper and tallied her scores: $740 + 780 + 800 + 770 + 650 = 3740$.

"Oh, that's interesting," said one of the other guys, who took the sheet of paper. "Let me see what I have." He wrote down his numbers. Sam squinted at the paper: a 3800.

"Let me see!" said another, and added his scores to the sheet. A 3830.

The friend who had told Sam about the party handed him the paper. "Can you write mine down?" she asked. "I got an 800, 700, 800, 750, and 750." 3800.

Sam looked over the other scores as he tallied his friend's. He smiled politely, as if he were enjoying the game as much as everyone else, but he was secretly disgusted. *This is Whitman, and it makes me sick,* he thought. At the same time, he couldn't look away: Two of the students who listed their scores were his competition in the Stanford early-application pool.

The other partygoers crowded around the paper. "Wow, those scores are really high," one of them said.

"Yeah, guys, that's insane. I'm definitely holding on to this. This just proves how crazy we are," said the hostess, who had invented the game. When the paper was returned to her, she scowled. "Look at these scores.

This is ridiculous!" she said, noticing how low her 650 on the Spanish SAT II looked compared to everyone else's scores. "The Spanish exam really sucks. If it wasn't for the 650, I'd have a really high number."

The conversation moved on, but Sam's thoughts didn't. Sure, his scores were lower, but he was a better writer and had done more interesting things in his life. His friends had gone to math camp while he was teaching English in China. Between the high-1500s SAT scorers with 4.0 GPAs or the Supreme Court intern, which one would add more to a well-rounded student body? Sam's mind spun. Everybody applying from Whitman was qualified to get into Stanford, but a Whitman graduate now at Stanford insisted that the admissions officers sorted the applications by last name, not school, so one person wouldn't be reading all of the Whitman applications. Sam still had a shot. At least that was what he kept telling himself.

It was only 11:15, but Sam had grown restless. He wasn't getting anything done. Instead of waiting to see if the party improved, he went home, worked for about half an hour, and then went to bed. As he drifted toward sleep, it occurred to him that rather than rushing out to what turned out to be an SAT 4000-game party, he might have been better off staying at home.

JULIE, SENIOR | PERCEIVED AS: THE SUPERSTAR

From Julie's journal:

My Life in Numbers
Yesterday I turned 17. I guess I am no longer sweet (as in sweet 16), but I do have some sweet new numbers attached to me. First, I got my SAT scores back this week and could not believe my eyes when I got a text message from my dad that said: "Congrats. New SAT score 1520 (760 V/760 M)." After resenting the SATs since I first started studying for them, it's crazy to think that I finally got a score I am satisfied with. I could thank the SAT gods for the birthday present, but the truth is, I did it all on my own. There was no luck involved. I spent more time with that wretched red 10 Real SAT book than any smart girl should.

Today I also finished 6th at Counties with a time of 19:14. The coach at Brown University told me that I would have to run under 19:30. For so long I resented that number because I knew I *could* run that fast, but I just hadn't done so in a race yet. It's just like the SATs. I knew I *could* do much better than a 1410; I hadn't been able to prove it. I hated how I was only described in numbers and letters and no words. Why couldn't colleges just take my word that I was a really good runner and just as smart as anyone who got a 1500 on their SATs? I don't know what happened, but something clicked. Now I have the numbers to go along with my life.

Chapter 5

October 25-November 7

COMPETITION

For thousands of families, school admissions processes begin before a child turns one; in several cities, that's how manic the competition has grown to get into elite preschools and kindergarten programs. With private preschools that accept children as young as two, many parents start searching for the right program years in advance. If they have their heart set on a particular preschool, parents have been known to try to sign up their child-to-be on a waiting list as soon as pregnancy is confirmed.

What follows is often a mad flurry of open houses, information sessions, tours, interviews, tests, letters, applications, and painstakingly written thank-you notes. Some couples take off from work and treat the preschool application process as if it were a job. In cities such as New York, where the preschool and kindergarten admissions frenzy has become legendary, the hysteria usually begins a day or two after Labor Day, when applications or tour appointments become available, sometimes in limited numbers. The application supply can vanish so quickly—at some schools, in a matter of hours—that some parents hire a team to call the schools, sometimes taking six hours to get through, pressing redial repeatedly as if trying to win a radio station giveaway. In other cities ranging from Aurora, Colorado, to Cleveland, Ohio, to Arlington, Virginia, some parents camp out overnight outside school buildings to sign up their children for private school spots.

For parents fortunate enough to snag the opportunity to apply, one of the next steps is to have their child tested, if they haven't already. In some areas, preschool applicants are evaluated by the forty-minute Detroit Test of Learning Aptitude. Children applying to kindergarten usually take the Wechsler Preschool and Primary Scale of Intelligence (informally known as the "ERB," for the Educational Records Bureau that administers it), an IQ test that measures a child's vocabulary, fine motor skills, and mathematical abilities.

Meanwhile, during the fall, parents might bring their child in for observation, while school staff members scribble on clipboards. Parents, too, are interviewed by admissions officers, who ask questions such as "What is your home life like?" or "What does your child do when she first walks in the door?" (One preschool director told me that the parent interview is superfluous "because they all lie. Everyone tells you the wonderful things they do with their child. Nobody ever admits they stick their kid in front of the TV to get ten minutes of quiet. People are so afraid to ask a question for fear they won't get in, which makes it a terrible experience for parents.") Once the application is complete and the letters of recommendation are signed, admissions procedures become a mystery to most parents, who must wait anxiously until the day they receive the decision letters.

Preschool tuition can hit nearly $16,000 per year and can come with an unspoken expectation of a parting donation upon graduation. Some New York City private kindergartens' annual tuition has surpassed $26,000. Why do parents put themselves and their children through the rigors of such a stressful, potentially costly process? Why does it matter so much where their two-year-old or five-year-old learns to color within the lines? Because an astonishing number of parents staunchly believe that the "right" preschool or kindergarten is a necessary stepping-stone on their child's march toward an Ivy League acceptance letter and, therefore, a successful life. If little Junior III doesn't get into an elite nursery school, many parents are convinced that he has squandered his chances with the Harvard admissions committee sixteen years down the road. Proper preschools are seen as feeders to elite kindergartens and lower schools, which tend to favor applicants from certain nursery programs. Those elementary schools in turn are viewed as crucial gateways toward top private high schools that send large numbers of students to highly ranked universities.

Consequently, many parents regard preschool admissions as a critical move to get an edge in the college admissions process. Preschool programs are perceived as a way to sift the wheat from the chaff while the grains are in their earliest years. Consider this anecdote from a *City Journal* reporter: One nursery school director "gently suggested that the child would be happier at a 'nurturing' (read: less academically high-pressure) school like Hewitt instead of Spence, the high-powered school she had hoped for. I asked another director about Hewitt. 'I have plenty of families who would rather die than say their child goes to Hewitt,' she sniffed. 'It paints 'loser' on your forehead.'"

Some parents will go to extraordinary lengths to avoid such indistinction. They donate large sums of money to the desired school, cozy up to school board members, or offer school officials gifts; one preschool director told me a parent volunteered to replace her entire wardrobe. Another director said a father who worked at a popular news program threatened to "expose" her if she didn't accept his child. Many couples join houses of worship before their children are born because the churches or synagogues are attached to preschools that give preference to members. A parent in Delray Beach, Florida, joined his local chamber of commerce specifically to get his toddler into a certain preschool.

In perhaps the most high-profile example of currying favor, former analyst Jack Grubman in 1999 allegedly exchanged a favorable recommendation on a stock he didn't believe in for then–Citigroup chief executive Sandy Weill's assistance with getting Grubman's two-year-old twins into Manhattan's 92nd Street Y preschool, which has been called "the Harvard of nursery schools." Weill not only wrote a letter to the school but also had Citigroup pledge a $1 million donation.

Meanwhile, a new breed of consultants has cropped up to help parents navigate the increasing insanity of preschool and kindergarten admissions. There are coaches to train children in interview skills and appropriate behavior, as well as consultants charging thousands of dollars to counsel parents on their own admissions interviews and to edit applications and accompanying essays. The preschool and kindergarten administrators I talked to said they couldn't stand these types of coaches. "It makes me sad because it puts outrageous pressure on very little children," said Peggy Marble, head of Manhattan's Christ Church Day School. "We're talking about two-year-olds. It's really unfortunate because the message it sends is one of pressure and panic. People are making money off parents' fears and worries."

The ERB doesn't even evaluate significant development markers, necessarily. "The tests don't measure creativity," Yale psychologist Alan Kaufman told *New York* magazine. "They don't measure social intelligence. They measure a relatively small band of mental functioning. They can't predict life success." Some parents go so far as to pay psychologists, who are allowed to order the single test version, a few thousand dollars to administer it, giving children a practice round. Die-hard parents have been known to take their child to several psychologists to squeeze in additional run-throughs. But parents tend to keep the ERB tutors and practice rounds hush-hush, scheduling playdates well after a tutor leaves their house. They prefer their child to seem innately intelligent, much like a woman might get her makeup professionally done to achieve "the natural look."

Preschool and kindergarten officials said the results are usually transparent. "Kids are truthful, and they'll say, 'Oh, I do this game with Mary at her house!' If a version of that quote from a child is said during an ERB test, that's the kiss of death," said Marlene Barron, head of Manhattan's West Side Montessori preschool. The Educational Records Bureau also frowns on test coaching. Still, there is no doubt in some psychologists' minds that a child's ERB performance can be improved not only by coaching but also by attending nursery schools that teach the children ERB-related tasks. A child's test scores can also vary based on the rapport he has with the examiner, which is why some preschools try to return to the same tester year after year.

Not that all private preschools mind the frenzy. A Manhattan nursery director admitted to *City Journal,* "Our admissions are driven by how easily or not we can place a child in kindergarten. We do let the occasional lowbrow family in. But if the mom's loud and is wearing garish colors, has bleached hair—I don't mean highlighted—I've got to say to myself, 'OK, nice family, terrific kid, but I'm not getting this mother past admissions at Collegiate.'"

Other preschool directors lament the madness. "There's a hype that's been set up in the market: If they don't go to this school, their child's life is ruined forever. For parents to feel like they won the lotto or lost something because they didn't get into a school, what a terrible thing to feel," Barron told me. "Sometimes I think that we could just put names in a hat and almost come out pretty much the same."

It's not unusual for parents to attach résumés to their toddler's pre-school application. A two-year-old's résumé might include music classes or membership in a prestigious church play group, foreign-language courses given to six-month-olds, a gym program, or Suzuki violin lessons. Even "gourmet cooking" has shown up on a toddler's curriculum vitae. And "there was a time when everyone wanted [their toddler] to speak French," a preschool director told me. "Now it's Mandarin Chinese."

Beyond the obvious effects that piling on structured activities will have on a one-year-old, there's also the way the single-minded focus on getting in can increase a child's anxiety. "When parents start with this pressure, children learn in an instant what the parents' agenda is," said Jean Mandelbaum, director of Manhattan's All Souls School. "When they find out that what's important is doing well on a test or showing off for strangers, they begin to develop that kind of personality where education is no longer about an interesting intellectual mind, but rather the way to get love and affection at home. Gold stars are the currency in the household rather than enjoying learning. Parents have a real risk of taking that away from a child. They send the message to kids that they have to be coached. Schools don't feel that way."

Several factors contribute to the growing madness over preschool and kindergarten admissions. Some schools reach far beyond the simple play-snack-nap routine. At a variety of Ohio preschools, children learn Spanish or French, take computer classes, do woodworking, or play tennis. At one New York City preschool, children learn to add or subtract in the thousands, and to square. The rise in applications might also be attributed to socioeconomic reasons: Some parents are receiving larger Wall Street or law firm bonuses and are choosing to stay in the city instead of moving to the suburbs.

The number of young students has shifted as dramatically as those of college-bound students. The Census Bureau reported that preschool enrollment increased from roughly 500,000 children in 1964 to approximately five million in 2003. Of about 100,000 state-licensed preschools in the country, only about 6,000 are accredited by the National Association for the Education of Young Children. In New York, the city with the largest preschool population, applications to private kindergarten increased between 30 and 50 percent in 2002, and then another 15 percent from 2004 to 2005, in a competition for only about 2,500 spots. Many of these spots go to siblings of current students, to whom schools often give preference, or to children of diverse backgrounds.

Rather than wait for the free public school programs that New York City offers four-year-olds, parents rush to get their two- and three-year-olds into one of perhaps fifteen exalted preschools. In 2000 the rising numbers of applicants began to get rejected by all of the schools to which they applied, which has now led families to apply to eight to ten schools rather than the four or five they might have applied to in the 1990s. As with the college admissions process, in the growing preschool and kindergarten applicant pool, parents believe students have to be that much more distinctive. A nursery school director told *City Journal* in 2001 about a family expecting to get their daughter into a prestigious kindergarten program. The director said, "They want a very competitive girls' school; they've limited themselves to the Ivy League. But the child is totally ordinary. . . . She's a darling, ordinary child who needs to go to Amherst, not Harvard. . . . This child will get in nowhere."

If, by "nowhere," the director meant "no elite private school," the child is hardly alone: An average of fifteen students apply for each slot in New York City preschools. Therein lies perhaps the most confounding aspect of the preschool admission process. Many parents battle to get their kids into an elite private preschool because they believe it will lead to an acceptance letter from a certain Ivy League institution. But the funny thing is, that institution has only eleven students competing for each of its available spots—meaning New York City's top preschools are tougher to get into than Harvard.

AP FRANK, COLLEGE FRESHMAN | PERCEIVED AS: THE WORKHORSE

AP Frank was napping early one night when his computer dinged to let him know he received an instant message. He stretched, yawned, and looked at the screen. The message was from a friend of his brother in Bethesda.

Richard's friend: [Richard] wasn't here today at all in school, and your mom
   just stopped by my house claiming he was "sick." And Richard's been
   going on about how his mom was threatening him to withdraw him from
   school if he doesn't shape up . . . I called Richard after [your] mom left
AP Frank: what did he say? i actually have very little idea about what's
   going on at home
Richard's friend: basically, he told [your] mom he's getting 4 Bs this
   quarter, 2 from ap chem
AP Frank: oh shit
Richard's friend: and mom now thinks he's slacking off and getting bad
   influences so she was on his case for roughly all of last night . . . he
   started homework around midnight, and then falls asleep in the
   morning, only to wake up at 11 am, when mom continues on her tirade.

Mrs. AP Frank had forced Richard to sign up for seven AP classes
that semester. Richard's friend told AP Frank that his brother, whose
friends had apparently taught to ride a bicycle during lunch periods at
school, had hopped on a bike and disappeared. When Richard's friend
signed off, AP Frank sat back in his chair, stunned. *Holy shit*, he thought.
It's happening. Someone was actually rebelling against Mrs. AP Frank.

AP Frank was torn. On the one hand, he didn't want to have to
worry about his brother this weekend. On the other hand, Richard was
taking his rebellion to an entirely new level. Their mother was clearly
trying to fit him into AP Frank's mold, and it wasn't working. Four Bs,
in Mrs. AP Frank's household, "pretty much equals death," AP Frank
explained to a friend. "One B on a report card is something to start
shitting your pants about. Four is . . . not good. At all." Once his
brother came home, AP Frank expected their mother would come up
with ways to punish him every day for at least the next few weeks.

AP Frank and his brother were completely different people. His
brother was popular because he had a magnetic, mellow personality. He
wanted to do well in school, but at a certain point, he was able to veer
off and have fun instead of studying. When AP Frank was a junior, he
was a self-proclaimed "stress freak" who hyperventilated at the thought
of earning less than an A. AP Frank wondered how long his brother
would put up with their mother. He remembered the January day that
had been his own breaking point, when Mr. Murphy had asked him,

"Can you just be brave for six more months?" Richard's departure, AP Frank realized now, was the move that required real courage. As a high school student, AP Frank had been paralyzed by fear and doubt, so he had stayed. He wished he had been brave enough to leave.

A few days later, AP Frank received an email from his brother. Richard had returned home the same night he left. He seemed to be doing okay, but he had some interesting news. Apparently, Mr. Murphy, ever the boys' lifesaver, had intervened. He had somehow gotten the message across to their mother that she needed to back off of Richard. AP Frank wasn't sure, but he thought that Mr. Murphy might have implied that he would call social services if her behavior didn't change. Supposedly, Mr. Murphy had gotten her to agree to let Richard do something besides studying—in this case, he could join a friend's band— and to let him go out on weekends after he finished all of his work.

AP Frank wondered why Mr. Murphy hadn't made that kind of phone call to his mother back in January. Maybe, he guessed, this time Mr. Murphy didn't want to see another breakdown.

JULIE, SENIOR | PERCEIVED AS: THE SUPERSTAR

At practice one late-October afternoon, Whitman's varsity cross-country coach gathered the fourteen runners in a huddle. "I'm really proud of you guys, especially Julie," he said. "She's been doing so great!" Julie smiled uncomfortably, the Queen of Awkward. Other girls on the team weren't happy with their times this season. She wasn't sure what good it did to have the coach remind them about her success.

"Yeah, Julie!" the boys on the team cheered.

"Boo!" C.J. said, laughing. Julie was surprised to sense something more behind C.J.'s joking grin. C.J., a junior who was one of the team's top runners, used to tell Julie, "I want to be like you."

As the team jogged in a tight pack during the long-distance practice run, the coach asked Julie about her college search. She told him she still wasn't sure about Williams or Dartmouth, because she liked them both. Behind her, she heard C.J. say to another runner, "She talks as if she's already into both schools."

"What?" Julie asked.

"You talk as if you're in both schools."

"Okay, well, that has to be your mind-set when you apply early somewhere, because you have to make the decision," Julie explained. "You have to choose which one you want to go to."

The next day Julie wasn't in a good mood. When she arrived late to the team room, none of the other girls said anything to her, so she didn't make conversation, either. She couldn't place the strange vibe she was getting. She followed the girls outside, where the coach was waiting. "All right, so we're ready to go?" he asked.

"Where are we going?"

"To Norwood." Norwood was a local park about three miles from Whitman.

"Okay, let me put down my long-sleeve shirt," Julie said. She went into the team room to put her shirt in her bag. When she got back outside, the team was gone.

Julie took off toward Norwood by herself. Why would they leave her? As she wondered why the team didn't seem to care about her, she started to cry. She had been respected more by the team when she was a freshman. *Maybe I shouldn't show up at practice,* she thought. *What would they do then?* She stopped running to consider this. She could turn around, run the mile back to school, and drive home. *No, Julie,* she told herself. *You're not practicing for them. You're practicing for yourself.* The rest of the way to the park, she considered what to say to the team. When she arrived, they were stretching. "What the hell just happened?" she said, her voice forceful though quivering.

"What the hell what?" asked the coach.

"You just left me?"

"I didn't realize you weren't with us," he said.

She turned to the girls. "What, I don't even matter?"

"Julie, you matter to me!" said a sophomore.

C.J. glanced up from her stretch. "Maybe if you weren't always late to practice . . ."

It was true. She was usually late to practice because of her environmental internship. But Julie was tired of being singled out. "C.J., shut up," she said. C.J. stopped stretching for a moment, her deep, dark eyes widened in surprise. The rest of the team cocked their heads, bewildered. Julie had never spoken so sharply around them.

As they started another run, though, Julie couldn't stay angry. She listened as C.J. talked about attending a stress workshop in school that day. "That's the stupidest thing I ever heard," Julie said. Talking about stress made her feel more stressed out. She still wondered if stress was the cause of her thinning hair. She had visited a pediatrician, a dermatologist, and a gynecologist, and no doctor had given her any medical explanation for the bare spot beneath her ponytail other than stress. But no one at Whitman knew about any of that.

C.J. laughed. "I just went because I could get out of class. Sam was there."

"Ohh," Julie said. "Sam loves to talk about stress."

When they finished their run, the coach and his assistant stood in front of the group. "We have a special activity for you," the coach said. He told the team to lie down in a circle and look up at the clouds. "C.J. was talking about being stressed, and then I looked up at the sky and saw how beautiful a day it was. I want everyone to relax and forget about all their stress. Just relax. Now I want you to think about what a great day it is today and what a great day Regionals will be. Picture your race."

Julie shifted into a yoga position, breathed deeply, and thought about her race. As she stared at the clouds, in a sudden moment of unexpected clarity between her visualization of the race and the minute she began to think about leaving for swim practice, she knew she could see herself at Dartmouth.

C.J., JUNIOR | PERCEIVED AS: THE FLIRT

When C.J. booed Julie at cross-country practice, she didn't mean to be rude. She tended to be unafraid to voice her opinions loudly and without much forethought, which meant she occasionally came across more assertively than she intended. She and Audrey shared that trait, which was partly why they were best friends. Or had been best friends, anyway, until they had argued heatedly over a school activity in the spring. Beyond carpool cordialities, they had barely spoken since.

C.J. admired Julie, who seemed naturally talented at almost everything she tried. But even though C.J. was a grade behind Julie, she constantly felt thrust into competition with her, and she didn't see how she could ever measure up in the eyes of the Whitman community. Julie was smart, stylish, athletic, hardworking, and participated in a multitude of activities. C.J. kept quiet as other juniors fawned over Julie in the locker room: "Julie, you're so cool," "Julie, I love your clothes." Especially on the cross-country team, people treated Julie as if she were some sort of goddess. Of course C.J. was annoyed when the coach singled out Julie for recognition. Like the rest of the team, C.J. knew very well, thank you, that Julie was having a tremendous season; C.J. had been running behind Julie for months. The coach didn't need to remind her of that.

C.J. and Julie had experienced friends-and-enemies phases throughout high school, but it wasn't necessarily Julie with whom C.J. was at odds. More often it was the idea of what Julie represented. To C.J., Julie symbolized the epitome of a Whitman student: one who was faced with the pressure to be "the best" and stepped up to it. It wasn't enough, at Whitman, to triumph over homework and tests, to battle academic stress, to put up with the constant grade comparisons. As C.J. explained to a friend, "You can't just be the smartest. You have to be the most athletic, you have to be able to have the most fun, you have to be the prettiest, the best-dressed, the nicest, the most wanted. You have to constantly be out on the town getting drunk and having fun, and then you have to get straight As and buy fancy clothes." The pressure soaked the school's ambience. C.J. heard people talking about their lives in the halls or at practice; she saw classmates' away messages, IM profiles, and Webshots simultaneously advertising their stress load and their social life: "I haven't started studying for tomorrow's tests but I'm going out with all my friends to have fun anyway!"

It was as if C.J. were being defined by what Julie was not, or vice versa. C.J. knew she was smart and articulate, but she was surrounded by people who were smart and articulate. When people compared C.J. with students like Julie, they placed C.J. in a different box, a lower tier. They dismissed her as someone who didn't care, which left her feeling like she had to struggle to keep up with the overachievers but at the same time not certain she wanted to. So instead of fighting against her second-tier image, she rolled with it. They didn't think she was smart, so she projected an image that was part mouthy, part ditz. They didn't think she was articulate, so she loudly told stories and made frivolous cracks, employing her goofy sense of humor. She knew that part of the reason top Whitman students weren't aware she had the same qualities they did was because she masked them. But it was painful to be seen as something she was not, or not to be seen for what she was.

Sometimes teachers' perceptions reflected the students'. In classes that involved student participation, teachers seemed to grasp that, despite occasionally being hyper and unfocused, C.J. was enthusiastic, vocal, and intelligent. In other classes, teachers treated her like a delinquent. One morning in September, C.J. came to school dressed 1980s-style for Decade Day, wearing a sports bra beneath an off-the-shoulder shirt, Converse sneakers, and a short denim skirt with spandex leggings underneath. The outfit covered more skin than her usual wardrobe, but when she walked into one of her classrooms, her female teacher said, "What day is it today, slut day?" The class laughed, as did C.J., who wasn't offended. She was positive that many people in the Whitman community viewed her as a slut, at least before they got to know her, because she was chesty and flirtatious (though she was convinced she consistently bungled her attempts to flirt).

On a warm day in another class, C.J. was wearing a normal-length tank top, but when she bent down to tie her shoes, a different female teacher came up behind her and said, "That shirt is not appropriate. Put on a jacket." Meanwhile, there were girls perceived as top students who wore tiny skirts and tight camis, and teachers didn't even look twice. Some of those girls—who were in five AP classes and boasted 4.0 averages—had, in C.J.'s opinion, "the common sense of a flea."

But not Julie. C.J. believed Julie deserved the accolades—just not the deity treatment, not the way one of her teammates obsequiously described her as "famous at this school." Sometimes C.J., too, was in awe of her, yet she was conflicted by the way Julie's image sometimes made her feel. It was strange that the semester C.J. felt most second-tier was the one when she was working the hardest. After getting a few Bs as a sophomore and freshman, this year C.J. had decided to buckle down, and her effort was paying off: This quarter she was getting six As and a B. That average put her nearly on par with students like Julie and Audrey.

C.J. thought about what a waste it was that she and Audrey hadn't spent time together since the spring. Once her senior friends—Julie included—graduated, next year would be awfully lonely if she and Audrey didn't patch things up. She picked up the phone and dialed

Audrey's number. "Hey," C.J. said. "Want to have milkshakes?" Like that, they resumed their friendship almost as if nothing had happened.

AUDREY, JUNIOR | PERCEIVED AS: THE PERFECTIONIST

Audrey was sitting in physics one Monday, trying to pay attention. She and her partner were almost done with their toothpick bridge, and Audrey was confident their hard work would secure them a spot in the Physics Olympics. She hadn't realized when she chose the bridge project how difficult it would be. Many of her friends chose other projects, started and finished them during classes, and received As. Meanwhile, Audrey and her partner had spent every weekend preparing for construction with such attention to minutiae that they even tested different kinds of glue. After researching bridges, they created drawings, including a life-size detailed design on posterboard. They put waxed paper on the posterboard and built the bridge on top of the drawing, using metal yardsticks as borders to keep the bridge straight. They had decided to build the bridge in four stages because it took more than a day for the glue to dry. With a week left to go, they had finished constructing the sides of the bridge. Now all that was left was to set up cereal boxes, tape the sides of the bridge to the boxes, and build the section in between.

The partner wasn't crazy about Audrey's overattention to detail, but Audrey reasoned that her partner had known she would work harder than anyone else. She laughed when Audrey obsessed over the length of the toothpicks. Audrey, however, was convinced she found the secret to the project: cutting the toothpicks instead of using them whole. Thus, they had spent hours with X-Acto knives, cutting each toothpick individually and rubber-banding bunches at each length.

Others teased Audrey for putting so much time into the bridge. Her posterboard scaled drawing was finished before other students started thinking about their bridges. Many students had begun the project only over the past weekend. Audrey's classmates expected her bridge to do well, but she tried to say as little about it as possible. If she told students she thought her bridge might win, they would work that much harder just to beat her. Audrey's peers seemed to thrive on competing with her for grades. Whenever she got a test back, inevitably classmates would surround her, asking, "Audrey, what'd you get?" She thought it was because they knew how much time she put into studying, so she rarely talked about her scores. As soon as she received a test or paper, she turned it over without looking at it and then put it away, resolving not to check the grade until she got home. When they saw Audrey hide her paper, other students grew angry, accusing her of withholding information. Audrey sensed they expected her to get the A, when in reality she didn't always get it.

"Audrey," the physics teacher said, interrupting his lecture and shaking her out of her thoughts. He held out a manila envelope. "This was delivered for you from guidance."

The entire class turned to watch Audrey walk up to him, pick up the envelope, and return to her seat. She wondered what she had done wrong and, flustered, tried to put the envelope aside so she could open it later when no one was watching her. As the physics lecture continued, however, her curiosity beat back her nerves. Inside the envelope, a Whitman staff member had placed a book about the best colleges for "high-achieving Hispanics." Audrey reddened deeply. It was one of those books that read in English one way and, when flipped over, was translated into Spanish. Audrey's bridge partner saw the book and laughed, as did the two girls sitting behind her, who knew why Audrey, who didn't look conventionally Hispanic, would receive the book. The seniors in the class looked confused.

"Well, that's not embarrassing or anything," Audrey said under her breath.

Audrey was proud of her culture but conflicted about how her ethnicity affected her high school career and the upcoming college application process. Other students sometimes made cracks about it; during a group conversation with fellow *Black & White* writers, when Audrey muttered offhand, "Why am I taking AP Spanish?" one responded, "Because you're Hispanic." In reality, she wasn't fluent in Spanish. She could understand the spoken language, thanks to plenty of cousins who didn't speak English, but she hadn't mastered the writing. Her lack of fluency, however, had no bearing on the assumptions other students made about her.

In the spring of sophomore year, Audrey's government class had debated affirmative action. The class was divided according to political party, which meant that Audrey, as a devoted member of Whitman's Young Democrats Club, had to argue in favor of affirmative action.

"Affirmative action rectifies the inherent inequalities in our society," Audrey stated. "And thusly, it's fair, given that it levels the playing field." Having prepared extensively, as usual, Audrey backed up her statement with statistics and court cases.

A friend who was sitting on the conservative side of the room looked Audrey in the eye and said, "Take, for example, our very own Audrey." Audrey cringed as the class gawked at her. Instantly, she knew her argument was shot. Her friend continued, "Why should Audrey have an advantage just because [of] her last name? How is that making things more equal? She's a model student *and* she gets the benefit of affirmative action." Students on that side of the room gave the friend high fives as she drove home the point that affirmative action was more of a reverse discrimination because it benefited minorities who didn't necessarily need it.

The room buzzed. Audrey grew warm. She wasn't sure how so many people knew she was Hispanic; her surname wasn't that obvious a giveaway. She supposed it was natural that in Whitman's competitive atmosphere, the same way that top students knew when someone failed a test or scored the highest grade in the class, they would dig up every advantage other students might have. The liberals were silent until a classmate tried to counter the point: "No matter Audrey's study habits, her father faced discrimination, and she is the exception, not the rule."

After class (and for the next week), Audrey's friend apologized profusely for using her as an example. But Audrey wasn't upset; she believed her friend was right. Why *should* she have the extra help? As liberal as Audrey was, she disagreed with the notion that affirmative action should be based on race rather than an equalizing system based on socioeconomic status. Audrey expected that when she applied to college, the fact that she went to a school like Whitman would nullify most of the advantage her ethnicity might grant her. She didn't deny, however, that having that extra edge provided her at least some comfort.

JULIE, SENIOR | PERCEIVED AS: THE SUPERSTAR

Julie wished the Dartmouth application left more room for creativity, but the questions were fairly standard, so she plugged in her answers. A short-answer question asked what five words she would use to describe herself. Julie stopped to think. She was tempted to use the words "More interesting than five words."

"Overachiever" would be an accurate description, Julie thought. She wondered how much these words would matter. She had already gone through several sheets of paper, trying to make sure the application was spaced out perfectly with uniform fonts. She guessed that despite the weeks she had put into her application, the admissions officers would probably spend about five minutes looking at it. Julie settled on "energetic, gutsy, driven, spontaneous, and compassionate" (but thought, *irritable, impatient, volatile, unpredictable . . .*).

As she was reviewing the application, the phone rang. It was the Williams coach, who wanted to know how her county championship race had gone.

"I got a 19:14," she told him.

The coach sounded pleased. "So are you still applying early?" he asked.

Julie squirmed. The Queen of Awkward, stuck again. "I don't think so," she said softly.

"Why not?"

"Well, I'm looking at Dartmouth."

"What does Dartmouth have that Williams doesn't?"

"I guess Dartmouth is a little bigger and not as quiet."

The coach wished her luck and told her that if her early application didn't work out, he hoped she would apply to Williams in the regular pool.

The day the Dartmouth application went out, Julie was temporarily elated. She forgot for a moment that while her academic life seemed to be settling into place, her social life still perplexed her. Classmates viewed her as part of the River Falls crew, though she still wasn't completely comfortable with that clique. Just a few days before, one of the girls had noticed her hair, which used to be luxuriously thick. "Oh my God, Julie, your hair's so thin I can see right through to your scalp!" she said, pointing. "We can do, like, Rogaine on a Friday night." Julie knew the girl was trying to be helpful, but still. After multiple blood tests, the vague diagnosis of stress, and, most recently, a sonogram, the issue was a touchy one. No matter. Julie wouldn't have to make any more decisions until she heard from Dartmouth on December 9.

In AP Spanish, the teacher told the class how exasperating it was to hear students freak out about their grades. Whitman students, the teacher said, had the wrong attitude. All they wanted to know was whether they were going to get an A and how many points each assignment was worth. This year's freshmen, she went on, were even worse. Thanks to the new grading policy, everyone was confused.

Julie only half listened, because the policy wouldn't really affect her. None of that was relevant anymore. Julie was free. Every to-do list she had made over the past eighteen months included SAT and college application matters. Now she looked at the SAT books in her homework cave and thought, *Ha!* When she encountered a word she didn't recognize, instead of looking it up and committing it to memory, she said to herself, *I don't care! It doesn't matter anymore!*

By nightfall, she started to worry that she had made the wrong college decision.

TAYLOR, SENIOR | PERCEIVED AS: THE POPULAR GIRL

On Halloween weekend, Taylor was still having trouble with her Stanford essays because she was convinced she had nothing original to say. She couldn't stop thinking about the other students who were applying early. At her last unofficial count, they all had better SAT scores than she did, even with her improved number from her October retake, a 1510. She was pleased for only a few moments after she saw her score, then remembered hearing that more than thirty seniors had broken the 1500 mark.

To her popular friends' dismay, Taylor hadn't gone to as many parties as usual this month because she had been cooped up working on her applications. She promised herself she would stay in tonight, but when one of her friends called, she wavered. She did want to get out of the house. "I have to work on applications, too, Taylor," the friend said. "Just go and have some fun, and then you still have two days to finish your Stanford application."

Taylor worked for another hour, then rushed around her house to put together a costume. Her friends had settled on a slutty theme: One friend was a "slutty bunny," with a short white skirt, a black bra visible beneath a knotted shirt, and a large balled tail; another friend was a "slutty ref," wearing a cropped black-and-white-striped shirt with a plunging neckline, a "booty skort," kneesocks, and a whistle. In keeping with the theme, Taylor tied an Abercrombie button-down shirt so it exposed her flat stomach, unbuttoned it past her cleavage, put on a short denim skirt and a cowboy hat, and dubbed herself a "slutty cowgirl." Taylor went to the party with a few friends and one of the Nastys. (Other Nastys made a brief appearance but left when they spotted a non-Nasty with one of their ex-boyfriends.) The party was fun, but Taylor couldn't get her mind off her application. The rest of her friends slept over at the party, while Taylor returned home to work on her application.

One short-answer essay question in particular was giving her trouble: *Of the activities, interests and experiences listed on the previous page, which is the most meaningful to you, and why?* How could she answer with a single activity that accurately represented her identity? She loved playing lacrosse, but her teams weren't great. Her leadership activities meant a lot to her, but even if she described all of the painstaking work that went into running the Mr. Whitman pageant, she doubted it would seem intellectual enough for Stanford.

She loved soccer, and the team had unexpectedly improved over the season, but the Whitman coach was now playing her less than half of each game. Her teammates said he underestimated her, but she didn't question him, both because she avoided confrontations and because she wasn't sure she had earned her spot. She had sprained her right ankle at a game in early October, after having gotten three hours of sleep the night before instead of her usual five and a quarter. Taylor returned to practice two weeks later and, in her first game back, had immediately sprained her left ankle. She prayed she would be able to make it back to the field for next week's playoffs.

Taylor deliberated how to package herself. Her interests in math and engineering were meaningful to her, but meaningful enough to portray an accurate picture to admissions officers? Her popular friends would think not. They counted on her to calculate tips at restaurants, but they thought her participation in math-related activities was funny. They made comments like "Taylor wasn't at lunch today because she was in the library with her math groupies!" They didn't know that the only reason she didn't go to math team meetings was because they were at the same time as soccer practice. They assumed she wouldn't socialize with the other math-oriented students; when they heard that a geeky junior invited Taylor to play Frisbee, they said, "Oh, Taylor would never do that." In fact, Taylor would have played had she been in town. When AP Frank invited her to a Frisbee gathering for his birthday the previous year, she enthusiastically went. She hadn't told her popular friends then, and she didn't tell them now that Derek had invited her to a chess team meeting, which she also attended.

Taylor berated herself for deleting solitaire from her computer, missing the distraction. She settled on writing the short essay about her book drive. The next night she finished her Stanford application and emailed it in. She could worry about Duke, Penn, and the other applications another time. She wrapped a sheet into a toga and went trick-or-treating with her friends.

AP FRANK, COLLEGE FRESHMAN | PERCEIVED AS: THE WORKHORSE

AP Frank was attempting to study for his math midterm the next day. The evening hours were slipping away from him, and he still had to go through several practice problems. *Gotta study,* he argued with himself. *I took this class in sophomore year of high school. This should be a cinch. Dammit. No, no, can't get overconfident. Gotta study. Geez, these problems can get annoying. Those assholes sure as hell better not give us a three-variable Lagrange problem.*

Half an hour later, AP Frank decided to give himself a short break. He wondered what zany things his old AP Chemisty teacher had been saying lately. Hoping to catch up on Whitman gossip, AP Frank called home. His mother answered, as usual.

"Hey, Mom. Lemme talk to Richard."

"Richard not here. He at friend's house," she replied.

"What's he doing at a friend's house?"

"Group project. Working with that crazy kid. He's wicked. His parents don't like to see Richard succeed."

"Mom, sometimes kids don't have a choice about whom they work with for projects. It happens."

"Did you do your laundry yet?" she asked him.

"Yeah, yeah. I did my laundry yesterday."

"Did you wash socks separately?"

"No, I did not wash the socks separately. Why the heck would I do that?"

"Because socks smell bad."

"Of course they smell bad, but washing them separately entails paying another dollar. I'm a poor college student, Mom. Speaking of which, you need to send me some money."

"Okay, I go to post office tomorrow and mail check."

"Thanks."

"Oh," she said, and paused before continuing in a tone of disbelief. "Mr. Murphy died."

AP Frank was stunned. The words didn't compute. "What?" he asked.

"He had heart attack. Died at home." She started to cry.

"What?" He didn't know what to say. "That's . . . terrible." AP Frank felt like the wind had been knocked out of him.

"He did so much for us. Life's not fair," Mrs. AP Frank said.

"Okay."

"You study hard, okay?"

"Yeah. I'll talk to you later. Bye."

AP Frank leaned back in his chair and stared off into space. *Oh, shit,* he thought. *Heart attack? Fuck . . . died in pain . . . He did so much for us. Shit. Mr. Murphy's dead.* AP Frank was again transported to the January day he had cried in Mr. Murphy's office. He remembered Mr. Murphy softly telling him to be brave, remembered his large hairy arms wrapping him in an awkward hug, telling him it would be okay. He thought about how Mr. Murphy was the only adult who stood up to his mother. How he had done everything he could for Richard. How he didn't take any shit.

I have to study for this exam. I don't have time to think about this, said a voice inside AP Frank's head. "You asshole," AP Frank thought back. "Don't have time to think about your own guidance counselor's death? What kind of heartless bastard are you?" *I fucking have to study. Me failing isn't going to demonstrate anything for him.* "But he's dead, he's . . . dead . . . No more Mr. Murphy. I never got a chance to tell him how I'm doing." *But is this what he would've wanted? Everyone has to die. Fact of life. Concentrate on what's at hand. Double integrals.* "Fucking human mortality." *Double integrals.* "He was a great man: compassionate, strong, generous . . ." *Go to sleep, man. You have class tomorrow.* "Okay."

Shaken, AP Frank put his head in his hands. Mr. Murphy had been his lifeline. He had been the one adult who knew exactly what was going on in Mrs. AP Frank's household, the one adult on his side. Who would look out for AP Frank and his brother now?

PETE, JUNIOR | PERCEIVED AS: THE MEATHEAD

The night before the physics bridge project was due, Pete and Hugh met at Pete's house to build theirs. Hugh, Pete's best friend at Whitman, was a top-tier student determined to get into an Ivy League school. They hadn't intentionally saved the bridge construction for the last minute. They had convened the previous weekend to give it an earnest effort, but the TV had proved more interesting than the bridge. This time they needed to get the project done. They blanketed the basement with newspapers, tuned the TV to a football game, and dumped out the toothpicks Pete and his father bought at the dollar store.

Pete and Hugh looked at each other and shrugged. They hadn't drawn up any plans. During commercials, they haphazardly tried to stick the toothpicks together with rubber cement, even though the rules stated they could use only toothpicks and glue. They coated the toothpicks with rubber cement until they were slimy, and built a roof out of toothpicks on the top. They stepped back and surveyed their work. The bridge was extremely lopsided, with rubber-cement chunks sticking out every which way. To Pete, it looked like a crooked canopy made by six-year-olds.

The next day Hugh brought their bridge in for testing during the first few minutes of their journalism class. Pete, harboring no illusions that their attempt would hold the weight of a brick, didn't bother going. The journalism adviser was talking to the class when Hugh walked into the classroom holding the bridge. From the doorway, he gave Pete the thumbs-down. When the teacher finished her announcements, Hugh came over and sat next to Pete with the bridge. It was still crooked, warped, and, now, sunken in the middle. To their credit, Pete thought, the weight of the brick hadn't really changed the composition of the bridge. At least it was still intact. "What happened?" Pete asked.

"Well, the good news is it weighed only eighteen grams," Hugh said. "But when they put the weight on, it kinda turned sideways and sagged in the middle but didn't break because of the rubber cement. So they couldn't get the brick to stay on the bridge."

Pete laughed. They would have to redo the project if they wanted a grade. Other students in the class were tapping him on the shoulder, snickering at the sight of the bridge, and asking if it had actually worked. "Hell, no!" he said. He turned to Hugh. "I'm gonna destroy it." Hugh grinned and handed him the bridge.

Pete tried to break the bridge in half, but the elasticized glue stubbornly held fast. It was too bendy to break easily. As Hugh cackled, Pete twisted the bridge until it separated. They couldn't reuse any of the materials anyway, especially after illegally coating them with rubber cement.

AUDREY, JUNIOR | PERCEIVED AS: THE PERFECTIONIST

The day before the physics bridge was due, Audrey glued on the last toothpick. She had a bat mitzvah catering job that afternoon, and her catering partner was dressed up and ready, waiting for her in the driveway. Audrey used a blow-dryer to dry the final toothpick enough for it to set. When Audrey came home from the reception that night, she and her father made sure all of the bonds on the bridge were secure, using X-Acto knives to shave away the extra glue so the bridge would weigh less.

Because Audrey didn't have a triple-beam balance to test the bridge's weight, she placed it on a scale she used to weigh chocolate when she made fudge. The scale was in ounces, but she tried to convert the measurement and came up with roughly twenty grams. She was confident that the bridge would be one of Whitman's best. There was no doubt that it would hold the brick. The only unknown was how much it would weigh on the physics department's calibrated scale.

In the morning, after one of her usual sleep-deprived nights, Audrey ran downstairs, late for carpool. She grabbed her lunch and a baggie of cereal off the counter, carefully hefted the bridge, and got into her father's car, where she held the bridge on her lap. When he dropped her off at school, he wished her luck.

"I'm nervous," Audrey admitted. She had no way of knowing how her bridge stacked up against the others until the weigh-ins began during lunch.

Her father smiled. "Don't worry. You'll definitely get an A."

Audrey walked straight upstairs to her physics classroom. Just outside the room, two smart, ambitious juniors were holding their bridge. "It looks really good," Audrey told them.

The girls glanced at each other. "Thanks," said one. Then she named a junior who was well known for his physics prowess. "He helped us with it, so we really just hope to pass and not get into Physics Olympics. How much does yours weigh?"

"I don't know yet. I'm going to go weigh it now," Audrey said. She didn't know what would be considered a good weight. "I weighed it at home and—I'm not sure because we don't have a good scale, but I think it's around twenty grams."

The other girls laughed and looked at each other again. "Oh. Ours is eighteen."

"Okay, well good luck," Audrey said, and walked into her first-period physics class. She didn't think it would be worth overtly competing with them before she knew how much her own bridge weighed. As Audrey walked to the scale at the back of the room, she could hear other people commenting on her bridge. "Whoa, that looks strong," said a classmate.

Audrey set the scale at eighteen grams, hoping to compare her bridge with the other girls'. The scale tipped; her bridge was even lighter than she had hoped. Audrey's heart raced. She moved the balance notch by notch until she had the bridge's weight. Audrey went to her seat and placed the bridge on the black Formica table in front of her. When the bell rang, the other two girls came in to drop off their bridge. "How much does yours weigh?" one asked Audrey.

Audrey tried not to grin, but she couldn't help it. Her braces shone. "Oh, it's 15.2 grams."

She couldn't stop beaming throughout the first part of class, as students marveled at her bridge. It was obvious that no one else's bridge, at least in this class, would match Audrey's.

When the period ended, Audrey's partner asked, "Do you think we should take it with us to our classes?"

Audrey pondered this. "No, I don't want someone to bang into it or step on it," she said. "I'd much rather leave it in the physics room, where I know it won't be broken." They looked around the classroom for a suitable place to leave the bridge for the few periods until the official test at lunch. About ten bridges were propped against the wall lining the right-hand side of the classroom. Audrey and her partner delicately laid theirs at the back of the line.

Throughout the morning, Audrey couldn't stop thinking about the bridge. The closer it got to lunch, the more keyed up she became. The bridge had the potential to be the most rewarding science project of her academic career. When the lunch bell rang, Audrey and her partner rushed upstairs. Another physics teacher was conducting the testing in the attached classroom. The girls followed the stream of students picking up their bridges and taking them next door.

Audrey and her partner practically skipped to the right-hand side of the classroom. Immediately, Audrey saw that the bridge wasn't where they had left it. She looked up, expecting to see a friend appear, chuckling, with the bridge in hand. Nothing happened. Audrey's heart fell. If someone had taken the bridge, even as a joke, that person could unintentionally break it. "Who would take it?" she asked her partner. "Someone must have accidentally used it to test their project. What are we going to do?"

Her partner didn't look worried. "Don't worry, it's gotta be here somewhere." Audrey stood dumbfounded while her partner searched through a stack of bridges at the back of the room. When Audrey turned around, she saw one of the junior girls with the eighteen-gram bridge. "Have you picked up or seen my bridge anywhere?" she asked.

"Why on earth would I take your bridge?" said the girl. Audrey believed her. The girl seemed scared that she would have to go to the Physics Olympics with a bridge that a junior physics star had helped her build.

Audrey approached her physics teacher, who was about to begin his class. "Excuse me, my bridge was sitting here, and now it's not."

The teacher, shuffling through things on his desk, didn't bother to look at her. "Bridges don't just get up and walk away. Look around," he said.

It crossed Audrey's mind that her teacher might not have seen her bridge on her desk that morning. If she couldn't find the bridge, he might not believe that she had constructed one in the first place. Audrey panicked. She ran through the storage room to the adjacent physics classroom where students were testing their bridges for another physics teacher. She approached each pair, asked if they had seen her bridge, and inspected their bridge to make sure it wasn't hers. The other students looked at her as if she were crazy, but Audrey didn't care. She walked up and down the long line of teams, staring at their projects as the students stared back. Her partner trailed silently behind her.

People noticed Audrey was agitated. "What's wrong?" one student asked. The others in line turned to look at her.

"I think someone took my bridge," Audrey said, a quiver in her voice.

"Audrey, calm down," said her partner, who led her into the storage room to look further. Nothing. The girls approached the teacher, who was weighing the bridges and testing the bricks. "Excuse me? My name's Audrey, and we can't find our bridge anywhere."

The teacher seemed frazzled. "Are you serious?" he asked. "Are you *sure* you looked for your bridge?"

Audrey assured him she had. She spoke quickly, trying frantically to get the words out before the tears came. "I can call my mom and have her bring over our poster that has what the bridge looks like so if someone tries to turn it in you'd know. I know it will work. It weighs 15.2 grams and holds the brick—"

"That's not necessary yet. Just wait. Keep looking and we'll see what bridges come through. If any bridge is fifteen grams, I'll make sure to come find you, because that's not something that's going to happen twice. I've never seen a bridge that weighs that little, so I'd like to see that," the teacher said.

Audrey returned to her classroom to continue searching. Her teacher was in the middle of a lesson, but all eyes turned to Audrey as she walked in. She rummaged through drawers and cabinets. After a few minutes, she gave up. On her way out of the room, her teacher stopped her. "Have you found your bridge yet?" he asked.

"No, it doesn't seem to be anywhere."

The teacher walked across the room until he was standing right next to her. "In thirty-five years, I've never seen a missing bridge. I have no idea who would take it," he said. Then he noticed that Audrey was on the verge of tears. "Don't worry, you won't have to remake the bridge."

"I want to remake the bridge because it was fifteen grams and I want to show that it works and I know it would do well," she said.

"Well, look on top of the cabinets."

Audrey scanned the old bridge projects on top of the cabinets. "It's not there," she said, her voice wavering.

"What does it look like?" the teacher asked.

"It has thirteen squares, three Xs in the middle, it's really light, it's rectangular, and it's a model of a Baltimore truss."

"If anything comes in like that, we'll make sure it comes back to you."

"I can call my mom and have her bring the poster over."

"There's no need to get your mom involved at this point."

"Thank you. Sorry for interrupting."

Audrey walked back through the storage room into the classroom where the bridges were being tested, and promptly burst into tears in front of the students. She borrowed a friend's cell phone and went into a stairwell to call her mom. As soon as her mother heard her voice, she asked what was wrong.

"It's gone," Audrey said through her sobs.

"What are you talking about?"

"Someone stole my physics project."

"Are you kidding me? What can I do? Have they seen it? How can I make sure that you get a grade?"

"I don't know. I don't know how I'm going to find it."

"The first thing you have to do is go to your teacher and make sure you get an A for this project, because we know you did the work."

"He's teaching a class now," Audrey said. "Can you bring over the poster so they'll see that we did the work?" Her mother said she would be there in half an hour.

Meanwhile, Audrey went to the tech ed and the art classrooms but didn't see the bridge. She got permission from her AP Art teacher to skip sixth period to look for the bridge, and returned to the physics testing room in case a student tried to present her bridge as his own. Audrey watched as the two ambitious junior girls tested their bridge and passed. She was happy for them but couldn't help thinking that if her project didn't turn up, they would likely go to the Physics Olympics with a bridge that wasn't all their own.

When Audrey's mother dropped off the poster, Audrey brought it to her teacher. "This clearly shows that you spent time on it. You'll get an A, and you won't have to redo the project," he said.

"I want to redo the project," Audrey said. "I want to show that it works!"

By the time Audrey went to bed that night, she realized she wouldn't have the time to remake the bridge. Later that week, she learned that the teacher had given her and her partner a 100 percent on the project. The juniors with the eighteen-gram bridge won the Whitman competition and moved on to the Physics Olympics.

∽

Audrey never found out what happened to her bridge. She believed the most likely explanation was that another student had stolen it in hopes of qualifying for the Physics Olympics but chickened out after Audrey loudly publicized its disappearance. Given the ultra-competitive atmosphere of today's high schools, Audrey's theory made sense: Another student probably did steal her bridge, either to use as his own or to sabotage Audrey, who was widely seen as an overachiever to beat. When teens are faced with unrelenting pressure to outperform classmates, cut-throat maneuvers aren't unusual. A midwestern junior told me, "You suck up to the teacher (subtly, of course). When [another] girl [gets] picked to be the star of the play instead of you, you pretend to hear about some nasty thing she's done with some nasty guy in the bathroom, and tell it to somebody you know will tell it to somebody else."

Remember Tracy Flick, the type-A Reese Witherspoon character in the movie *Election* (based on the Tom Perrotta novel), who "scratched and clawed her way to the top, lying and cheating when necessary"? She may no longer be an unusual type of student. A southern senior told me of a school election campaign during which a girl ratted to a supervisor that the top candidate abused alcohol. For a club officer appointment, a candidate told the supervising teacher that her opponent, who was new to the school, couldn't handle club president duties because she had a rigorous five-AP schedule. The teacher gave that candidate the position, not knowing that she, too, was taking five APs. Kentucky students told me about a scenario in which an officer called a secret meeting to hold club elections for the following year, conveniently told his friends and not his opponent about the meeting, and got himself elected president.

The competition is brutal. In 1968, 17.6 percent of college freshmen said they had an A average in high school; that number had jumped to 46.6 percent by 2003. At New Jersey's Tenafly High School, a senior with a B average in 2005 would rank no higher than 194 out of 225 in the class. Between 1997 and 2002, the number of students who took the AP BC Calculus exam—the test for the difficult class Taylor's college counselor told her to drop—rose by 84 percent.

Perhaps nowhere is the battle to overachieve more evident than in the fight for a high class rank. Countrywide, 81 percent of public high schools use class rank, which makes academic competition all the fiercer. The difference between top students' GPAs can come down to one thousandth of a point, leaving many excellent students at elite high schools stuck below the top quarter of their class. As a result, the feud for valedictorian has grown particularly heated. Since 2001, families in several states have gone so far as to sue for the title. In 2003 Michigan senior Brian Delekta, who was just shy of his class's top GPA, sued his principal, superintendent, and school board members because he was given an A rather than an A-plus for a middle school work-study credit he received for working at his mother's law firm. (The firm was located in a district in which the highest grade possible was an A.)

That same year, conflict erupted at Plano West Senior High School in Texas when senior Sarah Bird was awarded the number two rank with a GPA that was .00154 lower than the valedictorian's. She and her family hunted through the school district's policies until they found a discrepancy: Bird's participation on the school's basketball team counted as physical education courses, which were unweighted As. The family hired a lawyer, who persuaded the school board to name Bird co-valedictorian.

Also in 2003, New Jersey senior Blair Hornstine, who took most of her classes at home with private tutors because of an immune disorder, sued the board of education to prohibit it from naming a co-valedictorian—and asked for $200,000 in compensatory damages and $2.7 million in punitive damages. The school board had declared that her homeschooling gave her an unfair advantage and named as co-valedictorian a non-homeschooled student whose GPA was .055 lower than Hornstine's 4.6894. A federal judge sided with Hornstine, who was granted the solo title and $60,000. She was accepted to Harvard, but the admissions office revoked the offer after learning she had plagiarized material in columns she wrote for her local newspaper.

There are some who say that the fight for valedictorian prepares students for "real-world" clashes. An Indiana county school board member said he supported class rank because the valedictorian tradition "fosters healthy academic competition." One wonders how healthy the competition is when the push to excel encourages intense strategizing, not to mention the cheating epidemic described in Chapter Four. The so-called healthy competition encourages a Machiavellian win-at-all-costs mentality in which the number one class rank, and college acceptance letter, justify the means.

Then again, perhaps clawing to the top by any means necessary—cheating, lawsuits, manipulation—does prepare students for the real world. Haresh, a Georgia student I interviewed, said that "cutthroat competitiveness runs rampant in my school. It's immoral and unfair, but I also see that this type of behavior is probably what I should expect from the real world. It is a dog-eat-dog world, and to remain competitive, that is exactly what you have to do." In the 2004 Josephson Institute of Ethics study of 25,000 high school students, two thirds of males and 52 percent of females agreed that "in the real world, successful people do what they have to do to win, even if others consider it cheating." Nearly one in four students believed that "people who are willing to lie, cheat, or break the rules are more likely to succeed than people who do not."

This comes during an era when a string of high-profile CEO indictments have undermined the public's faith in business leaders, and dominating the headlines is a long list of prominent authors and journalists found to have plagiarized or fabricated material. In that context, Sam's fake Muslim seems less like cheating than like emulating American business as usual. As a student at a top Northeast college told ABC's *Primetime,* "The real world is terrible. People will take other people's materials and pass it on as theirs. I'm numb to it already. I'll cheat to get by." Obviously, he has company. In 2002 the percentage of high school students who said they would be willing to "lie to get a good job" rose to more than a third.

Likewise, college admissions officers told me that some students lie to get into a good college, inflating roles or making up titles to bolster their application. Grinnell College dean of admissions Jim Sumner, for example, recalled two athletes in recent years who boasted during the admissions process that they were being heavily recruited by other schools.

It apparently hadn't occurred to them that Sumner might be friends with the coaches they mentioned. He quickly uncovered their lies.

Because of episodes like this, some universities have modified their admissions process, randomly selecting applicants to prove their extracurricular claims, for example, or requesting that students submit a graded high school paper. But where is the line drawn that defines misrepresentation? In one survey, 91 percent of college students said it was unfair for a parent to write a child's college admissions essay, 42 percent to hire a college counselor for assistance, and 26 percent for a parent to correct a child's homework. Yet when Duke University began asking candidates whether they had received assistance with their essays, 95 percent of applicants said they did.

Surely, the gray areas between strategizing, embellishing, and cheating are cause for confusion. Half the students polled in a Rutgers' Management Education Center study said that copying questions and answers to a test (from friends in earlier classes) did not count as cheating. In a 2004 survey, 82 percent of high school students believed that working on an assignment with classmates when a teacher requested individual work was not cheating. In 2005, 77 percent of college students surveyed said that Internet plagiarism was not a serious form of cheating.

Immoral and cutthroat schemes have become so much a standard mode of academic survival—experts say it now begins in elementary school, and I've heard of kindergartners cheating on Field Day—that many students accept it as an unavoidable part of working the system. They view it as a natural result of the pressure of such a high-stakes competition; some students say their parents would prefer they cheat rather than get poor grades. They see it as a low-risk way to get an edge: According to a *Who's Who* survey, 95 percent of high-achieving high school students who cheated said they have never been caught. And they view it as necessary. More than half of high-achieving students do not believe that cheating is wrong. As a Virginia high school student told CNN, "The better grades you have, the better school you get into, the better you're going to do in life. And if you learn to cut corners to do that, you're going to be saving yourself time and energy. In the real world, that's what's going to be going on. The better you do, that's what shows. It's not how moral you were in getting there."

Chapter 6

November 7–November 21

PERCEPTIONS

When college admissions officers decide whether to admit applicants, they can use academic records and extracurricular performance as barometers. But how does one evaluate a toddler for placement
in kindergarten? To find out, I spent several days observing the lower-
school admissions office at Trinity School in New York City.

Trinity was founded about 300 years ago as a co-ed charity school
committed to educating children of the poor. Sometime since then, the
K–12 school did a 180 and became one of the most prestigious independent schools in Manhattan. Trinity's students also happen to fare unusually
well in the admissions process at prestigious colleges. Hank Moses, Trinity's headmaster and a former Harvard dean of freshmen, was emphatic
about the Trinity community's "deep commitment to education" over
prestige when I interviewed him. "Trinity would die if its families didn't
care about educating kids for good reasons. One of the things we do is admit *families,* not children," he said. "But it doesn't help that local newspapers publish competitive studies of the college-going record compared to
schools Trinity competes with." (At least two of Trinity's own promotional booklets list the college placement of recent graduates.)

Trinity's lower-school director of admissions, June Hilton, is a striking
blonde in her fifties whom Moses said is "passionately admired by families." Because June has been at Trinity for thirty years, she can analyze
whether four-year-olds will flourish at the school simply by remembering

similar children from past years. One day in November, I observed a typical afternoon for Hilton during admissions season. I settled on a plush couch in her office, a corner space that managed to feel both large and cozy, complete with a small nook filled with children's books, toys, and stuffed animals.

June and her staff were immersed in the early-notification stage of the process. Early notification was for families who were connected to the school, whether as siblings of Trinity students or children of alumni, faculty, or staff. "The parents take nothing for granted. The anxiety level is huge," she said. June hoped to have the acceptance and rejection notices in the mail by December 15. Much of June's office time was spent talking to parents and nursery school directors. "I'm sure she's definite. We'll take her," I overheard her say during a phone conversation with a nursery school director. "It's so stressful for parents . . . You mean the parents are thinking that? Oh no, that's horrible."

June hung up the phone and sighed. "All I wanted to know was when to expect the school report," she told me. "She said kids were getting labeled through this whole process by their ERB scores. She said parents are looking at the score and saying, 'That's my child, a seventy-ninth-percentile child,' looking at their own child that way."

June often told parents that all she could do "with great assurance and a lot of success" was to predict which children would be happy and comfortable in Trinity's kindergarten and perhaps first grade. "If anybody says they can do better than that, they're fooling themselves. There's nothing predictable. Like going to a doctor can tell you how healthy your child is, but only at the moment. People take it so far and make it so serious. People lose all perspective because the parents who are placing such a huge premium on this are incredibly successful in their fields. Most of them went to public school, and hey, those of us who did, we all made it. People forget that. A friend of mine, before his child was five, he said he wanted her to go to Harvard. I was aghast."

Ann Fusco, the Trinity admissions officer charged with evaluating children applying to kindergarten and first grade, came in to update June on the interviews she had conducted that morning. June explained to me that while most lower schools evaluated kindergarten applicants in groups of five to ten, Trinity evaluated them individually or in twos. Ann's work, June said, was the most important piece of the three major admissions factors—the others were the report from the preschool and ERB test scores—because Ann could determine how a child would fit in at Trinity specifically. Trinity wanted to avoid basing applicants' futures on what June called "the vagaries of testing four-year-olds."

Other factors also played a role. Trinity favored diversity and also gave preference to siblings of current students and children of alumni, faculty, and staff. In addition, June had to keep in mind the various preschools. "Some you have closer ties with than others, and you better make sure that each year you're taking at least a decent amount of kids, or if not, you'd better the next year. If you don't, then you're in some trouble. Even though they understand the numbers, too, it doesn't matter."

No sooner had June said that than the phone rang. After hanging up, June explained that the caller was another preschool head who wanted to know how Ann's interview went with a child having difficulties in the admissions process. The woman told June that the girl was "absolutely not right for Trinity" but asked for any information that might help her direct the child's parents on how to proceed at other schools. June said to me, "Heads of nursery schools, I feel so sorry for them, because these are very, very dedicated professionals. And they're spending eighty percent of their time on what's called exmissions, which is never what you thought you'd be doing. She works so closely with every single parent. But I know she'd much rather be working with children, curriculum, faculty, myriad things, and this eats up every piece of time."

Curious about how Ann managed to "interview" four-year-olds, I sat in a small chair in Ann's office to observe Trinity's evaluations of applicants for its kindergarten class. Formerly a third-grade teacher, Ann worked part-time at Trinity and part-time as a private tutor for elementary school–aged children. While Jen Levine, June's indefatigable associate director of admissions, interviewed parents, Ann would "interview" the children in her office.

The office was a tight space with walls full of bright posters of animals and the alphabet. Along the left wall was a table flanked on both sides by two small wooden desks. On each desk sat a tiny bear wearing a blue-and-yellow Trinity sweater in one corner, a small blue canister full of markers in another corner, and an 8½-by-11 sheet of white paper beneath a sharpened pencil. As Jen welcomed two pairs of parents into her office, Ann showed the boys where their parents were going, then ushered them into her office next door. She chatted with the boys about their birthdays and schools while she set them up at the desks.

"Here's a gold Trinity pencil," she said in her British clip, and asked the boys to write their names and to draw a person. The boys, one in an orange sweater and the other in a white shirt, got to work. When they wrote their names, Ann turned to Orange, showed him a card bearing a circle and a diamond, and asked, "Can you copy that little design onto your piece of paper?" She turned to White. "Now, you see those Magic Markers there; I'm going to give you a piece of paper, and what I'd like you to do is make a nice surprise for Mom and Dad."

"Done!" Orange interrupted.

Ann turned back to Orange. "How about a nice line of dots?"

He poked the paper. "Done!"

"Terrific job. Now, sweetie, how about some little circles right there?"

"Around the dots?"

"No, they don't have to be around the dots. Anywhere is fine."

Orange sang to himself as he drew across the page. "Little circles, little circles."

"Yeah, but look at the card so you do them the same," Ann reminded him.

Orange looked at the card, singing, "Little ovals, little ovals . . . Done!"

"How about a box that's grown a curly tail?" Ann asked, showing him the design.

"Done!"

"Now two nice wiggly worms," she said, pointing to squiggly lines.

"Done!" This continued through two more designs.

Ann checked in with the other boy, then returned her attention to Orange. "I'm going to ask you your letters. Have you learned your letters?" Orange began to sing his ABCs. "Wait a minute, I might try to trick you," she said, and showed him her lettered flash cards, which were out of order. Orange nailed them.

Next Ann showed Orange pictures to identify. He flew through them: "Letter, whale, broom, plug, snail, camel, shovel . . ." He paused.

"We're trying to figure what this man's job is," Ann prompted. "He's probably a . . ."

"Doctor?"

"Who else does Mommy take you to that begins with a D that looks in your mouth?"

"Dentist!"

He ran through more pictures. "Kangaroo, vegetables, mountain, chimney, toothpaste."

Ann stopped on the so-called toothpaste card. "Could it be anything else?" she asked. White had stopped drawing and was looking over at the card, too.

"Water?" Orange guessed.

White was now standing up and peering over Ann's shoulder. "Those are goggles!" he announced. Ann explained to the boys that the picture was of binoculars.

The last phase of the formal evaluation was to have Orange repeat sentences after Ann, such as "Tom has lots of fun playing ball with his sister" and "My baby brother wants Santa Claus to bring him a great big drum." When Orange finished, Ann showed him the markers on his desk and asked him to draw a picture for his parents. She took some notes, then turned to White, who mostly had been quiet and obedient. "Now tell me about that lovely picture, darling."

"This is my mom, that's me, that's Grandma, that's my dad, and those are my two dogs."

"What kind of dogs do you have?"

"I forget."

Orange stood up. "Okay! Now I'm going to do a light pink!"

Ann ran through the designs with White, then moved on to letters. "What is this letter?"

"I forgot that one."

She went through the rest of the letters, then returned to the one he had forgotten. "Have you thought of what that one might be?"

"F!"

"Excellent! You're absolutely right."

Orange was singing again to himself: "Gray, gray, graaay, gray gray gray."

Ann showed White the pictures, starting with a hanger. "Holder for coats!" White said.

Ann prodded him, "Mom says put it on the . . ."

"Hook!"

Ann moved on as White rubbed his eyes and Orange sang a new verse: "Red red reeed red reeed . . ."

"What is this, do you know?" Ann asked White.

"I forget."

"Let me give you the first letter: B." White looked blank. "Witches use them on Halloween."

"Broom!" he exclaimed.

Orange sharpened his pencil in the electric sharpener on his desk. "Sharpened up!" he proclaimed.

"And what is that?" Ann asked White.

"Um, some kind of bug or something?"

"Give me another choice." At White's puzzled look, Ann prompted, "Does it look like a snail or something?"

White smiled. "Snail! I forgot about snails!"

Orange was still sharpening his pencil. "Okay, I think that's sharp," Ann told him. She showed White the remainder of the pictures and ran him through the sentences. "Are you going back to school after we're finished?" Ann asked White.

"I have another school visit."

Ann raised an eyebrow and then took the boys on a tour of the school library while Jen finished meeting with their parents.

Everything Ann asked the children to do involved a measurable quality. When she showed them where their parents were going to be, she watched how they handled separation, especially after having just walked through Trinity's cavernous entrance hall, which Ann said could appear foreboding. (Most children whom Ann evaluated separated easily.) When she asked them to write their names, she observed the children's small motor skills. She asked them to draw a person so that she could check their developmental skills; for example, drawing a stick figure that sprouted arms and legs from its head might be cause for some concern. The exercise in copying drawings of shapes and designs measured hand-eye coordination. The reading of the alphabet letters determined whether the child had begun to learn them. The pictures of objects and people were vocabulary tests, and the sentence repeating was a way for her to analyze their retrieval skills.

Even the trip to the library was calculated. Not only did Ann want to observe the children in a change of scenery, but she also could see how they related to each other. Almost as important, Trinity happened to be a school with many staircases. By taking the children to the library, Ann made sure the children had the physical and emotional maturity to handle the stairs. Sometimes during the library trip, applicants (such as White) would be chattier in that more casual setting. They would say things like "Oh, I'm sick of visiting schools" or "We had to draw Mom and Dad like we did at all the other schools." The purpose of these assessments was mostly to check on the children's development and to see if the ERB scores were representative; for instance, a child might have been sick the day she took the ERB. Ann's tests helped Trinity to understand a broader picture of an applicant's personality and abilities. If, following her evaluation, Trinity had what Ann referred to as "real doubts, especially with siblings [of current students]," she would visit the applicant's nursery school to observe the child.

After the boys left, Jen came into Ann's office to discuss the interviews. "The parents were really nice, so we were having a good conversation," Jen said. "How were the boys?"

"They were cute, and they got on well with each other. By the end, they were dancing around in the library, quite friendly. They were lower-middle range, a little bit immature. Their small muscle was good." She told Jen about White. "He's only four and a half, and he's going to another interview today. I mean, he's only four and a half! That's a little heavy." Orange had scored slightly higher in Ann's evaluation because of his confidence.

Next, Ann had only one boy to interview because the other interviewee was sick. The boy entered quietly, wearing shiny black loafers and dark cords. Ann began with small talk about his birthday and his school, then asked him to draw a picture of a person. She showed him the first shape in the sequence. "Okay, sweetie, can you copy this design onto your piece of paper?"

The boy shook his head. "I don't want to make that," he said.

"I'll give you a hint," Ann said, unfazed. "It's a square standing on its pointy, and a circle, and they're stuck together! Do you think you could try that?" The boy tried, surveyed his work with dissatisfaction, and erased hard on the paper. "You don't need to erase it; just try it in another spot," Ann reassured him. "That's okay. Just do a square, don't worry about it . . . Now put a circle next to it . . . and now a line of dots."

"I can't see the dots," the boy said.

"Okay, how about some little circles, just like that. Can you see those okay, sweetheart?" The boy nodded and drew circles on the paper, slowly, meticulously. "Good boy. Now how about a box that's grown a curly tail, do you think you could try that?" The boy tried but erased his drawing. "You're not happy with that one? Okay, just try it in another place, you don't have to worry." The boy paused. "It's just a square without a top and a little curlicue on the side, darling. That's right, good boy. All right, and how about two nice wiggle worms, one crossing the other, that's right. And one last one." She showed him the final card.

"I don't want to do that one," he said.

"Okay, let me help you with it. Draw two straight lines, that's right, with a little pointy on each end."

"I don't want to."

"Allrighty."

The boy did well with the series of letters and the pictures, though he spoke haltingly when he repeated sentences after Ann. "Now I'm going to give you a piece of paper. See those Magic Markers there? Would you like to draw a picture for Mom and Dad?" The boy hesitated. "Are you a little tired this morning, sweetie?" The boy shook his head. When he reached for the markers, Ann erased some of her notes and wrote something else. Meanwhile, the boy tried to stick a marker back in his full canister.

"It doesn't fit," he said.

"Never mind, don't worry about it."

After he left, I asked Ann how he did, expecting her to comment on his disobedience. But disobedience wasn't the issue. Ann explained that he might have done better if there was another child in the room, as there usually was, but, she said, "He was a very precise boy, a little bit of a perfectionist."

"Is that a good thing or a bad thing?" I asked as Jen walked in.

"It can be good, it can be bad. He was very clear, if he couldn't do it well, he wasn't going to do it."

Ann turned to Jen. "He said, 'I can't see the dots,' " she said. "And then the next one I said, 'Can you see the ovals?' and he said yes. I wonder if there's a vision issue."

Jen replied, "Or maybe he couldn't do it perfectly."

PETE, JUNIOR | PERCEIVED AS: THE MEATHEAD

After finishing his sports article for *The Spectator,* Pete ducked out of the *Black & White* early to catch Whitman's "spirit bus" to the University of Maryland at College Park, where the field hockey team was playing in the state championship game. At the game, Pete met up with his usual crowd of ten guys, most of them football teammates who had persuaded Pete to join them regularly over the season to heckle for entertainment. The football guys had gone to so many hockey games that they had developed their own intricately constructed cheers designed to intellectually impress other schools' fans with complex linguistic units, which they now displayed:

Pete: "What's that smell?!"

Offensive lineman: "I smell *puuussyyy!*"

All: "We gonna bust these hos, we gonna bust these hos, we gonna bust these hos . . ."

Next the boys resurrected an old fave to bellow at Whitman's opponent, South River, a team from the eastern part of the state: "C-A-R, you don't have a car, 'cause you're poor, yeah yeah, you're poor."

The boys stood behind the cheerleaders, in front of bleachers full of boisterous Whitman fans. Pete chanted as loudly as his friends, forgetting for the moment that he took the free spirit bus because he didn't have a car, and that, while his family wasn't quite "poor," they weren't well off, either. Most people at Whitman didn't know this about him; many saw him as just another football meathead. Pete had told only Hugh and one other friend the details. Pete and his family were Russian immigrants who had been doing fine financially, with both parents working as computer programmers. Then the market took a downturn, and when the tech sector fizzled the summer before Pete's freshman year, so did his father's job. He was out of work for nine months before finding his present job in construction inspection, making less than half of his former salary. Ever since, he had been trying to get back into engineering, but because he had earned his degree in the Soviet Union, it was exceptionally difficult to find a position in the bleak U.S. employment landscape.

Pete's schoolwork wasn't affected when his father was laid off, but he could sense the pressure his mother felt to support the family. He thought she was incredible: She had kept her computer programming job, made time to help Pete and his brother with their piano lessons and other activities, and maintained a healthy social life. Even after his father began working again, Pete took care to be frugal. Pete's friends went out to eat frequently without concern for the cost because most of them used credit cards they didn't pay for. Pete felt uncomfortable asking his parents for money, knowing their financial situation. When he and his friends went out to lunch (regularly defying Whitman's seniors-only open-lunch policy), often Pete would go along for the company but not purchase a lunch for himself.

Pete didn't mind cutting back on material items. He didn't need access to a car to be happy. Not being on solid financial ground like his classmates didn't necessarily bother him; it was just a reality he had to live with. When he could, he worked odd jobs, including one as an aide at a Russian Sunday school. Even though the school had since lost the budget to pay him, he planned to volunteer there in the spring. He hoped to get a steady job over the summer so he could help shoulder his parents' burden. Pete's family was stuck in the limbo between being too poor to pay for college and not poor enough to qualify for significant financial aid. He couldn't plan to apply to any school early decision because he would need to be able to compare financial aid packages. This was something he couldn't talk about with his friends.

Pete didn't get sucked into Whitman's competitive whirlpool partly because he didn't put pressure on himself to battle his way into a top-tier college. More important, neither did his parents. Pete was convinced that Whitman students were no smarter than students at other high schools, but the pressure from parents and among peers to go to highly ranked colleges led the students to fight more ferociously. Pete was able to escape that stress because he believed that students had no better chance of getting an excellent job straight out of a top-tier school than out of an average one. He wasn't the type to think that far ahead, anyway.

As the South River Seahawk walked by the bleachers, Pete and his friends heckled, "Biiiiirdman, biiiiirdman."

Pete rarely gave any thought to what he and his friends shouted at games. He had thick skin and generally assumed that because it was difficult to offend him, other students weren't easily ruffled, either. As he saw it, he and his friends were merely playing a role; the students assumed the football meatheads would yell ridiculous things that came off as insulting, and so they did. The chants weren't meant to reflect reality. "C-A-R," the boys shouted again, "you don't have a car, 'cause you're poor, yeah yeah, you're poor."

AUDREY, JUNIOR | PERCEIVED AS: THE PERFECTIONIST

Audrey was chatting with a few friends in journalism class while they tried to get some homework done. As Audrey talked about schoolwork, C.J. perused *The Washington Post* personal ads. "Junior year is a lot harder than sophomore year," Audrey said. "Within the first week, I was ridiculously overswamped. I used to get homework done by 9:30 and get to bed by ten, but I haven't gone to bed before midnight all this year." Her friends nodded, except for C.J., who was engrossed in the personals.

"Now I wake up at the last possible minute, at 6:50, and I have three alarms," Audrey continued. "I tried putting the regular alarm clock across my room so I'd have to get up to turn it off, but now I think I'm sleepwalking, turning it off, and then going back to bed. So now I have my cell alarm set, too, and I put it in different places around the room every night so I actually have to think about where it is. But then this morning, I put the cell in my backpack in my closet, and after it rang, I still fell back asleep. I'm sleep-deprived."

C.J. glanced up from the personals. "She's late every single day!" she said to the others. "I refuse to drive her to school in three weeks, when I get my license."

At least she can get her license, Audrey thought. Most of Audrey's friends were celebrating their seventeenth birthdays, while Audrey wouldn't turn sixteen until January. Audrey hadn't much noticed the age difference until this year, when her friends started driving. Even when Audrey did turn sixteen, she wouldn't have time to learn how to drive.

"Here's one for you, Audrey." C.J. held up the page she was reading and cleared her throat. " 'Seeking great chemistry and warm hugs . . . Seeking a Democrat . . . Loves tulips. Well read.' " Audrey giggled, glad that C.J. was talking to her again.

Audrey and C.J., who lived two doors away from each other, had been inseparable since fifth grade. It was natural that they were so close. They lived in a neighborhood full of teens and parents who would often get together for a movie night at someone's house. More than that, Audrey and C.J. were close because of their similar personalities. Other Whitman students saw C.J. as a good-looking goofball and a flirt. She had a heart-shaped face, medium-brown hair, and dark, arresting eyes. Audrey still saw C.J. as the girl she was in fifth grade, with large glasses and braids down to her waist, neither of which she wore anymore.

Audrey and C.J.'s relationship had changed in the spring of sophomore year, when Audrey's overcompetitiveness had erupted in full force. It was a requirement for the sophomores in the journalism program to put together a mock issue of the *Black & White* in March, soon before they applied for positions on the following year's staff. In a class vote, Audrey had been elected editor in chief of "the mock." Because of Audrey's stress about the project, she and C.J., both outspoken, clashed so furiously that they ended up barely speaking until October. The friendship wasn't yet where it had been, but the girls were working on it.

Audrey wasn't sure why the *Black & White* seemed to be such a target for her frustrations. She wondered if it was because she cared about the paper so much. She supposed she could attribute part of her stress to the knowledge that her mother didn't approve of all the time Audrey spent at the newspaper office when she had so much homework to do. Particularly on "flat nights," Audrey wasn't able to give her mother a specific time when she could come home. Flat nights were the Monday and Tuesday nights before each issue was sent to the printer, when the staff would work at school late into the night to make sure the paper got out on time.

Meanwhile, Audrey's blunt assertiveness wasn't helping her make a case for her quest to be one of the top three editors of next year's paper. The appointments chosen by the current top editors wouldn't be announced until May, but the students had been gossiping since September about who would secure the coveted three spots. Some of the other juniors seemed to be getting annoyed with Audrey, the same way her sports teammates did when she took control in a way that unintentionally came across as overbearing. She never meant to take over a group, but that was exactly what would happen. Audrey had been actively trying to have more faith in others' abilities, because placing the burden on herself was both a cause and a result of too much stress. So far, she hadn't managed to get past it.

The girls at Audrey's journalism table had moved on to college talk. Audrey knew exactly where she wanted to go to college and exactly what she planned to study. Since eighth grade, she had known that she wanted to go to Georgetown University to major in political science and specialize in American government; she loved politics and history. Because of her passion for the *Black & White,* Audrey had extended her plan to include a graduate degree in journalism at Columbia. The problem was that, with her most recent grades, Audrey wasn't sure whether she could get in. In her four AP and two honors classes, Audrey had received three Bs this quarter, her worst academic quarter ever. When she came home with her report card the previous week, her parents faxed it to her grandparents. But instead of the usual congratulatory calls, within minutes one of Audrey's grandmothers called to ask why she had gotten Bs. Audrey's mother told her that she was getting Bs not because she wasn't capable of As but because she didn't have enough time in the day to get everything done.

At Audrey's journalism table, a senior was explaining that she had been absent from class several days recently because of a serious illness. "When I came back, I was behind from missing so much work, so I got stressed out and had a breakdown. I really couldn't take the stress of all that, school and college," the senior said. The other girls listened intently, except for C.J., who was now underneath the table.

"Where's my shoe?" C.J. was saying. "No, seriously, where's my shoe? How did I lose my shoe?!"

The senior continued, "I had to drop two of my AP classes down to honors and relinquish my club president duties to someone else. So I changed everywhere I'm applying to college. I had to look at the schools differently."

Audrey shook her head. "If only I was that open-minded," she said. "If I don't get into Georgetown, my life is over."

TAYLOR, SENIOR | PERCEIVED AS: THE POPULAR GIRL

One of Taylor's first soccer games back from her ankle-injury hiatus was the regional quarterfinal of the state playoffs. Taylor's left ankle was still painful, but she didn't have time to schedule physical therapy and didn't take pain relievers, afraid that they would slow her down. The varsity team was playing a school to which it had already lost during the regular season, a team that was undefeated, with only one goal scored against it all year. If this was to be Taylor's final soccer game for Whitman, she was going to be on the field. Taylor pushed herself to play through her pain. When the whistle blew, Whitman won 3–0.

The regional final was held at Whitman on a night so cold that as the game began, Taylor was huddled on the bench sharing a blanket with some of her teammates. In the bleachers, Whitman students and parents watched with varying levels of intensity. (One skinny boy muttered to another, "The Nastys must die.") Taylor played well and, with her height, fearlessness, and intelligent strategy, did a better job directing balls in the air than her teammates did, but the coach used her sparingly. She didn't tell him that her ankle still bothered her because she didn't want him to dock her additional playing time. When the game ended, Whitman had eked out a 2–1 overtime victory. Taylor played perhaps a quarter of the game.

Throughout the playoffs, Taylor had mixed feelings about the soccer team. She loved some of her teammates and was respected in her leadership role as co-captain, but the coach gave her less playing time the further they got into the playoffs. In the state semifinal, which no Whitman girls' soccer team had ever won, he put Taylor in with about ten minutes left in the first half, then took her out five minutes into the second. When he subbed her out, he put in a younger player who Taylor readily admitted was faster but couldn't keep possession of the ball like Taylor could. Taylor persuaded herself not to care about the coach's opinion anymore; she understood that he valued speed over smarts. But it hurt to know that her friends—the popular ones, at least—came to cheer for her game after game, yelling "Sexy!" when her name was announced, and she was barely out on the field. Even though they were always supportive of her at games, she felt like she was letting them down.

There she was, captain of the team, sometimes getting only fifteen minutes a game. But Whitman kept winning.

The varsity soccer state final was held at the University of Maryland, Baltimore County. Taylor was determined to do everything she could to contribute to a win, though she knew she wasn't starting. She was still feeling the effects of food poisoning from the night before, which she spent throwing up after eating bad sushi. Still, there was no way she was going to miss the championship game.

The bright stadium lights illuminated bleachers filled with fans from Whitman and from South River, which had beaten Whitman's field hockey team in the state finals earlier that week. The Whitman fans hung signs from the risers: MAKE HISTORY WHITMAN. REVENGE.

Taylor watched from the bench as South River dominated early in the game. For several minutes, Whitman and South River traded runs down the field, until, at the twenty-one-minute mark, the announcer called Taylor's name and, accompanied by cheers from the bleachers, she dashed to her center forward spot on the field. Taylor quickly distributed the ball to a wing, then retrieved it and rocketed a blistering shot that flew just wide of a post. Whitman kept up the pressure at its offensive end, out-juking South River until a South River wing collected the ball, sped down the side of the field, and launched a cross to a teammate, whose shot toward the far post flew past the Whitman keeper's outstretched arms.

The beginning of the second half was marked by Whitman's sense of urgency. In the bleachers, Whitman fans drummed on a cowbell and danced to the rhythm of a traditional Whitman cheer. Eighteen minutes into the second half, a Whitman sophomore took the ball from midfield, made a run of several yards, then fed it to a teammate inside the box, who hammered in the tying score. With less than five minutes left in the game, the atmosphere on the field was thick with fervor. Four Whitman shots sailed wide. "Let's go, Whitman, let's go," called the fans. The coach was practically on the field. By the time the whistle blew, Whitman had outshot South River 14–0 in the second half, but the game remained tied at 1. The championship went into sudden-death overtime. The next team to score would take home the trophy.

Again, Taylor's popular friends were in the stands to support her, and again, the coach had pulled her out of the game and didn't put her in for the second half or in the overtime lineup. Taylor struggled with the difference between how she was supposed to be perceived as a two-sport varsity captain, and the reality of what happened on the field. By senior year, she should have been playing the majority of the game, as were the other seniors, who were no more passionate about soccer than she was. She didn't delude herself into thinking that she was one of the best players on the team, but she was supposed to be *involved*—that's how she was known at Whitman. That was the assumption other students made when they saw her walking down the halls in her uniform, encouraging people to come to the games.

Off the varsity field, Taylor had gotten as involved with soccer as she had time to. Until her teammates graduated, she had played select club soccer on an older team. She had attended two soccer camps every summer since fifth grade, including a two-week camp at the University of North Carolina, one of the most prestigious soccer schools in the country. (These camps were in addition to lacrosse camps at Duke and the University of Maryland.) At an academic camp at Harvard the summer before her junior year, Taylor hired a Harvard assistant soccer coach to give her one-on-one training. They would jog three miles every day and run stairs every other day after the jog to warm up for two more hours of soccer training. By the time she returned to Bethesda for varsity preseason, Taylor was a better player and noticeably stronger. Now, however, she believed she hadn't done as much as she should have.

It wasn't enough anymore to love a sport and be good at it. It had to consume you. Most, if not all, of Taylor's teammates played on elite club teams. One of the team's top players regularly had two-a-day practices, got to practice early, went running afterward, and was seeing a nutritionist to gain weight and strength to impress college recruiters. Taylor knew high school football players who saw acupuncturists and wrestlers who wore layers upon layers of clothing and ate only Power-Bars for meals to lose weight. Taylor was a skilled, smart player in good shape who had been committed to her sports since she was little. But her devotion wasn't enough.

Just over a minute into the overtime period, a petite Whitman forward dribbled toward the middle of the field, held the ball for a moment as she waited for her teammates to catch up, then passed it to a senior co-captain on her left, who swung hard, connecting on a shot that rocketed toward the crossbar. The prior year's captains who came home from college to cheer at the game would later tell Taylor that she was a much better player than the coach realized, but it no longer mattered to her—none of it did: the playing time, the sprained ankles, the rocky season, the mixed feelings, the skewed perceptions—because after the shot hit the crossbar and ricocheted into the net, Taylor was off the bench and in the middle of the pileup on the field, jumping up and down, tears streaming down her face, arms around her teammates, celebrating the first girls' soccer state championship in the history of her school.

✧

Taylor's feeling that her camps, club teams, and individual trainer weren't enough to merit more playing time wasn't abnormal. Neither was the way she played through an injury without getting treatment. Julie, who constantly worried that if she didn't run on a college team, she would lose her athletic identity, wasn't an unusual case, either. Nor was Pete, who stopped playing football for Whitman because players were expected to make a year-round commitment, including off-season workouts before and after school and summer workouts four days a week, nearly all of which Pete attended because he wasn't "the kind of person who can half-ass something."

Like most other aspects of the school experience, sports now demand intensified commitment and competitiveness. Too often a sport is less a part of students' lives than a lifestyle that defines or consumes them. An Ohio student explained to me that her participation on the varsity basketball team didn't allow her to take part in any other after-school activity, even when her school team technically wasn't in season. It's no longer enough to play one sport in one season and do other things the rest of the year, no matter how talented the athlete. Many students feel obligated to also play on a year-round private club team (also known as travel, select, elite, or premier teams) with an incessant practice, game, tournament, and training schedule that destroys the concept of athletic "seasons."

These types of teams, which have exploded in growth in every area of the country, are operated like businesses. Team parents might handle paperwork, player and coach recruitment, uniforms, tournament registration, travel arrangements, schedules, and treasurer duties, and spend thousands of dollars in addition to their time and energy. They might sacrifice family vacations, not to mention family dinners, to revolve their schedules around a child's sports activities.

In addition, many coaches pressure their players to participate in off-season regimens and to attend development or skills camps, implying that athletes who don't go to camp or play club ball might not make the school team. For certain families, even a club team, a varsity team, and several weeks' worth of camps don't suffice. Some parents hire private trainers and push their children to practice individual skills in their "free" time, whether in the yard or on the street.

Not long ago, free time in the yard or the street defined youth sports. Extreme training and elite-level youth competition typically were reserved for a few chosen athletes in sports such as gymnastics and wrestling. In the 1980s, youth leagues became popular in sports including soccer, basketball, football, and volleyball, and in the 1990s, several factors converged to increase the intensity of these leagues. Urban sprawl and safety concerns lessened the likelihood that children would meet in a neighborhood playground or park for pickup games, and the median household income rose, which gave families the means to infuse more funds into private leagues.

Now, in the 2000s, experts worry about what they call a growing trend of "specialization": year-round, demanding commitment to one sport, often beginning at a young age. While experts say that specialization has led to the demise of the multisport athlete, I found anecdotally that overachievers often feel the need to specialize in more than one sport, leading students like Taylor to play on multiple teams and attend multiple camps for multiple sports. A Baltimore reading specialist told me how one such athlete woke up at three A.M. daily to do her homework. "It's like the students get caught in a trap," she said. "We're creating little robots."

Doctors blame specialization and the related pressures to excel in sports for escalating rates of school-age injuries; playing a different sport each season gives different muscles a chance to rest. Every year, more than 3.5 million children age fourteen and younger are treated for sports injuries. At least half of the sports injuries to middle and high school students are attributed to overuse, the repeated motion of the same body parts. Stress fractures, for example, have become run-of-the-mill for students who practice the same drills and techniques over and over again, and tendinitis can result when children aren't strong enough to undergo training regimens better suited to adults.

In 2003 fifteen-year-old pitcher Jeret Adair started sixty-four games for his Atlanta traveling team, more than most professional players pitch in a season. When the ligament in his elbow snapped, he had to have the kind of reconstructive surgery that was once reserved for veteran professional pitchers. The following year, Jeret's doctor performed similar operations on fifty high school pitchers. ("In young pitchers," one sports medicine pediatrician has said, "the growth plate gets pulled apart like an Oreo cookie.") In Rhode Island, an athlete swam 8,000 yards each day, despite arm pain. She intentionally began to dislocate a shoulder to lessen the pain so she could keep swimming, but after shoulder surgery and physical therapy, she quit competitive swimming at age fifteen.

In 2005 a nationally prominent orthopedist called children's overuse injuries an "epidemic." *The New York Times* reported, "Doctors in pediatric sports medicine say it is as if they have happened upon a new childhood disease, and the cause is overaggressive culture of organized youth sports." In an informal survey by the Minnesota Amateur Sports Commission, 22 percent of young athletes said they had been pressured to play while injured. Overuse injuries are often irreparable, with the only solution being to stop playing the sport causing the damage, yet some parents ask if doctors can operate so their children can keep playing. As a Philadelphia orthopedist told the *Times,* "I recently had a mother ask me if there isn't some kind of shot or fix-it procedure I could do for her 11-year-old daughter's ankle so she could be ready for an upcoming regional competition. I told her that if it were the Olympic Games coming up, perhaps we could treat this situation differently. But as far as I understood, her upcoming competition wasn't the Olympics. At this point, the daughter is giggling but the parent is in the corner crying."

Out of the forty-one million children under eighteen who play organized sports, 70 percent of them will drop out before age thirteen. The main reason for quitting? Pressure from parents and coaches. A Colorado dance teacher told me that at her studio, where parents routinely try to get their two-year-olds into a higher-level dance class, children have faked serious injuries to escape. Sometimes that pressure is painfully evident on the sidelines of the majority of youth games across the country. Competitive sideline parents are nothing new; in 1991 Texan Wanda Holloway was convicted of solicitation of capital murder for attempting to hire a hit man to kill the mother of her thirteen-year-old daughter's cheerleading rival, in the hope that the girl would be too distraught to compete for a spot on the junior high cheerleading squad.

But "sports rage" has been on the rise for several years. In 1995 an estimated 5 percent of parents watching their children's competitive sport exhibited abusive, overaggressive, or embarrassingly out-of-line behavior. By 2000 that number had grown to at least 15 percent and showed no signs of abating. In 2003 a survey found that more than 84 percent of young athletes, parents, coaches, and youth sports administrators personally witnessed parents acting violently toward children, coaches, or officials at youth sports events. As a result of this trend, the National Association of Sports Officials now offers "assault protection" coverage for officials who sustain injuries from a spectator or player during or because of a youth athletic event.

Sports rage shook up youth sports communities in 2000, when, at a Massachusetts ten-year-old boys' hockey practice, one child's father beat another to death—in a fight over whether the practice was too rough. Episodes of sports-rage violence have since occurred regularly. The head of a Florida anti-violence group was arrested after he stormed the field and punched a referee during his seven-year-old's flag football game. A Little League secretary in Massachusetts allegedly kicked and swore at an eleven-year-old boy who cheered for the opponent of her son's team. About thirty parents got into a brawl after a youth soccer tournament in Los Angeles. An Ohio father split the lip of a fourteen-year-old who tussled with his son for the ball during a soccer match. In Connecticut, after a girl was issued a three-game suspension from her high school softball team because she missed a game to go to a prom, her father clubbed her coach with a bat.

In July 2005 a Pittsburgh-area T-ball coach reportedly paid one of his eight-year-old players $25 to hit a mentally disabled teammate in the face with a baseball during pregame warm-ups so the coach wouldn't have to play the boy the required three innings per player. When the eight-year-old hit the disabled boy in the groin and walked away, his coach told him to "go out there and hit him harder," he said. The boy then hit his teammate in the ear, and the coach got his wish, along with several criminal charges. A state trooper explained to the press, "The coach was very competitive. He wanted to win."

Whether they want their team to win or their child to star, some adults' hypercompetitive sideline behavior hasn't gone unnoticed by their kids. Sadly, parents' anger is sometimes directed toward their own children, from yelling at them in the stands to berating their performance after the game. A Toronto father was charged with assault in 2003 for grabbing and shaking his ten-year-old daughter's face mask at her hockey game. In one poll, 45.3 percent of children said they had been yelled at, called names, or insulted during games or practices, and 8.2 percent were pressured to hurt another player.

Why has the role of soccer parent been redefined to sacrifice a child's health, assault children or other adults, and encourage a child to harm others? For some, the motivator is money. Parents took notice when teenagers Lebron James and Freddy Adu secured lucrative Nike endorsements. Many view sports as the ticket to a valuable college scholarship or an edge in the admissions process at schools like the Ivies, which don't offer scholarships but still must recruit athletes.

Child psychologist David Elkind has observed, "The pressure to make ordinary children exceptional has become almost an epidemic in sports. . . . The star mentality prevails, and the less talented youngster simply doesn't get to participate. Play is out and competition is in." This is why parents invest thousands of dollars in club teams and private training, sometimes forming their own travel team for the sole purpose of giving a child the opportunity for national exposure to scouts and re-cruiters. It's why some students sag so much under the weight of high expectations that they turn to performance-enhancing drugs. It's why parents send their children to sports psychologists, Pilates instructors, and chiropractors. Whether they're spending $3,000 a year on a club ice hockey team or $35,000 on figure skating lessons, hordes of parents see sports as an investment in the future of their child and their family.

Evidently, many people aren't aware of the odds. Fewer than 3 percent of high school athletes will play any sport in college, and only one in 13,000 high school athletes will be paid to pay professionally. Out of 6.9 million high school varsity athletes in 2004, only 126,000—or 1.8 percent—received scholarships to NCAA Division I, II, or III schools.

Annually, perhaps 15,000 of the available scholarships are for basketball, 5,428 for baseball, and 200 for ice hockey. Most soccer scholarships are awarded to foreign students. Parents would be better off saving the money they funnel into private clubs and training and investing it in a college fund.

Nevertheless, more parents are insisting their children join these elite groups. They're putting two-year-olds in weekly instructional sports lessons, three-year-olds in soccer programs, and twenty-month-olds in diapers on tiny bicycles. They're sending kids to five A.M. hockey practices at age four. Elite wrestling high school feeder programs start children at age six. Select soccer teams advertise in newspapers for players who are "committed, experienced, athletic, and competitive"—at age seven. Even non-pushy parents get the sense that they have to enroll their children in high-level leagues at the youngest ages possible so they don't get shut out of that option when they're older. As one Virginia father complained to *U.S. News*, "Where we live, travel soccer starts at the U-9 level. [If you resist,] you will be told, 'Your kids will quickly fall behind and not make the team when they are ten.' If you want your kid to play in high school, you have to start [travel] at ten, and if you want to travel at ten, you have to play travel at eight." Added a soccer mom, "It's an arms race."

Rather than teach children to play sports for enjoyment, adults give them the message that individual statistics and win-loss records are the marks of an admirable athlete—like some Whitman parents who paced the bleachers, parading a sign announcing the number of lacrosse goals their daughter had scored. Private youth club soccer teams as young as under-eleven are nationally ranked. There are national championships for eight-and-under soccer and basketball teams and a world championship for ten-and-under baseball teams. Elementary school–age basketball players are individually ranked at national tournaments where coaches and spectators insist they can pick out the six- and seven-year-olds who are future NBA players.

As with the chances of a college scholarship, parents usually aren't aware of the facts. Experts say that children's athletic skills in prepubescence are no sign of how they will perform as a teen; no matter how much they train, starting them early doesn't necessarily give them an insurmountable head start. Michael Jordan didn't make his high school varsity basketball team until he was a junior. But the notion of developing children at their own pace has disappeared. In its place is a mentality like this one: Trenton, whose story was featured on a Bravo documentary and an *Oprah* tie-in, is an aspiring football player training seven days a week, usually with his father, who shuns a full-time job to work five flexible part-time positions so that he can help his son practice. On Mondays, he runs Trenton through sand dunes. Tuesday through Thursday nights, Trenton's team practices. Friday nights, Trenton's father relentlessly pushes him to run up and down bleacher stairs in a football stadium. He rehashes Saturday's games with Trenton to go over "what he did incorrectly or correctly." On Sunday mornings, Trenton does the stairs again, before an afternoon of drills with a semiprofessional quarterback.

Every week Trenton sees a chiropractor so that, as his father says, he is "able to function at his highest level," and because in games, "he gets hit and hit and hit." Trenton's father explains his son's devotion to football this way: "I haven't exactly achieved the things that I set out to achieve in my life. . . . His future and my future is tied to football. . . . The major dream in my life that's unfulfilled is not playing in the NFL. I'm hoping that the dream that I didn't fulfill will come to life with Trenton." Trenton is eight years old.

SAM, SENIOR | PERCEIVED AS: THE TEACHER'S PET

When Sam emerged from the orchestra pit after the exhilarating Friday-night performance of *Les Mis,* a girl launched herself into his arms. Sam had known that his neighbor, a junior at a nearby private school, loved *Les Mis,* so he had expected her to come. He didn't, however, expect this kind of welcome and was pleasantly surprised when she agreed to go out with him the following week. But she wasn't Julie.

Sam first noticed Julie during sophomore year, when they had driver's education together. He found Julie attractive, with her wide smile and smooth ringlets, but he didn't know her that well. Junior year, Julie drove him to school every day, and their friendship strengthened. Sam was in awe of the hard work, multitude of activities and talents, and spontaneous social life he believed Julie managed to balance flawlessly. Then, a few weeks after junior year homecoming, a student who sat next to Sam in English class asked, "Have you hooked up with Julie yet?"

"Excuse me?" said Sam, dumbfounded.

"You didn't know?!" exclaimed the guy, who proceeded to tell him that Julie had been interested in Sam for six weeks before homecoming. Other friends told him that they always considered him and Julie a match that should have been. For the next two months, kicking himself for not asking Julie to homecoming when the dance had been such a disaster for him, Sam spent as much time as he could with her, though he tried not to let on overtly that he liked her as more than a friend. During winter break, they took long romantic evening walks by the canal in the snow.

One night in January, Sam worked up the nerve to ask her out for Indian food and a movie on a Friday night. She said yes. Excited, he talked it over with one of his and Julie's mutual friends, who agreed that it seemed like a date. On Friday, Sam IMed Julie and learned that she had gotten word of their big date, which was news to her. She was not pleased that everyone else seemed to know that their outing was a formal date. Sam apologized profusely.

What Sam found remarkable was that Julie still wanted to go out with him, and that they had a fantastic, albeit platonic, time. By the time they finished dinner, it was too late for a movie, so they drove to Georgetown, sat by the water, and talked candidly—not about anything important, not about their feelings. Sam believed he had never talked so comfortably with someone before, even if, unspoken, one topic was taboo. That was the way their relationship had been ever since: Each considered the other a great friend, and they were open to talking about everything except their relationship. Even on the rides to school that spring, they danced around the topic. It was like the flirtatious elephant in the room. Sam believed it was there for both of them, because one of Julie's close girlfriends had told him so.

He was proud that he and Julie had worked through that night; he called theirs "the best friendship that never should have worked out." And though he never told Julie, the fact that she could look past her anger to go out with him anyway made him admire her even more.

PETE, JUNIOR | PERCEIVED AS: THE MEATHEAD

Two days before their rebuilt physics bridge was due, Pete and Hugh met at noon at Hugh's house to construct it. For the first hour and a half, the boys worked diligently with Hugh's grandfather, who volunteered to assist them, using drawings that Hugh's mother had prepared. Then Pete flipped on the Auburn-Alabama game, and Hugh, who was gearing up for a date, got distracted listening to music on his computer. Pete stayed in the basement and tried to help Hugh's grandfather, who insisted on doing most of the work himself. The bridge was about three quarters done when Hugh drove Pete home on his way to pick up his date. Hugh's grandfather finished the project by himself that night.

On Monday Pete and Hugh took the bridge upstairs to their physics classroom and placed it on the scale. It weighed in at a respectable but unexceptional twenty-eight grams. They handed the bridge to their physics teacher, who placed it on the testing blocks. Pete gingerly positioned the brick on the bridge, and the boys held their breath. The teacher started the clock. Pete could hear the bridge creaking. He wanted the bridge to work mostly because he felt badly that Hugh's grandfather had spent eight hours working on it. His eyes wide, he stared intently at the bridge, willing it not to collapse. "Time up," the teacher said. Pete quickly grabbed the brick, in case the bridge couldn't hold up any longer.

"I think since our bridge held and is really light, you should give us a better B than an 80," Hugh said to the teacher. Pete remained quiet.

"What kind of a B do you want?" the teacher asked. He had been giving a 20 out of 25 for all redone projects that passed the tests.

"21.5 or something?"

The teacher smirked without responding.

In eighth period that day, Pete was sitting in the back of class, chatting with a senior acquaintance while the teacher handed out a quiz. "So, our bridge held the brick today," Pete said, laughing.

The senior pulled out his wallet. "Dude, I still have to rebuild my bridge. I'll buy your bridge so I don't have to spend all day tomorrow doing it. I'll give you thirty dollars for it. I'll, like, put a flag on it or paint it red or something so it looks different."

"I'll think about it," Pete said.

For the next two days, Pete weighed the idea of selling the bridge. Pete wasn't close with the senior, an Ivy League–recruited athlete who was known to take shortcuts on assignments. Pete thought he would feel like a jerk for selling it, but then again, selling it wouldn't hurt anyone, and, he thought, it was a dopey project to begin with. *We didn't really put in enough effort either time,* he thought. *I'm sure if he had an awesome grandpa, he could have gotten it done, too.*

The next night Pete decided to let the senior use his bridge. He considered the sale slightly unethical but rationalized his decision because of his perceived injustices about the project: His teacher hadn't taught the physics relating to the bridge, and he graded students on their performance relative to the best in each category. "So basically," Pete told a friend, "they pit us against each other and only give the best grade to the one whose bridge is the best." He wasn't even sure if he would accept money for it.

Two weeks later, Pete had abandoned all pretenses. "There's definitely a huge black market for these bridges," he told his friend. "I bet there are about five functional bridges that get passed around. A friend of mine tried to find his partner's brother's bridge from a few years ago, but he had given it to someone else already. And the girls who ended up winning had some other kid build their bridge." Pete had accepted the Ivy League athlete's $30 and had also given the bridge for free to another team, who painted the bridge another color to disguise it.

"Wait a minute," the friend asked. "How many teams have used your bridge?"

"Six."

AP FRANK, COLLEGE FRESHMAN | PERCEIVED AS: THE WORKHORSE

Every weekend, AP Frank was supposed to captain the Massachusetts Hall Intramural Frisbee team. For the first four weeks of the season, AP Frank and his team would arrive at the field, pumped up and ready to win, and then the other team would forfeit due to a lack of players. For their fifth game, the opposing team actually showed up. It was a cold, windy day, and the field was soaked in an inch of water. The players' fingers were numb. When they lost that game by two points, AP Frank took it personally. He wanted to prove that he could organize a winning team. Since then his team hadn't lost another game, including an overtime win during which AP Frank got hit in the head with a Frisbee twice and kept playing. Once he even persuaded a reluctant Kristen, who had just stepped out of the shower after washing her hair, to participate in a playoff game in the mud.

On the last day of the season, in late November, AP Frank and his team were confident. They won the semifinals 12–2, with five subs to ensure that the team would stay fresh and energetic. For the championships, they were playing Hollis, a dorm they had crushed in the regular season, 9–1. As the teams lined up, AP Frank recognized one of his Harvard Ultimate Frisbee club teammates, the captain of the Harvard B team. Usually, the Harvard captains refereed intramural games. But the captain didn't have a whistle. "What are you doing? Why are you lining up with Hollis?" AP Frank asked.

"I'm a prefect. Prefects can play."

AP Frank's heart sank. Prefects were upper-class mentors assigned to freshman dorms. Suddenly, AP Frank didn't feel like a Frisbee stud anymore. He hadn't even gone to club practices or games all month because of mild shin splints. One by one, the Mass Hall subs left the game, one for orchestra rehearsal, another to go to the *Crimson* newspaper office. Down to seven players with no subs, Mass Hall kept the game close, matching Hollis point for point. But as the team grew exhausted, they started playing badly.

With thirty seconds left and the score 6–8, AP Frank blocked Hollis's point and threw a point of his own to pull his team within one. A Hollis player whipped the Frisbee toward a teammate, but a Mass Hall Silencer intercepted. There were eight seconds left. With the right strategy, Mass Hall could win on a two-point play. Mass Hall threw the Frisbee, and Hollis picked it off and held it tight until the clock ran out.

AP Frank was disappointed. *We could have won in spite of the prefect,* he thought over and over during the fifteen-minute walk back to the dorm. At Mass Hall, AP Frank gave his teammates a little speech. "I'm really proud of you guys," he said. "You stuck through it." He looked around at his teammates and turned to the girls, like Kristen, who this time had cheered from the sidelines. "I'm really glad you guys came to cheer us on. We played a really good game, and we played damn hard."

Chapter 7

November 22–December 6

LEFT BEHIND

In late November, I returned to June Hilton's office at Trinity, where the Manhattan private school was allowing me unprecedented access to a series of events where many parents desperately want to be a fly on the wall: kindergarten admissions meetings. The purpose of the first session was to discuss siblings and children of alumni, faculty, and staff, who were especially important to Trinity. Before we stepped inside the lower school principal's office, June explained to me, "People tend to see this whole process as a big mystery. Parents think it's much more complicated or that the ERBs loom so large. People will call up and say, 'What do you mean, how did this happen, explain this to me.'"

One way to explain it is sheer numbers. There were fifty-eight spots in Trinity's kindergarten class, and forty-four siblings and alumni/faculty children had applied. June was counting on about a dozen of those candidates to turn down Trinity's offer of admission, but, she said, "Even so, it's going to be hard. And I'm going to need a lot of those spaces to create diversity, so it's going to be a battle royale over who has dibs on these spaces."

June took her seat on a blue sofa in the principal's office, joining the other admissions committee members: the principal, the assistant principal, a learning specialist, a kindergarten teacher, and Jen, the associate director of admissions. The first candidate June brought up was a child whom the committee wasn't sure would be mature enough for kindergarten the following year. His preschool report stated that he had trouble waiting for his turn to speak and he could become "very silly and loud." Yet he shared toys if others were sharing, and "because he is so bright, there are times when we forget he's just four." His parents happened to mention during their tour of the school that they were afraid he wouldn't be considered at Trinity because of his late birthday, though they were convinced he was ready. That was an admissions secret: Even on seemingly casual tours of the school, parents might be evaluated. At Trinity, after the tours, the guides—parent volunteers—wrote notes about the parents for the admissions committee.

As June passed around the boy's file for the committee members to read, she explained that the problem with requiring the boy to have an extra year of preschool was that Trinity might lose the family to another school. June wanted to provide an answer as quickly as possible, because if the parents chose to push for acceptance at the other school, she didn't want them to signal to that school that it was their second choice. I observed this kind of compassion repeatedly during meetings and in June's phone conversations. She was devoted to helping families gain entrance to a school, even if it wasn't Trinity. Every year in the weeks after admission letters were sent out in February, June spent hours guiding parents whose children hadn't been accepted to any schools.

The principal looked thoughtful. "I think in these situations, the most important thing to take into consideration is what would we say is best for the kid regardless of the circumstances. Forget his parents and that nursery schools don't always communicate clearly that a child needs an extra year before coming to our program. In this case, it's clear that if they would really like our school, the best thing is to spend another year at [his preschool]."

The learning specialist looked at his file. "Ann thought he seemed young and 'needed jollying.'"

"I think the biggest gift you can give kids today—when programs are pressured and kindergartens look like first grades did before—is time," the principal said. "Rushing this child with a set of expectations that seem to not match his normal development seems to be a mistake."

The committee agreed to remove the child from consideration for that admission cycle's kindergarten class. That was how the admissions committee members continued to analyze applicants: They gleaned as much information as they could from a child's file, formed a picture of the child, and tried to envision whether he or she would be a good fit for Trinity's program and vice versa. Strong or weak test scores were mentioned occasionally, but mostly the women stuck to more pragmatic topics. June mused to me at one point that while parents often let their imaginations run wild when envisioning kindergarten admissions committee meetings, the committee actually considered fairly ordinary issues. For example, Ann's observations of the children on the stairs during the library tour were particularly important. Other elements were the child's ability to handle transitions and willingness to trust adults, because kindergarteners were often shuttled off to various teachers for classes such as art, gym, and swimming. These factors, as June pointed out to me, were "not really all that complicated, esoteric, or impractical."

Throughout this and the next admission meeting I observed, the comments about candidates ranged from positives like "It's nice to see a girl with a passion for dinosaurs" to negatives like Ann's evaluation that a boy was "a serious child, small muscles undeveloped, difficult to understand, unfocused, young." They took into account a nursery school's concern about a child who "does not seem to have a special friend in school, lacks initiative, usually wanders, and is intractable." They discussed children's social skills and ability to share materials, problem-solve, take the initiative, and exhibit leadership behavior. They debated how to help a child whose mother wouldn't share the results of her child's speech evaluation with his nursery school. They reminded one another to keep diversity in mind, including children of same-sex parents. Some children received unqualified praise, some posed concerns, and others were put into temporary purgatory.

At that November meeting, June dropped a bombshell on her colleagues. "I've done some early polling of our families. It's going to be much worse," she said. "By our calculations, a year from now we will have more siblings and alums than we have spaces. Even if we took no other children besides siblings and alumni, we still wouldn't have enough space. With the whole issue of our being a family school, we can't see any way to win."

The committee members looked shocked. "Wow," one breathed. June told the women that Trinity's headmaster had asked her to put together an advisory group to come up with a new policy to deal with the numbers.

I returned to Trinity for another admissions meeting in January. It was cold and dreary outside, but it was Trinity's homecoming, a day when alumni returned, the school held athletics events, and women stood in the arched main hallway selling Trinity clothes. This time the committee sat around a wooden table in a small, hot room. June walked in looking weary and lugging a large cardboard box full of files. Despite a terrible flu, she had spent the last five days at home reviewing 400 files, as she did each year at this time. She was lucky if she got four hours of sleep a night during these marathon sessions, during which she ate while she worked and barely moved from her desk. Her goal was to narrow down the applications to a few dozen before the committee discussed the applicants without her—and her emotional attachments to the kids—in the room.

"You always say, 'Give me reasons not to take these kids.' Is that still the thinking?" the learning specialist asked June.

"Given the number of siblings and alums, there are so few spaces it's absurd, so I have to look at every space as needing to count for so much you wouldn't believe it," June said. "There are all the obvious things, like a good kid and family, but then there are huge political ramifications to all of this because there are whole schools important to us where we're just not taking kids from this year because we don't have the space to do it. So I've kept in some of the most serious trustee recommendations, but we told the trustees long ago what the space situation is. To my thinking, there's no child in here we would not want to have. I'm trying to look for ways to narrow this pack of sixteen boys down to nine, which is virtually impossible." The group nodded. "You'll see there's somebody from [June named a school], a school I'd really like to make a connection with. I have nineteen girls here, which we've got to drastically reduce. I've just come to where I can't do anymore. There's not one child I can take out of here. I think they're all wonderful."

"How many girls are you hoping to get the pile down to?" the kindergarten teacher asked. "How many should we like, is the question. You said nine for the boys."

"Six or seven," June replied. The committee members groaned.

This admissions meeting was similar to the November meeting: quiet reading of files and occasional discussions, in addition to coos over

applicant photos and comments about an impressively detailed stick figure a child had drawn during Ann's interview. There were, however,
two notable exceptions. First, this batch of files had a few applicants
who were children of celebrities, socialites, and icons. When I had asked
June during an earlier interview about the range of celebrity children at
Trinity, she responded that the school was "very light on celebrities, and
those that are here are really low-key."

The committee had an extended discussion about the child of a
semi-celebrity. The learning specialist said she had recently chatted with
a relative of that applicant who also had a child at Trinity. "The subject
of computers came up. She said, 'Do you want me to get you some
computers? I'll buy them for you.' I said, 'No, we have computers.'"

June said the applicant was "a brilliant kid—and will not come to
Trinity. We're just keeping her in here for now because it might be a thing
to offer even if they're not coming. The nursery school tells me that [the
semi-celebrity] really wants a girls' school." (When I asked June about this
later, she explained that she considered extending the offer because the
child had family at the school, not because the parent was well known.)

"The politics of all this are getting horrendous," June told the com-
mitee. "The days are gone when you used to just sort of fling your acceptances out there. There's so much brokering going on prior to those
decisions being put in the mail that it's unbelievable, some of it honest,
some of it dishonest. So thank you all very much. Jen is going to take
these home over the weekend. Help yourselves to goodies, too," she
said, gesturing to snacks on the counter. "I'm going home to bed."

June later explained to me what she meant by "brokering." Ten years
ago, children who applied to New York City independent schools were
likely to be accepted to four or five schools. Now, she said, because of a
lack of space, "the real danger is a perfectly wonderful child will not be
accepted to *any* schools. So we're all trying not to waste spaces but give
them to people who actually are going to want them." For some schools,
however, the politics of the process overtook its ideals. The independent
schools coordinated their response dates so that no school could get a
jump on the others. But while Trinity vowed never to pressure parents
for a commitment until decision letters were in the mail, other schools
were putting heat on nursery school directors to tell them in the midst of
the admissions season which families would commit to their schools.

Certain schools persist in hinting about acceptances to parents long be-fore the official decision letter date in order to try to secure a commit-ment. (This practice is not unlike the way some top colleges, including Harvard, send "likely letters" to students in February, giving them a heads-up that an acceptance letter will be on the way.)

Some schools rely heavily on asking parents to write "first-choice letters" during the admissions season, essentially promising that if their child is admitted, they will enroll. Because it was common knowledge that Trinity gave preference to siblings and alumni children, and the number of spots for non-affiliated children was slim, Trinity was put in a tough position. If a new family fell in love with the school, they would be less likely to write a first-choice letter to Trinity because of the low odds that their child would be admitted. Not wanting to waste their first-choice letter, they might send it to another school. Meanwhile, Trinity doesn't encourage first-choice letters. "It's just wrong. There's some undue pressure being put on parents to make decisions before they know what schools will be accepting their child, and that creates a lot of anxiety," June said. "I can sympathize, to some extent, because it takes all the risk out of it, only accepting people you know will accept you back. But it violates the spirit of the Independent Schools Admissions Association of Greater New York. If parents ask if it's necessary to write a first-choice letter, I say absolutely not. But a lot of people disagree with me."

In the spring of 2005, Trinity's board accepted the proposal put forth by June's advisory committee that despite the increasing numbers of sibling and alumni children, the school would hold fast to its policies of preference. Siblings of current students and children of faculty and staff would be turned down only in rare cases, and Trinity hoped to ac-cept as many alumni children as possible.

None of the five children whom I observed Ann interview were accepted to Trinity. Nor was the child of the celebrity.

TAYLOR, SENIOR | PERCEIVED AS: THE POPULAR GIRL

When Taylor came home from school, she opened the mailbox and pulled out a letter from the University of Michigan. *It's thick. They wouldn't waste that much postage on a rejection,* she thought, and opened it immediately. An acceptance. No matter what happened from now on, Taylor would be going to college. She was jubilant for several minutes, until she thought about telling her parents.

Taylor had a good relationship with both of her parents, who divorced when she was a toddler. But she didn't tell them when good things happened to her. She hadn't told them when she was elected co-captain of the varsity soccer and lacrosse teams. She hadn't even told them that she had applied for the University of North Carolina's Morehead Scholarship, for which she had recently learned she was a finalist, until her mother happened to come across a copy of the application. She didn't plan on informing them for a while that she got into Michigan, at least until enough time had passed that it would be less of a big deal.

It was difficult for Taylor to articulate why, exactly, she didn't want her parents to "know things," as she put it. She had no trouble telling her stepfather about her life, but she didn't like the attention she got from her parents when she told them about accomplishments. It was almost like she didn't want to boast to her parents, because then they might boast to others about her, and, as she told a friend, "You *know* parents get big heads about their kids."

Her parents weren't necessarily braggarts. They weren't the type of parents who would ask their children's friends what they got on the SAT, as several friends' parents had asked Taylor out of the blue. But as loath as Taylor was to admit it, if her parents were to say anything about her in her popular circle of friends, she was afraid it would seem as if they were bragging. When other parents asked Taylor's where she was applying to school, they would run down part of the list: Stanford, Duke, Penn, Harvard, and Georgetown. Her friends' reach schools were tiers lower than Taylor's safeties. By contrast, when someone asked Taylor where she was applying, she would list only a few schools that she considered good but not cocky-sounding, such as Michigan, UVA, and Duke. Taylor had heard her parents mention to other parents her leading roles in the book drive and the Mr. Whitman pageant. She knew that parents talked on the sidelines of the soccer field, but she hated how her mother had once offered Taylor as a tutor to a teammate's parents: "Oh, if your kid needs help, Taylor can do it."

This month Taylor didn't tell her parents she had competed in the first round of the University of Maryland High School Mathematics Competition, which consisted of a twenty-five-question test. Many students outside of the math team took the test because Whitman teachers often gave extra credit for the participation. Taylor not only passed the first round, she exceeded the qualification threshold for the second round by several points. She didn't compete in the second round, however, because she skipped school that day to work on her Duke application. A few days later, a popular student stopped her as she was walking with a smart boy in the Whitman parking lot. "You qualified for the Maryland math thing! Did you go?" the popular guy asked.

"No, I skipped school," she said.

"Oh yeah, I didn't go, either. When I read the list of people who qualified, you were the only name I recognized! I laughed to myself because the other twenty people probably applied to Stanford early and got like 1500s on their SATs," the popular guy said, his sarcasm evident.

The smart boy erupted in laughter. "Um, Taylor applied to Stanford early!" The smart boy also knew about Taylor's 1510 but didn't mention it.

A week after Taylor got the letter from Michigan, she was driving with her father to dinner, chatting about clothes she bought that weekend, when she casually slipped into the conversation, "By the way, I got into Michigan."

Her father's excitement was evident: "You can be a Wolverine now!" he exclaimed. "That's great! How many weeks ago did you find out?" When she told him, he was impressed that it had been only one. Immediately, he picked up his phone to call Taylor's stepmother and half brother, but Taylor said, "Not now," and he put the phone down.

PETE, JUNIOR | PERCEIVED AS: THE MEATHEAD

"It is raining outside today, so I wear my poncho to my place," Pete wrote. His junior AP English teacher had assigned this long-term project, "Journal of a Place," a month ago. The assignment was to visit a specific, meaningful place close to home on eight different days and write journal entries modeled after chapters from Thoreau's *Walden*. Pete had chosen an elementary school playground around the corner.

However, as Pete wrote his journal entry—his third of the night—it wasn't raining, he wasn't wearing his poncho, and he wasn't at his "place." Actually, he hadn't been to the playground in years.

The school wasn't even Pete's elementary school. Pete had moved to Bethesda before he started middle school. He had attended elementary school in another city in the area and, before that, preschool in Russia, where he was born. He chose to write about the playground only because he used to play pickup basketball there, so he knew the place well enough to write about it without going. Pete had played a lot of basketball in middle school, when he was the second-leading scorer on his club team. He had since stopped playing, but a few of his old teammates were headed to top-ranked college teams.

Pete didn't feel badly about taking a shortcut on this particular task. He was of the opinion that the assignment was inane, and he had other work he needed to finish. He felt strongly that he should put his effort into the assignments he would get the most out of, and this wasn't one of them. Anyway, Pete wasn't the only one writing eight journal entries without once visiting his place; he had heard several other juniors laughing about doing the same thing. Come to think of it, he didn't know anyone doing the assignment the "right" way. The girl who sat next to him in English wrote about Starbucks, for instance, but didn't specify which one she was referring to because she never went there. She was writing all eight of her journal entries that night.

Fifteen minutes after he started, Pete was almost finished with his entry. Still sitting at his computer, he wrote his concluding sentences: "Darkness stirs in every soul at this kind of weather. I brush the collected rain on my poncho and make my way home."

AP FRANK, COLLEGE FRESHMAN | PERCEIVED AS: THE WORKHORSE

When AP Frank's father picked him up at Baltimore/Washington International Airport for the long drive home before Thanksgiving break, AP Frank was glad to see him. During the ride, his father gave him the latest update on the mess at home: Richard was "breaking out" of his mother's mold, his mother was lashing back at Richard, and a social worker who was now involved with the family had laid down some basic rules that Mrs. AP Frank would have to follow. For instance, she could no longer sit outside Richard's room and watch him study all afternoon, and she had to let him take frequent breaks. AP Frank and his father talked about Mrs. AP Frank's unrealistic expectations. His father told him that in contrast to "AP Frank," kids at school were calling Richard "Regular [their last name]."

"Obviously, Richard's not the kid who can endure that kind of crap. I'm just a different person. That's how I was able to get through seven APs," AP Frank told his dad. "But it's college now. I'm like the perfect little son; I'm supposedly doing everything correctly. But I'm not going to maintain Mom's expectations. I'm not going to get a 4.0. She's going to have to be satisfied with the grades I get, because I'm doing what's best for myself. If she can't handle that, if she can't handle me not crying, not losing sleep over my grades and stuff, then she's got another think coming. And if she thinks all my life is about becoming a lawyer or doctor, then she's got another think coming, because next summer I'm not going to be at NIH. I'm going to be with my friend as a camp counselor."

"I don't share the same expectations your mom does," his father said. "I know what kind of crap she's put you through, and no matter what, I'm so proud of you." Deep down, AP Frank had known this was true, but it felt good to hear.

When they got home, Mrs. AP Frank rushed out of the house to give her son a hug. It was 10:30 P.M., and he had just enough time to get to a friend's birthday party. "I'm going to go out pretty soon," he said.

"What, this late at night? That's crazy," she replied.

AP Frank knew what card to play. "Mom, I'm getting good grades right now. I got a 97 on the math midterm, and the average was a 77." He didn't remind her that one reason he was doing so well in multivariable calculus was because he took that course at Whitman as a sophomore. A classmate, though, had noticed AP Frank's test grade, leaned over, and said, "Have you taken this class before?"

AP Frank froze. "Yeah, why do you ask?"

"Because you never pay attention in class."

AP Frank admittedly spent class time either sleeping or doing homework for other courses. He had chosen to retake the class because he was worried he might have trouble adjusting to freshman year. His AP cover had been blown at Harvard, anyway. Earlier in November, *Time* magazine printed an article discussing the Advanced Placement program and focusing on students who took an extraordinary amount of AP courses. At dinner one night, a friend showed him the article, cocked his head, and narrowed his eyes, chirping in his affable British accent, "So how many did you say you took again?"

"Uhh . . . seventeen," AP Frank said.

The friend looked down at the article and then back at AP Frank. "Shit! You got the bloke featured in *Time* magazine beat! This one only took sixteen!"

AP Frank told his mother that he had received an A-minus on his most recent expository writing paper, which, he explained, was practically unheard of. "Do you know what that means?" AP Frank said. "That means—"

Richard, who had been studying in his bedroom, peered through his doorway. "It means you work too damn hard!" he interrupted. AP Frank ran into his room, cackling, and happily greeted his brother.

The rest of Thanksgiving break seemed remarkably normal to AP Frank. During his brother's study breaks, they caught up on Whitman gossip, and AP Frank showed him wushu videos on the Internet. The subject of their home life came up only once; they rarely talked about their family. "So you know how I've been getting all these freedoms, just breaking out?" Richard asked.

"Yeahh," said AP Frank.

"Yeahh," Richard said. The conversation moved on, neither brother bringing up that they had heard the weekend Mr. Murphy had called the social worker again for them was the same weekend he died.

Ryland, junior | perceived as: The Slacker

Ryland trudged into school halfway through second period, as usual, relieved he didn't have a test that day. He couldn't recall the last time he had made it to first period. He didn't enjoy coming in late, but he was having problems lifting his head from his pillow in the morning. A heavy sleeper, he would snooze through his three alarms, through his mother yelling at him to get out of bed, through both parents leaving the house to go to work. No matter how much sleep he got, Ryland felt as though he couldn't get enough. The concept of getting to school on time now meant getting to first period ten minutes late. If it was already halfway through a period when he woke up, Ryland would think, *Why bother now?* and sleep until the next period. He would generally wake up at about eight A.M., forge a note from his parents claiming that he was sick, and rush to ceramics class, where he would plop a lump of clay in front of him and sit in a daze, pretending to be visualizing a masterpiece when the teacher walked by.

The students who served as aides in the attendance office rotated such that no one knew how often Ryland had been skipping his early-morning classes. If they had bothered to look in his file, they would have seen a stack of notes offering the same excuses, day after day. They also would have noticed that Ryland had progressively better class attendance as the day went on; he had near-perfect attendance in eighth period, even though it was physics, his least favorite class.

This wasn't the way Ryland preferred to experience high school. He enjoyed school. He liked having smart, serious discussions, and he appreciated learning about different perspectives. One reason he found it difficult to get engaged in math and science classes was that teachers presented—and accepted—only one way of looking at things.

But Ryland didn't have time to get a good night's sleep before a school day that began at 7:25 A.M. The varying hours of the new activities he had taken on this year had made his sleeping patterns irregular. Between community service, clubs, and the games and other events he had to photograph, on a typical day he didn't come home until eight P.M. or later. When the *Black & White* was closing an issue, he would be at school until 10:30 for consecutive flat nights, often having to skip classes because the seniors needed him to pick up the slack for other photographers who weren't willing to put in the hours. Sometimes he came in to school only to help with the newspaper and slept in the office the rest of the day. He devoted himself to the *Black & White* because he liked playing a leadership role in an intelligent activity. He worked well in groups and found the other students on the paper smart and friendly. The *Black & White* staff was like a family because they spent so much time together, time Ryland was desperate to spend away from his own home. He tried to finish his homework, tried to study for tests, but often there was just not enough time. On flat nights, he was never able to do his homework.

When Ryland got to second period, his ceramics teacher said, "Ryland, you have eleven absences in my class, six of which are unexcused."

"I can't wake up in the morning," he replied. He didn't tell the teacher how different his life would be if he only had more hours in the day.

AUDREY, JUNIOR | PERCEIVED AS: THE PERFECTIONIST

On Monday morning, Audrey's first and second alarms rang. She slapped them off and went back to sleep, as usual. When her father woke her up to tell her it was time for school, she realized she must have sleep-walked again to turn off her third alarm, on her cell phone. She had hidden it in the pillowcase on the other bed in her room, but she still woke up with the phone in her hand.

Audrey tried to sit up and immediately fell back, dizzy. She had always believed that it was better to endure a school day sick than not to go at all. Sick days carried the potential for an ominous cycle: If she stayed home, she would have to make up the work she missed, which meant staying awake later and losing more sleep to do the work, which would make her even sicker.

"You're just nervous. Get up," her father said. "Talk to your mom." Audrey did get extremely nervous whenever she had tests coming up; often the anxiety alone made her feel sick. Since childhood, whenever she said she felt sick, the first thing her mother would ask was what she had going on in school that day—a test or presentation, for example. But this time felt different.

"Mom?" Audrey said, padding downstairs in her pajamas. "I don't want to go to school today."

"At least try," her mother answered. "If you still don't feel well, you can call me."

In first-period physics, Audrey couldn't concentrate. She heard her teacher lecturing but couldn't register anything he said. After class, knowing it was a waste to be in school, she went to the art teacher's room, her safe haven, where she could use her cell phone to call her mother. Having never been to the Whitman nurse's office, she didn't want to make an appearance now. Audrey's mother picked her up and took her home.

For the next two days, Audrey lay in bed, trying to catch up on her sleep and stressing over taking sick days for the first time in her two and a half years of high school.

∽

I n some high schools, ambitious students fall into an unofficial competition regarding who sleeps the least. The less sleep they get, the more work and activities they can take on. A need for sleep is sometimes seen as a weakness, and the lower the number of hours a student can get away with, the brighter the badge of honor. A common refrain among overachievers is that it is necessary to sacrifice sleep for success. Perhaps it wasn't surprising, then, that some members of the Whitman community viewed Ryland as a slacker because he couldn't wake up in time for school. There are generations of Americans who claim that teenagers' sleep patterns, particularly a tendency to sleep late on weekends, indicate that they are lazy, that they are apathetic, that they are slackers.

Actually, they're normal. A 2002 study revealed that 87 percent of high school students can't wake up on school days without a parent or at least one alarm to arouse them. In a relatively new field of research focusing on the sleep habits of adolescents, experts have uncovered a wealth of evidence that explains why students like Ryland and Audrey need to set three alarms yet frequently sleep through them. It turns out that teens have vastly different sleep patterns from others.

When a high school student wakes up to get to a school that starts before eight A.M., the schedule is roughly comparable to an adult waking up for work at three A.M. This is because of a shift in teens' biological clocks. As teenagers go through puberty, melatonin—a hormone that helps control sleeping patterns—switches on later at night and continues to secrete for about nine hours. Because of this shift, a typical high schooler's natural bedtime is after eleven P.M. This change in circadian rhythms happens at the same age that teens' need for sleep increases. Unlike adults, who need an average of eight hours of sleep, teenagers require about 9.25 hours a night.

Obviously, they aren't getting it. In an informal poll I took of high school students across the country, many teens said they get six or fewer hours of sleep a night on school days, a figure that supports local and national polls. (The top-ranked student at a large public school in Illinois sighed, "If I got five hours of sleep every night the rest of my life, I'd die happy. Last year I got four to five hours of sleep per night. This year I get two or three, when I'm not pulling all-nighters.") Mary Carskadon, a leading sleep researcher, told me that teenagers are the most sleep-deprived age group in the country.

A 2005 *Pediatrics* study described the current high school schedule as so brutal that it is causing an "epidemic of sleep deprivation among adolescents." Like AP Frank, 20 percent of high school students say they fall asleep in class, and, like Ryland, as many as one in ten teens are late to school at least a few days each month because they are too tired to wake up. Jill, a high-achieving senior in a small Mississippi town, told me she was "so tired all the time" that she had taken to skipping school as often as once a week simply to catch up on sleep.

Audrey was caught up in a pattern familiar to many overachievers: Stay up late to get as much work done as possible, wake up in time for school, go through the school day working more slowly than usual because of exhaustion, then stay up even later that night to finish the old work and start on the new assignments. It was no wonder Audrey got sick. But the prospect of staying home for a day to recuperate—or adhering to her mother's 10:30 bedtime rule for even one night a week—caused anguish because it meant time away from schoolwork, and not keeping up meant being left behind.

Audrey, at fifteen, was already taking on the mentality of driven adults in the workforce for whom staying home sick carries a brow-raising stigma. Stepping off the hamster wheel on which the rest of her class sprinted, even if only for a moment, would have consequences that Audrey considered worse than physical illness. If she could have concentrated that morning in class, she would have stayed at school that day no matter how ill she felt.

For teens, sleep deprivation can have a more dangerous outcome than missing class. Research has linked insufficient sleep to depression and other health issues, low grades, disciplinary problems, poor concentration, and strained relationships with family and friends. The National Sleep Foundation reported that, especially for students like Audrey and Ryland who are "heavily involved in school and community activities, their jobs and other responsibilities," sleep deprivation can cause negative moods, decreased school performance, increased likelihood to try stimulants, and a higher risk of accidents and death.

The latter category includes teen drivers who fall asleep at the wheel. A North Carolina study found that more than half of all crashes due to driver fatigue were caused by drivers age twenty-five or younger. In 1990 a seventeen-year-old who six months before had been named the safest teenage driver in the U.S., crashed the car he was given as a prize into another vehicle, killing himself and the other driver. Investigators concluded that he had fallen asleep while driving.

Mary Carskadon calls school start times one of the biggest contributors to adolescent sleep deprivation. "When a school administration says [students] just need to learn to sleep at the right time and meanwhile are putting this burden on them, it isn't fair, and it makes it impossible or extremely difficult at best for teenagers to get adequate sleep," she told me. "In some kids, it can lead to really serious problems with learning, behavior, motivation, emotion, and there are inklings that not getting enough sleep can affect metabolic rate, weight gain, and so forth." She and other experts have called early start times "abusive."

Some groups of parents, educators, and government officials have ardently lobbied for delayed school start times. Starting high school in the seven o'clock hour when students can't naturally fall asleep before eleven P.M., the groups have argued, is irrational, and it places yet another obstacle in front of students striving to be successful. Remember, Ryland's attendance in eighth period was the best of any of his classes, even though it was his least favorite course. Illinois researchers reported that adolescents performed better on alertness tests in the afternoon than they did in the morning. The study's lead author pointed out that standardized tests, which are typically administered at eight A.M., should be pushed back by two hours.

As should high school schedules. Some schools across the United States paid attention to the emerging research on teen sleep patterns and adjusted their schedules accordingly. In 1996 the Edina public school district in Minnesota delayed its high school start time from 7:25 to 8:30 A.M.; the following year Minneapolis shifted its start time to 8:40. When University of Minnesota researchers studied about 7,000 of those high school students, they found that compared to students with earlier start times, the students had better class attendance, were less sleepy during the day even during the first two class periods, were more likely to show up on time, and experienced fewer mood swings and feelings of depression. Fewer students fell asleep in class, more had time to eat breakfast, and the number of disciplinary problems and dropouts decreased. Parents said their children were easier to live with. Students felt they were able to finish more of their homework during the school day and got higher grades. Some schools reported that their school atmosphere was calmer and that fewer students sought help for stress relief because of academic pressures.

In 1998 Congresswoman Zoe Lofgren (D-CA) first introduced in the U.S. House of Representatives the "Zzzzz's to A's" Bill, whose purpose was to provide grants to school districts that moved their high school start time after nine A.M. Lofgren told me she became aware of the teen sleep problem when her children hit puberty and couldn't wake up in the morning. Lofgren did some research. "I felt very relieved I wasn't a bad mother," she said. "This is a biological phenomenon, and at the same time, for no very good reason, we start making kids wake up earlier. I thought, *Well, why do we do that?*" Lofgren, who sent the bill to every school district in California, was surprised by the emotional responses. Districts that delayed their start times sent her thank-you notes. Others revealed what she called a "hostility toward young people—make them get up early and walk through snow uphill both ways."

On June 30, 2005, she reintroduced Zzzzz's to A's as a resolution. "It's never been acted on and it never will—I know that. I'm a Democrat in a House that is ruled by Republicans, and no bill with my name on it is ever going to move," Lofgren said. "So one of the questions I had is, what can I do that will be helpful where the bill introduction alone accomplishes the task" by disseminating information.

"Why are you reintroducing it?" I asked her.

"Because not every school board in America has yet studied the science," she replied without hesitation. "I think that having healthy, happy teenagers is a good thing."

One argument Lofgren heard against delaying start times was that with later start times, students would simply go to bed later. Minnesota found otherwise; students reported getting an hour more sleep a night because they kept the same bedtime. Other opponents take the no-sympathy-for-teens approach. In 2004 Connecticut state representatives successfully repealed a prohibition against giving standardized tests to seventh-to-twelfth-grade students before nine A.M. "Jobs in the real world require you to have a reasonable amount of self-discipline to get a decent night's rest and start work well before nine A.M.," argued a representative who opposed the prohibition. But unlike teens, adults in the "real world" don't need 9.25 hours of sleep, and they don't have an innate natural bedtime past eleven P.M. Furthermore, "a decent night's rest" might be impossible. "Districts that have very early start times are deluding themselves if they think their mission is optimal," Mary Carskadon said. "In the twenty-first century, in our culture, given the teen biology, it's very hard for any child to get adequate sleep, under the circumstances."

Ultimately, school districts' decisions on school start times appear to come down to the cost of changing bus schedules so that they don't overlap with those of elementary and middle schools. One wonders how school officials weigh transportation costs against student health. Edina Public Schools superintendent Kenneth Dragseth told me that delaying start times was "one of the most significant things I did in my tenure. If the only reason people aren't doing it is because of busing, then get creative and try to figure it out."

SAM, SENIOR | PERCEIVED AS: THE TEACHER'S PET

On Friday Sam left for a debate tournament at Princeton, relieved to escape Bethesda for a while. The only potential drag for Sam was that Debate Girl, a judge in the competition, had asked if she could ride to Princeton with Sam's friends, and he had agreed. Sam was able to maneuver the rides so that they weren't in the same car, but at dinner that night, she clung to him and his teammates. Sam was so unresponsive to her aggressive overtures that eventually she seemed to give up.

On Saturday Sam aced the preliminary competitions, the qualifiers that narrowed down the field to about two dozen finalists. Sam later learned he had finished the day in first place. That night he began to prepare his speech defending the finals topic: withdrawal from the United Nations. He arranged for the hotel to make two wake-up calls so that he had plenty of time to get to the nine A.M. final round, and went to sleep.

Sunday morning, the day of the finals, Sam woke up and looked at the clock, which blinked 8:59. The hotel wake-up calls hadn't come. His teammates hadn't called. The finals were fifteen minutes away by car. Sam threw on his suit, found a teammate's parent outside the hotel, and asked for a ride.

When Sam arrived at the Princeton classroom, he waited until the student who was orating finished his speech. He spotted his Whitman teammates, who had either forgotten him or purposely left him at the hotel, and the student legislators, who wouldn't give high marks to a student who arrived fifteen minutes late to the finals. Sam had blown it. He ignored his friends while, per proper procedure, he announced to the session, "Point of personal privilege to enter the chamber."

"Granted," said the presiding officer. All eyes turned as Sam made his way to his empty chair in the middle of the room. A half hour later, when Sam delivered his speech, he was still frazzled. After the finals, his ranking fell from first.

The next day Sam's anger grew progressively explosive. It wasn't just the tournament. He was sure he had failed his math test. He missed the camaraderie of *Les Mis* rehearsals. He believed he was in a social rut. He couldn't escape a gut feeling that everyone else was moving somewhere, going places, their lives changing, while Sam was staying the same.

Every morning he woke up grumpy, put on clothes, went downstairs, ate the same breakfast, drank his orange juice, put a sandwich in his backpack, tried unsuccessfully to back his car out of the driveway, tried again, went to Brad's house, where Brad would usually still be sleeping so Sam drove Brad's younger sibling instead, took the same assigned Whitman parking space, attended the same classes, went to his extracurriculars, returned home, and sat at his desk to work and chat online until he went to bed. Weekends were a change, but he knew that on Monday he would be back in the same place again. He felt that he spent his weeks fighting to get through them, rather than enjoying them; he called this sentiment the "academic weird survival thing." He had taken on the commitment to *Les Mis* precisely because it was a new, different activity to shake up his schedule, but now that it was over, his attitude had soured again.

After school, alone in the house and hungry, he threw open the refrigerator to take his anger out on the sub sandwich he had stuck there before the Princeton tournament, found it was gone, and blew up. "Fuck!" Sam yelled, slammed the door closed, saw a plastic cup on the counter, and bashed it into the wall with his palm. Ignoring the shattered pieces, he tromped into the living room, where he hurled his PlayStation 2 controllers at the floor, threw pillows across the room, and kicked over the chairs.

When his mother came home, Sam apologized to her for breaking the cup. "Don't overdramatize it," she said. "It's no big deal."

"I don't think you know what's going on," Sam replied. His mother sat down to listen. "It's just a general frustration with everything and anything: school"—*girls, friends,* he thought—"life, everything. I'm just sick of the monotony. I'm sick of school. I'm bored out of my mind because there's a pattern of no change in my life. Every day the exact same things happen. My classes are exactly the same. Nothing changes. I'm just so frustrated. I'm just . . . accomplishing nothing and succeeding at nothing in my own eyes."

Sam's mother nodded sympathetically. "I understand. Let's think of something new for you to do."

"We'll see." Sam shrugged and went upstairs. In his room, he thought about what was truly bugging him. Much of it was the feeling that he was wasting time, that in the eyes of others, he was a "success," but from his own perspective, he was worthless. He knew his outburst wasn't a cry for help, because he wasn't depressed; he was simply unhappy. He was so sick of the stress of what he called "the monotony of being a high school senior" that he felt pressured to apply to Middlebury early decision 2 before he had even heard from Stanford because he wanted the college process over with already. Then, he was confident, the pressure would end.

That night Sam's parents wanted to talk. "Sam," his mother called from the family room, "come in here. We have a few ideas." His parents suggested that perhaps Sam should get a job or do volunteer work, and told him that he might feel better if he had more exercise, maybe running, biking, or lifting weights after school. Sam wasn't listening. He had already vented to his mother, and he just wanted to go back upstairs to his bedroom.

"One sec," Sam's father said, and went into the next room, motioning for Sam to follow. "Okay, Sam. What's up?" he asked.

"I'm just sick of everything. It's like a Möbius strip. Everything is a pattern, and there is no change, and I just can't stand it anymore. School is worthless. I'm bored with *Black & White,* with everything . . ."

His father chuckled sympathetically. "A week ago you were fine," he said. "What's up now? Is there something else?"

Sam liked talking to his father because he could usually make sense of the world. But there were things Sam wouldn't talk about with his parents. "Nope," Sam lied.

"Well, I'll put my thinking cap back on, but meanwhile, let's finish those college applications and get you through January. With all that you have planned"—the extracurriculars tended to heat up in the spring, and varsity tennis and a spring break trip would join them—"it sounds like February through May will handle themselves." Sam doubted it.

Chapter 8

December 8–December 20

VERDICTS

I t was clear to me, as an observer, that Julie, Sam, and Taylor ultimately would do well at whichever colleges they attended. Because of their drive, curiosity, and passion for learning, I knew they would take advantage of new experiences, bond with professors, and further their knowledge in their chosen fields. But all three of these varied personalities were convinced that Stanford was their dream school, and all of them felt pressure to get into a university with a name that others respected. As Sam explained to me in only our second meeting, if he didn't get into a school whose prestige reflected his exhaustive work and the nights he spent studying until three A.M., he would feel he had "done a lot for naught," even if he fell in love with a non-elite school that was perfect for him.

Overachievers across the country told me they felt similarly, that all of the effort they had expended to present themselves as attractive applicants—the grades and test scores, the extracurricular stardom—would be a waste if they weren't admitted to highly ranked universities that would justify their sacrifices. A Nebraska junior explained, "Schools on my list have to be in the top twenty-five schools in America, with only a select few who get in. Why? Because that way, *when* I get into one of them, I feel that I'm good enough to be one of the chosen ones. I feel I've achieved something."

I conducted a group interview on this subject with top seniors at Vermont Commons School, a tiny independent school in South

Burlington, Vermont, where the college counselor joked, "We have thirteen seniors, so almost everybody's in the top ten." The school fostered a cooperative attitude among the students, who believed the teachers were extraordinarily understanding about their multitude of activities and worked hard to play down the notion of competition within the class. And yet the students I spoke with were zeroing in on name-brand schools. "I like the idea of having a school with a name that's respected. It's a really attractive idea because of the push to go to a school that people have heard of for the prestige," one boy said.

"If you go to someplace that nobody's heard of, there's always the question of why hasn't anybody heard of this place? What's wrong with it? What's wrong with me for wanting to go to a place that nobody's heard of?" said a girl who the college counselor told me was one of the most impressive students in the school's nine-year history.

I asked if any of them had crossed off schools because of a lack of prestige. One boy nodded furiously. "I was looking at colleges in Pennsylvania and read about Muhlenberg. It sounded like a great college. Then I read about the ones that seemed to have rank, like Swarthmore, ones that other people talk about. I thought those sounded like better choices because I've heard of them. So you don't really look at the one no one else is talking about, because you don't want to say, 'I'm going to Muhlenberg' and have someone say, 'Where's that?' "

"People are constantly asking us, 'Where are you applying?' And that's a horrible question, because you feel like you have to prove yourself," the girl said. "They're going to judge you by that list."

The obsession over name-brand schools is the most frenzied it has ever been; paradoxically, as it has become more difficult to get into selective schools, students' and parents' expectations that students will attend those schools have gone up. A new form of high school peer pressure has the same effect: Some overachievers look down on peers who don't aim for top-tier schools. Certainly, college applicants have reasons to gun for top-tier schools beyond the ego trip. Many parents and students are convinced that a degree from an Ivy or other elite school is necessary for success in life and, worse, that without one, a student is doomed to failure. A prestigious degree, they think, will translate into a higher salary, a better job, and an easier life. College is seen less as a vehicle for deeper learning and growth than as a passport to financial success and higher social status.

It must be noted that in some fields, a university name carries disproportionate weight, no matter how ludicrous. Some law firms claim they won't even look at résumés of candidates who didn't graduate from prominent law schools. But is it true that an undergraduate degree from an elite institution is a golden ticket to lifelong dreams and achievement? And is it worth the stress and money it takes to get there?

In 1999 Princeton economist Alan Krueger and Stacy Berg Dale, a researcher at the Andrew W. Mellon Foundation, sent shock waves through Ivyland when they concluded after a twenty-year study that graduates of prestigious colleges did not earn more than graduates of other schools. After examining the salaries of students who were accepted at elite institutions but chose to matriculate somewhere less prestigious, Krueger and Dale concluded that earnings disparities could be explained by the caliber of the students, not the university they attended. The students who turned down acceptances from selective schools averaged the same income as those who attended them. Krueger and Dale attributed the result to students' initiative and motivation to learn, traits that engaged students display regardless of the prestige level of their school. In terms of future earnings, merely going to college is a larger factor than the school a student attends.

What's more, surveys of top business leaders do not support the idea that a degree from an elite institution is necessary for success. By 2005 the percentage of CEOs at S&P 500 companies who did not graduate from an Ivy League school had risen to 90 percent from 84 percent in 1998. Also that year, the number of S&P 500 CEOs who graduated from the University of Wisconsin matched the number from Harvard. In 2004 and 2005 the CEOs of Chiquita Brands, Continental Airlines, Intel, Kellogg's, Kmart Holding, Sara Lee, Time Warner, and Walt Disney had received their undergraduate degrees from Southern Illinois University, University of South Carolina, University of San Francisco, DePaul University, University of Houston, Augustana College, University of Hawaii, and Ithaca College, respectively.

The truth is, while families spend years hyperventilating over and strategizing how to get into an impressive-sounding school, the educational and social experiences at hundreds of other colleges are just as good, if not better. Much of the name-branding has carried over from a different era, when fewer students attended college and there was a sharper divide between the elite universities and the rest. Since that time, many schools have caught up in quality to those traditionally considered top-tier. It's only the attitudes—in many cases, of adults from that era—that haven't. Hordes of parents each year sacrifice facets of their children's well-being, and their own, to get them into schools that are overrated.

Or perhaps a better word is "overranked." Every year brings a plethora of new ordered lists of colleges; in fall 2005 the rankers included the Princeton Review, *Peterson's Guide, Newsweek, Forbes, Rolling Stone,* and *Golf Digest,* among others (such as the *Campus Squirrel Listings* report, which suggests that "the quality of an institution of higher learning can often be determined by the size, health and behavior of the squirrel population on campus").

The most powerful instigator is *U.S. News & World Report's* "America's Best Colleges" issue, which, since 1988, has annually ranked every regionally accredited four-year college in the country and reaches tens of millions of people. The *U.S. News* rankings began in 1983 as a biennial survey based only on college presidents' opinions of other schools; the magazine now ranks schools on criteria that include graduation rate, percentage of returning freshmen, student-faculty ratio, average faculty salaries, student selectivity (including acceptance rate, matriculants' SAT or ACT scores, and class ranks), per-student spending, the rate of alumni donations, and "peer assessment."

Every back-to-school season, college officials anxiously anticipate the *U.S. News* issue. Armies of students and parents take its word as gospel. Many parents tell college counselors to get their children into the "highest-ranked" school possible. Counselors at a Virginia public high school even use the rankings of Virginia universities to divide their senior class. They rank the students in academic order, then tell parents which group their child falls in: the University of Virginia tier, the Virginia Tech or James Madison tier, and so on down the line, regardless of whether that school is appropriate for the child. The *U.S. News* rankings themselves often become a self-fulfilling prophecy: A college that moves up is likely to see a swell in applications, while a school that dives draws complaints from disappointed alumni, who then might be less likely to donate, which could further lower the ranking.

Despite massive public perception, the *U.S. News* rankings are not designed to present a factually based ordered list of the best colleges in the country. The rankings are designed to sell magazines, to continue to grow a franchise, or, worse, to fuel the frenzy. A former *U.S. News* staff writer and "America's Best Colleges" contributor has said, "The rankings are completely ridiculous. But they totally pay your salary."

When the magazine's first rankings algorithm produced a number one school that wasn't considered elite, the algorithm (which rewarded diversity) and the statistician who created it were dumped. Instead, *U.S. News* went with a formula that resulted in a top ranking for Yale. *Washington Monthly* reported that since then, *U.S. News* "essentially put its thumb on the scale to make sure that Harvard, Yale, and Princeton continued to come out on top, as they did every year until 1999." Furthermore, the magazine reportedly penalizes uncooperative schools. When Reed College refused in 1995 to submit statistics to the magazine, rather than omit the school from the list, as Reed requested, *U.S. News* dropped it from the second quartile to the bottom.

Also, the statistics by which *U.S. News* judges schools can be misleading. One category, faculty resources—which accounts for 20 percent of a national university or liberal arts college's total score—rewards schools in part by their number of full-time professors with the highest degrees in their fields, and by how much the school pays those professors. But the accomplished, well-known professors who earn the highest salaries are often the same ones who build and maintain their reputations by doing research and publishing papers, neither of which directly have to do with teaching students. In many cases, the more famous a professor, the less time he has for teaching and for student interaction. The head of UCLA's Higher Education Research Institute found that students at more elite schools tended to be *less* satisfied with teaching and faculty relationships and reported *worse* educational development than students at other schools. Students at colleges where professors were focused on classes rather than research, by comparison, reported increased satisfaction with most aspects of the school and improved skills in every academic category examined.

The rate of alumni giving is another dubious measure: The higher the rate, the better a school's score. The size and quantity of alumni donations, however, could be attributed to anything from a winning football season to the freebies the school awards students who spend hours on the phone soliciting alums for money. Besides, undergraduates don't necessarily benefit from alumni donations. At Harvard, the wealthiest university in the world, an administrator has said, "There are more claims on Harvard's money than on any other college. Teaching undergraduates is a very small part of what Harvard does," given its ten graduate schools, several museums, and the largest private library in the United States.

Additionally, a full quarter of a school's rating, the largest percentage assigned to a single statistic, is based on "peer assessment." Illogically, rather than polling current students or faculty to determine their satisfaction with the school, *U.S. News* asks *other* university presidents, provosts, and admissions officers to rate about 220 other schools on a one-to-five scale. *Washington Monthly* reported that these officials' opinions seemed to be linked to how much schools spend on faculty research and development.

Over the last decade, several researchers have declared the *U.S. News* rankings invalid. Even the National Opinion Research Council, which was commissioned by *U.S. News* to critique its methodology, issued a report in 1997 stating that "the weights used to combine the various measures into an overall rating lack any defensible empirical or theoretical basis." Yet the rankings still continue to drive the lives of millions of students—and the jobs and ethics of college officials. *U.S. News* manipulated the ranking algorithms to keep elite schools elite; as a result, schools have manipulated their data to stay afloat, some going as far as to hire consultants to show them how.

Some schools are so obsessed with moving up on the *U.S. News* charts that they shift priorities and funding to boost the statistics the magazine measures, even when those statistics don't improve the undergraduate experience. Schools might determine the size of their freshman class or the students for whom they'll bid with financial aid packages, or decrease need-based aid in favor of merit scholarships, based not on what's best for the class but on what would produce the most impressive class-average SAT score.

As the education consultants remarked in Chapter Three, even the admissions practice of early decision is part rankings strategy, because ED students must enroll in the school that accepts them. Many colleges have actively tried to recruit more applicants—including students they would never accept—because the more applicants they reject, the better their *U.S. News* "selectivity" rating. Most college officials interviewed by *The Atlantic* unmasked other schools "playing the market" that way.

In many cases, schools have gone beyond manipulating rankings data to flat-out lying about them. In 1995 *The Wall Street Journal* published an investigative piece about colleges cheating on the rankings data for *U.S. News* and other guidebooks. For example, New College of Florida jacked up its average SAT score by not counting the lowest 6 percent of student scores. This wasn't inadvertent; the then–admissions director called the duplicity "marketing strategy." Other colleges employed similar "strategies," despite being prohibited from doing so by the guidebooks: Northeastern University upped its SAT average fifty points by not including scores of international and remedial students, a fifth of the freshman class. Boston University counted the math scores but not the verbal scores of hundreds of international students because their math scores were often better than those of American students. NYU didn't count scores from poor students in a state-sponsored program. Other schools didn't count scores of alumni children or minority students. Monmouth University simply fabricated the SAT scores it reported to a College Board guide, inflating them by 200 points.

The *Journal* also compared the statistics colleges provided to debt-ratings agencies, which by law had to be accurate, with the statistics given to magazines and guidebooks, which did not. The paper revealed that colleges reported different figures to different companies for the same criterion, depending on who was asking and why. Kent State University was reported in *U.S. News* to have a 33 percent acceptance rate, but its credit report stated the rate was actually 86.7 percent. Even Harvard was inconsistent: Its mean SAT score in *U.S. News* was 1400, while its credit report score was listed as 1385.

For many colleges, the discrepancies weren't limited to test scores; schools fudged enrollment and acceptance numbers as well as graduation rates. Some schools doctored acceptance rates to make them seem more selective by first funneling hundreds of students whom they planned to accept onto a waiting list, because they could then officially count the students as rejections. Rensselaer Polytechnic Institute rejected approximately a fifth of applicants from specific undergraduate programs, then accepted them into other programs yet still reported them as rejections. Even alumni giving rates can be manipulated. *Washington Monthly* reported that one West Coast college reclassifies alumni who haven't donated in five years as dead.

These circumstances are reminiscent of Julie's "My Life in Numbers" essay. The rankings reduce centers of learning to mostly meaningless numbers, just as schools strip students down to grades and test scores. And just as students feel they need to cheat to keep up, so do schools. Colby College's former director of communications admitted that the school shot up from twentieth place to fifteenth in the 1992 *U.S. News* rankings because of "numbers massage" and a mistake. Colby officials then had "a meeting that could only be described as a strategy session on how to cheat on the survey" in order to "preserve our competitive advantage and forestall a subsequent plunge in the rankings that would have to be explained to concerned alumni." As a former Colgate dean of admissions told *The Wall Street Journal*, "This is awful stuff, but when the American public comes to you and says you're not in the top 20 and they're going to make their decision based on that, it puts incredible pressure on you to have the right-looking numbers."

The rankings don't address what students actually get out of the college experience, much like a student's SAT scores reveal nothing about his or her personality. They are partly to blame for parents judging colleges not by the educational value but by the glamour of the degree. Would we accept this kind of unscientific ordering in any other aspect of our lives? Let's say *U.S. News* ranked potential spouses instead of schools. The equivalent rankings for a wife would be based on what the woman's friends thought of her looks on a scale of one to five, the length of her previous relationships (over only the last year, because this is an annual ranking), the average looks of previous boyfriends or husbands, the average salary of those boyfriends or husbands, the number of those previous suitors who wanted her back this year, the size of her salary, and the frequency with which her parents handed her pocket change. A large chunk of the potential wife's rating is based on her selectivity: The more likely she is to like you, the worse her rank. There would be no analysis of her personality, intelligence, kindness, or humor, not to mention whether you might get along. Forget her interests, passions, and tastes. Will she love you, care for you, and make you happy? Unimportant.

Some students are beginning to realize that happiness comes from more than a name. In 2005 an internal Harvard memo was leaked, revealing details of a confidential survey of students at thirty-one colleges, including all of the Ivies, MIT, Stanford, Wellesley, Amherst, and others. The results? Student satisfaction at Harvard, that magical beacon of overachiever dreams, ranked near the bottom of the group. Students at Harvard were unhappy with the unavailability of faculty, the quality of instruction and advising, the lack of sense of community, and the campus social life (the last of which would not be news to AP Frank). Harvard students were less likely to be taught by professors than at other colleges and were often divided into sections led by inexperienced graduate students. Professors and students described to *The Boston Globe* a "hurried and stressful atmosphere on campus." Harvard may regularly sit atop the *U.S. News* rankings, but in the ranking that really matters— that of student satisfaction—only four schools surveyed were worse.

As contributing editor Gregg Easterbrook wrote in *The Atlantic,* "It is genuinely ironic that as non-elite colleges have improved in educational quality and financial resources, and favoritism toward top-school degrees has faded, getting into an elite school has nonetheless become more of a national obsession." So has the idea that a traditional four-year college is the ideal path for every student. Good students are often pressured to go to a four-year college (and to pay for it) even when there is no reason to go. If an overachiever shuns typical college life for a culinary institute, nursing program, or trade or technical school, he's automatically viewed by many to have lost his ambition, wasted his potential, or squandered his academic efforts. He'll be absent from his high school's published list of the percentage of graduates who go on to traditional four-year colleges, even if he might someday become a four-star chef, a Broadway choreographer, a hairdresser to the stars, or achieve another celebrity status that will inspire that same high school to loudly trumpet him as an alum.

Sometime in recent years, this country abandoned the notion that students should follow individual paths suited to their own passions and skills. That definition of success—happiness in the pursuit of personal goals related to personal interests—has disappeared behind the rising shadow of the rankings. What was once a simple, unscientific list of subjective favorites has become the be-all and end-all for parents, students, alumni, and school administrators. Once parents send a child, whether at age five or fifteen, down that elite route, at what point will they stop being consumed by name-brand fever? Parents or students accustomed to prestige might, upon an Ivy college graduation, insist exclusively on a name-brand graduate school, a job at a top-ranked company, a home in a pedigreed neighborhood, marriage to a spouse from a prominent family, a couture-only wardrobe, children who attend elite preschools, and a casket from a designer company.

Scads of students spend their high school years, if not the majority of their academic experience, panicked because of the desire to get into a highly ranked school on a for-profit rankings list that is fixed, useless, and wrong. Those same senseless rankings have college administrators scrambling to improve statistics that diminish a student's college experience. In terms of educational quality and value, then, perhaps the colleges that rank highly on name-brand lists actually may be the least desirable schools to attend.

JULIE, SENIOR | PERCEIVED AS: THE SUPERSTAR

Julie couldn't concentrate. She had indoor track practice followed by swim practice, but all she could think about was that the day that for so long had seemed to be far in the distance was tomorrow. As she circled the track, she remembered running around the same track back in September, pretending she was on a college team and trying to decide where to apply.

The last month had been mostly a blur. As winter drew near, her spirits dampened and she obsessed over whether she made the wrong choice in applying early to a campus where the weather might depress her. Julie knew she had distinct ups and downs. When her life was going well, it went exceptionally well, and when it frustrated her, she broke down. For a week, Julie debated withdrawing her Dartmouth application, but by early December, she decided that if the university accepted her, she would be grateful and relieved.

All day people came up to her and said things like "Don't stress: You're in!" She found this annoying. It only added to the pressure, because if her classmates expected her to get in, how could she tell them if she didn't? Unlike in September, this time at track Julie didn't envision herself running on a college team. She hadn't heard much from the Dartmouth coach, but at this point she thought she would try running in college, see if she liked it, and keep in mind that it wasn't and shouldn't be the most important thing in her college years.

The next day, when Julie visited another dermatologist for yet another opinion about her thinning hair, she was able to stay collected. But now, driving home alone in the pouring rain, she was excruciatingly nervous. She had told her friends at school not to ask about her Dartmouth letter. "You'll just know," she said to them. "You'll be able to tell."

As soon as she got to her house, she went to the computer room. Her mother, who had driven separately from the doctor's office, wasn't there yet, but Julie didn't care. She didn't want her parents to find out before she did, as they had with her SAT scores. She turned on the computer and tried to calm herself down. *This is completely out of my control,* she thought. *I'm just checking it.* As she waited for the computer to boot, she wished she had finished her other applications. The prospect of doing them after being rejected or deferred only added to the pressure she felt now.

I can do this. Julie took some deep breaths. The computer was taking an awfully long time to boot. Finally, her home page popped up. She typed in the Dartmouth URL and waited, drumming her fingers and swiveling around in her chair. Of course, her Internet access speed was the slowest it had ever been, on the day when she most needed it to be swift. "This is hilarious," she muttered. When the Dartmouth page finally appeared, she typed in her user name and password, her eyes fixed to the screen.

The page was about to load when Julie's instant messenger automatically popped up, stalling the Dartmouth page. "Oh, God," Julie groaned. She put her hands to her head. Immediately, a guy from indoor track whom she didn't know well IMed her: "you racin on saturday?" She minimized his window, trying to ignore the insistently blinking orange bar. A junior friend IMed her: "hey so remember how it's really cold today?"

"Agh!" Julie said aloud. "hey 1 sec," Julie typed back to the junior, and minimized that window, too.

The Dartmouth page looked like it wanted to load. Julie cringed and swiveled her chair in the opposite direction, looking away. "I can't look, I can't look," she breathed, fanning herself. Then the page was up. "Congratulations! It is with great pleasure that I inform you of your admission to Dartmouth College as a member of the class of 2009 . . ."

Julie was overcome with relief. It was over. She read and reread the letter. She responded to the track guy, who in the meantime had misinterpreted her silence and written, "oh i'm sorry. forgot that we don't communicate at all."

"What?" Julie typed back. "i just got into college." Random Track Guy was the first person outside the room to know. She IMed back her junior friend, who was so pleased that she immediately put up a tribute to Julie in her own IM away message. Other students saw it, and soon Julie was flooded with IM messages of congratulations, even from C.J.: "JULIE IM SO PROUD OF YOU. YOURE AMAZING. IM SO JEALOUS. IM SO HAPPY FOR YOU YESSSSSSS. YAYAYAYAYAY!"

"you're an ivy leaguer now," Derek joked. "feel free to look down on common people."

After several minutes of responding to IMs, Julie realized she hadn't told her parents. She called her mother's cell just as she walked in the door. After showing her mother the letter and speaking with her father, Julie returned to the IMs. She had forgotten about Random Track Guy.

"OH DANG. no shiiiit," he had written. "where buddy? dartmouth?"

"yep!"

"you excited?" he asked.

"super," she typed. And she was.

SAM, SENIOR | PERCEIVED AS: THE TEACHER'S PET

In preparation for his date with his neighbor, Sam got his hair cut short and relatively spiky. He picked up his brother from the library, argued with his parents about his '90s haircut, took a shower, and zipped around the house to get ready. He spritzed on some cologne and went next door.

After the opening performance of *The Nutcracker,* they walked toward the Mall, the Washington, D.C., area encompassing museums and monuments. The night was crisp. Sam put his leather jacket over the girl's shoulders. "Close your eyes," he said. When her eyes closed, Sam guided her with a hand on her back toward the center of the Mall.

"Fifteen more yards . . . ten more yards," Sam counted. "Okay, you can stop. Open your eyes." Her eyes widened. She was facing the U.S. Capitol, lit up in the night. "Turn around," Sam said. Now they were looking at the Washington Monument, bright against the sky. They were the only two people in the area, which seemed hushed, removed from the city.

"Wow," she whispered, leaning close to Sam. Sam wondered if he should put an arm around her. She had an innocence that he found both endearing and exasperating, because he wasn't sure how she felt. If it was the right time to make a move, wouldn't she let him know? He suggested they go to dinner at the downtown Bethesda hot-spot strip anchored by the local Barnes & Noble.

On their way into Cosi, a popular café, they ran into Ellie, the artist Sam had dated and dismissed, who gave Sam's neighbor a look he couldn't interpret. Sam and his neighbor took a table next to two Whitman students who were celebrating college acceptances to the University of Pennsylvania and Georgetown. Sam was happy for them but at the same time disconcerted. On a daily basis, the Whitman senior class was inundated with news of college early acceptances. It seemed to Sam that most of his friends and acquaintances were faring well in the early pool, that everyone else already knew where they would be going next year, while he was caught in an uncertain fog.

After dinner, Sam parked his car at his house and walked his neighbor to hers, his hand again on her back. When they reached her front door, he hesitated. Her father was sitting in the living room watching them. Sam cleared his throat. "Thank you for coming," he said.

"It was a lot of fun," she responded. Eyeing her father, Sam gave her a hug and went home, wondering whether the date had gone well.

The next night Sam got an IM from Brad, who had chatted with Sam's neighbor about Sam's creative, romantic date. "she says that if someone she likes, ie whats his face from her school, had done what you did, she would have fallen for him," Brad typed. "but that she likes her relationship with u the way it is."

Sam couldn't figure out what he was doing wrong. Only an acceptance to Stanford, he thought, would fix senior year.

RYLAND, JUNIOR | PERCEIVED AS: THE SLACKER

Ryland was hanging out with his girlfriend and some of their friends in his girlfriend's kitchen. He tried to spark a smart, interesting conversation with a question that could lead to in-depth philosophizing: "If you won so much money that you didn't have to work another day in your life, what causes would you commit yourself to, and what would you do with the money?"

The friends looked pensive and tried to answer. "I'd do stuff to help animals," said one. "I would commit myself to science and to curing a disease," another volunteered. Ryland's girlfriend laughed at him for asking such a serious question and immediately changed the subject. Upset, Ryland went to the living room and found a book to read.

Later that night, Ryland's girlfriend still didn't understand what she did wrong. "You have no interests in life," he told her. "I don't feel I can talk to you about serious things." He wanted to tell her that she didn't seem capable of having an intelligent conversation but decided against it. The non-conversation was the last straw for Ryland. His girlfriend didn't *do* anything and couldn't understand why Ryland did so much. Within the last week, she had told Ryland about how a friend's boyfriend said to her friend, "I have soccer practice, then a tutor, then some meetings later, but I have an hour in between when I can come see you." That was what Ryland's girlfriend wanted him to do. He didn't see how he could find the time or, truthfully, why it would be worthwhile.

After several days of losing his nerve to break up with her in person, Ryland called her. "I want to break up," he said when she answered the phone.

"Okay. Why?"

Ryland told her that he wanted to be by himself and that it was difficult to break up with her because she hadn't done anything wrong.

"You know you're not going to be hanging out with my friends anymore," she said.

Ryland was irate. It was her fault that their friends would think they had to choose sides, because they knew it would make her angry if they spent time with Ryland, whereas he didn't mind if they split their time. "You know I hate it when you say that, because before we were going out, they were my friends, too, and now, suddenly, they're your friends," he said.

"Well, I mean, you won't see them all the time now that you're not with me," she said.

"I know that. I have to go," Ryland said, and hung up.

THE STEALTH OVERACHIEVER, JUNIOR | PERCEIVED AS: ?

The Stealth Overachiever was working on math homework with class-mates, but the others were more focused on PSAT scores than they were on derivatives. "Every school but ours has gotten their scores already," one girl said. Stealth didn't get involved in the conversation, feeling rel-atively calm about the numbers that seemed to be causing other juniors to hyperventilate.

One friend, who was especially obsessive about school-related numbers, had even gone to the guidance department a few days earlier to try to get his scores early. "That score is so important for my ré-sumé," he had said to Stealth after his unsuccessful venture.

"No, it's not," Stealth assured him. "PSAT scores are only necessary if you need the money."

The next day the juniors were on edge as they walked the halls, anxiously enduring the long hours until they could go home and check their mailboxes. At home, Stealth spied among the college mail an enve-lope from Whitman and tore it open: a 227 (which calculated roughly to a 2270/2400). Stealth didn't consider the score outstanding, and it was not as high as recent practice exam scores, but it was satisfactory. With a sigh of relief, Stealth picked up the phone.

"Hi, Mom, I got my PSAT scores."

"How did you do?" she asked. Stealth told her. "Didn't you do bet-ter on the diagnostics?" She sounded worried.

"Yeah, but I think this is enough."

"Okay," she said. "That's good."

TAYLOR, SENIOR | PERCEIVED AS: THE POPULAR GIRL

Because so many other early applicants had already received their letters, Taylor had a feeling she would hear from Stanford. She left school at lunch to peek in her mailbox, and sure enough, there it was. A letter from Stan-ford. A thin one. She opened it in her car. Taylor had purposely lowered her expectations because it was easier to hear bad news that way, but the deferral still stung. She crumpled the letter into the bin on her driver's-side door and drove back to school, annoyed. She knew a deferral wasn't an outright rejection, but it felt like a door had been closed. She was confident she wouldn't be accepted in the spring. Her affair with Stanford was over.

When Taylor got back to school, she happened to see Derek and another Stanford acceptee walking into the building at the same time. Taylor firmly believed that the three Whitman students who had gotten in early were smarter than she was. In her opinion, however, none of them "impacted the school environment at all." People at Whitman *knew* Taylor because she was so involved with school activities. Taylor's deferral made her feel as if her contributions to her high school had gone unrecognized. After her next class, Taylor and two of her friends were walking down the hall when a popular friend stopped her. "So did you hear?" the friend asked. Taylor choked up. She couldn't help it. All of the months—years, really—of anticipation had come down to a flimsy letter in her mailbox. "Okaaay," the friend said, and walked away.

In English, a classmate asked her if she got in. When she told him she was deferred, a student who had gotten into an Ivy turned to look at her. His face fell. "I was sure you were going to get in," he said. "I'm so sorry." A classmate who had just been deferred from Yale sympathized with her. Somehow, the students she considered her "smart" friends made her feel slightly better.

Later that day, Taylor told her parents. She had no problem telling them about things that she believed she failed at.

∽

Many Whitman students didn't have accurate information about the college admissions process, like the graduate who told Sam earlier in the year that Stanford applications were read alphabetically. But then, with the flurry of admissions myths ricocheting across the country, it seems few applicants (and parents) are able to distinguish truth from rumor.

When I first checked in with Matt Lawrence, the Stanford admissions officer who was the "territory manager" for Whitman's region, he had just picked up his second round of early applications from the admissions office. The position of territory manager was only in its second year at Stanford. The admissions office had decided to use territory managers for two reasons: High school counselors would have one point of contact at Stanford, and the manager reading each application would be able to view it in geographical and cultural context. As territory manager for one of the larger territories—Maryland, Washington, D.C., Virginia, and Pennsylvania—Matt routinely retrieved a batch of fifty green color-coded folders from the admissions office. The order in which he picked up the folders was random, having nothing to do with when applications were submitted, the candidates' schools, or the alphabetical order of the candidates' names.

It was Matt's fourth year as an admissions officer, his fourth year of putting his life on hold from November to April. On that first day of reviewing early applications for the Class of 2009, he sat at the dining room table in his home near campus and did a quick read-through to see what the group looked like. "I pick up a folder, get the context of the school that year, the pool, to get an idea of where things might fall out. I don't put them in piles—others in the office probably do," he told me.

The next day he did the full examination, reading every piece of every application closely. At that point, he said, "I'm looking first at information about that school, the transcript, teacher recommendations, counselor recommendation, what students tell us in their essays, to get to know who these students are and what they believe. I'm still just reading and making some notes. All final decisions will be made by the director, but the recommendations I'll be making to the director are starting to shape up." For all of November and part of December, Matt's daily routine involved "sitting pretty much nonstop all day," with a few quick breaks to check email and voice mail and to get caught up on travel expenses, though Stanford admissions officers don't do as much travel as their peers at other schools.

On Wednesdays, the Stanford admissions officers congregated on campus for their weekly staff meeting, during which they talked about admissions trends and how they were feeling about the process. The day of my first conversation with Matt, the staff meeting had addressed general topics, such as where they were in the process, how many folders had been "pulled," how many completed, and what they thought the time line was going to be like that year. They were on schedule to mail their early-action letters in mid-December.

If the process sounds boring, that's because it is. There's no magic to reviewing applications for college admission. At many colleges across the country, applications are read by at least two admissions officers and sometimes reviewed by additional officers or discussed in committee meetings. "One of the myths is that there's a secret to it that nobody knows except a few people, and if parents and kids figure it out, they'll get in. There's a real feeling out there that if you can figure out what the key is, you can unlock the door into anyplace," said Brown University dean of admissions James Miller, who has also worked at Bowdoin and Harvard. "The other big myth is that you have to package yourself appropriately, like an exercise in commerce, and if you package your child appropriately, he stands the best chance of gaining admission. Neither is true. The truth is there is no real key, no formula, no index, no nothing."

The overwhelming amount of time that overachievers spend on piling up extracurriculars solely to bolster a college résumé may be a waste. According to the National Association for College Admission Counseling (NACAC), only 7.5 percent of colleges considered extracurricular activities of "considerable importance" when evaluating an applicant in 2004. Several admissions officers told me versions of the banality that Matt Lawrence used during our first conversation: "We're not looking for a well-rounded student; we're looking for a well-rounded student body."

Attention to extracurriculars depends on the campus, of course, but Harvard dean of admissions and financial aid Bill Fitzsimmons told me the idea that applicants have to do unusual things to distinguish themselves is a "misconception." "In broad terms, there are three ways to get into Harvard," he said. Each year, out of 23,000 applicants and 2,100 admits, about 200 to 300 students get in because "they are among the most exciting potential scholars of the coming generation." The second category consists of "people who do something extraordinarily well," 200 to 300 excelling in, say, dance, drama, or athletics, whose achievements "are almost surrogates for energy, drive, and commitment." The third way to get into Harvard is the most common: students who achieve "plain old accomplishments on a day-to-day basis. It's not about gimmicks but about substance."

Swarthmore dean of admissions Jim Bock calls this idea "the Whys versus the Whats," because colleges are much less concerned with what students do than why they do it. "We're not wowed by the event but what it meant to you, what you learned about yourself," he said. "Some are what we call 'pointy': They excel in one thing; they're a scientist, poet, or activist. But your pointiness may not be what we need in a given year, so you shouldn't do something just to make a school happy. When someone asks, 'Are you looking for well-rounded students or well-rounded classes,' my answer is both. Institutions have needs, too. Students can't control what the needs of the school are, and they change over time. These kids are on a treadmill, spinning their wheels, but they're not asking why—'why am I taking every AP class, joining every club'—and then [they're] wondering why people aren't getting in. We can see through that on some level."

Other admissions officers echoed the refrain: A student should pick a couple of activities she is passionate about, rather than spreading herself thin. As Grinnell dean of admissions Jim Sumner put it, "Think of doing one or two things outside the classroom well, but don't run yourself ragged trying to do a dozen things, because that's not going to do you any good in the college admissions process. It's depth, not breadth."

At the 2004 NACAC annual conference in Milwaukee, I sat in on a session titled "College Admissions: Urban Myths Exposed." One myth NACAC's panelists hoped to debunk was that the SAT is the major factor in admissions decisions at highly selective colleges. Panelist Michael Keaton, Haverford's associate director of admissions, blamed the SAT myth on the media. "Great SAT scores aren't going to guarantee a student admission, and in many cases, scores that aren't the most competitive will not bar a student from getting into the most selective colleges and universities," he said. "While the SAT is important, often representatives in the media elevate the status to where it probably shouldn't be."

In response to the frenzy over those selective colleges, some schools have changed their emphasis. During recruiting trips, Harvard tells students there are hundreds of excellent college choices, and while Harvard might be one of them, another school might be a better match. Grinnell admissions interviewers are trained to spend about a third of the hour-long interview calming down the student and his family. Swarthmore is close to adding an application question asking whether students have had test preparation and similar help. In 2003 MIT revised its application to decrease the number of spaces for students to describe extracurricular activities, and asked counselors to evaluate applicants' humor, integrity, and "warmth of personality."

In 2005 Bowdoin adopted a question from the MIT application that asked applicants what they do for fun. "I thought it sent the right message. It said to kids back up a little bit; right now you're sort of engaged in this orgy of credentialing. What other things make you happy?" said James Miller, who "stole" MIT's question as Bowdoin's dean of admissions before he left for Brown. "A lot of the joy for students has been taken out of the admissions process. I'd never claim it's easy, but to sound hokey, it can be sort of a journey of new places and new people. Or it can be a death march. The truth is, you can end up in the same place."

Stanford even changed the way it reviewed transcripts. Matt Lawrence told me a joke that was popular around his office when he began working at Stanford. A student asks, "Should I take regular English and get an A, or AP English and get a B?" The admissions officer responds, "Take the AP class and get an A." (Admissions humor. Hilarious.) Matt said that while previously officers wanted to see students taking any AP and honors classes they could, now they wanted to see a "reasonably demanding" curriculum that fit in with students' interests.

Other admissions officers agree. "People assume that ten APs are better than eight. That is absolutely not true, but I see kids taking masochistic curriculums," said Vanderbilt dean of admissions Bill Shain. "Any admissions process that rewards that kind of planning is damaging to kids. It makes sense to challenge yourself—within the limits of good health."

When I pressed Matt Lawrence on what would make an applicant stand out in the Stanford pool, he said the catchphrase was "intellectual vitality," which involves "students' passion, curiosity, excitement, and engagement with the world of ideas. Those are things that make Stanford unique, and that we're specifically trying to find in those applications. It translates into a process that needs to be thorough and thoughtful. We want a really holistic view of that folder. What we're often looking for is the potential for them to be doing amazing things here at Stanford. It's the idea of context, family background, what it is about this student's individual perceptions and beliefs that will make them stand out in our pool."

Students don't necessarily have to agonize about standing out in their high school's pool. Several admissions directors told me it's a myth that applicants compete directly against their classmates. "If there are that many we really want, then we'll take them," James Miller said.

Matt agreed. "We're not looking at them against each other. That perception is out there right now. It's something we're really struggling with."

I asked him what he looked for from Whitman students. "In a school like Whitman, we look at the usual things in a large public school, but added to that, there's the dynamic feature of living in the D.C. area, which really adds something to these students' worldviews: a sense of service, commitment to the larger world, students who want to work internationally, ability to travel, to have internships at places like the National Institutes of Health, the ability to apply things they learn in class to the real world," he said. "You see so many students who you know can do the work here. The distinction we often make between students who are competitive is the idea of the intellectual vitality."

Near the end of our first conversation, I told Matt what Vera von Helsinger had said—that to get into Stanford, Julie "would have to have lived in Mongolia for two years or have been in a civil war." He laughed. "Students feel there's nothing they've done on their own that would make them stand out. That's wrong. It's that idea of packaging and coaching, students trying so hard to make themselves stand out— we're not able to see how they really are. There are no life experiences that would get you into Stanford. It's not what you've done; it's how you've experienced whatever has happened to you."

SAM, SENIOR | PERCEIVED AS: THE TEACHER'S PET

On the way to his mailbox on December 15, Sam had a feeling that the Stanford letter had arrived. Shaking with nervousness, he pulled out the mail and immediately saw an envelope from Stanford. The envelope was small. *Oh, no,* Sam thought. *I got deferred.* He placed the rest of the mail on the ground and ripped open the Stanford letter. He skimmed it: . . . *unable to grant you admission* . . . He slumped over, numb. A rejection. Stanford had outright denied him admission without even letting him compete with the regular admission pool. Sam was devastated. *Stanford completely rejected all the hard work I've done,* he thought. *They're saying I'm not good enough. Did they even read my application?*

That evening Sam put up an IM away message: ":'(Every year admissions people make mistakes. I just happened to be one of them. Only nice messages please . . ." He spent the night moping around the house, watching television, and ruminating over his future. *Why wasn't I deferred?* he thought. *What will this mean when all the other schools look at my applications?*

When Sam returned to his computer before bed, he found dozens of IM messages from friends across the country. "tough luck man, they made an egregious error," wrote one friend.

A message from C.J. read, "oh sam youre brilliant. ill kick the shit out of those bitches and dont worry youll be happy no matter where you end up going. sluts."

There was one from Audrey: "we all love you and know how much you will accomplish. Don't worry about it too much, you know you are capable of getting into the hardest universities across the nation. your scores prove it, your accomplishments prove it, and the school knows it. whatever college you go to will be the better for it, and you will get the best education ever simply because you are studious and care about learning—which is a rare gift."

Even Sam's neighbor had chimed in: "i baked you some cookies?"

From Debate Girl: "Oh Sam . . . I'm so sorry!! Were u deferred or rejected? they arent worth having you in their class. You can do so much better . . . like [she named her university]."

Julie wrote, simply, "but hey—you have more guts than i do."

Sam stared at the computer screen for a long time, smiling through misty eyes. Then he took down his away message and put up a new one: "Having friends like you guys EASILY beats getting into a stupid college. There is no question about what I would want more :-)!!"

JULIE, SENIOR | PERCEIVED AS: THE SUPERSTAR

Once Julie had gotten into college, she wasn't sure what to do with herself. She felt antsy, as if there were things she was supposed to be doing but had forgotten what they were. That feeling diminished somewhat when she visited yet another doctor. The doctor looked over the test results, said in a matter-of-fact tone, "You have a heightened level of testosterone," and prescribed birth control pills. Julie was too upset to listen attentively as the doctor explained how her hormone levels might have led to the thinning hair.

Testosterone. Julie was embarrassed, even though her mother assured her that one in ten women had that hormone imbalance. Once she started taking the pill, however, Julie began to feel like she had a sense of direction. Now that she didn't have to worry about school, she could take control of her life. She resolved to focus on reevaluating everything so she could figure out how to make herself happy. For starters, she went on a mission to learn to be more in tune with herself. First stop: facial.

Afterward, Julie went to indoor track practice, her face puffy. She warmed up with the team and headed to "The Hill," a 300-meter mound behind Whitman. The team would have to sprint up and jog down twelve hills without stopping. Julie used to love to run hills because they challenged her, and she would be the first one to finish every time. But today, on three hills in a row, two small freshman girls beat her to the top. She wasn't fatigued; she just . . . didn't care.

After the third hill, Julie gave up. She found her coach. "I am so burned out," she said, breathing heavily. "I'm trying so hard to stick with it. I don't know what's wrong with me. I want to get a good time so I can run at Dartmouth, but right now I don't even know if I want to run." Her voice cracked.

The coach put a hand on her shoulder and smiled understandingly. He told her to do whatever she needed to regain her desire to race. She could take time off, he told her—the entire season, even—or come to only a few practices a week, or bike while the others were doing track workouts. Julie left practice feeling as though her coach truly cared about her well-being.

She was still restless, however. Getting into college had given Julie some security concerning her near future, but, contrary to her expectations, it hadn't provided her with any certainty about who she was behind the numbers on her application. If anything, the process had muffled her identity. The next day Julie wrote the following in her journal:

"So you got into college! You must be so relieved," a junior says to me. "Yeah!" I exclaim with a big smile. It's true—I can get a B without fear that the world will end and I can relax. But for me, it's harder to relax than be in productive-work mode.

For as long as I can remember, I have had two after-school activities every day followed by a long night of homework. Occasionally I would take breaks to eat dinner or call a friend, but for the most part I was plugging away every day. During this time I had tons of problems—with friends, with acne, with depression—but mostly I just pushed these issues aside because I was too busy. Just like my room, I may look organized and put together on the surface, but under my bed and in my closet where I hide junk, my life is a mess.

It's weird to put time and effort into things that make me happy. I have never been one to do activities because "they look good on my college application" because I genuinely like to be busy and have a lot going on in my life. But now that college applications are a thing of the past, I need to focus on my needs for the first time in my life. Yesterday I got my first facial. "How long have you had acne?" the beautician asked me. "Um . . . since I was about 12," I responded. The beautician went on to censure me about how I should have gotten a facial a long time ago because some of the blackheads have been in my face for a long time. Lovely.

I am an athlete—a triathlete. I love to be part of the team, but my head isn't in it right now. My body feels great, but I'm a mental disaster. I lost my competitiveness. I think I lost it because I've always been so competitive in school—with my grades and, unfortunately, my peers—but now that I'm into my Ivy League college I no longer have to view my classmates as obstacles to run over so that I can get to a good place. I'm going to a good place. But without being an athlete I don't know who I am. I don't know what I like to do. I feel so lost.

I have had some problems, like blackheads, for so long. Now I am giving my life a facial to cleanse out all the blotches that have festered for so long. At first everything will be inflamed and puffy, but just as the beautician reassured me, "It will calm down and in the long term you will be so much better off."

AP FRANK, COLLEGE FRESHMAN | PERCEIVED AS: THE WORKHORSE

AP Frank worked steadily throughout December, even skipping club Frisbee practice, but his bigger projects still loomed. He wasn't procrastinating, exactly. He wasn't happy with the two research papers he had written, so he was rewriting them from scratch. Now it was the early hours of the morning, and he was stuck with two papers due that afternoon. He was already operating on only two hours of sleep, having spent every midnight since Monday chugging Red Bulls to stay up for as many hours as possible.

AP Frank wasn't dead set on getting As, even though a friend had told him recently that the statistic about no Harvard students attaining 4.0s in the last twenty years was inaccurate; his friend said that four students in the last five years had managed that achievement. AP Frank knew his mother couldn't watch over his shoulder from Bethesda. But he felt he couldn't turn in an essay that didn't represent the best he could do. He needed to improve it until *he* was satisfied. Whether a professor deemed his best effort worthy of an A was out of his control.

As he had all week, AP Frank, hepped up on Red Bull, worked at his desk with Andrew studying on the bed, as he usually did, because Mike, Andrew's roommate, played loud music and was hysterically disruptive. AP Frank needed Andrew's calming presence because he would be pulling his first all-nighter. They had been working diligently for four hours straight when, at about two in the morning, there was a knock at the door.

Andrew looked up and said, "It's Mike. Don't get it. He'll ruin us."

Apparently, Mike could hear from behind the door. He trilled in falsetto, "Housekeeping? Anybody home? Housekeeping here!"

AP Frank laughed and opened the door. For the next hour or so, the three lounged around, chatting. Then Mike picked up AP Frank's guitar and said to Andrew, "You're never downstairs anymore, man. I miss you," then proceeded to strum the few chords he knew. Before long, Mike had turned up the amplifier and was serenading Andrew at the top of his lungs with a song he composed on the spot: "Andrew . . . is a man I once knew / All I know is that he's had more lovin' than you / The reason, you see / Is 'cause of his giant wee-wee / Magnums! Magnums! Magnums!" (The latter part was the chorus.) Soon other Mass Hall students were crowded in AP Frank's room, crying with laughter as Mike earnestly strummed away.

Eventually, the dorm's proctor appeared in his pajamas. He looked at Mike. "You know what time it is?" he asked.

"Yeah, it's about 3:45," said Mike. "I'm sorry, I didn't mean to wake anybody up."

"Yeah, well, you did," the proctor said, and left.

The Mass Hall gang dispersed, and AP Frank and Andrew were again studying alone in the room. *I love these guys so much,* AP Frank thought. Before coming to Harvard, he had dreamily envisioned getting reprimanded for playing his guitar in the middle of the night in the quietest dorm, an image that, although he wasn't the busted guitar player, had just come to pass. He glanced at Andrew and, still giddy with the hilarity of the evening, reentered "the zone" and returned to work. He finished one paper by 6:30 that morning and the second by 1:15 P.M., forty-five minutes before class.

AUDREY, JUNIOR | PERCEIVED AS: THE PERFECTIONIST

Monday was the first of two flat nights for the *Black & White*'s annual extended holiday issue. Audrey was one draft away from finishing four articles for the print edition and one for the online edition of the paper, an unusually large number of articles for one student to write. She still had her heart set on being elected one of the top three editors in May, but the competition was fierce. As much as she loved the paper, merely being in the atmosphere of the office stressed her out.

Audrey was just as meticulous about her newspaper articles as she was about her schoolwork. First she typed out a list of the names and numbers of each source she planned to interview, the questions she wanted to ask them, and a short speech to use as an interview script. She could write the actual article within an hour, as long as it was about 600 words, but then she took at least another half hour to edit and rewrite it. For each article, she also wrote three or four different options for lead paragraphs and then, at the end of her editing process, eliminated them one by one until she had a lead that satisfied her.

After school, Audrey's mother took her home for five minutes to pick up the hard copies of her drafts and the disk with the electronic versions. Audrey went to her attic bedroom, where she had left the hard copies, but didn't see them. The new cleaning lady hadn't put all of Audrey's things in their usual places. On the days surrounding flat nights, Audrey's papers were typically strewn about the room. Thanks to the cleaning lady, the room was sparkling, but Audrey couldn't find anything. She looked everywhere, rifling through stacks of paper, digging into file cabinets, but the drafts were gone. Her mother was waiting for her downstairs. Audrey snatched her disk and ran out the door.

When she got to the *Black & White* office, Audrey stuck her disk in a computer, expecting to print out her articles for Sam to edit. An error message popped up. Her disk was corrupted. When Audrey remembered she had emailed herself an earlier draft of one of the articles a few days before, she pulled up the email and clicked on the attachment. The document was blank. And Audrey was off—maniacally running around the office, not sure what to do or whom to talk to, but snapping at students who got in her way. (As C.J. later described it, "Have you ever heated up a pot of water and put a cover on and it's to the brim and you're freaking out because you don't want to go near it because the water's coming out and it's heating everything? That was Audrey. I just wanted to fix it so my kitchen wasn't destroyed.")

Audrey nervously approached Sam. "I don't know what happened to my drafts. I don't know how to get my articles," she said.

"Don't worry, let's just go get them right now," he replied. "It's no problem."

Sam drove Audrey home to help her find the documents on her computer. Audrey ran upstairs to her study, praying that the articles were still saved. She opened the word processor, sighing with relief when she saw the titles of her articles. She opened the documents. They were empty. Her face pale, she turned to Sam. "Oh my God, what am I going to do? How am I going to pull this off? I'm so sorry!" Sam tried to calm her down.

Audrey spent the next day and a half rewriting her articles from scratch. By Wednesday afternoon, when the paper went to the printers, Audrey had completed all five articles. During that time, she didn't do any of her homework assignments or study for her tests. Bombing a test was worth it to her. The *Black & White* came first.

⁓

Twice in December, I checked in with Matt Lawrence, the Stanford admissions officer in charge of Whitman's territory. The first time I called, the early admissions decisions had been made, and the mailing was two days away. Matt was spending much of his time double-checking folders while other staff members reviewed the admissions letters to make sure students received the right ones. The number of applications had risen 6 percent since the year before, with 2000 more applicants than two years earlier. The number of admissions staffers had not changed in that period.

Matt was also spending time on the phone with high school counselors. During the last ten days, Matt had regularly called counselors and teachers to check on items as minimal as one sentence in a recommendation letter to ensure that he understood fully what the writer was trying to say about the student. Meanwhile, counselors were calling Matt to update him on students' recent accomplishments and to ask for an early read. Like other admissions officers, Matt indicated to the counselors how their students were faring so they would be prepared to deal with the aftermath. Usually, he spoke in admissions code, with either a "He looks very good in our pool right now" or a "[She's] not emerging at this point." For the most part, Matt said, "the counselors know what's going to happen anyway. Oftentimes the call goes the way they think it will." Matt believed the early-admissions season had been tough but rewarding. For him, the last couple of weeks had been a coffee-dazed blur. By two days before the mailing, he was relieved that the decisions had been made but knew better than to be relaxed. He knew what was about to come.

Applicants and their families aren't the only ones stressed out about the admissions process. Admissions officers told me about long hours, exhausting travel, emotional attachments to rejected candidates, and angry parents. A former Harvard admissions officer even had a gun pulled on her by the parent of a rejected student. A student wait-listed at Swarthmore mailed the admissions office a nasty poem about its "mistake," accompanied by a smiling photo of herself wearing the sweatshirt of an Ivy League school that accepted her. ("We put that up on the wall because we thought it was so obnoxious," Swarthmore dean of admissions Jim Bock said. "We felt we had made the right decision about her character. That's just mean.")

At the 2004 NACAC conference, keynote speaker Michael McPherson, former president of Macalester College, explained, "There's high anxiety on all sides in this admission race . . . Nobody really likes this. Everyone feels trapped. Admissions officers feel uneasy."

In a panel discussion on anxiety, a panelist said admissions officers were under such pressure that one dean had discovered an officer was hiding applications in his apartment and fudging how many he had read. She added that other stresses included "finding a balance between dealing with the immediate and long term . . . You overenroll? Bad news. You underenroll? . . . Bad news."

In the early-admissions season for the Class of 2009, Stanford accepted 860 students, slightly higher than the 803 it had accepted early the previous year. By April, the admissions officers expected to offer admission to 2,400 students. They did not report how many students had been deferred, but Matt said that the number was small.

Two days after Sam and Taylor received their letters, I called Matt again. Letters had gone out on Friday, and by Monday the office was flooded with calls, mostly from parents wanting to know why their child was denied or deferred. The admissions officers took shifts with calls throughout the week. In less than five days, Matt fielded about sixty calls, some from repeat callers, many who spoke through tears. "There are always people who have a hard time hearing no. To have to explain to a parent that your son or daughter is amazing and could do extremely well at Stanford, and will do wonderfully at whichever school they attend but just didn't make it in our pool . . . it doesn't give them the closure they want," Matt said.

I was reminded of something Brown dean of admissions James Miller told me during an interview. "We make choices, and we have very few spaces," he said. "But for the kids, it's very personal. It's the first time in their lives they've ever really said to someone, 'Here I am, what do you think?' The frustrating thing is you want to say to these kids, and it's true, 'There's nothing wrong with you.'"

Chapter 9

Winter Break

FAMILY MATTERS

AP Frank, college freshman | perceived as: The Workhorse

———————————————————————————————————————

A P Frank was both looking forward to and worried about returning home for winter break. His thoughts would be with his Harvard friends, especially Lydia, who often stopped by his room to tell him about guys she turned away because she had promised herself that she wouldn't have a relationship freshman year. She worked even harder than AP Frank did. He couldn't help wondering why she told him about other guys, though he was positive she didn't know about his burgeoning feelings for her (unlike about a third of his dorm). Instead of telling Lydia, he poured his heart out to Kristen. Cheerful but sarcastic, Kristen was an independent spirit and well versed in movie culture. AP Frank regularly visited her at midnight and talked until four A.M. about everything from his issues with his mother to his interest in girls.

AP Frank was afraid of what he would find at home, but he wanted to see his brother and his high school friends, eat good food, and sleep late. He also worried that once he got there, he would want to go back to college; and when he retuned to college, he would only want to go back home, thanks to classes and a dining hall where even the pasta tasted funny. Which place was "home"?

The ride from the airport included another debriefing session with AP Frank's father. It was almost certain, his father said, that he would leave Mrs. AP Frank over the summer. AP Frank felt detached. It seemed that he always came home after a blowup, or left just before one.

This made it easy to pretend these things weren't happening to him. A divorce would make life better for his father, he thought, but he pitied his mother. His father's main concern was Richard. He wanted to help his son get through high school and into college so he could get out of the house.

At home, AP Frank learned that two of the social workers assigned to his family had asked Richard what he wanted for Christmas. "Nothing," Richard told them.

"We're not leaving until you tell us what you want."

Richard blurted out the first exorbitant thing that came to mind, thinking that if the item was expensive, they wouldn't bother getting it for him: "a good-quality bass guitar." AP Frank knew about this because he was awakened one morning at eight by his mother arguing into the phone, telling the social worker that his brother didn't need their presents, that they should use taxpayer money for kids who needed help. A bass would have been nice for his brother, AP Frank thought. They didn't really celebrate Christmas this year.

The social worker wasn't Mrs. AP Frank's only target. AP Frank hadn't told his mother that he was increasingly interested in majoring in environmental science and public policy. He could put his science-heavy background to good use without having to spend hours memorizing minutiae, as he would for biology. But his mother picked up on his reluctance to confirm his NIH internship for the summer. She repeatedly ordered him to read a *Washington Post* article about a famous lawyer, hoping it would inspire him to go into law. AP Frank laughed, refusing to read the article.

His mother glowered at him. "You waste Harvard education if you don't go into law or medicine," she yelled. "And AP Frank, so legendary, why have so-so life, so-so job, die so-so? Not good story!"

෴

When Julie jokingly called her non-intrusive mother a "hovercraft" for standing near her while she instant-messaged, she didn't know what AP Frank was going through, or that she had independently hit on a phenomenon that leaves teachers and college officials flummoxed and child development experts dismayed. In recent years, the term "helicopter parents" was coined to refer to a new breed of parents who hover over their children and swoop in to solve or prevent their problems.

Not all helicopter parents watch over their children's shoulders while they do their homework, as Mrs. AP Frank did. Then again, many parents go even further than Mrs. AP Frank, by doing the homework themselves. An Iowa high school counselor fielded a phone call from a parent complaining about a C her child received on an essay. As the parent argued every point on the paper, the counselor realized why she was protesting so vehemently: The parent had written it. In 2005 a Maryland mother—like Japanese *kyoiku* mamas—sat in her ten-year-old son's math class for two hours each week so she could help him with the work at home.

Today's helicopter parents do more than merely hover. They are obsessed with their children's statistical achievement and with doing all they can to make sure their children end up at the top. A study of academically talented sixth-graders revealed that 73 percent of their parents said it was "very important" for their child to attend a top-level college and 81 percent said it was "very important" for their children to be highly successful in their careers. A Detroit tutor told me that parents asked him to begin tutoring their son for the MCAT, the Medical College Admission Test that college upperclassmen take to get into medical school. The boy was ten.

In what has been called "parenting as product development," parents often strategize even more than the students. Principals say that parents of freshmen call high schools to ask, "How can my kid get to number one?" Some parents hold their children back from kindergarten or first grade so they will be smarter in class or stronger than their peers by the time they play high school sports. Many parents push for their children to be labeled "gifted" when they're not. Others visit psychologist after psychologist until they find one who is willing to diagnose their perfectly healthy child with a disability that will allow him to take the SAT and other standardized tests untimed. For example, a suburban teacher was surprised to find that one of his brightest, most conscientious students, "the type who'd get to school to turn in a paper on time, even if she were dying of stomach flu," was conveniently diagnosed with "difficulty with Gestalt thinking," defined as the inability to "see the big picture," which allowed her to take all of her tests untimed.

College admissions officers and guidance counselors contend that surging numbers of parents are overinvolved in the application process—editing applications, writing or rewriting essays, calling admissions offices, and threatening lawsuits against schools that deny their children admission. Some colleges have seen parents fax daily updates on their child's life, request that they be allowed to double-check their child's spelling on an already submitted application, try to attend their child's admissions interview, or make excuses for their child's grades. "I see this type of behavior at least twice a week," MIT dean of admissions Marilee Jones has said. (Schools warn that applications and essays bearing signs of heavy parental help can hurt a student's chances at acceptance.)

Increasing numbers of parents are taking over their children's college course registrations, calling to complain about professors, administrators, and housing assignments, and bombarding officials with questions during freshman orientation. College officials are also reporting rising numbers of students who have been so sheltered that, as young adults, they lack interpersonal skills, common sense, initiative, and problem-solving abilities. As a result, some schools are holding separate orientations for parents and creating new departments to deal with parents' phone calls and emails. Northeastern University holds a seminar for parents called "A Time of Holding On and a Time of Letting Go."

Once they have delivered their children to college, some helicopter parents continue to wield control. Because students have had parental help with their homework since elementary school, it's not unusual for them to email college papers and problem sets home for corrections. (Meanwhile, tutors whom parents hired to help their children in high school have said that the students, in college, still tried to send them homework for editing.) Multiple students told a Syracuse professor that they were late for class because their mothers didn't call to wake them up in time. At several schools, in the middle of classes or adviser meetings students called home to complain about a low grade, then gave their cell phones to the professor or adviser so the parent could intervene. As University of Georgia professor and former administrator Richard Mullendore put it, the cell phone has become "the world's longest umbilical cord."

The process of child "development" has become more about the parent than the child. Several experts have argued that parenting has become this country's most competitive sport. "Our children are experiencing a childhood that is no longer just a preparation for adulthood but a full performance in its own right," child psychiatrist Alvin Rosenfeld has said. "We parents act as the producers; our children are pushed onto the stage and scored on every single thing they do. American parents have been persuaded that average is no longer good enough."

Why would parents suffocate their children for an A, risk their children's health for athletic recognition, and sacrifice their own reputations for their children's entrée to an elite college? Psychologists cite several factors they believe contribute to the current trend of parental overinvolvement. Because it costs much more to raise a child than it used to, some parents might view a successful child as a return on their investment. Similarly, when parents pay thousands of dollars a year to a private school or college, they might expect to have as much input as possible on the education they're funding. Today's parents are often successful and expect nothing less for, and from, their children. A successful child reflects a successful parent, the thinking goes, and parents become anxious that if they ignore any opportunity as soon as it presents itself, their children will lag behind.

Parents might also feel that in this era of educational budget cuts and rising safety concerns, their role has become more vital. Many schools have increased class sizes and eliminated subjects because of budgetary constraints; when schools and teachers have less time for students, parents may believe they need to step in to help fill the void. Parents who look ahead worry that in the increasingly competitive economic landscape, their children will need extra help to land stable and rewarding jobs.

Add in the guilt factor, and parents' motives become even clearer. Approximately 70 percent of married mothers and more than 60 percent of mothers with children younger than age six work outside the home, and working hours generally are on the rise. "Many of these kids are with babysitters, so they program them to the gills to make sure the child is occupied doing something using their brains," All Souls School director Jean Mandelbaum said about preschoolers. (She added that with many nannies' lack of English skills, some parents want to ensure their children are occupied with instructive classes.)

With less in-person quality time to devote to children, parents can overcompensate by jumping headlong into their children's lives whenever possible. "We baby-boomer parents are not very good at just sitting back and watching *anything* that has to do with our kids," wrote a parent who scripted his son's phone calls to college admissions offices and gave him "briefing papers" before interviews. "We are a generation of type-A personalities. We are a generation of control freaks." Some parents have taken up to a year off from their jobs to manage their child's college application process. Many are thoroughly convinced that the more they are involved in their children's lives, the more they will be able to control the adults their offspring will turn out to be.

But that strategy is likely to backfire. As psychologist Robert Evans told the San Francisco Bay area's *Diablo* magazine, "Parents are just much more hurried and harried than in previous generations. They have less time to spend with their kids, and even when they do have time, they tend to be more highly strung. The time that many parents spend with their kids is focused on their accelerating skills or being more productive. But kids need more than that—they need parents to play with them, read with them, or, as they get older, listen to them, and just plain be with them. Without that kind of nurturance, kids basically make do with a starvation diet, in terms of emotional contact. Eventually, their resilience in the face of stress diminishes." Children who are too stressed out over the pursuit of success won't be able to pursue it to the best of their ability.

More important, while parents' self-esteem might soar when their children succeed, the children can lose self-esteem and, worse, plunge into depression. They can lose faith in their own abilities when their parents intervene or cheat on their behalf—calling a teacher to argue a grade, for example, or weaseling extra time for SATs and other standardized tests when the child isn't learning-disabled. A Colorado junior told me that her mother persuaded her geometry teacher to change her B to an A, and "though I truly earned Bs for the rest of the year, As were given on the report card. That made me so mad!" Many students in these circumstances come to believe that their success is due to their parents' intrusion, and they lose the joy they might have experienced from achieving on their own.

Petrified of failure (a B), students can stop taking risks and thinking independently because they're driven only to get good grades and high test scores. In the aforementioned study of overachieving sixth-graders, 39 percent said they feel "a lot of pressure from their parents to always be an exceptional student." The researchers speculated that the number would be even higher had 99 percent of the eleven-year-olds not reported that they were confident in their academic abilities and probably believed at the time that they could live up to their parents' high expectations.

The same study reported that children of parents who defined academic success by performance goals (such as high grades and top college admission), rather than as learning for understanding, "were significantly more likely to exhibit dysfunctional perfectionism than children of learning goal parents, reporting a combination of high concern about mistakes, doubts about actions, parental expectations, and parental criticism." Many students told me that the expensive ways their parents tried to boost their résumés, such as tutors, trainers, private coaches, and standardized-test-prep classes, caused them more stress because they didn't want to waste their parents' investments. Essentially, helicopter parents are setting their children up to believe that if they don't beat their peers to the top—top grades, top athletic accolades, top schools—they are failures. Talk about performance anxiety.

In a controversial study, Harvard psychologist Jerome Kagan proved that parents who try to protect their children from stressful experiences can create anxious children. Other early-childhood experts report that children who sense parents' tension about certain achievement-oriented goals grow nervous and inhibited. "Children need to be gently encouraged to take risks and learn that nothing terrible happens," said Michael Liebowitz, head of the Anxiety Disorders Clinic at New York State Psychiatric Institute. "They need gradual exposure to find that the world is not dangerous. Having overprotective parents is a risk factor for anxiety disorders because children do not have opportunities to master their innate shyness and become more comfortable in the world."

A Massachusetts junior told me the most pressure she felt in her life came from her mother, who threatened to punish her if she didn't get excellent grades. "No matter how hard I try, it seems that she isn't happy; she is constantly expecting more. When it comes to sports, my mom wants me to be the star and gets almost upset with me if I make a mistake." As a result, "I have a constant feeling of stress. I feel like I will be seen as a disappointment by everyone if I mess something up. I feel that I'm dumb if I don't make the honor roll and that I'm a bad athlete if I make a mistake during a game, and I get worried once something starts to go wrong. Very often the pressure causes me to fold. I get worked up knowing that it will be my fault if we lose, and I crack under the pressure. In softball I tend to fly out because I strive so hard to make contact. In soccer I let people by me. Sometimes I get flustered and fake an injury so I won't have to play."

Parents' efforts may or may not land a child at an Ivy, but if the price is a young adult who is a basket case, one wonders why they think it's worth the trade-off. "Parents themselves have created many of the stresses and anxieties children are suffering from, without giving them tools to manage them," Hara Estroff Marano wrote in *Psychology Today* in 2004. "However well-intentioned, parental hyperconcern and microscrunity have the net effect of making kids more fragile. That may be why the young are breaking down in record numbers." And cheating. Instead of learning how to develop into independent, self-aware adults, many children are being taught by their parents how to game the system. Some parents have sued schools for expelling their children for cheating, claiming that teachers were at fault for leaving out tests that were too easy for students to steal.

Meanwhile, children are desperately missing their parents as parents rather than as micromanagers. In 2000 a national YMCA survey reported that 21 percent of teenagers said two aspects of their lives tied for being their top concern: educational worries and a lack of time with their parents. In the last twenty years, children's structured sports time has doubled, while family discussions, dinners, and vacations have dropped precipitously, all of which affect more than the children.

As they are consumed by their high expectations for their children's lives, parents overlook the damage they are inflicting on themselves. Parenting becomes less fun, less joyous, when adults with toddlers already dread the college admissions process. In 2005 *The Wall Street Journal* ticked off "warning signs" of helicopter parents: They "fall into a lasting funk" when their children's achievements don't meet their standards, and lose enjoyment in other aspects of life; they are preoccupied with details of children's activities, practices, schedules, and performances; and they start sentences about their children with the pronoun "we," as in "We're applying to Harvard." These parents are increasingly commonplace.

Today's parents can become more overinvested in their child's ups and downs than the child is. Duke director of admissions Christoph Guttentag has said, "The problem, I'm sure, is related to larger societal issues—how we define success, what parents want for their children, the idea that parents can help their children create their success rather than letting the children find it for themselves . . . The issues of prestige and ranking tend to be more a concern of parents than of students." In 2003 MIT dean of admissions Marilee Jones shared this story in a *USA Today* op-ed: "Last April, a few weeks after sending the acceptance/rejection letters for the Class of 2006, I received a reply from a father of one of our applicants. It was curt and written on his corporate letterhead: 'You rejected my son. He's devastated. See you in court.' . . . The very next day, I received another letter, but this time from the man's son. It read: 'Thank you for not admitting me to MIT. This is the best day of my life.' "

Parents can lose their own lives in their children's. As a child once said to psychologist David Anderegg, "I wish my parents had some hobby other than me." A 2005 study found that a fifth of parents base their own self-worth on their children's successes and failures. Those parents, the researchers found, had worse mental health than parents who weren't overinvolved in their children's lives. They were "much more likely to feel symptoms of anxiety and depression, less likely to be satisfied with life." Another finding in this study was even more striking: Even when their children succeeded, the parents' well-being didn't improve, because they were already worried about their child's next attempt at success. "All parents feel bad when their children don't do well," the study's coauthor said, but only overinvolved parents "feel bad about themselves."

If for no other reason, that should help to persuade parents to back off. In 2001 a *City Journal* reporter described a mother who spent practically a year in tears. She had difficulty speaking in complete sentences, lost fifteen pounds, and was in such bad shape that her behavior caused a friend to worry that she was suicidal. The woman called it "the darkest year of my life." Why? Her son was rejected from a private kindergarten. The distortion of priorities and values in many of today's overachieving families is staggering. Happiness and health—of children and parents— have taken a backseat to success and recognition. In 2005 the parents of a senior at Shenendehowa High School in upstate New York protested that their daughter had been named salutatorian rather than valedictorian of her 640-student class despite her 99.33 GPA and six-AP course load. The parents wrote to school district officials, "There are no words that can express our pain." If a number two class rank represents the worst pain that family experiences, one word comes to mind: lucky.

SAM, SENIOR | PERCEIVED AS: THE TEACHER'S PET

The night before New Year's Eve, Sam went out with friends. They were chatting about colleges on the way home when one said, "Sam, I really could see you at Middlebury. All your nuances fit."

"How do you know?" he asked.

"I don't know. But I know this one girl that goes there, and you're sort of like her. It's just a school that seems to fit."

"Okay, when I make my decision because you say so, maybe I'll go," he said, keeping his sarcasm light.

When his friends drove off, Sam was pulling the mail out of the mailbox in front of his house when it hit him. Several dozen people had said he would "fit" at Middlebury. Why wasn't he applying early decision 2 to Middlebury? The only reason he was "staying in the game" of regular admissions, as he put it, was Harvard. Just the day before, he had aced his Harvard interview. It was scheduled to last thirty minutes, but the interviewer seemed so interested in what Sam had to say that their discussion lasted eighty minutes. "It won't be hard to write a good letter," the interviewer told him. "I'm glad you chose Harvard. It's a really good school." But even if Sam's Harvard connections came through, was it right for him? Over lunch that week, AP Frank told Sam that Harvard students were exceptionally focused and seemed to care less about meeting people than studying. Sam wondered if Harvard would overwhelm him. The only reason he was focused on Harvard, he realized, was because of its prestige.

Sam wanted a friendly, non-homogenous student population, and at Middlebury, he could meet plenty of international students. He didn't know any Middlebury students who didn't like the school. The academics at Middlebury were just as good as at Harvard, he told himself, the classes smaller, and the professors, well, as much as he hated to look at rankings, Middlebury was ranked number one for professors bringing material to life. Maybe it was more important to go to a prestigious graduate school than an undergraduate school. Maybe it was more important to have fun as an undergrad than work too hard. Was the name of a college really that important in the end? As he had learned, a student could dream about a certain college for seventeen years only to find out that he didn't have a chance, coming from Whitman. *Okay, this makes sense now,* Sam thought as he went inside his house. *Now I know what I'm going to do.*

Before Sam left his house on New Year's Day, he had a ninety-minute conversation with his father about his choice to apply to Middlebury. His father told him he agreed with the decision, despite his belief that Sam had a 60 percent shot at getting into Harvard because of the number of people pushing for him. "I think you've made the right decision. I just don't want you applying to Middlebury for the reason that you want to get in somewhere early and that you're relapsing after the Stanford rejection, afraid of a Harvard rejection."

"I think I'm applying to Middlebury for the right reasons," Sam said.

"I hope so."

In the afternoon Sam and Julie took her dog for a walk on the Billy Goat Trail, a popular hiking path along the Potomac River. Sam told her about his decision to aim for Middlebury. "But I sort of still want to hold out for Harvard," he admitted.

"You're better than that," Julie said. "Don't hold out for Harvard just because you want to be a Harvard student."

"No, that's not the reason," Sam fudged. But at that moment, when Sam knew full well that Julie was right, he finally was able to let the Ivies go.

JULIE, SENIOR | PERCEIVED AS: THE SUPERSTAR

For New Year's Eve, Julie planned to go to dinner with two girlfriends, pick up Derek and his friend, go together to a party, and then host a sleepover at her house. At dinner, when the girls were alone, one of them asked Julie if she liked Derek.

"Well, I mean, I have for three years," Julie said.

"Oh," one nodded. "It's one of those forever crushes."

"You and Derek are cute together," said the other. "You should totally date him."

Julie wished she could talk to Sam about Derek, but Sam had begun acting strangely toward her, insisting on paying for dinners and giving her thoughtful presents. For reasons she couldn't articulate, she intuitively thought it might be better for their friendship if she created some space.

The next day Julie learned from a friend that Derek had broken up with his girlfriend. That same night Derek IMed Julie to tell her that, now that he was newly freed, he was interested in hanging out with another girl but he didn't know who was available.

Derek: **no seriously. Who is there?**

Julie's eyes widened. Was he really clueless, or was he giving her an opening? Should she be blunt and tell him, "Me, me!" or should she be as coy as he usually was? He was waiting; she had to think of something quickly.

Julie: **sometimes the girl is right under your nose!**

They went back and forth for about an hour with vague non-statements before Julie decided she couldn't stand the games. Perhaps, she thought, she should say something she might regret.

Julie: **have you liked any other girls while you were going out with [your ex]?**
Derek: **well i mean i couldn't really let myself think like that but a little bit yeah . . . Taylor for a bit. i don't really remember who else**

Oh. Of all the girls at school, Julie hadn't expected him to name her friend. She tried to be encouraging. "ok well you could go for her?"

Derek: **nah, she's out of my league anyway**

Another forty minutes of conversation passed before Julie typed, "I think we're looking for the same thing."

Julie's mother popped her head into the room. "I hope this is a life-changing conversation, because you should really go to bed," she said to Julie. *Well, it* could *be,* Julie thought.

Derek: i know what you are thinking and i have too of course but i don't think it is a good idea

It took him an hour and a half to get there? "That's obvious," she typed, then had second thoughts.

Derek: i don't know, i just don't think it is smart. you are too much my friend. So what do you think.

Julie: i like you and would be willing to "try" but maybe im not seeing the whole picture right now?

She wasn't sure how the conversation had shifted from cryptic to honest, but now it felt much more productive.

Derek: what if we try and fail? would it ever be the same? we have such a good thing going. it seems stupid to risk it

Julie: ok now riddle me this: do you think we will be able to go on being JUST real good friends after this? and forget that this convo ever happened?

Derek: haha well i think so yeah. you have plenty of boys. i mean i always knew there was something . . . maybe i was wrong . . .

Julie: this is up to you . . . you have more baggage than me

Derek: but you also have to think: i just got out of a long relationship. right now i mean i am looking for some rebound thing

Julie: and i dont want to be that girl

Derek: i wouldn't let you be that girl

Julie: is that it? we just are destined to be friends?

Derek: i don't know. i think for the time being yes

Julie: ok deal

Julie liked Derek, but she didn't want to be his rebound girl. At about midnight, the conversation ended, three hours after it had begun.

RYLAND, JUNIOR | PERCEIVED AS: THE SLACKER

Ryland had intended to spend winter break catching up on schoolwork from classes he had slept through in December. Some of his teachers seemed to try to thwart his efforts by assigning extra homework, which called into question the point of a break. In addition to his constant weariness, Ryland had also fallen ill. He spent most of his vacation sleeping, except for Sundays, when he diligently prepared the usual meals for the homeless people in Washington who counted on him. His mother had relayed to him his doctor's orders to take it easy, sleep well, and eat well. Nevertheless, school started up again tomorrow, and she expected him to go, no matter how tired he was.

Ryland's mother was already riding him about getting to bed early so he could wake up in time for school, but he was so far behind in his classes that he didn't see how he would be able to catch up on both work and sleep. His energy was gone. Worse, semester final exams loomed only a couple of weeks away. Just thinking about the exams made him squirm. Ryland supposed it was no great mystery why he had such severe test anxiety. On certain kinds of tests, his mind would go blank because he was afraid of what would happen if he got a B or C. More specifically, he was afraid of upsetting his mother.

The pressure had erupted full force at the beginning of freshman year, when, suddenly, everything "counted." Ryland's mother started up with the college talk: He needed to keep up his grades, add more extracurricular activities to his schedule, and become more "involved." Ryland had tried to comply, studying hard and taking a photography class outside of school, but then the tone of the college talks changed. He wasn't doing enough, his mother told him. That was when she began a refrain she would repeat for years: "You're not going to do any better than Montgomery College"—the local community college—"and you'll end up being a waiter for the rest of your life." She also told him she didn't want to scrounge for the money to pay for a private college unless it was clearly worth the cost.

Because Ryland was only in ninth grade at the time, he didn't know anything about the college process. When his mother told him he wouldn't get accepted into a good college or be able to support himself, he believed her. As he explained to a friend, "I felt completely hopeless, like I had already ruined everything. I was like, what's the point? My life is basically over now." Unable to concentrate in school, Ryland started to skip class. He left his house for long walks in the middle of the night and would lie on the roof of a nearby community center to collect his thoughts. One night he spent a few hours sleeping on a bench at a local elementary school. Inside his house, Ryland locked himself in his room and cried.

Midway through freshman year, Ryland's Whitman guidance counselor suggested that he see a psychologist. That first doctor was cold and clinical, and Ryland couldn't bring himself to open up to her. It was abundantly clear to Ryland that he was depressed, but the psychologist insisted that he wasn't. Ryland wondered if she was convinced he was fine because when she asked him questions, he only shrugged and smiled the nervous smile that he couldn't help when someone made him feel uncomfortable.

It was important to Ryland to see a doctor he liked, so he could be treated properly, and also because he needed to get out of the house, away from the pressure, and, eventually, to college, where he finally expected to be stress-free. Ryland convinced his father to take him to another doctor, a psychiatrist this time, who quickly diagnosed him with clinical depression and ADD. Ryland's mother, who was fanatically anti-medicine, was skeptical but allowed Ryland to be put on Zoloft and Ritalin.

Within days, Ryland was feeling better. His crying bouts became less frequent, and he began to find school-related activities interesting again. By sophomore year, Ryland was back on track, with improved report cards and a few new extracurricular activities. He dyed his hair closer to its natural auburn color, rather than the burgundy, purple, and blue-black hues with which he had experimented. He even signed up for journalism class as a way to coax himself outside of his comfort zone. He hoped to be a writer, but the teacher pushed him into photography, which he had been doing on the side with what he called his "moody-broody friends," a group that wore black clothes, black nail polish, and metal concert shirts. He remained on the Ritalin until the summer before junior year, when he stopped taking it because his mother had convinced him he didn't have ADD and because he thought the drug changed how he acted in social settings.

With the beginning of junior year, however, came more activities, tougher classes, the new grading policy, and heightened pressures. When his mother told him he didn't have enough extracurriculars, he accepted more extensive responsibilities at the *Black & White* and joined more clubs, taking on leadership roles. His mother continued to tell him his efforts weren't good enough to get him into a worthwhile college. He tried to intensify his schedule, but the pressure had made him exhausted and, now, sick.

He couldn't complain to his parents, and he couldn't complain to his friends. Only when Ryland's ex-girlfriend went away for part of winter break did his former clique hang out with him. Once she came back, they stopped calling.

Worn out and unwell, behind in most of his classes, Ryland felt like he was falling into a deep black pit, where the farther he plummeted, the less likely he would be able to climb out.

Chapter 10

January 10–January 30

BREAKS

AP Frank, college freshman | perceived as: The Workhorse

After getting reaccustomed to being home, AP Frank was back at college and feeling discombobulated. In addition to the shift back to the college mind-set, it didn't help that Harvard students returned from winter break to Reading Period, unstructured days to finish final papers and prepare for the upcoming final exams. Punctuated with intramural dodgeball games, AP Frank's routine went something like this: Go downstairs to B31 to play video games; wander around and talk to people; write a few sentences of a paper; go out to grab a snack; come back to the room to eat the snack; notice that the trash needed to be taken out; take out the trash; then, because he was out anyway, he might as well do the laundry; write another few sentences; go downstairs to B31 . . .

A few nights after his return to school, AP Frank told Andrew he was thinking about dropping the Harvard Ultimate Frisbee club team. He believed he lacked speed and endurance, qualities necessary to be good at Ultimate. Shin splints had kept him out of practices and games in November, and December was too hectic academically. The decision weighed on AP Frank, who liked his teammates, enjoyed the exercise, and wanted to improve. The heaviness he felt lifted slightly when Andrew reassured him that quitting a team was no big deal. Andrew was probably going to quit a team himself; besides, he pointed out, two major extracurricular activities amounted to an enormous time commitment.

AP Frank slept on it. When he woke up the next morning, he felt wistful, like he already wasn't on the team anymore. He decided that Andrew was right. As much as he liked his teammates, he would quit Frisbee to focus on wushu. He sadly emailed the captain his regrets and removed himself from the Frisbee mailing list.

It was during this uneasy transition period that AP Frank experienced the least responsible moment in his otherwise illustrious academic career. He was casually chatting online with a classmate about the final expository writing paper, a colossal assignment on which AP Frank hadn't yet done much work.

"Do you think [the professor] will be mad at me if I run over the page limit by two sentences?" his friend asked.

"Nah you're fine," AP Frank responded. "How's the paper going?"

"Fine. I'm revising it."

"Oh man, what are you worrying about? You have a whole week!"

"A week?" The friend paused. "It's due tomorrow, Frank."

AP Frank felt light-headed. "You're kidding me, right?" he asked. She wasn't kidding. It was nine P.M., and the final paper for one of the most difficult courses AP Frank had ever taken was due at five P.M. the next day. He had twenty hours, minus class time—which included a French test—to write a good paper.

AP Frank froze. He hyperventilated for a few minutes, unable to think beyond the only words that coursed through his mind: "Ohh shit. Ohhh shit."

His friends mobilized. Kristen raced to CVS and bought him a pack of Rollos and three cans of Red Bull, the first of which AP Frank chugged at 1:30 A.M. Andrew came over to calm AP Frank by studying in his usual spot on the bed and forcing him to take breaks. AP Frank was able to relax until Andrew left at three A.M. to go to sleep. He blanked, momentarily paralyzed at the thought of the task ahead of him. At four in the morning, he choked down his second Red Bull of the night, his throat burning, his eyes watering. At seven, AP Frank realized he couldn't spell correctly, let alone form coherent sentences, so he got dressed, brushed his teeth, and fell into bed. As soon as he woke up, he sprinted straight to his French classroom for his test.

After the test, AP Frank downed another Red Bull and resumed writing. He felt physically ill not only from the stress but also because he was letting his dorm down. He was the only student he knew of in Mass Hall to have a shot at getting the elusive A in expository writing, having gotten a B, an A-minus, and an A on his papers. "You've got to do it for us!" his friends had said. Now that chance was gone. He would have to turn in the worst paper he had ever written. At 4:45, AP Frank submitted his paper with a self-deprecating cover letter about how terrible he thought the paper was. "In formulating my argument and proving my argument, I have utterly failed," he wrote. "I'm dissatisfied with this paper and I'm very sorry to turn in one that is not an improvement over the last one."

When he got back to his room, AP Frank had something to eat for the first time all day. A B on the paper would at least give him a chance at an A-minus in the course, but he didn't expect to score that high. He was at peace with that. He told a friend, "If I get lower than a B, I'll just take it in stride. I did my best. I screwed up. But in the grand scheme of things, T. S. Eliot got a B-plus, so I'm no better than that."

C.J., JUNIOR | PERCEIVED AS: THE FLIRT

In the most simplified landscape, C.J. had three major circles of friends: Audrey and the other students in her neighborhood, the cross-country and track teams, and a group of four girls led by a junior with whom C.J. had been close since elementary school. C.J. and Audrey were back to being best friends, but the group of four girls appeared to be pulling away from C.J. as their social activities had increasingly become dominated by drinking, smoking, and skipping school. So C.J. was especially excited when she got an invitation in the mail for a hot yoga party that Julie was hosting.

C.J. and Julie had smoothed things over in the fall, and C.J. was genuinely thrilled for Julie when she got into Dartmouth. But lately, the relationship had grown rocky again. Julie had skipped three weeks of the indoor track season because she wasn't sure whether she wanted to run. Meanwhile, the team had elected C.J. captain, which seemed to cause issues when Julie decided to return. One day C.J. entered the team room and asked her teammates when they thought the team should have a dress-up day in school. Julie responded, "Why should I care? It's not like I'm captain." Another day, the team was on a practice run and Julie sprinted away, far ahead of the group. When the team caught up to her at a stoplight, C.J. said in a way meant to be light-hearted, "Hey, where's the fire?"

"You don't have to follow me," Julie sniped.

"Look, it's not my fault you didn't join indoor until three weeks in! It's not my fault I'm captain!" C.J. snapped back. "I'm trying to include you, but there's nothing I can do. Why are you blaming me?" Later Julie apologized, explaining that she was finding it difficult to be a senior and not a captain. C.J. wondered why it would be so challenging to be Julie. Earlier in the month, in one of her first indoor track meets back, Julie had breezed through a two-mile race in 11:57, breaking the twelve-minute mark she needed to qualify to run at Dartmouth. It wasn't as if C.J. could ever replace Julie, whose party invitation convinced C.J. that she and Julie were back on good terms.

C.J. supposed her increasing distance from the group of four girls partially led her to get back in touch with Derek. Few Whitman students knew that she had ever spoken to him. Last year, when she was a sophomore, she had known who he was: the guy who got a 1600 without trying. The first time she talked to him, she was walking out of class and marched right up to him—she was even brasher then—and said, "You're Derek!" He gave her a strange look. "How do you know that?" he said. Ever suave and sophisticated, C.J. responded by immediately running away. She later heard from friends that, as a result, Derek thought she was weird. They chatted several times online that year before they lost touch.

Now C.J. found herself wanting another friend who could have smart conversations that didn't include color commentaries of the latest alcohol-and-drug-fueled escapades. One night she found an excuse to IM Derek, and they resumed talking online regularly. Eventually, they made plans to hang out in person and, over the next several days, started to get to know each other as friends.

It took no time at all for the random-hookup rumors to swirl.

RYLAND, JUNIOR | PERCEIVED AS: THE SLACKER

The Sunday before his physics final exam, Ryland and a few friends went to a guided meditation session at a Buddhist temple for a comparative religion assignment to observe a religious ritual other than their own. Ryland was surprised to see that the temple resembled a large house. A nun greeted them at the door and led them to a side room past the kitchen. The room was chilly and expansive, with red, green, blue, and purple fabric wall coverings. A monk wrapped in layers of fabric welcomed them and gestured toward ten people sitting on the floor in a circle. The monk talked about the importance of posture, then told the group to close their eyes as he guided them through some deep-breathing exercises. "Count slowly as you breathe in," he said, "and exhale to the same count."

Ryland inhaled—one, two, three, four—and slowly exhaled—five, six, seven eight. The monk led the group through three sets of deep breathing, then talked about how nice it was to forget about all of the distractions in the world around them and to clear their minds completely. Ryland tried to forget about his upcoming exams and the SAT he would have to take in the spring. That week, no sooner had his father bought him an SAT workbook than his parents began barging into Ryland's room to remind him to do the practice sections.

The monk continued the deep-breathing sets. Inhale: one, two, three, four. Exhale: five, six, seven, eight. The heater in the room clicked on, distracting Ryland from clearing his head. He opened his eyes at every noise, curious about the other students in the class. Ryland's mind wandered to that morning, when he was late leaving his house for the temple, which somehow had led to yet another argument with his mother about school. "You're not going to get into college," she had said slowly and deliberately.

Ryland had mentioned at the dinner table that week that he was interested in attending the prestigious school that both of his parents had attended. "You can't get in there," his father had said. When Ryland pointed out the benefit of a double legacy, his parents countered that they hadn't donated any money.

Inhale: one, two, three, four. Exhale: five, six, seven, eight. Ryland's heartbeat slowed. The heater clicked off, but he wasn't interested enough to open his eyes. His parents weren't here. There were no tests here. There was nothing he could do here for his extracurricular activities. Ryland felt relaxed and focused at the same time. When the session ended, he felt more at peace than he had since starting high school.

Half an hour before the physics final, Ryland's legs were shaking and he couldn't help fidgeting. He had finished his comparative religion exam early, breezing through it because the test was easy and the teacher was engaging enough for him to remember her lessons. Physics was different. He had met with a tutor—a Whitman senior—for a few sessions to prepare for the exam. The best advice the tutor could give him was to cheat by programming the physics formulas into his graphing calculator "like everyone else does." Ryland didn't see the point of programming formulas when he didn't know how to use them. He had asked the teacher for extra help preparing for the exam, but was refused.

Ryland turned in his religion exam and left the room. *I might as well try,* he thought. He sat at his assigned seat in the middle of the empty physics classroom. He sat up straight, closed his eyes, placed his hands palms up on the table in front of him, and did some deep breathing. Inhale: one, two, three, four. Exhale: five, six, seven, eight. As he tried to picture ocean tides gently lapping at the beach, Ryland's breathing grew louder, deeper. When a thought about physics tried to creep into his mind, he let the ocean carry it away. Inhale: one, two, three, four. Exhale: five, six, seven, eight. Ryland could feel his muscles loosen. His heartbeat slowed down considerably. By the time the exam began, Ryland was relatively relaxed.

Ryland sailed through the multiple-choice questions, able to forget for the moment that he was taking a final exam. He wrote a sentence for a short-answer question. And then he blanked. His old fears resurfaced. He tried to close his eyes and do a set of deep-breathing exercises, but it didn't work. His breathing was shallow, quick. *I'm not going to try to rack my brain for stuff I don't seem to remember,* he thought. *I'm not going to pass anyway.* He closed his test booklet and didn't bother to look at the rest of the exam.

PETE, JUNIOR | PERCEIVED AS: THE MEATHEAD

While other Whitman students spent the three-day break between semesters being productive, Pete had other plans. He got in touch with Yuri, the son of the woman who gave Pete his weekly lessons in Russian, which his family spoke at home. Pete and two other Russian students, Steve and Victor, went to Yuri's house to play video games in his basement. Pete and Yuri kept easily beating the other two, who were growing visibly irritated. Slightly before midnight, Steve, who had just gotten killed for about the dozenth time, yelled, "Fucking shit, I *shot* you!" and threw his controller across the room.

Unfortunately, the controller happened to hit Yuri's cat, which immediately went berserk. The boys stared at the cat as it maniacally tore around in circles, clawing at the furniture. "Dude," Pete said, "you need to castrate your cat."

"I *did,*" Yuri said. Steve carefully reached for the controller he had thrown. Immediately, the cat turned and stared at Steve, its eyes as wide as they could get. Then it emitted a loud screech, charged toward Steve, leaped onto his leg, and attacked it. The other three boys howled with laughter.

"Your fucking cat knifed me!" Steve yelled. He looked down at the hole in his pants and the blood dripping down his leg. The cat was motionless now, watching them from slitted eyes about fifteen feet away. The others were still cracking up.

"Shut up, it's not funny," said Steve. Suddenly, it dawned on him: "Hey, that cat has cat AIDS!" he gasped. "I'm gonna die!" The other boys lost it again. It was commonly known among Yuri's friends that his wild cat had cat AIDS.

"*Cat* AIDS." Yuri laughed.

"It's still AIDS! I want to be cleaned out," Steve insisted.

Pete found the breath between laughs to spit out, "We can do it here."

"Hell, no," Steve said, "I don't trust you guys."

At Steve's insistence, the boys piled into the car and headed for the hospital. As they parked, Victor said from the front seat, "I'm not gonna be the one to tell the nurse," and put his finger on his nose. Pete, who hadn't realized they were playing the nose game, was the last to put his finger on his nose.

In the emergency room, Pete and Steve approached the reception desk while the other guys watched with amusement from the waiting area. The nurse glanced at the gauze pad on Steve's leg. "What happened?" she asked.

"Umm," Pete said, "my friend kinda got clawed by a cat, and he thinks he got cat AIDS." Then he cracked up.

The nurse glared at him. "Are you serious?" she asked.

"Yeah," Pete replied. "He got clawed by a cat, and it has cat AIDS." He tried his best to refrain from bursting into laughter again, but it was difficult.

"I seriously doubt he got cat AIDS, but we can check him," the nurse said.

For three hours, Pete and his friends played a loud game of poker in the lobby while Steve waited to have blood tests done. When they got back to Yuri's house at close to four in the morning, they went to sleep. Pete could think of better things to do during semester break than spend three hours in the ER, waiting for his friend to find out he didn't have cat AIDS, but at least he ended the semester 40 bucks ahead.

THE STEALTH OVERACHIEVER, JUNIOR | PERCEIVED AS: ?

After debate practice ended, Stealth went upstairs to the AP English classroom to see if the teacher had posted the first-semester grades yet. Stealth wasn't too worried, not with straight As in six other classes. Stealth always got As on English exams, but it was tough to guess how the teacher had graded the second quarter; she seemed to have a grudge against Stealth, who didn't come across as a typical Whitman overachiever. She hadn't given Stealth an A on an essay until the second-to-last one of the semester, whereas when her composition assistant graded essays, Stealth usually got a 100 percent. Funny, Stealth mused, that the assistant who didn't know any of the students' reputations consistently gave Stealth high grades, while the teacher who made assumptions graded Stealth down.

The white sheet of paper taped to the classroom door came into view. Stealth looked up the corresponding student number and followed the line with a finger. First quarter: 89. Second quarter: 92. Stealth breathed a sigh of relief. And then—Exam: 89. Final grade: B. Stealth was horrified. A B on an English exam? *Why'd I put in the work to get an A second quarter?* Stealth thought. Stealth stepped inside the classroom and politely addressed the teacher: "I'm fairly certain I did well on the exam. Can I take a look?"

She rifled through her grade book. "You got a five out of nine on one of the essays," she said.

Bullshit, Stealth thought. *There's no way I did that badly.* "May I please see the essay?"

"I don't have it," she said. "You can come in next week."

"Okay," Stealth said, and left the room.

Stealth didn't expect to be back. The B was less irritating than the fact that Stealth had worked relatively hard over the semester without learning anything. The B wouldn't have been a big deal if the teacher had actually taught. But Stealth wasn't the type to argue for grades, unlike many other juniors. Stealth got annoyed when classmates tried to wheel and deal for grade bumps. The ability to dispute grades made them meaningless. One of Stealth's friends argued for grades all the time; he constantly tried to switch his schedule to get teachers who would give him As, and complained to his counselor if they didn't give him the grade. Stealth's friend had a different AP English teacher, had scored lower than Stealth in both quarters and on the exam, and yet had managed to get an A for the semester.

The friend, who constantly chattered about his grades, test scores, and college plans, was someone whom teachers and students saw as smart and high-achieving. He made his reputation known, and teachers treated him accordingly. Meanwhile, Stealth, who often got higher scores, participated in more activities at a higher level, and never boasted about grades, was viewed by students and some teachers in an entirely different way. Stealth wondered if colleges would be able to discern the candidates behind the reputations.

✦

Stealth never went back to see the teacher. But many students would have, in high school and in college. In 2005 Alicia Shepard, a journalism professor at American University, wrote an article for *The Washington Post* magazine about grade grubbing. She described an atmosphere so panicked that some students challenged their final grades within an hour of her posting them to an electronic bulletin board. "I have never received a B during my career here at AU and it will surely lower my

GPA," one student argued. A B-plus student "harangued" Shepard until she changed the grade to an A-minus.

At the end of the following semester, which brought continued pestering for better grades and second chances on papers and tests, Shepard received an email from a student who bemoaned his A-minus. He said he had assumed she was a tough grader, but when he talked to classmates about their grades, "it appears that the grade was handed out more readily than I thought." He wrote, "I know it's a great pain in the ass to have an A-minus student complain, but I'm starting to wonder about the way grades are given. I would be very curious to know who the A students were." When Shepard agreed to change the grade to an A, the student responded, "With grade inflation being what it is and the levels of competition being so high, students just can't afford to be hurt by small things. I thought that you did a great job with the course."

When I read Shepard's article, the surprise for me wasn't that A-minus and B-plus students grubbed for an A, but that the professor had granted their requests (the last of which was rejected by an administrator). But just as overachiever culture pressures students and parents to get ahead, it pressures teachers, too. What's more, these teachers are often compelled to cater to the highest-achieving students, the ones who least need the help. When parents complain about a child's grades, principals often side with them, in some instances to avoid what's been called "bright flight"—an exodus of overachieving students whom a school needs to maintain its reputation. At the college level, professors can feel obligated to raise the grades of students on scholarships that require a minimum GPA. An educational organization in Georgia reported that pressure to change grades was one of the most frequent complaints it received from high school teachers.

There have been several reports of teachers who hesitate to grade students down or report them for cheating or misbehavior out of fear that parents will sue them. In some regions, high school parents threaten lawsuits over disciplinary measures that could taint a college transcript. Because of this trend, in 2003 Emory College began requiring students and parents to disclose any instances of misconduct. Meanwhile, the number of teachers purchasing liability insurance rose by 25 percent between 2000 and 2005.

It's not only parents and students who are pressuring teachers. Some teachers told me that they have been forced by administrators to compromise their ethics for top students. High school guidance counselors told *The Atlantic* they are under constant pressure to "produce" by getting students into elite colleges. Schools crave scores and statistics such as high rates of graduates going to Ivy League schools, which can affect everything from the quality of incoming students—and the money that incoming parents have to donate for fund-raisers or auctions—to the property value of homes in the area. Some administrations are apparently willing to do whatever they can to get those numbers.

A high school art teacher told me she was forced by her school's guidance department to give high-achieving students A-pluses instead of As and B-pluses. In one case, a guidance counselor told the teacher, "Because of her GPA, giving this child an A is like giving another student a B. You're affecting this kid's future by not giving her the A-plus." The teacher was forced to make exceptions for other "AP kids," because, as an art teacher, she was "lucky" that these students would be willing to risk their GPAs by taking a non-honors class in the first place. For one high-achieving student whose parents refused to allow him to take art because it would lower his GPA, the administration instructed the teacher to allow him to take the class pass/fail so it wouldn't count in his GPA. When she asked if she could do this for other students, the administration refused, saying this was "an extenuating circumstance."

That teacher, like many others, followed her administration's orders because she was a young employee who did not yet have tenure. But even some veteran teachers feel they have no choice. An Ohio private school teacher told me that on several occasions, administrators asked her to grade some students on a different scale than others or to give extra credit only to certain students, often because those students' parents were community VIPs or on a school board or committee. A private school teacher in Silicon Valley said that because of the pressure to get eighth-graders into competitive high schools, teachers and administrators have "arrived at a pact with the devil" to give selected students better grades than they deserve. Some top students are well aware of this bias. A Maine senior told me that because she was consistently her class's highest-ranking student, "by my sophomore year, my reputation had preceded me, and it was almost impossible for me not to ace a class."

In some cases, administrators directly engage in dubious practices to make their students—and, subsequently, their schools—appear more impressive, manipulating grading policies and other statistics. In North Carolina, a principal and guidance counselor at North Moore High School were caught skewing the school's average SAT scores by using state remedial money (allotted to help weak students) as an incentive for higher-achieving students to retake the test and improve their scores. In all, twenty-two high-scoring students received a total of approximately $2,200—a dollar for every point over a hundred-point improvement, plus bonuses for top scores—to take the SAT again, even if they had already been accepted to college.

Meanwhile, the same school's administration discouraged weaker students from taking the test at all; only 28 percent of students at that school were taking the SAT, compared to about 70 percent statewide. The school held assemblies during which the names of students *permitted* to take the SAT were announced, while letters were sent to parents stating that the school could not afford for students to take the SAT if they were going to score below 1000. At a different Moore County school, guidance counselors hid SAT registration forms to dissuade potentially low-scoring students from bringing down the school's average.

In another case, a Bethlehem, Pennsylvania, school district abolished D grades in 2002 because, an assistant principal said, "it's very competitive to get into schools . . . More and more employers are looking for higher grades, and I think colleges are doing the same."

There may be a bit of a chicken-and-egg situation here. Is it that college admissions officers expect higher grades or that they've become accustomed to high schools inflating them? Neither scenario bodes well for students, parents, or teachers, all of whom might feel obligated to get or give the A. Bs, teachers say, have become the new "gentleman's C."

At colleges, too, grades have been on the rise for years; some experts calculate the rate at an increase of .15 points every decade. Harvard's average GPA rose from 3.17 in 1985 to 3.39 in 2001; Stanford, from 3.04 in 1968 to 3.44 in 1992; Dartmouth, from 2.70 in 1967 to 3.33 in 2001; and Duke, from 2.90 in 1970 to 3.37 in 2001. In the 1990s, the A overtook the B to become the most frequently given college grade, while the mark of mediocrity, the C, has dwindled. At schools including Princeton, Pomona, Harvard, Columbia, and Duke, approximately half of grades given are in the A range. A 2001 *Boston Globe* investigation uncovered that 91 percent of Harvard students were graduating with honors; several months later, Harvard decided to limit its number of honors graduates.

Some experts trace grade inflation to a confluence of several factors: roots during the Vietnam War era, when students with low grades could be drafted, a trickle-down trend from graduate schools in which only As and Bs are passing grades, and a feeling among parents that if they pay expensive tuition costs, the institution owes As in return. These circumstances can put teachers in an awkward spot. As Duke professor Stuart Rojstaczer wrote in *The Washington Post* in 2003, "If I sprinkle my classroom with the C's some students deserve, my class will suffer from declining enrollments in future years. In the marketplace mentality of higher education, low enrollments are taken as a sign of poor-quality instruction. I don't have any interest in being known as a failure. Parents and students want high grades. Given that students are consumers of an educational product for which they pay dearly, I am expected to cater to their desires not just to be educated well but to receive a positive reward for their enrollment. So I don't give C's anymore, and neither do most of my colleagues. And I can easily imagine a time when I'll say the same thing about B's."

With pressure coming from all sides—society's grade inflation, administrators' abuse of authority, students' pleas, and parents' threats—a disturbing number of teachers go down a path that by now is familiar to many overachievers. Like time-crunched students in need of an A, the teachers resort to a last, drastic measure: They cheat.

The prevalence of teacher and administrator dishonesty on student standardized tests is astounding: A 2004 paper listed teachers or staff members caught cheating on state tests in at least thirty-four states. In Dallas in 2005, one district's school board was dissolved after it was discovered that *two thirds* of the elementary school personnel who administered state tests cheated on them, some by giving students answer keys, others by ordering students who finished early to correct classmates' tests. In Tennessee in 2003, teachers in two counties reported 124 episodes of school personnel cheating on state tests, including staffers making potentially low-scoring students watch movies in the library for a week while other students took the state test, teachers pointing to wrong answers during the test, and counselors supposedly changing answers afterward.

A high school teacher in Nevada gave students a handwritten study guide that included fifty-one questions from the state test. In California more than 200 teachers were investigated for cheating between 1999 and 2004. A Staten Island high school staff member told the *New York Post,* "The students of the school benefit because they pass. The school benefits because the pass rate is up. But it's grade inflation. It's cheating. You're falsifying exams. It's totally corrupt." A fourth-grade teacher in Spokane reportedly showed students answers to the state math test before they took it; in the space where students were supposed to show their work, one student wrote, "my techre told me."

One might argue that "techre" simply wanted more money. Many schools offer teachers financial incentives—up to $25,000 in merit pay increases—if their students do well, or withhold bonuses if the students aren't up to par. It is a motivator more powerful than money, however, that links today's educators with the children they teach. A New York fourth-grade teacher who helped her students cheat defended herself this way: "Teachers are under a lot of pressure to get good grades."

SAM, SENIOR | PERCEIVED AS: THE TEACHER'S PET

When Sam told his parents he was going to Brad's house, he didn't tell them that Brad's mother was out of town and that Brad was having a party for a few dozen people to celebrate the end of the semester. Sam was surprised to see at least ninety Whitman students packed into the house. Some of them were Brad's friends, some were strangers, and many of them were people whom Sam had never seen at a party before, mostly seniors who were celebrating that their schoolwork no longer mattered.

"The overachievers are letting loose!" Sam crowed. Derek and C.J. were goofing off in a corner, *Black & White* editors and River Falls girls were milling around, potheads were smoking outside under the deck. The mix of students crammed into the basement and hooking up in bedrooms was so eclectic that Sam found himself saying, "Heyyy, *you're* here! Whoa!" over and over again. Sam thought it looked like a high school party from the movies, except that in the movies, people spilled out into the backyard, whereas in reality, everyone except the smokers stayed inside so neighbors would be less likely to alert the police.

Sam tried to help keep the party in line so Brad could enjoy it without worrying that his mother would find out about it when she returned to town. "Don't smoke that in here," Sam told a group. "Please don't mingle in the front yard," he said to another. "Don't hook up in their bedroom; go somewhere else!" He turned down the hip-hop music. Other students teased Sam for being uptight, but he was adamant about protecting his good friend.

At ten P.M. the phone rang. Brad came running upstairs from the basement. "It's your mom!" he said to Sam.

Fuck, fuck, fuck, Sam thought. He had told his parents only that he was going to hang out with Brad that night. "Please shut up for a second!" he pleaded to the mass of people surrounding him. They quieted.

"Hi, Sam," his mother said. His father was on the phone, too. "We just called to tell you that somebody just dropped off a love note!"

"Oh." Sam guessed his parents were beside themselves with excitement because they rarely knew what was going on in his social life.

"It has your name on it," she added.

"Oh."

"The envelope is also covered in kisses."

His father chimed in: "I bet it's a bunch of your junior girl admirers. A white car pulled away from our house."

"Okay, I'll come home soon and get it," Sam said. "Hey, can I sleep over at Brad's tonight?" His parents said yes.

When he got home, his parents wore dopey grins. They watched him closely as he opened the envelope—addressed to "Samuel, my love"—and silently read the letter, printed on hot-pink paper.

> *My love for you has grown so strong,*
> *I've waited for you for oh so long . . .*
> *On the court you pulse and thrust,*
> *You make me want you, I must, I must.*
> *Your points in debate make me sweat,*
> *Let's get under the sheets, let's get <u>wet</u>.*
> *Sam _____ please don't make me wait,*
> *You are my one, my perfect mate.*
> ❤ *Yours Truely . . . [sic]*

"So?" his parents pressed. Sam was amused that his parents had unknowingly stared at him while he read an erotic note. Back at Brad's house, Sam read the note to a small crowd of friends, one of whom identified the author as a girl writing on behalf of Ellie, the artist who had a crush on him junior year. Now that Sam and Ellie had AP Physics together, he was making more of an effort to get to know her, and she seemed to be forgiving him gradually for the way he had dismissed her after their junior-year date. But Sam guessed the letter was a joke, assuming she hadn't warmed to him *that* much. He spent the rest of the party playing beer pong. At five A.M. he and a friend, the only ones left at the house, went out to get stain remover to help Brad clean up a bong-water spill on the carpet. They scoured the house, positive by the time they left that Brad's mother would never know they had been there.

Alas, it was not to be. Soon after she got home, Brad's mom found one beer cap and grounded Brad indefinitely. "One cap!" Sam complained to a friend. "One! That's like getting a ninety-nine percent on a paper and it's not good enough. That's like the Whitman mentality. One cap!"

AP FRANK, COLLEGE FRESHMAN | PERCEIVED AS: THE WORKHORSE

Exams seemed to go fairly well for AP Frank. He spent time with his friends and took comfort in not knowing what his first college exams held in store because there was no way to flawlessly prepare for them. He saved his studying for the two days before a test, so the stress was compacted into only those forty-eight hours, rather than present all year. He was surprised to find that he felt free, that without the rigorous routine he had followed in high school, he felt more in control.

During intersession at the end of January—Harvard's semester break—Cambridge was buried under more than two feet of snow. AP Frank and Mike watched marathons of the television show *24* on DVD. One afternoon the two were sprawled on the B31 couch when AP Frank's mother called his cell phone. "Frank."

"What."

"Where are you?"

"I'm in my dorm." He always said that, even when he wasn't actually in his room or his dorm. "What do you want?"

"How did exams go?"

"They were okay. They were fine." AP Frank motioned to Mike with a finger that he could unpause the DVD in a minute.

Then his mother said, "Richard's in foster care."

"What?!" For a moment AP Frank couldn't digest the news.

His mother told him that she had gone to school to pick up his brother, but he wasn't there to meet her. She waited a half hour and no Richard. She went to the transcript office to have some transcripts printed. An hour after school ended, he still hadn't shown up. She went to the guidance office to have him paged, and someone there told her that child protective services had picked him up that afternoon.

AP Frank slouched in his seat. He felt terrible. What had happened was momentous, and he needed to talk to his little brother, but he didn't have the contact information. Still, this was his break from school.

"Mom, I don't want to hear this right now," he said.

"What?!"

"I'm with people right now."

"Oh, okay. I call you later."

"Okay."

He hung up the phone. "Ahhh, shit."

Mike looked concerned. "Hey, what's wrong? Is everything okay?"

AP Frank told him about his brother, leaving out much of his own story. At Harvard, only Kristen knew the details of his family life.

"You want to talk about this some more?" Mike asked.

"I don't want to think about this anymore," AP Frank said. "Let's watch Jack Bauer save the president."

Chapter 11

February 2-February 12

SUPERLATIVE

JULIE, SENIOR | PERCEIVED AS: THE SUPERSTAR

O n cap-and-gown measurement day, held during third period in the cafeteria, Julie had an uneasy sensation in the pit of her stomach. An assistant principal gave a short lecture about second-semester senior-year attendance, and then came the part that Julie had dreaded. Senior Superlatives. The Nastys ringleader and the other class officers passed out the ballots.

For the next several days, seniors would be talking about whom to mark down for such distinctions as Senior Sex Symbol and Most Self-Assured. The winners would be announced at the Senior Banquet in mid-March. Julie hated what the Superlatives did to students. She referred to the upcoming week as "talk about people week." For days people would gossip about friends, comparing their classmates. Senior Superlatives, in Julie's eyes, were a thinly disguised popularity contest. Groups of friends voted in blocks, and whoever had the most friends would win the most flattering awards.

The second the sheets were passed out, seniors began campaigning. Julie didn't know how people got away with it; she certainly wouldn't have been able to pull off that kind of blatant lobbying. An artistic senior asked Julie's table to vote for her for Most Creative. When a guy sitting next to Julie mused aloud, "Who should I put down for Best Eyes?" a girl nearby shouted, "Put me!" Some of the scrambling was more subtly manipulative, but Julie saw through it. When some of Julie's friends chose a member of the group to stump for Class Sweetheart, the girl said, mock-complaining, "Oh, if I get that award, people will make fun of me: They'll call me 'sweetheart.' " She said this loudly and frequently enough so that other seniors in the room would know that she was a contender.

The River Falls girls, Julie's longtime friends, were already divvying up the awards. Julie had heard that the crew was going to have a Superlative sheet get-together over the weekend, but she wasn't invited. It was a good thing that Derek and his ex had broken up; otherwise there would have been three Best Couple nominees in that circle of friends. When Julie had learned that Derek and C.J. were hanging out, at first she was annoyed. Derek wasn't the kind of guy who would truly have a rebound girl, and Julie had let her opportunity slip by. Julie and Derek were gradually resuming their friendship, but he didn't talk to her about C.J., and Julie didn't ask.

In Spanish class, someone asked, "Who for Best Hair?" Julie suggested a girl she didn't know, who had shiny blond curly hair and occasionally straightened it to glistening flat perfection.

"Ew!" a girl responded. "I hate her hair. It's totally fake. I hate when you can see the roots." As the conversation continued along those lines, Julie tuned out and took her first good look at the list of awards, in case there was one she could win. Until this year there had been a Most Likely to Win an Ironman Triathlon category, which Julie would have won handily. This year the category had been changed to Most Athletic, which was vague enough to be a popularity award.

"Oh! Julie for this one!" When Julie heard this, from a friend who had been campaigning relentlessly for Best Couple, she tuned back in.

"For what?" Julie asked.

"Best Dressed!"

Julie knew she couldn't compete against the girls who spent weekends at the mall and hours getting ready for school each morning, but she was flattered. Then she saw it. A new category that had been added this year for who knew what reason: Most Awkward. Initially, Julie, the self-proclaimed Queen of Awkward, was invigorated. *Hey! That's my award!* she thought.

At lunchtime, Julie's River Falls friends were having a field day lobbying for Julie to win Most Awkward. At first Julie thought it was appropriate. For the next few days, she went around telling people, "Isn't it funny that they're campaigning for me for Most Awkward?" She didn't think lobbying for that award was tacky because it wasn't a title people wanted. It seemed to fit with her personality; she usually referred to herself in public as a geek or some other similarly self-deprecating term.

By midweek, after her friends had spread the word to other circles to vote for Julie, the prospect of winning Most Awkward began to bother her. She liked to tell funny stories about her awkward moments to her friends, but strangers didn't think she was awkward, she thought. It wasn't like she had that reputation. Or if she did, would she even want to know? At the end of the week, Julie wrote the following in her journal:

This is what we have been waiting for. We have endured three years of stress, peaking from February of junior year to December of senior year. But now it is second semester. Just when we are no longer competing against each other for grades, awards, and positions, our senior class officers hand out the sheets for Senior Superlatives. One would think that these fun, good-natured awards would bring the class together to share some laughs and memories. However, in a class as talented and competitive as ours, there is no such thing as good-natured fun.

I see the award Class Sweetheart and a resentful feeling comes over me. I wish I had remembered to be a sweetheart in high school, but I have a feeling I was too concerned with my own well-being. At lunch, a not-so-good friend said, "Oh yeah, I voted for you for Most Awkward." When I said, "Haha did [___] tell you to?" she responded, "No, I just think you are awkward." Ok, now that is awkward. And uncalled for. I'm not *actually* awkward, am I? Later that day, some random kid comes to me and says, "So I hear you are campaigning for Most Awkward? You're going to win by a landslide."

I was right, there has been some incredible gossip this week. In my opinion, no one is qualified for Class Sweetheart. The truth is, this is Whitman and everyone wants to get ahead.

RYLAND, JUNIOR | PERCEIVED AS: THE SLACKER

At the end of the first semester, when students were approaching the physics teacher to check on their final grade for the second quarter, Ryland had crept up behind the teacher's desk, trying to look over his shoulder to see the grade without having to talk to him. The teacher spotted him. "Congratulations!" the teacher said. "You got a D! You passed!" The teacher acted as if Ryland's D were a monumental achievement.

"Fantastic," Ryland muttered.

Ryland was tired of teachers assuming he was a poor student just because he had test anxiety, sick of adults talking down to him as if he were dumb. The teacher had no clue who Ryland really was. Ryland wondered whether his teachers would treat him differently if they knew that until he entered high school, he had been a straight-A student. The D in physics was Ryland's first high school transcript grade below a B. The rest of his grades were surprisingly decent, given that he had missed so much school. He had As in journalism and ceramics and Bs in every other class but physics. He wasn't proud. He knew he could do better. He used to have a 4.0.

Even Ryland's mother occasionally mentioned that he was much smarter than his grades suggested. Teachers who took the time to talk to him recognized his intelligence. Throughout middle school, Ryland had been an excellent student who could understand most of the material taught in classes without needing to take many notes. He still thought of himself as a good student. But when he got to Whitman, suddenly everything "counted." It was as if his entire academic career before high school had been mere rehearsal, and now he was thrust to center stage beneath a bright spotlight and an audience full of admissions officers.

The pressure was enormous. Ryland got overwhelmed and put off homework and studying because he didn't want the stress to suffocate him. When he wasn't behind in class, he found school easy. "But when I get behind, it all goes to hell," he told a friend, "because I panic." Freshman year, his depression had caused him to fall behind. In the first semester of junior year, he had lagged because of his rocky adjustment to his new sleeping patterns. He desperately hoped second semester would be different.

Already there was a bright spot in his high school life. During semester break, he went to a dance party at a classmate's house. Soon after
he got there, he noticed an attractive girl standing to the side of the
crowd. He introduced himself, danced and talked with her the rest of
the night, and they had been together since. A sophomore with a 4.0
GPA, she was a member of two of Whitman's athletic teams, played in
the school orchestra, and had an array of interesting hobbies. Ryland
couldn't fathom how she kept up that schedule without exhaustion, but
as he got to know her more, he grew increasingly proud of her. She was
smart, involved, and kind. She inspired him.

Shortly into the second semester, Ryland sat down for his first
physics test with his new teacher. As he waited for the tests to be handed
out, he fidgeted. He was accustomed to either not knowing the material
or thinking he knew the material and then blanking as soon as he saw
the test. But this teacher was different from his first-semester teacher,
more laid-back, less stern, more straightforward, and not sarcastic. After
the teacher passed the tests through the rows of students, Ryland hurriedly scanned the first page. The test was multiple choice. *I know this,*
he thought. *I remember this!* By the time he finished, fifteen minutes
early, he had the feeling he had gotten an A.

AUDREY, JUNIOR | PERCEIVED AS: THE PERFECTIONIST

When first-semester report cards were distributed in homeroom, Audrey
held her breath. She looked at the grades, stupefied. Accustomed to seeing a line of As at the end of the semester, Audrey was dismayed with
herself. *I could have done better if I had applied myself more,* she thought.
Next semester I'll do better. There were five Bs and two As. She had expected the B in physics. During the first day of the semester, her physics
teacher had as much as admitted that he made a mistake in his adoption
of the county grading policy over the first semester. This semester he was
counting homework and extra-credit points like he used to, and Audrey
had a 100 percent. But the teacher wouldn't revise any of the grades for
first semester. Audrey's other Bs were in math, AP English, AP Spanish,
and AP Art. Assuming the art grade was a mistake, she found the teacher,
pointed out the error, and convinced her to change the grade.

Audrey's Spanish teacher had warned her that because she hadn't answered the semester-exam essay question, she would get a D on the test. This meant that even though she had gotten As in both quarters, her semester grade technically was a B. Her Spanish teacher was considering changing the grade to an A because she knew that Audrey was a diligent, devoted student who happened to have testing issues. She never had enough time to get through a test. She would go through it slowly, question by question, methodically making sure each answer was right. Those answers would usually be correct, but because she was so meticulous about answering them—and so distracted by her fear of not being able to work quickly enough—she wouldn't have time for the last half-dozen or so questions, and her grade would suffer.

Audrey arrived home before her mother, fretting over how to handle the situation. In eighth grade, Audrey had brought home a report card with a B in math. Her parents were furious because the course had been easy, but Audrey had been lazy that semester. It was the first time Audrey had blatantly not done all of the work assigned for a class, and her parents knew it. Audrey cried hysterically on and off for a week because of that B. Her parents were strict, but Audrey was harsher with herself, mentally beating herself up when she didn't do as well as she expected to. Her self-flagellation tended to get her in less trouble for grades because her parents knew she was harder on herself than they were.

Audrey decided that if she confronted her mom before she had the chance to ask about the report card, she could have more control over the reaction. She left a message on her mother's cell phone: "Hi, Mom, it's me. I'm just calling to let you know I got my report card back and it's a lot worse than I thought it was going to be. I'll talk to you when you get back, but I'll talk to the teachers and I'll get the report card changed."

When Audrey's mother came home, Audrey was impressed with her calmness and understanding. She looked at Audrey's report card and said, "All right, well, I know how hard you worked." Her mother looked as if she didn't know how to react. Like Audrey, she was used to seeing As. "Just talk to the teachers and get back to me."

Audrey guessed what her mother was thinking. They had argued about grades many times over the course of the year. Audrey's mother believed that the *Black & White* was the source of Audrey's slipping grades because it took up so much time. Whenever Audrey's mother told her to consider quitting the *Black & White,* Audrey would retort that journalism was her favorite class, she loved the paper, and she planned to be a journalist someday. Audrey knew her mother was absolutely right, though. If the newspaper weren't on her plate, she would be earning straight As.

AP FRANK, COLLEGE FRESHMAN | PERCEIVED AS: THE WORKHORSE

AP Frank flipped open his laptop at his desk and, battling nerves, pulled up the website that displayed his first set of college grades. He looked down the list: A in French. A in math. A-minus in expository writing. A few days before, he had gone to his writing professor's office to get the paper he had written last-minute, convinced it was the worst he had ever done. When she handed him the paper, he was stunned to see the green A-minus. There was only one final grade AP Frank hadn't guessed in advance. There on the screen was his first official grade lower than an A: a B-plus in music. AP Frank was angry because he thought he had done well on the exam, but after some thought, he brushed it off. This was not the earth-shattering moment others might have expected. He accepted that he had done his work as well as he could, and got over it. He hoped that when his mother received his grades in the mail, she could get over it, too.

When AP Frank sat down in his academic adviser's office for the beginning-of-semester meeting, the first thing he noticed was that his adviser still wasn't wearing a shoe on his right foot. Grinning at the bright purple sock, AP Frank glanced around the office and found the other shoe sitting underneath a table. He didn't say anything, afraid to come off as rude.

"What courses are you taking?" the adviser asked.

"Chemistry, biology, I'm continuing with French, and I'm applying for a freshman seminar in forestry." He didn't plan to inform his mother about that last class, which involved four weekend trips to the Harvard Forest, two hours away.

The adviser told AP Frank he was in good shape. The schedule AP Frank had chosen balanced the heavy course loads of chemistry and biology with two lighter classes. "How's your social life?" the adviser asked. "Are you going to a lot of parties?"

"Well, Mass Hall is twenty-three kids. We do everything together, but it takes a lot of effort to get out there and meet new people."

The adviser nodded. "Are there any girls you like?"

AP Frank told him a little bit about Lydia. "The girl works all the time," he said. "I hear from everyone that she doesn't want a relationship, but I get this weird-ass vibe that she's into me."

The adviser gave him the name of a casual Middle Eastern café that he said was a good place to take a girl. "Looking for a girlfriend is like shopping for courses," he opined. "You put yourself out there, see what's available, and test the waters, try things out." AP Frank smiled. He liked this guy.

"How are the extracurriculars?" the adviser asked. AP Frank told him about quitting Frisbee to concentrate on wushu. "That's a good idea. Most freshmen take too many extracurriculars and have to drop a couple to learn how to manage their time better." The adviser's words were reassuring, but by that time, AP Frank had already convinced himself that he had done the right thing. He had improved so much that he could now help wushu teammates who were having trouble with certain movements. Usually, there were three practices a week, but with a big performance coming up at the city's Cultural Rhythms Festival, the schedule had ramped up to five practices per week. AP Frank went to all of them.

Later that day, as he was talking on the phone, Lydia walked in and made herself comfortable. He raised an eyebrow; recently, Lydia had started coming into his room to hang out even when he couldn't pay attention to her. As he finished his conversation, she sat on his bed, going through his things and looking around. When he hung up, he and Lydia talked for a few minutes before the phone rang again.

"Frank." It was his mother.

"What."

"I have to talk to you. Richard's in foster care," she said.

"You told me."

"We have to go to lawyer to get him back. It'll cost me so much money."

"Mom, I'm with people."

His mother started to cry. "Frank, you my only son. I have to talk to you."

"Mom. You can't do this to me," he said. "I have people over. I'll call you back." She was still crying when he hung up the phone.

Lydia was a good distraction. He loved having long, in-depth conversations with her. Plus, she was cute. "Guess what I did during intersession," she said. "Oh well, maybe I shouldn't tell you."

"Lydia, you can't prelude something like that and then end it with 'maybe I shouldn't tell you.' That's not fair."

"Well, okay, I'll tell you. I made valentines."

Oh, for other people, AP Frank thought. "Okay, that's great!" he said.

"See, now you're not going to be excited."

Oh. I guess I'm getting one, he thought. *I suppose I should make one for her.* He decided to make one for all of the girls in her suite so as not to be overly conspicuous.

When Lydia left and AP Frank called his mother back, her attitude was completely different. "Frank!" she barked. "You have to write Richard email. Richard talking about not going to good school. He wants to go to University of Maryland. It's a terrible time. There is no control."

AP Frank rolled his eyes. Maryland was a good school and a place that he would encourage Richard to apply to, if he only knew how to reach him.

PETE, JUNIOR | PERCEIVED AS: THE MEATHEAD

It was another lazy day in journalism class. Pete had written articles here and there, but he had spent much of the previous issue's flat nights sitting in the third-floor stairwell playing poker with several other guys. Having ended the last round up $50, he now had lunch money for the next few weeks. Today he was spending the journalism period debating Hugh, one of Whitman's top students, on whether stress was unavoidable.

"Stress is where you have [sports] practice six times a week, and *Black & White,* and It's Academic, and debate, and four APs," Hugh argued.

"Please," Pete said. "You do *Black & White* occasionally, and you only did three debate tournaments this year."

"For the last two years and most of junior year so far, I just worked hard and basically didn't have too much fun. And now I get six hours of sleep," Hugh said.

"No, you don't, you sign off IM at three in the morning. I try to go to bed at ten-thirty," Pete said. "My schedule goes sleep, physics, homework, sleep, physics."

Hugh huffed. "I gave you the physics. You copied it during the Super Bowl."

Pete's attitude toward school had changed only slightly since September. He still didn't allow himself to worry much about his grades, but his GPA had barely dipped since sophomore year. He attributed this success to the classes he enjoyed. "I used to care more about grades, but I guess I've figured out how to treat learning as an end, not a means of getting into college," Pete told a friend. "I can write a good enough college essay that colleges will see what I can do. I don't need a 5.0 or to bitch to teachers to get what I want, because I think if I'm meant to go to the school, they'll take me either way."

Cliff, Pete's offensive-lineman friend, lumbered over to say hello. He clapped a hand on Hugh's shoulder and announced, "This kid got a broken nose because we sandwiched him."

Hugh looked up. "You sat on my face."

Even Cliff's attitude had changed over the year. Doubting his band's potential to get signed by a label, Cliff had applied early to a state university out west and not only got in but, to his amazement, had been accepted into an honors business program. The boys talked about why he had chosen that school.

"Warm weather, hot girls, and I can get in," Cliff said. "With a 2.2 GPA, that's a pretty big deal."

"You did well on the SATs, though," Pete pointed out.

"Yep, 1300 SATs, that's why I got in." Cliff had stayed out late the night before the SAT, taken the test on about two hours of sleep and a Red Bull, and scored 200 points higher than he thought he deserved (out of 1600).

"You're the definition of the uncommitted smart kid," Pete said.

"Uh-huh, wasted potential."

"I'm sure if Cliff cared about school, he'd be a genius," Pete said to Hugh.

"Probably, but that's not half as fun," Cliff said. "I'm in an awesome band, I get hot girls, and I'm going to the number two party school in the nation."

"One time Cliff was stressed," Pete said, and snorted.

"Oh yeah," Cliff agreed, "one time I had this test and it was worth like eighty percent of the grade, so I went to sleep because my brain hurt thinking about it."

TAYLOR, SENIOR | PERCEIVED AS: THE POPULAR GIRL

For Taylor, the winter was a whirlwind of college alumni interviews, almost daily trips to the gym, and, once she finished her college applications, parties. Gradually, she got over the sting of her Stanford deferral. It wasn't that the deferral, which she viewed as a rejection, didn't matter to her, but she found that the more she immersed herself in her usual activities, the more she realized that the thin envelope mattered less than she had thought it would. Life went on.

Taylor's alumni interviews were usually held at coffee shops, sometimes more than one in an afternoon. She dreaded the inevitable awkward moments when the bill came and she would do the pseudo about-to-take-out-the-wallet move, even though it had been the interviewer's idea to meet over coffee. The interviewer would insist on paying, as Taylor would think, *Shouldn't I be sucking up to you?*

Taylor didn't mind the interviews themselves. She was naturally a friendly person and able to view the interviews as regular conversations. She even prepared beforehand by Googling the alum to find out as much about him as possible. She figured that with the schools she was applying to, there had to be other applicants who were much more awkward and less social than she was.

Nonetheless, Taylor was surprised when, in February, one of her interviewers emailed her the recommendation he had sent to the admissions committee of his prestigious alma mater. In the recommendation, which he asked her to keep confidential, he praised her intelligence, eloquence, enthusiasm, and maturity. He spoke about her passions inside and outside of school, her dedication to service and to learning, and her "interesting array" of friends. He concluded that

Taylor was "the very best candidate" he had ever interviewed. She didn't tell her parents about that last line. She kept it to herself.

AP FRANK, COLLEGE FRESHMAN | PERCEIVED AS: THE WORKHORSE

AP Frank was listening to music and talking online when he got a Facebook message. (Facebook is a popular online directory connecting college students to one another and displaying their photos and profiles.) The message was from a college senior across the country. The girl, a Whitman graduate, wrote that she knew where Richard was: He was staying with her parents. AP Frank immediately asked for the phone number.

She sent him the number and a message: "I find it amusing [that] glancing at your profile, and discovering that of all the random kids you could be, you are 'AP Frank' (yes, unfortunately the grapevine extends to seniors in college)."

Relieved to finally have an opportunity to talk to Richard, AP Frank dialed his brother. "You fool! What are you doing?!" AP Frank teased when Richard answered.

"What? Who's this?"

"This is Frank, you dumbass." The brothers laughed.

"Oh, oh, ohh!" Richard sounded happy to hear from him. "How'd you get this number?"

Richard gave a bare-bones version of what had happened, and AP Frank didn't press for further details. Richard had emailed child protective services, which picked him up from school. When he was safely in their care, one of his social workers had presented him with a belated Christmas present: a new bass guitar. They took him to live with foster parents who were nice, but, to Richard, seemed slightly odd. Their daily greeting when he woke up in the morning was "Would you like a hot dog or a hamburger for breakfast?"

When a spot opened up in the Whitman school district, Richard was then sent to live with his current family, including a son at Whitman whom Richard hadn't known. The two were becoming fast friends, jamming on Richard's new bass and his foster brother's guitar and drums. These foster parents had a laid-back style that, to AP Frank, seemed like a dream. "I'm super-motivated now," Richard said. "I get all my homework done in two or three hours, because then I can go out."

AP Frank understood this. He and his brother used to drag out work for as long as possible, knowing that if they finished early, their mother would come up with more work. He changed the subject. "So, is it nice at the house?"

"Yeah, dude, it's so pimp. These people have a sixty-two-inch flat-screen TV!" Richard seemed to be doing fine.

"You asshole!"

"Yeah, I just reached for my remote and turned down my stereo system," Richard said. AP Frank could hear his brother grinning.

When AP Frank hung up the phone, he marveled at the way the world worked. AP Frank had been the "good son." Without too much of a protest, he had done everything his parents asked him to. He simply "sucked it up," in his words, and quietly hoped that eventually things would improve. Richard, by contrast, had defied his parents and busted out of the house. Now he was living in a mansion with caring foster parents and few rules. "His life is so frickin' sweet now. I was like, 'Damn you,'" AP Frank told a friend. "He's doing better than I ever did."

The phone conversation led AP Frank to two realizations. First, he now knew for sure that, against his mother's orders, he would abandon his summer position at NIH to work with a friend as a camp counselor in Pennsylvania. And second, as happy as he was for Richard that his life was working out, AP Frank was undeniably envious.

◈

There were many things AP Frank would have done differently if he could have experienced high school on his own terms. He would have joined Whitman's Frisbee Club, practiced the guitar more often, and taken photography and drawing classes—he loved to draw. He would have devoted more time to friendships. He might have kissed a girl. He might have been happy. Instead, his mother insisted his high school life be devoted to looking perfect on paper.

In an ideal world, high school would be a process of exploration, about developing a knowledge base in various subjects and honing an assortment of skills so that a student could discover which paths he might like to pursue while easing into adulthood. But in today's achievement-oriented race toward perceived prestige, high school isn't about learning any more than youth sports are about enjoyment. A 2005 survey revealed that nearly half of student respondents didn't believe that what they learned in high school was useful. Several students explained to me that they were told (by parents, administrators, college counselors, etc.) to avoid classes they would "take for fun" and subjects that might become passions because "they won't look as good to colleges."

Many students I talked to didn't take art, sports, music, yearbook, or home ec classes because they weren't honors or because they needed the time for an AP class. During graduation season in 2004, a Rhode Island principal asked one of his best students what she regretted most about high school. She responded, "Not taking an art class because it would have hurt my GPA."

Students are taught to intensify their efforts when their work "counts," and things are counting earlier and earlier. AP classes are billed as college-level; middle school classes now include many high school–level subjects. In Whitman's Montgomery County, the Board of Education decided in 2003 that grades for high school courses taken in middle school—such as Algebra I or introductory foreign-language courses—would appear on a student's high school transcript, leading the community to despair over how an eighth-grade misstep could impact a high school GPA.

At a group interview, four of the top seniors at Henry Clay High School in Lexington, Kentucky, discussed these issues. "There's a constant pressure throughout high school to always have in the back of your mind that clubs and activities are going toward building a résumé," an athlete said. The students told me about a battle for valedictorian in which a student got straight As but ranked behind another student who took an advanced course freshman year. "He didn't take that course," one boy said. "He took a class he thought would be interesting, but he lost out because of it and regrets it."

A girl shook her head, resigned. "People say, 'What are your hobbies outside of school?' I was like, 'I can't even read a book till I'm done with my applications,'" she said. "I always wondered if I was just wasting my high school years trying to get into college, and then I'll be wasting my college years trying to get into grad school."

"Yes! Yes!" the other students shouted.

In the fall of 2005, I traveled to Winnetka, Illinois, to visit New Trier High School, which is often hailed in the media as one of the best schools in the country. But as some of the school's most successful students shared with me, New Trier also happens to be a pressure cooker. "Everyone says if you were at any other school, you'd be top of your class. The people who get onto varsity or the fall play are the best in the country, not the best in the school," said Carolyn, an aspiring pre-med student who didn't let herself apply to Ivy League schools because, according to the TCCi scattergram, her statistics didn't match those of her classmates. "My high school career was planned out for me probably in sixth grade. You need to know, coming in, what you want to do. Once you're on a path, you can't switch paths. If you don't start things freshman year, you can't just come into something. And colleges say they want to see continuity."

"It's the same with sports," said Thomas, a standout student athlete. "There's no point in trying out for the golf team after freshman year." When Thomas tried out for the volleyball team as a sophomore, he was told that he played better than the boy he competed with for the last spot, but because the other player had been on the team as a freshman, the coaches took him instead. "You have to be in the system from the beginning. You have to know what you're going to do when you get into high school."

"It takes out a lot of personal growth," said a girl who had been listening to our conversation. "There's no room to explore anything you want."

"Everyone talks about how many classes and opportunities New Trier has, but I think it's set in stone what we're supposed to take. There's not as much choice as everyone thinks, because if you're not in AP English junior year and BC Calculus senior year, you can't get into an Ivy," Thomas said.

"I'm viewing college as my high school experience. In college, I'm going to take the classes I want, I'm going to have fun, I'll be less stressed out, get to hang out with my friends," Carolyn said. "Now I feel like I'm in a prison of prep."

"You gotta get on the train and go, immediately," said Matt, a fellow senior.

New Trier's top-ranked senior nodded from across the table. "My mom calls it a conveyer belt. You get on the conveyer belt to college."

The prospect of having to choose a path quickly and stick to it to look good for colleges and graduate schools is terrifying to many students. They can get so caught up on that conveyer belt that rather than working to understand and appreciate classroom material for the sake of learning, they are working to game the system. Some top students strategize from the beginning of their freshman year, plotting which classes to take and which teachers to switch to, all with their GPA in mind.

In 1997 scandal erupted at Sarasota High School in Florida when Denny Davies was named valedictorian over another student who had the same GPA. According to an apparently little-known school policy, tiebreakers in class rank competitions went to the student with more credits. Davies had discovered this rule and furtively taken extra classes, including an easy independent study, to gain the valedictory edge. Both the school principal and Davies' guidance counselor defended the senior's actions. "He's very clever," his counselor told the local newspaper. "He said, 'I want to be valedictorian. I've figured out I need to do this and that. Can you help me?' Denny had a good strategy, and this strategy was available to anyone who was a competitor."

That sentence alone could sum up why the high school experience has spiraled so dangerously out of control. Students aren't praised for grasping or for appreciating classroom lessons. Rather, they're exalted for strategizing their way to the top, for proving they are competitors. In the fast-paced race toward college, emphasis in schools has shifted precipitously from a love of learning to a battle for statistics. As Julie suggested, students' lives become defined by numbers. Denny apparently chose his courses not because he was interested in the subjects but because they would elevate him to number one in the class.

Recalling Sam's Senior Stress Week observation, many high school students today are like robots, programmed to go mechanically through the motions of academia in a desperate attempt to craft a competitive college résumé. They live their lives not in the moment but for that distant day in the future when the college acceptance letters arrive. A senior in Virginia explained, "The stress of getting into college starts the day you enter high school. The administrators always tend to focus on the future, and everything is focused around what will happen in four years."

When students aren't doing something "productive"—studying, working on an extracurricular activity, practicing a sport—they often feel guilty and anxious, as if they're wasting time. When they get tests back, instead of trying to understand material they missed, many spend their energy wheedling the teacher to grant extra points elsewhere (or they switch teachers entirely). They are so caught up in climbing to the top, in achieving recognizable accomplishments *right now*, that they don't stop and reflect whether the direction of their climb makes sense for them personally. And how could they? Such a pause would take too long, because behind the grades, test scores, and awards, they have no idea who they are. Their identities have been lost in a pursuit of perfection.

It's not just parents who are pushing perfection; I found self-driven perfectionist students in several regions of the country. Caitlin, a junior in rural Minnesota, said, "I do not let myself settle for less than my best. This can be both extremely rewarding and tiring to keep up. My parents tell me I have trouble relaxing. I agree, but then I decide there is just so much to do and continue doing it." Haresh, a Georgia senior who was participating in eleven extracurricular activities at the time we spoke, said, "I often feel like there is too much to do in too little time. I feel like I'm never doing enough, and what I'm doing is not good enough. I can't do the things that I used to do, like hang out with friends or go to parties and such." Haresh had to quit tennis, which he loved, because it "interfered" with his studies.

Several students described breaking down in class or in the hallways, sobbing at their desks when they didn't get As or berating themselves for 99s. Matt, a Texas senior, explained his obsession: "When .004 of a point separates individuals in the top five or ten, then every point matters. Anything less than a 100 is unacceptable to me. The idea sounds crazy, but when you have people at the top scoring 98s, 99s, and 100s on all of their assignments, a simple A just doesn't cut it." Matt had a 98 semester average in AP U.S. History, notoriously the most difficult class at his school. "During the last marking period of the first semester, I did poorly on one of my quizzes, and as a result, my grade dropped a single point. No big deal, what's one point, right? Wrong. I beat myself up over that one point for about a week because it could have raised my semester average up to a 99." A New England student said, "My seventh-grade science teacher told me, after I received a 98 on a test, that, because she was offering retakes, I should retake the exam because a 98 was not the highest-quality work."

These are the perfectionists who anguish over "failing" a test or paper—i.e., getting less than an A. Several students called a B-plus "below average." A Connecticut junior said, "When kids at my school get an 89, they'll start hysterically crying and argue with the teacher. It's not 'I'll do better next time.' It's like life or death, and if you don't get that grade, your life's over."

To get that grade, increasing numbers of students are turning to tutors. It has been estimated that in 2005, tutoring nationwide was at least a $5 billion business, expected to grow by an average of 12 to 15 percent a year over the next few years. Tutoring has become a natural way to push B-plus or A-minus students to get As, even at the elementary school level. One Michigan tutor received a call from parents whose overachieving eighth-grader had been begging them for months to hire a PSAT tutor. The parents called the tutor not to appease their son but to enlist him to convince the child that he didn't need tutoring for a test that didn't count.

It's one thing for a child to be what's called a "normal perfectionist," someone who strives to excel but accepts personal limitations. When children are routinely judged by their achievements, however, they can become "neurotic perfectionists." These are the perfectionists who chastise themselves over mistakes, who obsess over the lone A-minus on an otherwise straight-A report card, who come to adopt the attitude that if they aren't perfect then they must be below average. In today's schools, the middle ground is shrinking; so-called middle achievers can be ignored because they're not the weak test takers who will drag down No Child Left Behind scores, and they're not the stars who will increase a school's number of National Merit Scholars or Ivy League admits. As child psychiatrist Alvin Rosenfeld has said, "Every kid is either gifted or learning disabled. 'Normal' has been abolished." That's why C.J. felt like a nobody even though she was a good student, terrific person, and skilled athlete with many talents. Surrounded by perfectionists, she thought she was subpar.

While students who don't consider themselves gifted struggle to stand out, overachievers can stress out over keeping up appearances. "I often feel pressure to impress everyone around me, to keep up my reputation," said Lindsay, a Louisiana junior. "Many think that being a 'smart kid' makes life loads easier, but it doesn't. Once you get the grades to prove that you're smart, you have to keep it up, no slacking allowed, and that's the toughest part. If you're considered 'smart,' then you've always got to be the best. Even if something is difficult for you, you can't let it show, for the better person can take it and use it to their advantage."

An International Baccalaureate student who gave up horseback riding to focus on varsity sports because she wasn't "riding competitively" said her personal perfectionism drove her to maintain her overachiever image. "I'm my own biggest source of pressure. I am extremely hypercritical of myself. I will rewrite lists because I don't like the way they look in the handwriting, not because the information on them is wrong. All the time, I tend to overorganize instead of getting things done, making tons of lists of all the things I have to do in class order, in difficulty order. I get really stressed out. The only time I let my guard down is when I go to church, which I have started doing recently by myself. I usually start crying for no reason at all, I think because it's the only time where no one is asking anything of me and I don't have to keep up an appearance since my family isn't known at the church I go to."

It is drilled into today's children that they should prioritize quantity of extracurriculars over quality of life, and success over happiness. They are taught that success in today's world is defined primarily by how an achievement looks on a school application. They seek perfection and frequently find they cannot be content with anything less. Even the idea of contentment is foreign to them. This is a by-product of overachiever culture. As a high school student told *The Washington Post* in 2002, "I see what's missing instead of what's there and I'm not alone. So many kids get pushed at such a young age to do everything. . . . So many people who don't love what they are doing, don't enjoy half of it, and spend more time crying than learning anything because someone told them the only way they'd ever be successful in the future was to take a class that was way beyond their ability or desire. Can't there ever be a time when all you're supposed to do is 'be'?"

SAM, SENIOR | PERCEIVED AS: THE TEACHER'S PET

Sam didn't check his computer immediately when he awoke. By then the results of his early decision 2 application to Middlebury would be accessible. But why rush? The decision wasn't going anywhere, and Sam's computer was slow to boot up. He lay in bed reading and otherwise procrastinating while a voice inside his head muttered, *I hope I get in, I hope I get in.* At eleven o'clock, his father, who Sam knew was doing everything he could not to bother him that morning, came upstairs and gently said, "Sam, look, you can tell me about Middlebury."

"Dad, let me handle it," Sam said, pretending he had looked at the Middlebury website. For all of the years his parents had nagged him about tests and grades, today was the day he was going to get back at them, albeit marginally, by making them wait.

Sam tried to be confident. He had "played every card," as he put it, to present himself as a desirable applicant. "If a damn college can't recognize that, then I have absolutely no faith in the system," he told a friend. He was more nervous than he let on. Even if he did get in, he felt like a weight wasn't going to be lifted off of his shoulders—the Stanford rejection had jaded him—but at least he would know.

Sam got out of bed and turned on his computer. He loaded the Middlebury College admissions decision page and typed in his user name and password. "Congratulations . . ." he read. He collapsed back into his chair. "Thank God," he said aloud. He finished reading the letter and made a mental note of the orientation date in September. Sam went downstairs and circled the rooms on that level of the house, knowing his father's eyes were on him. Reveling in the suspense, he showed his father a *Sports Illustrated* article. "So when are we going downtown?" Sam asked.

"We can go now. Why?" said his father.

"Well, you have to buy your college boy lunch."

His father hugged him. Sam wished he could celebrate with Julie, but she had seemed distant lately. Instead, he spent the day with his father.

Chapter 12

February 12–February 25

THE SPACE BETWEEN

JULIE, SENIOR | PERCEIVED AS: THE SUPERSTAR

Second semester, Julie and three other girls in her math class regularly
got together to do their calculus worksheets. Julie liked this easygoing new group of friends whose relationship focused on getting the
math homework done. During one homework session in mid-February,
the conversation drifted from math.

"Okay," said one of the girls. "Who is the one person you can tell
anything to?" Each of the girls in turn named her closest confidante.

"Julie, who's yours?" one asked.

"Uhh." The Queen of Awkward shrugged.

"Oh, that's so sad," said another, sounding genuinely concerned.
"You don't have, like, a best friend?"

"No, I never had one," Julie mused. "I don't have that one person
whom I can trust not to tell anyone. I sort of feel like I have all fair-
weather friends who are there when I'm in a good mood. When I'm not,
there's, like, no one there for me." The girls gave her sympathetic smiles.
She didn't add that she was so close to her family that she didn't necessarily feel the need to find peers in whom to confide.

Julie was socializing more than usual these days, now that many
second-semester seniors were going out on weeknights. She had moved
her swimming practice so that she woke up at 4:15 to swim before
school, instead of at night, when she might miss out on a social activity.
It was still difficult to get close to people, especially when the lengthiest

conversations occurred online. Julie considered IM the epitome of social laziness. You could "talk" online to people for two hours and still not know anything more about them than before the conversation began. But IM was how most students found out what was happening on a given night, and how they made their plans.

Julie hadn't told any of her friends about her wildly vacillating emotions. She knew the hormones she was taking could affect her moods, but she worried that maybe she should see a professional to help her manage what were becoming increasingly frequent breakdowns. Neither her 1520 SAT score nor acceptance to a prestigious college had fixed her unhappiness and insecurity.

The math group's conversation moved on to boys. Julie wasn't going to tell them about her interest in Derek. Their friendship was nearly back to where it had been before their three-hour online conversation. With Julie, he was what she called "ATNA": all talk, no action. Meanwhile, Julie and C.J. were once again on good terms. Julie felt badly, recognizing that she had taken out on C.J. her frustrations with her own uncertainties about running.

She half listened to the girls' chatter, saying nothing until one asked her, "Hey, Julie, who's the oldest guy you've been set up with?"

"What?" Julie hadn't quite tuned back in, but they mistook her non-answer. They hadn't known her ex-boyfriend from the summer.

"Oh! No one?" The three girls looked shocked.

Julie laughed and rolled her eyes self-deprecatingly. "I don't have any friends, I don't have any guys," she said.

One of the girls shook her head emphatically. "No, you get guys all the time, left and right. I mean, what about Sam?" This girl was close friends with him.

"What are you talking about?" Julie asked.

"You guys are really good friends, right? Didn't more happen last year?" When Julie shook her head, the girl looked confused. "Oh," she added. "He deeply, profoundly cared for you."

Julie suddenly understood the strange vibe she had felt the last few times she had been around Sam. She thought he was wonderful, kind, thoughtful, and chivalrous, but she wasn't interested in him like that; she never had been. The only guy on her mind was Derek.

AP FRANK, COLLEGE FRESHMAN | PERCEIVED AS: THE WORKHORSE

AP Frank was watching a movie with a dormmate when his cell phone rang.

"Frank." It was his mother.

"What."

"I calculated your GPA. A is 4.0. A-minus is 3.67. B-plus is 3.33. So you got 3.7. Is just okay," she said. "You shouldn't take music course. It's very difficult, and it's stupid course because you are not genius in music and you can't get A-plus."

"I'm watching a movie. Why do you always have to call and lecture me?"

Five minutes later, AP Frank's father called to tell him that his mother was angry. "She isn't happy with the way you talk to her."

"How would you feel if the only time your mother ever called was to evaluate how you were doing—not to say 'How are you?' 'How do you like college?' 'How are you feeling?' 'Are you having a good time?'"

"How about you talk to your mom and apologize."

AP Frank braced himself to check his pride and apologize. But as soon as his mother picked up the phone, she yelled at him. AP Frank tried to get in a word to say he was sorry. He could hear his father in the background, imploring, "Just listen to him! He's apologizing to you!"

AP Frank sighed. He hated this. With his mother still shouting in his ear, he hung up the phone. It seemed that no matter what he did, she maintained control over every aspect of his life, and his life ultimately boiled down to the numbers on a 4.0 scale.

Late at night Taylor IMed AP Frank. "I hate boys," she said. *Ohh boy, it's another one of these,* AP Frank thought. When his female friends vented to him about boys, they would say things like "Guys are the three Gs: gay, girlfriend, or gross." Well, what about AP Frank?

"What's the matter this time," he typed. She told him about the two guys she was interested in: a popular athlete and Derek.

AP Frank: you shouldnt be having trouble with any of these guys because youre one of the most popular girls in school.

Taylor: no, im not so much "popular" now. im more of a "smart person."

AP Frank: i really wouldnt be able to tell the difference, having never been popular myself.

Taylor: no, its not that big of a deal. just a lot of really fake people that get on your nerves after a while.

AP Frank: if youre not a fake person like that, why dont you just be yourself around derek and start spending some time with him and then hell start liking you back.

Taylor: no, Im such a loser. i always lose.

AP Frank: what are you talking about?! look who youre talking about.

Taylor: look who *im* talking to. ap frank, all As, 1600. taylor, not all As, not 1600.

AP Frank: yeah well, ap frank has never kissed anyone, never had a girlfriend, and never been on a date.

Taylor: ive never had a boyfriend or been on a real date either.

This surprised AP Frank. He knew she had at least hooked up with several guys.

AP Frank: oh. sorry. im a loser.

Taylor: youre not a loser, im a loser.

AP Frank rolled his eyes. Taylor was smart, funny, and hot. AP Frank didn't see how she would have any problems attracting guys, including the two she was interested in.

AP Frank: okay taylor. lets make a deal. if i initiate, then you initiate.

Taylor: okay, deal.

AP Frank didn't tell Taylor that he had already taken a step toward making a move on Lydia. He had spent the previous night making her a valentine, sweating over how to craft it so that if it didn't go over well, he could say it was only a friendly gesture. He hadn't made many valentines as a child. Were hearts optional?

A few days earlier, Lydia had told him, "Frank, I think if I were stranded on a desert island, I'd like to have you there with me. It'd be a lot of fun." Then she asked, "Who would you like to have with you on a desert island?"

It was obvious what she wanted him to say. "Can't say," he replied. "They'll hear."

Lydia looked behind her, where Mike and other friends were busy laughing over something else. "No, they won't. Here, just tell me."

He shook his head. He didn't mean to be coy—he was just shy about these sorts of things—but it might have appeared that way.

"Frank, I'm disappointed in you!" she said, and stormed off.

That night AP Frank put the finishing touches on his card, on which he had pasted a *Far Side* comic showing a couple stranded on a tiny desert island with only a palm tree and a ten-piece band, captioned "Care to dance, Mrs. Hollings?" He signed it, "Your desert-island buddy (you knew who it was all along)."

AP Frank went to Kristen's room to make sure his valentine for Lydia was appropriate. "That's the cutest valentine ever," Kristen said.

AP Frank hoped so. If it didn't work out with Lydia, he didn't know whom to ask to the Freshman Formal, which he had recently learned was only two weeks away. The idea of a formal-date dance, a party that his classmates would attend in couples, intimidated AP Frank.

As soon as AP Frank woke up on Valentine's Day, he remembered it was the day he had to give his valentine to Lydia. His heart raced. When he opened his door, he found a lacy heart pasted onto glittered red construction paper. "Happy Valentine's Day! xoxo Lydia." AP Frank smiled. She had been flirtatious lately, playfully stepping on the backs of his shoes when they walked together, and practically asking to be tickled when they studied. Then he looked up, glanced down the hall, and realized that there were valentines from Lydia outside every door he could see.

For the rest of the day, AP Frank was jittery until Lydia came over. He was in the middle of chemistry homework, which gave him an easy excuse to stall. "How do you do number three? Is it a weak acid reacting with a strong base?" he asked. Finally, he whipped out the valentine.

She read it, expressionless, then said, "Who's Mrs. Hollings?"

Dammit, AP Frank thought. *She doesn't get it.* "Oh . . . it's just a cartoon," he said. "Happy Valentine's Day, Lydia." He gave her a hug, and they chatted for a few minutes about classes. When the conversation lulled for a moment, she smiled up at him. AP Frank so badly wanted to lean in and kiss her, but he didn't. He went to sleep kicking himself for a week of anticipation that had led to nothing but dashed expectations.

AUDREY, JUNIOR | PERCEIVED AS: THE PERFECTIONIST

After a hectic long weekend at a Model United Nations conference that required Audrey to miss school on Monday, she woke up feeling sick on Tuesday. She and her mother went through their usual back-and-forth:

"Mom, I can't go to school," Audrey said.

"What test do you have today?" her mother asked. "Audrey, you're not sick."

"No, I am. I just threw up. I'm definitely sick."

"You're not sick. You're making yourself sick," her mother replied with compassion. "You know you psych yourself out. You have to stop letting your stress get to you." She had been telling Audrey this since middle school, when Audrey began vomiting before exams because of the time pressure.

"I feel like I don't have any control over that."

"But you do."

This year was different; Audrey knew that she hadn't taken a total of six sick days last semester because of nerves. (The sick days *caused* her anxiety, because she panicked about the work she was missing.) She was making herself sick because she didn't have time to sleep. Audrey stayed home.

Audrey spent the following Sunday at a *Black & White* work session at school, desperately trying to be as useful as possible to the seniors so she might have an edge in the newspaper staff elections. She was extremely worried that she might not get one of the top three positions. As hard as she worked, it seemed like there were always other students working harder. Home at 5:30, she had to study for Monday's work: two makeup tests, math homework, an AP Spanish oral exam, and an AP Comparative Politics test for which she hadn't yet read the chapter, which meant she would need at least four hours to do the reading, type her notes, and rewrite them in longhand. She hadn't yet started an AP English paper due Tuesday because she had to study for Friday's tests in four classes. Plus, she was already two paintings behind in her AP Art class, even though the quarter had begun only two weeks ago.

Above it all, the SAT loomed constantly over Audrey's head. She had been obsessing over her vocabulary flash cards since August. Her guidance counselor had already warned her that her PSAT and diagnostic SAT scores were so low that they seriously threatened her chances at Georgetown. Unless she improved the numbers, admissions officers were likely to put her application in the reject pile without looking past the scores. Just thinking about the SAT sent Audrey into a tailspin. She assumed she wouldn't do well when she took the new SAT for the first time in March. Her only comfort was that she could retake the test in the fall.

Audrey couldn't fathom how she could study for the SAT, do her homework, keep up with her extracurriculars, and be in bed by 10:30 as her parents wanted. Monday and Tuesday were *Black & White* flat nights, from which she didn't get home until at least 10:30, and then she had the English paper to write and tests to study for. Unwilling to give up flat nights, Audrey hit upon another solution. Her study was too close to her parents' bedroom for her to work without her mother knowing, so Audrey began a habit that continued throughout the year: She pretended to go to bed at 10:30, waited until her parents went to sleep, then crept downstairs to the kitchen, borrowed her mother's laptop, brought it back upstairs, and, in the darkness of her bedroom, stayed up working on the laptop until two in the morning. "I'd rather risk being sick and be caught up than go to bed early and get further and further behind," Audrey reasoned to a friend. "I guess either way I'm digging my own grave."

TAYLOR, SENIOR | PERCEIVED AS: THE POPULAR GIRL

Taylor's calculus tutor, a geeky Whitman graduate, checked over her last problem. "You're wrong," he said.

Taylor checked over her work. "No, I'm not. You're wrong," she said.

"No, I'm right. You're wrong," he shot back. Taylor made him do the problem over again himself and told him to check the answers in the back of the textbook. "Oh yeah," he said, "you're right."

Taylor pumped her fists. "Yesss."

The popular kids made fun of Taylor. "Why do *you* need a tutor?" said a student from the Nastys' corresponding guy group. "You're good at math, and it's second semester!"

It had been Taylor's idea to get a tutor this year. With his help, she almost got an A first semester in arguably the most difficult class at Whitman: the AP BC Calculus class her college counselor had told her to drop. Unlike the popular students, the "smart kids" didn't think twice about Taylor's tutor, because they had tutors, too. Even Julie had asked her parents to hire a tutor to help her with junior year AP Chemistry, although she had an A. In the one class Taylor had with Derek, he made fun of her for doing her work when, for a second-semester senior, it didn't really count. But Taylor did it—and kept her tutor—because falling behind in class would make her stressed. It was easier to take it as it came.

It was also easier to take Derek's teasing now that she had a full-blown crush on him. Taylor didn't think she could "initiate," as she had promised AP Frank. Sometime after Derek broke up with his girlfriend in January, Taylor realized that when she had joked with her friends that if she and Derek went to Stanford she could marry him, deep down she wasn't necessarily joking. Taylor distracted herself from what she assumed were her unrequited feelings toward Derek by hooking up occasionally with the jock she was attracted to, but she knew AP Frank wouldn't count that as initiating. The problem was, she didn't know how to initiate with someone like Derek. "This has never happened before, liking the 'smarts' over the 'athletic' or 'popular,'" she told a friend. "My game isn't mastered in different groups." With a popular guy, all she had to do was call him and say, "Want to hang out?" and he would know she was interested. She showed up to a few of the jock's varsity games—just the right number, without overdoing it—and she knew he was on board. With someone like Derek, she didn't know the appropriate strategy.

Her popular friends urged her to go for the jock instead. "You'd work better with him," one friend said. "I just see you guys going together better than you and Derek."

"Derek and I have better conversations," Taylor said. "They're more interesting and less awkward." Usually, she and the jock couldn't think of much to talk about other than sports.

At that, another popular friend grew angry. "You don't just have to go for smart guys. I don't know why you're stereotyping like that," she said. "[The jock] can be interesting, too. I think you're underestimating him."

This was the same friend who couldn't understand why Taylor shared a parking spot with a junior she considered a nerd. "It's so weird you share a spot with that kid," she said to Taylor once. "I don't even know what his name is."

Taylor told her his name. "I love him!" she said.

"Whatever, Taylor," her friend muttered. "You and your math boys."

At a party in mid-February, Taylor hung out with the jock. She left at about 12:45, but when she got into her car, she realized she didn't want to go home. She called Derek. "Hey, what are you doing?" she asked him.

"I'm at home," he said.

"Oh, well, I was going to ask if you wanted to go for a walk," she said, "but if it's too late, we can do it another time." Taylor wasn't using a euphemism; she frequently took walks in the middle of the night to clear her head.

"No, a walk sounds good," Derek said.

As they walked around the neighborhood, Derek opened up to Taylor. He told her that he liked C.J. but that her signals confused him. Taylor attempted to conceal her surprise. Derek and C.J. seemed like such a random pairing, two people from completely different Whitman circles. There was no way Taylor was going to initiate now.

C.J., JUNIOR | PERCEIVED AS: THE FLIRT

For C.J., lunch on school days had become a repeating scene. Because she was desperate to hold on to her small group of elementary school friends, who often broke Whitman's senior-only open-lunch rule, C.J. would go with them. At a pizza place in Bethesda, the four of them would sit there chomping on slices while C.J. ate her healthy bag lunch. The other girls would spend the meal prattling about their latest escapades, many of which involved getting drunk or high. These were some of Whitman's top students—straight-A students who had been scoring well on SAT diagnostics—and yet their conversations often centered on what they did when they forged notes and skipped classes. C.J. listened to them, eating quietly, wishing her friends hadn't changed.

By mid-February, the lunches had grown worse. The four other girls decided to name their clique, which didn't include C.J.; they now referred to themselves as the "MaryJanes" and gave themselves secret code names. They told C.J. they had settled on the name both because it was a slang reference to marijuana and because when the girls went out to smoke hookah together, the lie they told their parents was that they were seeing the movie *Spider-Man 2* (the hero's girlfriend was named Mary Jane). Lunch discussions now revolved around MaryJanes this, MaryJanes that, still focusing on drunken escapades. When C.J. did pipe up, the others gave her a sarcastic "Good story, C.J." look. They chattered about their inside jokes, leaving C.J. out of the loop.

"C.J.," a MaryJane said at one lunch, "go get us a Coke. The Mary-Janes can't be seen in the security camera because we're badass. It's incriminating evidence." C.J. knew that behind the joke, the girl was further etching the boundaries of the clique. When they sauntered out of the pizza place, C.J. trailed in back.

C.J. had no desire to be part of the MaryJanes. She thought the idea of naming a clique was lame, not to mention their choice of label. She would sit through the lunches, bored, not saying much, but unable to escape the thought that some of these girls had been her friends for so long she didn't want to lose them. And yet, as they moved through more adult-sounding worlds of alcohol, pot, and hookups, C.J. felt they were clearly leaving her behind.

Because she didn't want to drink or smoke, C.J. was spending more time with the track team and with Audrey and their neighborhood friends. She spent one day a week with Derek and IMed with him the rest of the week. Her track friends teased her about hooking up with him, because at Whitman, students without boyfriends or girlfriends didn't date so much as hook up. Presuming C.J. and Derek were now a couple, people would come up to her and say, "Hey, do you know where Derek is?"

"How am I supposed to know where Derek is?" she would respond. "I don't have a Derek GPS system."

C.J. and Derek were not hooking up. She was scared to cross the platonic line because she didn't want a boyfriend and the title and obligations that seemed to accompany it. It was fun to spend weekends with someone because you wanted to, but if you were boyfriend/girlfriend, then certain commitments were expected. C.J. didn't have time. Instead, they mostly spent hours hanging out, watching movies and *The OC,* playing pool, or going to parties together. Usually, their interactions consisted of C.J. ribbing Derek about the chess club or his ability to solve a Rubik's Cube in eighty-eight seconds, and Derek dishing it back, needling her about her outfits or silly things she said. C.J. was convinced one of the reasons Derek liked hanging out with her was that she didn't revere him like other students did—though she hadn't known the extent of his reputation as a genius until the rumors circulated about the two of them.

Now, from students in the hallways, from teammates, from friends, she heard about his intelligence all the time. When they passed by her, friends would twist imaginary Rubik's Cubes, hands flying. C.J. wasn't blown away by his accomplishments; she thought he had the potential to be more ambitious than he was. Derek was so mellow and prone to goof off that she couldn't think of him as someone like AP Frank. She still sometimes thought of Derek by his IM screen name, which made her ponder how weird it was to be spending time with the screen name in the flesh.

RYLAND, JUNIOR | PERCEIVED AS: THE SLACKER

Ryland was hanging out with his girlfriend, who, to his delight, was content with the fact that many of their "dates" consisted of naps because his parents didn't allow him to nap at home, for fear it would "ruin his sleep cycle."

So far the semester was going fairly well. Ryland received As on his first two physics tests and was up to speed in most of his other classes. He was even feeling better about his college prospects. He had read a magazine article that argued high school was relatively unimportant and that the name of the college a student attended was less significant than how that student performed. The message resonated with Ryland, who didn't care about prestige. As he told a friend, "If I'm interested in something, I commit to it and am successful. I don't think I'm going to have a problem, even if I'm not in the best school."

When he shared this outlook with his mother, she responded, "You're right, you don't have to get into a name-brand school or an Ivy League school. But you're not going to get into any school. You're going to go to Montgomery College."

"Actually," Ryland replied, "the University of Maryland has a good environmental science program, and I'm really interested in that." He knew that a high percentage of Whitman students who applied to Maryland got in.

"You can't get in there," she said. Still, Ryland had soldiered on with his schoolwork.

The shrill ring of Ryland's cell phone interrupted his date. "Ryland, you need to come home now," his father said. "I need the car. Your grandmother is in the hospital." Ryland rushed home, where his father was standing in the doorway, ready to leave immediately. Ryland's father called from the road to tell him to call his mother, break the news to her, and compile his grandmother's medical information. For the next several days, Ryland served as the go-between for his parents. He was so distraught by his beloved grandmother's failing health and bogged down by the responsibilities his parents placed on his shoulders that for the rest of the week, he hardly went to school.

AP FRANK, COLLEGE FRESHMAN | PERCEIVED AS: THE WORKHORSE

At about 2:30 in the morning on the Friday after Valentine's Day, AP Frank and Lydia were coming back from turning in their chemistry problem sets when he suddenly decided that now was the time. "Lydia," he said. The words seemed to fall from his mouth: "Lydiawouldyouliketogotothefreshmanformalwithme?"

She paused for a few seconds, smiling uncertainly. "Well, I don't know if I'm going, but if I am, I'd love to." AP Frank hurriedly changed the subject and went to his room.

A few days later, AP Frank was asleep when there was a knock at his door. He crawled out of bed and opened it to see Lydia. "Hey, Frank!" she said. "Let's go to the freshman formal together!"

Still half asleep, he replied, "Sure, that'd be fun," and rubbed his eyes. When she left, he sat back on his bed and thought, *Whoa, she said yes.* As he gradually woke up and went about brushing his teeth, getting dressed, and combing his hair, he thought, *WHOA. She said yes!* Each time he reminded himself, it meant more. Later, he learned from Kristen, ever his informant, that six other freshmen had asked Lydia to the formal, but she turned them all down. She had chosen him.

AP Frank thoroughly enjoyed the freshman formal. He later posted on his blog for his Whitman friends that the night was "easily the most fun night I've had at college, possibly ever—and without alcohol. The wonders that dancing with a girl you're crazy about can do for you . . . unbelievable."

That night AP Frank decided he couldn't take it anymore—listening for her to stop by, walking away from a conversation with her and thinking, *Oh, man, I could have said something so much funnier there.* He needed to know how Lydia felt about him. He went downstairs to tell the B31 guys about his resolution. They discussed it for two hours, late into the night, putting aside work to chat over burritos and chips. He told them he wanted to confront Lydia immediately.

"I really don't think that's the way to play it," Andrew said. "You have to spend a lot of time with her, not necessarily just you and her. You know, just be like, 'Hey, let's go explore Boston' or 'Let's go out with friends,' until at the end of the year it's just patently obvious that you should go out, and next year you make your move."

This strategy made sense to AP Frank, but he couldn't wait until fall. "I can't. It's just eating me up inside," he said. He was stirred by the doleful strains of the orchestral theme song from the movie *Meet Joe Black* that Mike played on repeat throughout the night.

"Well," Mike said, "a man's gotta do what a man's gotta do." As soon as he said it, violins swelled with a clash of the cymbals. AP Frank looked at Mike, smiled a sad smile, and nodded at the computer screen. Mike closed his eyes and nodded back.

"Mike, this is how you're going to know if things don't work out," AP Frank said. "I'm going to come down here with my USB stick, and I'm going to ask you for these songs. Because I'm going to need them. A lot. That's how you'll know I've done it, or rather, have failed at doing it."

"Frank," Mike said. "Please just tell me you won't be crushed."

"I don't know if I can, man. I've invested a lot of emotional energy in this whole ordeal. I don't know how I'll be able to take it." Eventually, Andrew convinced him to wait a week, until after the chemistry exam, because Lydia would be stressed out for the week leading up to it.

The next day AP Frank participated in his first wushu performance, a mix of martial art, dance, and gymnastics. The adrenaline rush of appearing onstage to the roar of a crowd, which he had experienced only at the Mr. Whitman pageant and graduation, was one of the most exhilarating feelings he had ever had. The weekend couldn't have gotten better, until Mike happened to say to the boys of B31, "Me and Frank pretty much make up the Fun Contingent of this dorm. I mean, without us, think of all the work you'd get done." AP Frank grinned. He had succeeded in reflecting the person he had hoped to become at college, away from home. He had finally broken the "study-hard-no-social-life nerd" image that had been dogging him all his life. At the end of the weekend, AP Frank blogged about how much he loved his Harvard friends.

He ended his blog with the line "I love my life, but I'm still scared of the future."

C.J., JUNIOR | PERCEIVED AS: THE FLIRT

C.J. needed something to take her mind off her stress. She felt bombarded by schoolwork and disheartened by her track times. Tired of listening to the MaryJanes brag incessantly about their alcohol consumption, C.J. decided she should try getting drunk so she could relate to their stories. A house party at the end of February gave her the perfect opportunity. It was her week off between indoor and outdoor track seasons, she was sleeping over at a track teammate's house, and the senior hosting the party apparently had told his mother to stay in a room upstairs and not come out until the party was over. C.J. yearned to do something out of character. It seemed as if everyone else was moving on to a mature style of partying while C.J. was still stuck in the Dance-Dance-Revolution-in-the-basement phase.

Sam picked C.J. up and took her to the party, where about thirty students were already drinking. C.J. found Derek and said hello to a few other people before Sam offered to get her a drink. When Sam returned with a shot of vodka, C.J. made Derek and Sam turn around, worried that because she had never done a shot before, she might accidentally toss it all over herself. Derek seemed to think she was an experienced drinker, and she didn't want him to know that she had never actually consumed alcohol.

There was a lot Derek didn't know about C.J., because she was convinced he had a different first impression of her than anyone else had, and she didn't want to change it. He seemed certain that she was the most secure-with-herself girl he had ever met. "I like the fact that you're different from other girls because you don't worry about your weight or appearance," he told her once. He seemed to think she was a fascinating, boy-crazy girl because she was ambiguous about her past experiences at parties and with other boys. He made C.J. want to be someone she wasn't, so she pretended to be that girl. She liked Derek, she liked the idea of having a Derek, but the piece that didn't seem to fit was her. In front of him, C.J. was determined to live up to that first impression.

C.J. did the shot and spent some time talking to friends, but she didn't feel drunk. She didn't feel any different at all. She did another shot and watched a game of beer pong. Still feeling nothing, she found the bottle of vodka, did a third shot, and resumed talking to friends. Now slightly tipsy, she downed more shots because she didn't consider herself drunk. *I can sober up at any time,* she told herself. *I'm just being hyper.*

When the partiers heard rumors that the police were coming, the crowd scattered, and a girl drove C.J. to her track teammate's house. C.J.'s teammate made her drink several bottles of water. "I'm not drunk!" C.J. said. She lay down in the street and called Derek on her cell phone.

"I wish you cared," Derek said.

"I licked Sam's finger," C.J. replied. Then she ate some snow.

When she woke up the next morning, C.J. was disappointed in herself. She recognized that she had put herself in a potentially dangerous situation—and yet she had a good time. She wrote the following to a friend:

To adults, it's just a teenage kid getting drunk; not being able to handle pressure, working all week, and sentencing her liver to death

on the weekends. But it's so much more than that. It was this suffocating pressure that accompanies everything in Whitman, this same panic you get when you have to stay up all night long. How can I explain that all my friends I've had since elementary school have left me behind in this world of inebriation and slurring words and all the great stuff that accompanies Bacardi and that I'm losing them? When I go out to lunch with my friends (yet another instance of breaking the rules that's really an attempt to stay in contact with these kids I've loved since elementary school . . .) I'm 100% on the outside looking in, hearing all these jokes and knowing that (a) I wasn't there (b) I don't know what it feels like (c) I'm no longer in their little world? How can I explain why I've essentially changed all my friends so I wouldn't have to drink and smoke every night and yet I still got drunk . . . There was no peer pressure. I'm pressuring myself. If I don't want to drink, why did I drink?

⁂

The first time I met AP Frank, before he left home for Harvard, he told me about a philosophy of his that worried him. He said, "When you cage up an animal for all of its life and then you let it free, it's going to go crazy." He was afraid that once he got to college, he would experience that fate.

Many students don't wait until college to attempt to break free. As C.J. suggested, high school students might not drink because of peer pressure. They drink because of pressure, period. They drink because of pressure to be superlative. They drink because of pressure to be perfect. Consider all of the other factors that high school students have to deal with in addition to academic stress. Besides the full-time job of over-achieving, students deal extensively with social, psychological, romantic, identity, and family issues while at the same time trying to navigate adolescence. None of these pressures lets up after the bell rings at the end of the school day.

Students can get so tightly wound, it's understandable that they search for outlets to let off steam. Drinking alcohol happens to be one of the most popular methods, perhaps not surprisingly, given adults' habits of imbibing to unwind. Like adults, many students say they "need a drink" to escape the stress and pressure of their daily lives. By the time they reach twelfth grade, almost 80 percent of students have consumed alcohol, and nearly a third have engaged in binge drinking, defined as having five or more drinks on one occasion. By eighth grade, almost half of all students have tried alcohol, and more than 20 percent say they have been drunk. At the college level, campuses report record increases in binge drinking. As University of Virginia professor John Portmann told *Psychology Today*, "There is a ritual every university administrator has come to fear. Every fall, parents drop off their well-groomed freshmen, and within two or three days, many have consumed a dangerous amount of alcohol and placed themselves in harm's way. These kids have been controlled for so long, they just go crazy."

The statistically good news is that nationwide, illicit drug use is on the decline. (Illegal use of prescription drugs is on the upswing, however, as discussed in Chapter Fourteen.) But the sad fact is that students who try these substances often do so less out of rebelliousness than out of escapism. As a Massachusetts junior told me, "I turned to drugs and alcohol because I felt the need to escape everything. I no longer do any of that because I realize it was dangerous and stupid. Sometimes I do think about it, though. Everything seemed much simpler when I could escape the pain and loss of control."

For many students, there's another outlet that falls under the umbrella of "partying" to relieve stress: sex, or just fooling around. "I suppose I went to extremes because of the amount I was working and the reputation I had," a California senior said. "I enjoyed being the valedictorian who could still get drunk or high or have sex on the weekends. My friends knew me as someone who would study until late at night, then go out with a guy, and wake up on Saturday morning to go running and then study all day. It's funny to think that being a good student led to me trying dangerous things, but I think I was just trying to break the mold."

When I asked her what adults might not know about today's high school experience, she expounded on why she partied. "I was definitely very stressed, and I worked very hard. Long nights studying, job shadows, college classes, internships, SATs, sports, all at the same time as balancing a social life. This could be why students do things to such extremes. There is a sense of urgency and pressure. Many of my friends and I would drink to the point of blacking out. Every time. I would have sex with guys the first time I hooked up with them, because I didn't want to waste time. I think I came out fine, and I was happy with how I balanced work and play. But I don't think adults realize what high schoolers are capable of. They think that if we work hard and appear to follow the rules, then we won't make mistakes."

More than 60 percent of twelfth graders have had sex, and health centers say students are experimenting with sex at younger ages. In recent years, middle schoolers have been caught having sex on school buses. In Pennsylvania, a group of middle school girls who called themselves the "Pop-Tarts" offered blow jobs at parties. And in high school, some students are using sex as a tool to attempt to break out of the cage.

A midwestern Latina student felt imprisoned by her parents' pressure to be the perfect college applicant. They refused to allow her to take art or music because the classes weren't APs, and they forced her to take Spanish classes, even though she was fluent, to get the easy A. They also insisted she become a cheerleader, though she disliked it, so she would have an extracurricular activity to bolster her college application. When she wasn't at school, her cage became more literal: Her father locked her in her room, where she was expected to do nothing but study. Because she wasn't allowed to leave the house during the weeks before the SAT, she took to sneaking out late at night. Just before the test, the sixteen-year-old sneaked out to have sex with her boyfriend to relieve her stress—and had a pregnancy scare. To this day her parents don't know about the home pregnancy tests she frantically took then and twice more in the ensuing months, or that she then turned to alcohol as another escape.

Locked in her room as the SAT neared, she was forbidden to take breaks, relax, or chat with friends. Burned out and stressed beyond belief, the non-drinker skipped school soon after the test to try to relax at a friend's house, where she had two beers. A police officer happened to catch the students, arrested them, and jailed them for the day. Her parents didn't speak to her for a week, but not because of the arrest. They were furious because of her 1300 (out of 1600) SAT score.

Chapter 13

March 4–March 25

TESTED

A P Frank's day was going so well that he resolved to ask Lydia out before the end of it. He had been agonizing over her since the formal. They spent the weekend studying together for the chemistry exam, taking brief breaks to poke and tickle each other. For her work space, Lydia made herself comfortable in his bed. She woke him up in the mornings to study, rapping on his door and then barging in, wearing her red hoodie and her backpack, announcing, "Chemistry doesn't sleep!"

AP Frank walked away from the chemistry exam feeling confident about his grade. The weather was warm enough that he could wear a fleece instead of a jacket, and he spent much of the day socializing with friends. He talked to Richard, who was now on Whitman's varsity volleyball team and in a band, happy in his foster home, and doing well in classes. AP Frank was in such a good mood that he even raved to friends about that day's biology lecture, which was supposed to be about inversions and gene locations but instead covered *South Park*'s Mr. Hankey the Christmas Poo.

Despite his glee, AP Frank spent the day wringing his hands, thinking, *Gotta do it. Today's the day.* He was in bed getting ready to take a midafternoon nap when he saw Lydia in the hallway. His heart leaped into his throat. *Now? Should I?* He let the moment pass.

The next night AP Frank was combing his hair in the bathroom when, in his glasses' reflection, he saw Lydia walk into the hallway.

Okay, game time, he thought. As he walked out of the bathroom, Lydia peeked around the corner to see if it was him. AP Frank had never been more ready to tell a girl how he felt about her. They went into his room, where she sat at his computer to show him some people she knew on Facebook. He was kneeling on the floor next to her. *This is as good as it's going to get,* he thought. *Just wait for the right moment. It'll come . . .* The conversation stopped. She looked at him expectantly. AP Frank was about to speak when Isabel, a Mass Hall dormmate, walked in. "Frank, can I use your printer?" Isabel asked.

Dammit dammit dammit. "Uh, sure, go for it," he said.

Isabel sat at his computer and proceeded to load up a website that featured a photograph of an extremely obese woman—certainly more than 500 pounds—in skimpy clothing on all fours on a bed. "OH MY GOD, WHAT ARE YOU DOING?" AP Frank yelled. The mood killer was exquisitely timed.

"Eww, what are you doing?" Lydia echoed, wrinkling her nose.

"I need to print four of these pictures as a reminder to keep to my diet," said Isabel, an already slender girl.

"Okay, this is gross. I'm leaving," Lydia said. *This is the worst thing that could happen, ever,* AP Frank thought.

Once Lydia had turned the corner, AP Frank kicked the wall a few times. "Arghh!"

"What's wrong?" Isabel asked.

AP Frank sputtered incoherent syllables before bellowing, "I was going to *do* it!"

Isabel, like many members of Mass Hall, knew immediately what he was referring to. "Oh my gosh, I'm so sorry!" she said.

"No, no. It's okay. It's not your fault," AP Frank said, trying to calm down.

"Really?"

"Actually, no. It is your fault, but that's okay."

When Isabel left, AP Frank killed time by doing homework before Lydia returned. After a few minutes of idle chatting, AP Frank thought, *Here goes.* He closed the door, cleared his throat, and began. "Lydia, I wanted to ask you what your status on relationships is at this moment. Because this past month, we've spent a lot of time together, and I've realized that I really enjoy your company and I love spending time with you, so I was hoping . . . that you'd make an exception once, for me."

There was a pause. Lydia looked pensive, and unsurprised. "Frank, I really enjoy spending time with you, too," she said. "But I just got my chem exam score back, and I got an 81."

"That's fine," AP Frank said. He didn't tell her that he got a 96.

"No, it's terrible!" Lydia replied. "I studied *really* hard for this, and it bothers me that I came out thinking I did well when I didn't. So I don't really think I can date right now."

AP Frank furrowed his brow and put on his most serious "Mm-hmm, I totally understand" face. The room was quiet for a few beats. "Well, that's okay. I just needed to know," he said. "So. This doesn't change anything between us then, right? You'll still hang out with me, you'll still come by?"

"Of course," she said.

"Thanks."

Silence again. AP Frank picked up the T-shirt graphic he was designing for the Mass Hall intramural team and started to yammer: "Hrm, I don't have everyone's sizes yet, but I think I can guess. He's a small, she's a small . . ."

Lydia sat on his bed and listened to him for a few minutes. Then she said softly, "Frank, come sit by me." He did. She put her arm around him. "Frank, let's look out for each other—not just this year—and let's keep in touch and stay close."

"Sure thing. That sounds great."

"I want to avoid regrets by working hard," Lydia said. "I don't want to look back and think, 'If only I had just focused.'"

"I want to not have regrets by enjoying my time here, by having fun," said Frank, his AP prefix shed at last. "I don't want to look back and think, 'If only I had just relaxed a little.'"

After Lydia left, Frank opened his desk drawer and saw his bright red USB memory stick. He trudged slowly downstairs, nudged open the B31 door, and walked into Mike's room, where he was doing homework. "What up, Frank," Mike said without looking up.

"Mike, I'm gonna need those songs," Frank said, and held up the memory stick.

Mike stood up and gave Frank a hug. "Aw, man, I'm sorry." One of

Mike's roommates came up to Frank, shook his hand, and said, "You're a good man, Frank. I'm proud of you." Mike put on the song, and Frank lay down on Mike's bed, shuffling cards as he did when he was nervous. He stared off into space as Mike sat down to resume his homework. "You gonna be okay, man?" Mike asked.

"Yeah, I'll be fine." Frank continued to shuffle for a while, then went back upstairs to try to get some work done.

That night Frank put up on his blog: "Leave it to a Harvard girl to not want to date because she has to focus on academics."

AUDREY, JUNIOR | PERCEIVED AS: THE PERFECTIONIST

During the week leading up to the SAT, Audrey was already a wreck. She divided her hundreds of vocabulary flash cards into three piles: words she knew, words she kind of knew, and words she kept forgetting. The latter pile was still a daunting size.

On Tuesday afternoon one of Audrey's friends came over to hang out, but their casual conversation gradually shifted to the SAT. After several minutes, the friend said, "You're overly stressed." She grabbed Audrey's flash cards from the ledge near the stairs to Audrey's attic bedroom, took the rubber bands off the three piles, and meshed the stacks together, pulling cards out of order and reinserting them haphazardly into the combined stack.

Audrey was astonished. "Oh my God, you did not just do that!" she shrieked as her friend smirked menacingly at her. "Those were in specific piles!" When it dawned on the friend that Audrey's wrath was real, she tried to run away with the cards, but not before Audrey caught her with an Indian rug burn on her arm. "Give them to me right now!" Audrey yelled. The friend tossed her the cards and skittered to the other side of the room, where she hid under Audrey's bed. Audrey asked her to leave, which she did, sheepishly.

For the next hour and a half, Audrey went through the deck card by card, until she had reorganized it into her original three piles. She couldn't help thinking that at least reassembling the cards forced her to review the words again.

On the Thursday before the SAT, Audrey and her parents were sitting in the kitchen discussing colleges; the following day they had a conference with Audrey's guidance counselor to plan the application process. Audrey wasn't overjoyed about engaging in college talk two days before the SAT.

While Audrey's mother looked up colleges on TCCi to see the SAT scores and GPAs of accepted Whitman students, Audrey flipped through one of her vocabulary card stacks. She had carried the cards around all week. She had even gone on a one-day art department field trip to New York for the sole purpose of spending four uninterrupted hours on the bus each way, studying the cards.

Abruptly, Audrey's father grabbed the vocabulary cards. "You're done with these," he said. "You're not getting these back. You have to stop. It's a mental game, and I know you can do it. But you can't do this to yourself. You did this for the PSAT. You can't do it again."

The PSAT, for which she had studied for months, had brought Audrey the most heartache she had felt all year. When she had received her score in December, she had a panic attack. Her numbers sent her into a fit of hysterics; short of breath, she couldn't stop crying for hours. "I'm not going to get into college!" she bawled. Her parents tried to calm her down, but she screamed at them to leave her alone.

Now, faced with a threat to her SAT preparation, Audrey panicked again. "You need to give those to me!" she said to her father, who was holding the flash cards up high. "I'll fail if I don't get those back. What happens if there's a question and I blatantly don't know the words? I'll have no chance!"

"Audrey, you're going to fail if you keep stressing out," her mother said gently. "You get so worked up that you don't do well because you get it in your head that you're going to fail."

Her father gave her a serious look. "It's two days before the test. If you don't know it now, you're not going to know it then."

Audrey stormed off. She grabbed her other card stacks from her room and angrily rifled through them. She had been trying to memorize the cards all week, and yet she found herself looking at words she had reviewed only five minutes before that she still couldn't remember. Audrey tried to relax, but her nerves were out of control. She had only two days.

Fifteen minutes later, her father came into her room and handed her the cards. "You have to chill out. Promise me you won't study tomorrow." She took the cards and walked away.

❧

I t is probably safe to say there is no test that students and parents agonize over more than the SAT. The test has become an obsession. High
school students often take it multiple times, praying to boost their scores
by even a few points. Tutors and test prep centers report that parents are
signing up for their services for children as young as twelve; in 2003, 17
percent more seventh- and eighth-graders took the SAT than in 1993.
Experts warn that tutoring children for the SAT at young ages can lead
to excessive stress, but hordes of families do it anyway. As Columbia
University president Lee Bollinger said at a College Board conference,
"The SAT has become a symbol . . . of all the anxieties, concerns, fears,
and frustrations in the college-admissions system." Or, as a New York
SAT tutor phrased it, students "feel that everything they have done for
the past four years comes down to the SAT."

One problem is that so much effort and faith are put into a test
that for decades researchers have proved to be flawed. Julie, for example, was not a different student when she scored a 1520 than when she
scored a 1410 four months earlier. Until 1994, "SAT" stood for
"Scholastic Aptitude Test." But generally, students' "aptitude" increased
by thirty points for every $10,000 their parents earned in yearly
income. A California study found that the level of parents' education
alone explained more than 50 percent of the difference in students'
SAT scores. The SAT has historically been accused of racial bias, with
minorities regularly scoring below the national average for white
students. And in March 2006, the College Board confessed that the
tests of more than 5,000 students who took the October 2005 SAT
were mis-scored, some by up to 450 points lower than they deserved.
By the time the College Board admitted the errors—three months after it first learned about them—it was too late for seniors to change
where they chose to send college and scholarship applications.

Furthermore, several researchers have concluded that the SAT as-
sesses little more than test-taking skills. One study examined how students' different learning styles corresponded to their SAT scores. Students
were categorized as taking a "surface approach" to learning (a superficial
memorization of facts), an "achieving approach" (a focus on grades and

scores rather than understanding of the subject), or a "deep approach" (a genuine commitment to learning). The study found that the higher-scoring students were those who used the surface and achieving approaches, while the lower-scoring students were more likely to use the deep approach, their love of learning unrewarded by the SAT.

Administered by the College Board, the SAT was purportedly designed to predict students' grades during their freshman year at college. However, studies have revealed that the test alone is practically worthless for that purpose. Beyond freshman year, students' SAT scores have even less of a correlation with their college grades, and almost no correlation with their success in the workplace as adults.

In a landmark twenty-year study of its optional SAT score submission policy for applicants, Bates College found no differences in academic performance between submitters and non-submitters, stating, "Testing is not necessary for predicting good performance." William Hiss, Bates's vice president for external affairs, told me he would recommend without hesitation that other colleges adopt the optional policy. Test scores "become a false negative to turn applicants down. And worse than the false negative are students taking themselves out of the college aspiring pool in the first place. Standardized testing is artificially truncating the pool of people who will be successful in college."

Despite these findings, schools have continued to teach to the SAT. In 2000 Richard C. Atkinson, then-president of the University of California system, visited his grandchildren's upscale private school, where he observed twelve-year-olds studying analogies to prepare for the SAT. "I learned that they spend hours each month—directly and indirectly—preparing for the SAT, studying long lists of verbal analogies," he later said. "The time involved was not aimed at developing the students' reading and writing abilities but, rather, their test-taking skills." The story goes that, struck by the visit, Atkinson decided if his students had to take the SAT, then he should give it a try, too. After taking several sample tests, he called his deputy to complain about analogies.

In February 2001 Atkinson announced his recommendation that the University of California, the College Board's biggest client, stop requiring its applicants to submit their SAT scores. "SAT scores can have a profound effect on how students regard themselves," he said. "All of us have known students who excelled in high school, students who did everything expected of them and more, suddenly doubt their accomplishments, their abilities, and their basic worth because they scored poorly on the SAT."

Faced with the prospect of losing the University of California's 76,000 applicants per year and the $2 million they generated (at that time, students paid $28.50 each time they took the SAT), the College Board eventually kowtowed, promising to revamp the SAT to woo Atkinson back.

RYLAND, JUNIOR | PERCEIVED AS: THE SLACKER

When the mail came one day midway through the third quarter, Ryland shuffled through the envelopes. He spotted a letter addressed to his parents and tore it open. Whenever he saw mail addressed to his "parent or guardian," he opened it and squirreled it away. He wasn't shocked to see that he had received his first serious interim, a warning letter teachers sent out midquarter if a student's grade was in jeopardy. His Modern World teacher had written, "Ryland is not engaged in Modern World. Awaiting submission of work. Needs to take test preparation and assignment completion seriously." Ryland slumped. *I need to talk to her about why I'm behind,* he thought. *My teacher thinks I really don't care about anything.*

In truth, he hadn't caught up with his work from when he missed classes because of his grandmother's hospital stay. Once he had fallen behind, he grew increasingly dejected because he felt he had to do his work methodically, in chronological order, the old assignments before the new. He had completed much of the work but didn't feel comfortable turning it in piecemeal; he wanted to finish all of it and hand in the whole stack. Because he hadn't completed the old assignments, he didn't jump ahead to finish the new ones, which he otherwise might have submitted on time.

Ryland was now regularly going to sleep after three A.M. The county environmental group and the group who prepared food for the homeless were meeting at Ryland's house every weekend; the *Black & White* was coming out more frequently, which meant more photos and more flat nights; and the newspaper editors were starting to assign him articles to write. He had failed his last two math tests because he didn't know the material. Oddly enough, with his new teacher, physics was his least stressful class. Ryland put his interim in a drawer where his parents wouldn't find it, and resolved to see his Modern World teacher that week. Overwhelmed with homework that night, however, Ryland unintentionally slept through half of his classes and got stuck in a new cycle. He continued to forge notes for the attendance office. In case someone looked at his file, he listed his cell phone number as his parents' point of contact.

Ryland didn't want to come across as the kind of student who would receive an interim. He was trying hard to improve. He wasn't socializing much and had resolved not to take on any more extracurricular activities beyond those to which he had already committed. His girlfriend understood his schedule and was flexible with it.

When he got up the courage to face his Modern World teacher, Ryland went to school early to find her. He timidly poked his head inside her classroom. When she spotted him, he said, "I want to talk to you about why I'm so behind in this class."

"Okay." She ushered him to a desk and pulled out a seat for him.

How could Ryland tell her that he was stressed out of his mind because of his myriad activities and the pressure of junior year? All Whitman students were stressed out of their minds. Instead, he explained that he had shut down for a while because his grandmother had been hospitalized and that he hadn't been able to catch up on the work. As he told her this, Ryland felt guilty. Even though his grandmother's illness had caused him to fall behind, he didn't feel good about using it as an excuse. "I'm trying to catch up," he added. "I'm behind in all of my classes. I'm planning not to go out this weekend so I can start to catch up in everything."

The teacher was caring and understanding. She had assumed he was simply uncommitted to her class. She told him he could have an extension.

Ryland did plan to catch up over the weekend. He succeeded in catching up in his other classes because he hadn't talked to the other teachers and didn't want to make excuses to them. But he didn't catch up in Modern World, because a new activity was taking up his time. Starting this month, on top of everything else, he had a three-hour SAT prep class twice a week. While sitting in his first prep class, he had grown furious. He didn't have time for the class, and taking it certainly wasn't going to change his level of intelligence.

As he told a friend, "I think the way everyone takes these preparatory classes is bullshit. It's gotten so that even if I am a lot smarter than some-one, if they have an SAT class or two, of course they will do better than me. But that doesn't mean that I'm not as smart! I'm against wasting time on massive preparing for the SATs. But colleges won't look at my scores and say, 'Oh, but he didn't take a class because he's busy doing other im-portant things that he actually is interested in.' So I basically *must* do something, just to be judged on the level of everyone else."

C.J., JUNIOR | PERCEIVED AS: THE FLIRT

On the Thursday before the SAT, C.J.'s father drove her and a few other teammates to a rural Maryland town for the state tournament in business management. The tournament was held Thursday afternoon though Sat-urday afternoon, but C.J. arrived later, not wanting to miss school and track practice. The competition consisted of a hundred-question multiple-choice business management test, for which C.J. crammed in the car, and two role-playing exercises instructing teams to solve a business problem and present their solution to a panel of judges who interviewed them. Last year C.J. and her partner had come in first in the state tournament in two categories and in the top 10 percent at the national tournament.

C.J. and her partner looked forward to the role-playing exercise. They immediately got to work when a judge handed them a piece of paper with their prompt: They were managing a resort that attracted businessmen and the elderly, with the goal of expanding to attract fam-ilies with children. They came up with an advertising campaign, a mar-keting plan complete with statistics, a summer camp program, and profit projections. When their fifteen minutes were up, the judges fired ques-tions at them. "How are you going to handle risk management?" one asked. C.J. and her partner were smooth. "We have trained profession-als," C.J. said, "and there's a children's hospital right down the road." The duo left the room feeling like they had nailed their presentation.

As soon as her last competition ended on Friday afternoon, C.J. left the tournament to get home in time for a good night's sleep before the SAT. On Saturday she spent the SAT thinking about her partner, who was still at the tournament, waiting for their names to be called during the morning's award ceremony. The top two teams would qualify for the national tournament. After the test, she called her partner. "We sucked," her partner said as soon as she picked up the phone.

"That means we got second," C.J. said. "That sucks."

AUDREY, JUNIOR | PERCEIVED AS: THE PERFECTIONIST

The day before the SAT, Audrey and her parents met with her guidance counselor. Audrey's mother brought along an organized list of the colleges Audrey was considering and the average unweighted GPA and SAT scores for accepted Whitman students to each school.

When the meeting began, the counselor handed Audrey's parents a copy of her unofficial transcript. As they looked at it in silence, Audrey guessed that everyone was thinking the same thing: Last semester's grades had sunk her below the average accepted GPA for Georgetown, her do-or-die first choice. Before her parents could say anything, Audrey quickly pointed out that there were two Bs that the teachers had promised to change to As.

"Oh, right, I don't know why those haven't been changed," the counselor said. "That would definitely put you back in the thick of it." Audrey could sense the room relax.

About halfway through the meeting, Audrey's mother reminded the counselor that Audrey was Hispanic. The counselor looked thoughtful. "You have to stack all the cards you can get, and this is one of those things that could really help you," he said. "It depends on each school. It always helps, but there's no set rule."

As the counselor went over the list of schools, he repeated about a half-dozen times, "That's a bit of a reach school, but since you have the Hispanic card, who knows . . ." Audrey wasn't as uncomfortable with this line of thinking as her father seemed to be. She had come to grips with the fact that her father's place of birth automatically expanded her choices.

On the morning of the SAT, Audrey jolted awake in terror. *Oh, no,* she kept thinking. *I can't do this.* She had fulfilled her promise to her father by not studying the day before, though she was able to do so only by inviting friends over to make sure she watched movies and did other non-SAT activities. When Audrey came downstairs, an omelet, toast, and orange juice were waiting for her on the table. She wolfed down the meal.

On the ride to Whitman, Audrey and C.J. insisted that the radio stay off, worried that if they listened to music, they would get songs stuck in their head, which might push out more important SAT-related factoids. They frantically volleyed reminders of SAT terms they tended to forget: "Dangling modifiers!" "Parallel structure!"

By the time she got to Whitman, Audrey wondered if she would be able to keep her breakfast down. When the proctor opened the door to the classroom, Audrey showed her ID, sat down at her desk, and panicked, butterflies squirming impatiently in her stomach. She thought she was going to be sick, which added a new list of worries to the litany. *What do I do if I'm going to be sick? I'm not allowed out of the classroom and back in!*

Once the test began, Audrey focused, fully aware that she needed every available second. She went through all of the questions in a section, circling numbers of questions she wasn't certain about and drawing squares around those she could only guess at. When she finished the section, she went back over the squared questions, then the circled ones. All the while, she calmed herself down by reminding herself that, unlike the PSAT, the SAT could be taken and retaken several times.

∽

On March 12, 2005, Audrey and C.J. were among the first group of students to take the College Board's new SAT. The exam time now totaled three hours and forty-five minutes, forty-five minutes longer than the old SAT. Analogies, Richard Atkinson's nemesis, were noticeably missing from the revised verbal section, which contained longer reading passages and a section in which students had to match pairs of words. The math section now tested Algebra II skills. The new SAT also added a writing section that included a twenty-five-minute essay graded on a one-to-six scale and a multiple-choice section about grammatical errors and improving sentences and paragraphs. Overachievers now had a new magic number to strive for: a perfect SAT score of 2400.

Atkinson never axed the SAT, thanks to the College Board's revisions. But did the new SAT remedy concerns about the old one? Arguably not. For example, the gap between black students and white students had been smaller on the analogies section than on the test in general, but analogies were now gone. In fact, on the new SAT, the gap between white and minority scores widened in some states.

Meanwhile, the new SAT raised new problems. Kaplan Test Prep surveyed nearly 2,000 students, many of whom said the test length exhausted them and they didn't have time to finish the essay. "The students described themselves as drained, bedraggled, bewildered, and completely overwhelmed," reported Jennifer Karan, national director of Kaplan's SAT program. She said that in some cases, administrative matters kept the students at testing sites for an hour longer than the test, meaning that for nearly five hours, students were not allowed to eat or drink, and, depending on the proctor, some weren't even permitted five-minute breaks between sections.

The National Council of Teachers of English questioned the validity of the essay section, fearing pressure to teach formulaic writing. Nearly half of 374 schools surveyed by Kaplan, Inc., planned to disregard the essays entirely. Schools such as MIT, Ohio State, and the University of Chicago refused to consider the essay for admission in 2006, in part because of a possible link between essay length and score. Students' essay scores could vary depending on whether they liked the essay topic and to which essay grader they happened to be assigned. The essay changed the nature of what had previously been an objective, machine-scored multiple-choice test.

In 2003 *Time* reporter John Cloud participated in a mock scoring session with the College Board's writing-development committee. The fifteen readers assigned fifteen essays anywhere from one to six points. In an example of just how subjective the writing section was, none of the essays received the same score from every reader, and on most of them, the difference varied by at least three points. On a larger scale, the College Board hires thousands of readers to grade about 2.3 million student essays per year, with the graders expending about a minute or two per essay. "The pressure to read fast and to reward competent but formulaic essays will be massive," Cloud wrote.

Educators fear that teaching to the essay test will stifle creativity, originality, and revision processes. In 2004 *The Atlantic* published a piece by Princeton Review officials that discussed the College Board's grading criteria. They advised, "To receive a high score a student should write a long essay of three or more paragraphs, with each paragraph containing topic and concluding sentences and at least one sentence that includes the words 'for example.' Whenever possible the student should use polysyllabic words where shorter, clearer words would suffice. The SAT essay will not be a place to take rhetorical chances. Flair will win no points; the highest-scoring essays will be earnest, long-winded, and predictable."

To show how the new SAT essays would be scored, staff at the Princeton Review graded passages penned by famous writers, SAT-style. An Ernest Hemingway essay garnered only a three because it lacked "specific examples and clear topic sentences" and was "too undeveloped to be good." Shakespeare notched a two, with a "poorly organized" passage "riddled with errors in syntax, incomplete sentences being the most noticeable problem." The graders did lavish praise on one writer for an essay that was "well developed, displays an impressive vocabulary, and makes good use of supporting examples." The elusive six was granted to Ted Kaczynski, the Unabomber.

Even before the new SAT was administered, overachievers began strategizing a new plan of action: Take the ACT in addition to the SAT to boost the chances of getting a good standardized test score—and take each test twice. The strategy makes sense; while all SAT scores are sent to the colleges where a student applies, the reporting of ACT scores is optional, which means students can take the ACT as many times as they want and don't have to report the scores.

The ACT, which tests English, math, reading, and science, is a more curriculum-based test than the SAT, and unlike the SAT, it doesn't penalize students for wrong guesses. The ACT's optional essay test uses more practical questions than philosophical. In decades past, the ACT was the test of choice for midwestern students, while students on either coast traditionally took the SAT. With the advent of the new SAT, however, the numbers shifted. Among 2005 graduates, ACT takers numbered almost 1.2 million, closing in on the SAT's 1.4 million. The number of students who took the February 2005 ACT increased by 22 percent over 2004.

University of California President Emeritus Richard Atkinson told me he is "very satisfied" with the new SAT. But it remains to be seen how much other universities will value it. In the months surrounding the new SAT's debut, Holy Cross and Lawrence University added their names to the list of more than 700 schools that do not require SAT or

ACT scores. "There was so much angst developing around the writing test, with kids starting to stress out," Steven Syverson, Lawrence's dean of admissions, told *The New York Times*. "When we heard the test-prep industry say it would add $200 million a year to coaching revenues, we just said, 'That's it. It's out of line, it's out of whack, and we don't want to be part of it.'"

Indeed, the test-prep industry has profited enormously from the new SAT. The month it debuted, Kaplan Test Prep reported an increase in business "well north" of 20 percent. For years the College Board had insisted that students' scores could not be improved by coaching. But companies like Kaplan and the Princeton Review said that the new SAT was even more coachable than its predecessor. After the first new SAT was administered, College Board spokeswoman Chiara Coletti accused the test-prep industry of hyping the anxiety of students and their families to make a buck.

With the new SAT, the College Board itself suddenly was pushing new test-prep products. The College Board sells a $19.95, 889-page guide described this way: "This new book is the only one with practice tests created by the test maker according to proprietary new SAT specifications . . . [S]tudents: Gain experience by taking 8 practice tests and receiving estimated scores. Raise confidence by reviewing concepts, test-taking approaches, and practice questions. Increase understanding of the new PSAT/NMSQT® and the new SAT. Plus, book buyers receive free online score reports and a discount on The Official SAT Online Course™ with auto essay scoring." The changes to the SAT also increased the student test fee to $41.50, adding more than $30 million a year to College Board revenues. Students who want to send their scores to more than four schools pay $9 for each additional school. Who, exactly, is trying to cash in?

Some parents and students might already be familiar with the College Board, which describes itself as "a not-for-profit membership association" composed of more than 4,700 schools, colleges, universities, and "other educational organizations." In 2006 the College Board, which also sets AP curriculum standards, planned to audit AP classes nationwide by reviewing descriptions of course syllabi, sample assignments, and sample exams.

But many families don't realize how powerful the College Board is.

Regardless of the debate over whether the SAT is a useful tool, the Board knows full well that in this era of hyper-competitiveness, schools will teach to it. In fact, it is the College Board's mission that every school in the country do so. The *point* of the new SAT is to change what students across the country are taught in schools, by forcing teachers to teach to a test. In 2003 some school districts were already scurrying to change their course offerings so their students would be better prepared for the new SAT. Other schools offer SAT prep courses during the school day for elective credit.

The College Board can determine how students write, what skills teachers emphasize, and which books classes read. When the Board issues specific recommendations—such as math courses including radical equations—schools adopt them. Through the use of the most feared test in the United States, these non-elected officials have ensured that a single private group can dictate a national curriculum with no input or approval from the general public. Back in 2001, Richard Atkinson, who spurred this revolution, said, "America's overemphasis on the SAT is compromising our educational system." With the new SAT, that doesn't appear to have changed.

Even the College Board's title "New SAT" is a marketing tool, which, for the periods before and after the debut of the test, theoretically would sell more of its own preparation books. In 1994 the College Board changed the test's name from the Scholastic Aptitude Test to the Scholastic Assessment Test. Now, according to the College Board, the letters don't stand for anything anymore. Perhaps that in itself is symbolic.

SAM, SENIOR | PERCEIVED AS: THE TEACHER'S PET

In a black suit and blue tie, Sam walked into the hotel hosting Whitman's Senior Banquet, the pre-graduation, pre-prom send-off night of food, dancing, and the announcements of the Senior Superlatives results. During a dinner of pasta with vegetables, Caesar salad, breaded chicken, and petite desserts, Julie left her table and pulled up a chair next to Sam. He smiled. He knew she wasn't interested in him, but that was okay. She was someone who had been a stranger before junior year and now was one of his closest friends. Maybe, Sam thought, he should forget about romantic prospects with anyone for the rest of his senior year. Maybe he should focus on cultivating the friendships he wanted to sustain. It occurred to him that there was no one he would rather go to prom with than Julie, even as a friend.

The two senior class officers and the head Nasty walked up to the dance floor. "Now," the DJ bellowed, "your class officers are going to announce the Senior Superlatives!" The room hushed. One by one, they went through the categories: Best Eyes, Most Athletic, Senior Sex Symbol, etc. "And Most Stressed goes to . . ." the Nasty began, ". . . Sam!" *What?!* Sam thought. *That's bullshit.* Cheers of "Saaam!" ricocheted around the room. Embarrassed, he accepted his certificate from the Nasty, who cooed, "Crazy Sam. I love you, Sam!" Back at the table, Julie laughed sympathetically. She seemed relaxed; probably, Sam guessed, because she was in no danger of having to accept an award in front of the room. Rumor had it that the Nastys had turned on one of their own as Most Awkward, and the category mysteriously disappeared from the list.

A few superlatives later, the officers announced, "And Teacher's Pet goes to . . . Sam!" Sam wasn't surprised by that one. He meandered toward the stage, spied some teachers sitting near the front of the room, and, to his classmates' laughter, exaggeratedly strutted over to shake the teachers' hands and give them high fives.

The next day Julie took Sam to RFK Stadium to buy him a Washington Nationals baseball cap as a belated gift for his eighteenth birthday. They walked through a nearby market, joking about Senior Banquet. On the ride home, Sam's stomach was in knots. Even if he were going to ask Julie to prom as a platonic date, which he assumed any event with her would be, asking her still loomed as the culminating event of his years in high school. He slipped a jazz piano CD into the car's player and nervously tried not to think about his date disasters at past Whitman dances.

When Julie pulled into Sam's driveway, he got halfway out of the car. "Don't forget your hat!" Julie said.

Sam took a breath. "Oh," he said, casually poking his head back into the car, "I have a question."

"Yeah?"

"Would you at all be interested in going to prom with me? I think it'll be really fun."

Julie paused.

The Stealth Overachiever, junior	Perceived as: ?

Stealth loved debate. It fulfilled Stealth's competitive nature—Stealth was the kid at fourth-grade basketball camp who would cry after losing a game. But more importantly, debate was an intellectual challenge. As Stealth saw it, while high school was "just a mad scramble to turn in a lot of work and get everything done," debate was "the kind of place you can challenge yourself intellectually by doing things you want to do, like you can make up the easiest case position, or you can go read Heidegger and see what he has to say about a topic." Debate also provided an opportunity to meet great people, like Geoffrey, Stealth's favorite debater, who was the most brilliant and hilarious person Stealth had ever met. At tournaments and camps they both attended, they were usually inseparable. At Whitman, Stealth often regaled friends with stories about Geoffrey's antics.

Stealth cruised through the first three rounds of the district debate championships. Top debaters from Virginia, Washington, D.C., and some parts of Maryland were competing for the two Mid-Atlantic slots at the national tournament in June. After the third round, only three students were still undefeated, including Stealth and another Whitman student. In the fourth round, Stealth was up against the third undefeated contender, a girl from Virginia. Stealth expected to lose. Local judges tended to favor students who, as Stealth put it, "speak pretty," and this girl was a former national qualifier who was known for her eloquence. Stealth was one of the fastest local speakers and a good debater but didn't speak pretty.

Stealth was right. The round was close, but the judges tallied Stealth's first loss of the weekend. One more loss and Stealth was out. After an easy fifth-round win, Stealth went to the hallway to hang out with the other Whitman debater while they waited for the judges to post the next round's matchups for the five remaining students. When a judge taped the sheet to the wall, Stealth was irritated. Instead of scheduling a matchup against someone new, the judges had slated a second faceoff against the Virginia girl.

Neither Stealth nor the well-spoken girl dominated the debate. While waiting for the judges to post the scores, Stealth saw the girl and went over to chat. She was wearing sunglasses and talking quietly to a few other students. "Hey, guys," Stealth said. When Stealth got up close, the girls' teary eyes behind her sunglasses were evident.

"You picked up," she said, debate-speak for "you won." Stealth felt badly for her. She had gone to nationals the year before, and now Stealth had knocked her out of contention. Stealth gave her a hug.

Round seven was the semifinal. Stealth's personal RadioShack timer showed that the allotted four minutes were up, just as a judge raised two fingers, signaling that there were still two minutes remaining. Confused, Stealth checked the RadioShack timer again. The four minutes were up. Why was the judge trying to extend the time illegally? Stealth wrapped up the speech and sat down, rejecting the chance to cheat in a debate tournament.

Stealth and the other Whitman debater arrived late to the tournament's awards ceremony. They slipped into the back of the room and waited for their category to be called. "In the first semifinal, the semifinalist trophy goes to . . ." The announcer named a girl from Virginia. "In the second semifinal, on a split decision, the semifinalist trophy goes to . . ." The announcer handed a trophy to a boy from Virginia. "And the two national qualifiers, both from Walt Whitman High School . . ." Stealth and the other Whitman debater shook hands and made their way to the stage to receive their trophies. Stealth had never placed first in a debate tournament. Despite the excitement, Stealth also couldn't help feeling guilty that in order for Stealth to place first, the eloquent girl had to be eliminated.

JULIE, SENIOR | PERCEIVED AS: THE SUPERSTAR

Julie had waffled over what to get Sam for his birthday. She wanted to get him something special because he was a close friend, but she didn't want to get him something that could be construed as leading him on. Her father had thought of the Nationals cap, which seemed to charm Sam.

When Sam asked her to prom, Julie was stunned. If she wanted to go to prom with a friend, she would be happy to go with Sam, but almost two months away from the dance, it seemed extremely early to give up on the idea of going with a guy who might have more-than-friend potential. She could think of three mild crushes she currently had. Weren't friends supposed to decide to go together closer to prom, after they had exhausted the list of potential romantic dates?

She wasn't ready to make a decision, but it was cute that Sam had asked her, and it would be easy and comfortable to go with him. She had been somewhat dreading the idea of hunting for a date. As Julie tried to mull this over quickly—she'd had no warning—she smiled. Evidently, Sam took her smile as a yes. He beamed back and practically floated to his door. It had happened so quickly. Suddenly, she was taken for prom.

Over the next week, Julie's track teammates told her that it was way too early to commit to going with a friend; Sam and Julie were one of the first "couples" to be lined up for prom. They said she deserved to leave open a window for guys she liked who might also be interested in her.

Unfortunately, one track teammate told Sam about the conversation. Over the next few days, the Whitman rumor mill churned: "Sam asked Julie, but she doesn't want to go with him!" "Julie never actually said yes!" Sam and Julie didn't speak directly, instead making assumptions based on what other people told them. It got back to Julie that Sam had said, "Julie always second-guesses herself," which irked her. Maybe she did tend to second-guess herself, but that wasn't what she was doing in this situation. She hadn't had time to first-guess!

The night before Julie left for spring break vacation with her family, she called Sam for a heart-to-heart. "So, I'm sure you've heard from the track girls," Julie said. They discussed what they both wanted out of prom.

"I thought it would be a good idea to have prom be undramatic, and that's why I asked a friend, and already it's dramatic, so that's wrong," Sam said.

"I don't know what I want to do with prom. What am I supposed to be saying to a good friend, off the cuff?" Julie asked. "I'd like to not already be sure I'm going with a friend, because while that's fun . . . I don't want to go with someone just to have a date, but going with a friend could be awesome."

"It's okay, we're on the same wavelength," Sam said.

"Okay, talk to me in a week when I get back from Florida. I don't know what I want to do right now."

Julie felt better when she hung up the phone. *That's why I'm good friends with Sam,* she thought. *He's really considerate, and he understands me.*

SAM, SENIOR | PERCEIVED AS: THE TEACHER'S PET

Sam was a wreck. He didn't understand Julie at all; hell, he didn't understand girls, period. "Julie changed her mind!" went the gossip headlines. Through that night and the next day, his friends told him that Julie was playing him and that he should somehow get back at her. But Sam didn't believe that. He would wait to see what she said at the end of spring break and then go from there.

C.J., JUNIOR | PERCEIVED AS: THE FLIRT

C.J. was having a bad week. First she realized that she wouldn't be able to go to the business management national tournament for which she had qualified. Not only would it cost $800, including registration and travel to California, but the tournament was scheduled right before AP exams and her SAT II date. She had been looking forward to competing, but she couldn't afford to take time away from studying for some of the most important tests she would ever take. Not to mention that missing at least two full days of school during her all-important junior year would distract her throughout the tournament. She was disappointed that, because of tests, she wouldn't get the chance to excel in an activity she loved.

AP exams were six weeks away, but C.J. was already starting to worry about them. Actually, these days she was worrying about everything. She saw a copy of her high school transcript and immediately regretted not working as hard as she could have during sophomore year. She had been satisfied with her mix of As and Bs back then. She wasn't now. It bugged her that she had a B in physics despite occasional help from the smart kid who sat next to her—a kid whom she flirted with to pass the time in class (she privately referred to him as her Slinky toy) and who seemed to think she was an idiot.

On her way home from school, C.J. would sometimes spend ten minutes driving past her street two, three, four times before finally pulling into her driveway, because going inside meant she would have to start the homework that never seemed to end. There were too many other things to worry about. She ate lunch with the MaryJanes much less often and had stopped hanging out with them outside of school because she was tired of hearing about drinking, smoking, and hooking up. Every night she stayed up late doing homework and patching friendships over IM before falling asleep for a few hours and waking up to start all over again.

There was more. Derek's earlier comment to C.J. that she was different from other girls because she didn't obsess over her appearance was inaccurate. Even though she was slim from running, she had begun to worry about her weight because of a new habit. When C.J. felt excessively stressed, which was more often than she cared to admit, she would come home and binge-eat. She would see six cupcakes on the counter and eat them all.

She knew why she did it—she could follow her thought process the same way she could when she drove around the block repeatedly. She knew she came home and binged because it was how she dealt with stress. She couldn't stop herself. She would sit at the kitchen table, read the comics, and eat, occasionally hiding boxes of cookies from her mother while making mental lists of all the work she had to do. *Oh my God, I have to do the Shakespeare project,* she would think. *And I haven't started my World essay.* Afterward, she would feel gross, but still, she would do it again. Once, around first-semester exam week, after a particularly gluttonous binge, she spent a long time contemplating whether to vomit it up, which she had never done before. She decided to run it off instead.

Spring break was in less than a week, but C.J. couldn't look forward to it, because it meant college visits. Even when C.J. worried about college, it wasn't just college she was worrying about. She was scared she would never find a job, that she wasn't happy and would always be unhappy, that she would wake up one morning and realize she had wasted her youth in front of a physics textbook and AOL Instant Messenger. She was also afraid of losing the senior friends she loved, and wanted to spend every minute with them. At the same time, she despaired that when in the fall the seniors were off having fun and forgetting about her, her friends in her class would forget her, too, and she would be home alone and miserable. So, in addition to fretting about what she called Whitman's "food chain of competition," she agonized that she wasn't having fun, as she traveled from one worry to the next in a constant whirlwind of second-guessing and apprehension, worrying about kid things and worrying about adult things, caught in the middle, stressing about both the future and the past.

C.J. didn't tell her friends or parents about her worries. What did she have to stress about, compared to everyone else? She didn't tell them because she had two AP classes to her friends' four, a transcript dotted with Bs to her friends' straight As, a few extracurriculars to her friends' laundry lists. She didn't tell them because she doubted everyone else felt the same way; she was probably, in her words, Whitman's "black sheep that got dropped on her head as a baby." Most of all, she didn't tell them because the hardest thing to deal with, more than schoolwork, college, life, and friends, more than, as she put it, "alternating between not caring and caring and regretting not caring when I care," was that on top of everything—on top of driving themselves to be smart, pretty, thin, and athletic—perhaps the most difficult pressure for high school students was that despite it all, they also had to push themselves to appear happy.

One night in late March, after C.J. and Derek went to a horror movie, Derek put his arm around her and leaned in. She blurted, "Good-night kisses are kind of awkward." C.J. mentally kicked herself—*Shoot, why did I say that?*—and then, finally, kissed him.

Later, Derek asked her, "So am I not supposed to tell anyone about this?" He knew she didn't want a boyfriend, although she hadn't told him the real reasons why. He seemed to think it was because she was so boy-crazy that she wanted to be free to see other people; he told her once that she talked about boys more than any other girl he knew.

"I don't care," C.J. replied. But she did. Behind her goofy smile, she was worried that if she insisted he wasn't her boyfriend (because she didn't want the stress and gravity that came with the label), people would think she was hanging out with him only to hook up, which would be worse. Even Derek was still under the impression that C.J. was an experienced junior. She didn't tell him that she was closer to what she and her friends called the NHU—"Never Hooked Up"—Club than he knew, and that Derek was only the second boy she had ever kissed.

FRANK, COLLEGE FRESHMAN | PERCEIVED AS: THE WORKHORSE

The eve of the last day of classes before spring break, Frank went to Lydia's room to work on a chemistry problem set. While Lydia compared their answers, Frank dozed off in a large green hemisphere chair on her floor. After she finished, she stood up and said, "Move over." Frank cocked his head and shifted in the seat, which was barely big enough for two. Lydia sat next to him. When he put his arm around her, she laid her head on his chest. He kissed her lightly on her temple.

"Frank," she said, "I think I know what you want, but I don't want to hurt you."

"What do you mean?"

"Frank, I like you. I like you, too. But I have to think about this. If we start something now, we're going to have to deal with three months of summer vacation."

Frank didn't know what to say. He was euphoric, relieved, and confused. Lydia had feelings for him! Three months of summer didn't seem like a big deal. After a long pause, he said, "Lydia, I just really want to try this. I think we could really work things out. And my friends always told me, and what I try to live by, is 'Don't cry because it's over, smile because it happened.'"

"Frank, don't worry," she said. "I'll think about it over break."

Before he left, Frank turned and asked, "Lydia, can I kiss you?"

"Now?" she asked. Frank half shrugged as if to say, "Why not?" Lydia shook her head.

That night Frank went to sleep dreaming of the day when he would have Lydia in his arms at last. Spring break wasn't that long a wait.

JULIE, SENIOR | PERCEIVED AS: THE SUPERSTAR

Julie had expected that after her conversation with Sam, she would feel free because her prom possibilities would be wide open. She didn't. She talked to some friends and then made a list of a few guys she liked, but she wasn't the kind of girl who could target a guy and then pursue him. She was going to be gone for most of spring break. Whom would she be able to pursue from Florida? That afternoon, in the car with her family, she told them her concerns. "I'll probably end up going with a friend anyway, like someone I won't know as well, so maybe I should go with Sam," she said.

"If that's what you're thinking about, you should probably tell Sam before it's too late," said her mother.

Julie sent Sam a text message: "I always have to do things the hard way. I will go to prom with you."

He texted her back immediately. "This made my day!"

AUDREY, JUNIOR | PERCEIVED AS: THE PERFECTIONIST

Over spring break, when Audrey received her copy of the extensive *Black & White* staff application, she spent several days soul-searching. All year she had been focused on the top three editors' positions. But as hard as Audrey had worked for the newspaper, with her thick portfolio of articles and late hours at flat nights, there was a handful of students who had done even more. Audrey wanted to be the best, as usual, and she wanted to see her name at the top of the masthead. She wasn't sure, however, if the highest positions were the right places for her. As a senior, she would hold leadership roles in many other activities; she worried about the consequences of being spread too thin and the chaotic pressure of running the *Black & White*.

Audrey looked over the list of editorial positions. There was a relatively new position, just below the top three in seniority: online managing editor. The OME, who was essentially in charge of the newspaper's Web coverage, was a top editor but unconstrained by print deadlines and flat nights. The OME had the ability to make her own schedule and impose her own deadlines yet was also viewed as one of the paper's leaders. Audrey thought carefully about what she wanted out of her senior-year position on the newspaper. She wanted a role in which she would be able to contribute. She wanted a title that was respected, that would indicate to the class below her that she was an accomplished editor. OME had the potential to be that position, even if the name recognition wasn't as prestigious as Audrey might have hoped. But maybe she didn't always have to be The Best at everything she did. Maybe, sometimes, simply great was good enough.

A weight lifted off Audrey's shoulders as she filled out her application, indicating that her first-choice position was online managing editor. She was confident that the number four position was the ideal place for her. She hoped the seniors on the paper would agree.

Chapter 14

April 2–April 24

KEEPING UP

TAYLOR, SENIOR | PERCEIVED AS: THE POPULAR GIRL

W hen Taylor got home at 2:30 A.M. from spring break in Cabo San Lucas, her college mail was waiting for her. The last month had gone by quickly. On the social side, she had given up on Derek and was enjoying a friends-with-benefits fling with the jock. Neither one wanted a relationship, but they had agreed to go to prom as friends.

Taylor had kept busy with her varsity lacrosse co-captain duties. She wished the Whitman team were more like her club team, which was doing so well that Taylor was convinced if it had performed as solidly last year, she would have been able to play lacrosse in college.

The Morehead Foundation flew Taylor to the University of North Carolina for a long weekend during which she attended classes and had interviews. Taylor had such a good time at UNC that she decided if she were offered the scholarship, she would take it, maybe even if she had a choice between UNC and Stanford. But the scholarship didn't come through.

Now back at home, as Taylor ripped through the envelopes, she was excited but mostly too tired to have any strong reactions: acceptances from UNC, Duke, Penn, Georgetown, Rice, Vanderbilt, and the honors program at the University of Virginia, rejections from Harvard and Williams, and no word from Stanford. As she drifted off to sleep, sure that she would excuse herself from school that morning, Taylor decided that going far away for spring break was the best thing she could have done. If she had been home, she would have obsessed about the mail, waiting for the letters, anticipating each verdict. Instead, she spent the week on the beach, barely thinking about college. Receiving nearly all of her college mail at once, with no time for her nerves to build up, made the rejections easier to take.

A few days later, when she received her second thin envelope from Stanford, Taylor was so prepared for the rejection that she hardly cared anymore. She had already shed tears over Stanford, and December seemed long ago. She wondered if she would have been happy with the Stanford student population, anyway. She told a friend, "I know a lot of the schools I'm looking at aren't that different, but I think Harvard-Stanford-Princeton-Yale attract a group of kids I wouldn't get along with so well. I'm friends with them, but they're not like the people I want to hang out with on the weekends. They're not the kids who were my best friends."

With her long list of acceptances, she figured she had plenty of great schools from which to choose. "Fuck them," she said to herself, threw her Stanford rejection in the trash, and went to lacrosse practice. Taylor decided to put off choosing a college. She had until April 30 to decide.

FRANK, COLLEGE FRESHMAN | PERCEIVED AS: THE WORKHORSE

The first thing Frank noticed when he sat down in his adviser's office for their last meeting of the year was that his adviser had both shoes on. Frank proceeded with his announcement, one that he didn't know how or when to share with his mother. "I'm thinking of switching from concentrating in bio to environmental science and public policy," he said. His adviser didn't bat an eye. They went over the list of courses Frank had tentatively mapped out for his next three years at Harvard. As his adviser approved the course selections, Frank realized that the ESPP concentration felt natural. *This is what I'm supposed to be doing, and I'm doing it,* he thought.

When they finished, Frank told the adviser about his progress with Lydia. By the end of the ninety-minute session, the adviser said, "It sounds like she already said yes."

A few days later, Lydia came into Frank's room for their first in-person conversation since before spring break. His spirits lifted. He had awaited this moment for what seemed like ages.

"Frank," she said, "I told you I had to think about whether I wanted a relationship or not." Frank could feel something clench in his chest. *This isn't going right,* he thought. "At the beginning of the year, I promised myself that I wouldn't have a relationship during freshman year. You know, Harvard is a once-in-a-lifetime opportunity. I wanted to start on the right foot, and—" She paused, not making eye contact. Her tone was focused, as if she had rehearsed the lines. "I just don't want to break a promise to myself."

Frank calmly picked up his water bottle and took a swig. "That's fine," he said, keeping his voice cool, although he was torn up on the inside. "That's understandable."

"But I still want to be friends," she said.

"Yeah, of course."

Frank let her jabber about her spring break, but his mind was elsewhere. *I need to freaking get back to work. I don't know what to say to her anymore.* He was disappointed but too weary to be sad. Instead, he was irritated. Irritated that she again had made him think there was a chance only to shoot him down. It was time, Frank decided, to do whatever he needed to do to forget about Lydia and move on.

THE STEALTH OVERACHIEVER, JUNIOR | PERCEIVED AS: ?

As the AP English teacher handed out the final grades for the third quarter, classmates sighed in relief at their 85s. The class was a difficult one, and the workload had been intense. Stealth didn't mind the effort it took to keep up in the class because this teacher taught useful lessons, as opposed to last semester's teacher. For the first time at Whitman, Stealth had requested a teacher switch.

The switch paid off. When the teacher placed Stealth's grade sheet facedown on the desk, Stealth turned it over. A 97. As far as Stealth had heard, that was the highest grade in the class. Other students had no idea what Stealth's grade was and didn't ask; the only grade they knew of was the four out of ten Stealth had scored on the first practice essay of the quarter and told friends about. Stealth had appreciated the four because there was more constructive criticism on that single essay than there had been during the entire first semester with the other AP English teacher. As usual, Stealth kept the high grade quiet.

RYLAND, JUNIOR | PERCEIVED AS: THE SLACKER

Ryland still hadn't turned in an English paper that had been due the day before spring break. He had almost finished writing it longhand over the vacation but didn't have time to type it up and edit it until the end of his first week back. He gave it to his teacher. "I put the paper on Turnitin, but I just kept forgetting to bring you a copy," Ryland lied.

"Okay, you need to bring me the receipt before I can accept it," she said.

When he got home that afternoon, Ryland submitted his paper to Turnitin.com. Within minutes, he received an email confirming that the site had received his paper. He pasted the email into a word processor document, backdated the receipt date to the day it was due, changed the time on the receipt, repasted the revised confirmation text into an email to his teacher, and forwarded it to her.

Ryland felt awful. He had sunk to a new low: cheating on the receipt to a cheating-prevention website. He was tired of making up excuses and sliding through back doors because he couldn't finish his work on time. *I'm done,* he thought. *This is the beginning of fourth quarter. I'm not going to lie to my teachers or skip class again this year.*

The next time Ryland visited his psychiatrist for his regular appointment, he told the doctor about his struggles with school and asked whether it would help to resume taking Ritalin. From the beginning, the doctor had been convinced that Ryland had ADD. He wasn't hyperactive, but he found it difficult to focus on conversations, didn't always register what he read, and had trouble taking notes when people were talking. Ryland's mother still didn't believe the doctor, and neither did Ryland, until the doctor showed him a questionnaire he had filled out during his freshman year. The questions asked whether Ryland got distracted easily, switched from important tasks to less important ones before he had finished the former, and had difficulty processing information he read. Not only had Ryland checked off that he had problems with nearly every item listed, but each of those issues had since grown worse. Ryland couldn't remember why he stopped taking Ritalin after sophomore year, other than his mother's determination to keep him from taking pills he might not need. The psychiatrist suggested he give it another try. Ryland decided not to tell his mother he was going back on the drug.

Two days later, Ryland took Ritalin before he went to school. He forgot that he had taken the pills until second period, during a physics test. Because this physics teacher was so much more low-key than Ryland's first-semester teacher, he hadn't experienced test anxiety in that class—until now. Ryland was breezing through the problems when, all at once, he felt like his heart was in his throat, racing uncontrollably. Then he remembered the Ritalin. *Okay, it's okay,* Ryland told himself. *Keep it down.* He began to feel anxious about the prospect of being anxious, and worried that he wouldn't be able to stay on the Ritalin because of the anxiety. *My whole promise to do better will be foiled,* he thought.

Now he remembered another reason he had stopped taking Ritalin: While it did make him feel more confident that he could concentrate on schoolwork, it also made him jittery. *It's okay,* he repeated to himself. *The anxiety comes a certain amount of time after you take the pills, and then it fades away. It won't escalate. I have to do this. It's going to go away.* When Ryland finished the physics test with time to spare, he wanted nothing more than to put his head down on his desk to relax. But he had a Modern World test to make up during the next period. He kept pushing the anxiety out of his head and spent the rest of the class looking through his notes.

The next period, Ryland sat at a desk in the hallway to take the Modern World test. He took a deep breath to try to quell his jitters. The hall was quiet. He looked at the front page of the test, was surprised to recognize all of the terms, and got started. He was anxious, yet not so much that he blanked. This was a different kind of anxiety; he wasn't hyperventilating, shaking, crying, or wishing he could sit on the bathroom floor and disappear. When he realized he could remember the material, he smiled inwardly. The Ritalin was helping, despite his skittering heartbeat. Ryland finished the test more quickly than he had completed Modern World tests before. After the test, his anxiety disappeared, the Ritalin gradually wore off, and he was fine.

Over the next few days, Ryland came to the decision that he was going to keep taking the Ritalin no matter how anxious it made him, because he was determined to do better in school. He told a friend, "If it's going to help with school, it's worth the anxiety, because bringing my grades up will appease my mother and help me get into a better college. Hopefully, my mother won't yell at me about my grades as much."

Ryland got an A on the physics test and did better on his Modern World test than he had on any other test in that class.

∽

Ryland was legitimately diagnosed with ADD, but the debate over the accuracy of an ADD diagnosis, and whether or when to medicate, underscores a much more insidious trend. For high school and college students across the country, Ritalin and Adderall, the two most common ADD medications, have become black-market drugs.

Why? The pills are considered universal enhancers, meaning that even students without ADD could gain a longer and more focused attention span from the pills. "It won't make you smarter, but if the material is hard, you'll be able to stick with it longer, plow through it. You're able to concentrate better," said California pediatrician Lawrence Diller. "People with ADHD who are performing below average on mental aspects that require continued concentration and attention to detail, when you give them Adderall or Ritalin, their performance improves to normal levels. If you give [non-ADHD] people who are performing normally in these tasks low doses, their performance improves to supranormal levels."

Many teenagers have figured this out, buying friends' prescription pills or faking ADD in order to get their own drugs, especially before tests, papers, study sessions, or all-nighters. Because Ritalin and Adderall are sanctioned treatments that their classmates use, students tend to view the pills less as drugs than as study aids. Doctors report that the largest percentage of students trying to get Adderall and Ritalin are non-ADD students who want to use the drugs for studying. High-achieving high school and college students are coming to doctors' offices in droves, hoping to score an ADD diagnosis with the accompanying prescription. "It was simple," Rutgers senior Jeff Ghusson told his school newspaper. "I went to a child psychiatrist in my hometown. I admitted to him that I've taken Adderall before and it helped me study." When the doctor gave him a written diagnostic test, Ghusson said, "I knew what answers he was looking for, so I lied."

Several recent studies revealed that high numbers of teens—and up to one in four college students—are using ADD drugs without a prescription. In 2002 a University of Wisconsin–Madison internal quality improvement report stated that 20 percent of students with an Adderall prescription had abused the pills, shared them with friends, or sold them. Because illegal use of prescription stimulants spiked during finals week, the campus stopped conducting ADHD evaluations for the two weeks preceding each finals period.

Bill Frankenberger, director of the Human Development Center at the University of Wisconsin–Eau Claire and an author of several studies on the topic, said, "We heard repeatedly that the mecca for illicit use was at some of the elite schools. The word is out that [Adderall and Ritalin] can help your performance on exams." In a 2005 study, Frankenberger found that students "felt pressured by time commitments, and that sleepiness and fatigue made it difficult for them to study. This combination of not getting enough sleep and feeling pressured by academic and social demands may lead college students to seek other forms of energy boosters and study aids."

Between 1992 and 2003, the number of teenagers who abused controlled prescription drugs more than tripled, a rate much greater than that of adults during the same period. In 2005 the Partnership for a Drug-Free America revealed that for the first time since 1988, abuse of prescription and over-the-counter medications was more popular among teens than drugs including cocaine, ecstasy, methamphetamines, heroin, and LSD.

Even more startling, Adderall, sometimes called "kiddie coke" in the media, has become known as the hot drug among high school students. High schoolers as young as fourteen have been arrested or suspended for non-prescription Adderall use in cities from Tucson to Pittsburgh. Teens from Boulder to Palm Beach report using friends' Adderall to perform better on tests. The black market for drugs like Adderall is pervasive; pills are usually sold for $2 to $5 apiece, sometimes jumping to $10 during exam periods.

A southern high school senior who took Adderall for the SAT told me he easily procured a thirty-milligram pill from a friend who purchased surplus pills from ADD students. "My school is by no means a bad school, but we have a large 'underground' drug system, basically, so getting illegal drugs is no problem at all," he said. "I decided to try it because many kids told me that it helped them a lot for taking the SAT."

Not long before Sam's Senior Stress Week, Whitman administrators suspended a junior for distributing Ritalin on school grounds to at least five other students. A source told the *Black & White*, "He gave a whole bottle of Ritalin to [his friend] for one gram of weed, which costs about 20 dollars. After the trade the kid who got the Ritalin was bragging about how much he ripped off the other guy, and how people kill each other to get [Ritalin]."

Buying, selling, or using other people's Adderall or Ritalin is illegal and dangerous, but it also raises an interesting dilemma: Is it cheating? Psychiatrists have called Adderall an "academic steroid," equating non-ADD students who use it to score straight As with athletes who use banned substances to hit home runs. "The drugs enhance wakefulness, delay time to fatigue when someone's doing a difficult task, and increase ability to stay on things," said Eric Heiligenstein, clinical director of psychiatry at the University of Wisconsin–Madison. "The drugs allow them to learn more." The drug effectively turns overachievers into super-achievers. But, then, students use other substances to similar effect: Pete took diet pills, Frank chugged Red Bull energy drinks, and several students told me they popped NoDoz or other caffeine pills, "even though they make me sick sometimes," a Kentucky junior said. Where does one draw the line?

Apparently, some parents don't. Some have gone to the extreme of persuading doctors to prescribe ADD medications when their children don't need them. Bethesda internist Ava Kaufman told me that parents have called her to request specific Adderall dosages to get their children through final exams. "They come in like they're shopping," she said. In the spring of 2005, a mother of a private school junior called Kaufman a few weeks before final exams to demand Adderall for her daughter. "I'm sure she has ADD, and she really needs to get good grades so she can get into the college of her choice," the mother said.

"You want this now? A couple of weeks before finals? Isn't it a little late?" Kaufman asked.

"We really need it," the mother said. "She needs to get As. She needs to get into [she named a prestigious college]."

Kaufman said that she didn't treat patients with those drugs unless they had been tested by a psychologist. "You can't get this all done in three weeks, and then she'll need to get adjusted, because we start with a low dosage. We're not going to get her Adderalled by finals."

"Fine," the mother said. "I'll find a psychologist."

The mother found a psychologist who gave her the recommendation she wanted. By the end of the summer, Kaufman learned that the daughter felt so pressured to succeed that she became anorexic and bulimic, sexually promiscuous, and "really out of control," Kaufman said. The girl contracted a sexually transmitted disease, ended up in therapy, and was rejected from her first-choice college. "Most of the parents I see are lovely," Kaufman told me, "but those others make me feel uncomfortable. They make you wonder if they have their kids' best interests in mind, or if it's about their own needs."

JULIE, SENIOR | PERCEIVED AS: THE SUPERSTAR

Throughout the week after spring break, most of Julie's classmates were distributed among various college campuses. She couldn't help feeling slightly relieved when Taylor didn't get into Stanford—not because she didn't want Taylor to get in, but because she assumed they were so similar, with their interests in athletics and sciences, that if Taylor didn't get in, then Julie wouldn't have, either. She watched as friends who had deemed certain universities "perfect" for them in the fall got rejected. Even Derek got wait-listed at Yale.

Until Derek and C.J. escalated their relationship into the more-than-platonic stage, Julie had held out hope. There was one snowy night when Derek asked her to come over, and she frantically shoveled her driveway to clear a path for her car before her father said she couldn't go out in that weather. Once, Derek came over to study math, and they ended up chatting on the couch, his arm around her. There were more cryptic IM chats. And then she finally nudged him away.

C.J. had confided in Julie that she liked Derek, but she had learned from a friend that another senior planned to ask her to prom. Because C.J. and Derek weren't "official," and Derek hadn't said anything about prom, she wasn't sure what to do. So one day at school, when Julie and Derek were walking through the halls, Julie told Derek about C.J.'s dilemma. As he processed this, Julie thought about how she loved C.J.

and Derek separately but didn't think they seemed "right" together. Julie didn't believe she could ever completely give up on Derek; there probably would always be something intangible between them. Nevertheless, she took a breath and said, "You should ask her."

"She wouldn't want to go with me," he said. "She doesn't like me. She tells me all the time she likes other guys."

"You're quasi-dating," Julie said.

"No, we're not."

"Yes, you are. You seem to like her, she seems to like you, you hang out and hook up, but it's nothing official."

"Oh," Derek said. "If that's the definition, then I guess we are."

When C.J. approached them, Julie discreetly walked away so that Derek could ask her to prom in private. Within weeks, C.J. and Derek were officially dating.

PETE, JUNIOR | PERCEIVED AS: THE MEATHEAD

Pete couldn't think about checking his SAT scores, mostly because he was preoccupied with a stomachache that had started the night before. But by the time he got to his fourth-period *Black & White* class, he was restless. As unconcerned as he could seem about grades, standardized tests were different. He needed high scores in order to get the best possible financial aid packages from colleges the following year. With his classmates busy chattering, Pete crept to a computer at the back of the classroom, opened the College Board Web page, checked his scores quickly, then closed the window before anyone happened to look over at him.

He went back to his seat. At the other end of his table, girls were talking nonstop about SAT scores. Audrey was telling her friends that she wasn't going to check her scores until she got home because she didn't want to freak out about them, but then she continued to talk about freaking out. By the end of the day, Pete had told just three people his score, and only because they asked him. Their reactions ranged from surprise to downright shock.

Pete was relieved and content. A senior friend with a similar score hadn't done well in English first semester and still got into Carnegie Mellon and the University of Maryland. He and another of Pete's friends had chosen full rides at Maryland over acceptances at Carnegie Mellon. If his friends could get a free ride to Maryland, Pete thought, maybe he could, too.

AUDREY, JUNIOR | PERCEIVED AS: THE PERFECTIONIST

On April 11 Audrey promised herself she wouldn't check her SAT scores before or during school. That way she wouldn't have to deal with the inevitable feelings of inferiority as other students pranced around comparing numbers, and she wouldn't have to lie when classmates accosted her with a barrage of "what'dyougetwhat'dyouget"s. She could honestly say that she didn't know.

Students checked their scores online throughout the school day. The computer lab was packed. Audrey grew nervous when she heard other people talking about their scores but managed to block them out. Instead of listening to the score babble, Audrey threw herself into her schoolwork and ran around checking up on her quarter grades, which teachers had posted outside their rooms. Tabulating her six As and a B soothed her.

Several students, however, managed to pierce her shield of ignorance. The conversation repeated nearly two dozen times: "Audrey, what'd you get?"

"I'm not looking in school, so I don't know."

"Why aren't you looking?"

"Because I don't want to break down in front of people."

"Yeah, right, you know you did awesome," the interrogator would inevitably scoff.

"I just don't test well," Audrey would try to explain. "I never have."

The interrogator wouldn't believe her, which frustrated Audrey to the point where she almost wanted to look up her SAT score in front of him to prove her inferiority.

During one of these conversations, an overachiever continued to push. "Yeah, right, Audrey," he sneered. "I don't believe it."

It was late in the school day, and Audrey was tired. To get him to leave her alone, she blurted out something she had told only one Whitman friend because it was a number that shamed her. "Look, I got an 1870 on the PSATs."

"No. You didn't get that," the kid said. "Whatever. I don't believe that for a second."

"Fine, don't believe it," Audrey replied. "Why would I lie to you about that? Why would I make my scores lower than they are?"

When Audrey got home, she decided to wait until just before bed to check her scores, in an effort to avoid the afternoon's SAT talk. She made vanilla milkshakes for herself and the friend who drove her home, then went upstairs to do homework. But she couldn't concentrate. The knowledge that her numbers were a click away gnawed at her until she relented. *Who am I kidding?* she thought. Alone in the house, she went to the College Board website. As she moved her mouse over the "Get Scores" button, Audrey became nauseated. These numbers could make or break her fate at Georgetown.

She clicked. Digits flashed onto the screen, but Audrey had been worried about the numbers for so long that now that they were in front of her, she couldn't register what they meant. *Oh my God,* she thought, *those are my SAT results.* Eventually, she snapped out of her panic, which grew the longer she stared. She ran to get her calculator, too discombobulated to analyze the numbers in her head. Then she was flooded with an immense feeling of relief. She had scored a 2140, nearly 300 points better than she had scored on her PSAT. She hadn't failed.

Audrey was bursting to tell somebody, but her mother was across the street, talking to one of Audrey's friends and her mother. Audrey darted outside barefoot, her calculator still in hand, to share the news with her mother. "I have the scores!" she blurted out. While she hated the idea of talking about her scores in front of people, her friend was like family, and she wanted to tell her mother without waiting.

Back inside the house, Audrey's enthusiasm dimmed. Her score was still lower than most of her friends'. She was glad she had improved from the PSAT, but the number was nothing to get excited about. She had tested well by her individual standards, but those standards were not of the caliber she wanted to be held to, not if she was aiming for Georgetown. A friend who also tended to test relatively poorly called to tell her that she had gotten the same overall score.

The difference in their score breakdowns, however, was important. Audrey had scored a 770 on the essay, but on the standard math-verbal sections, she had totaled a 1370. Her friend had received a 720 on the essay, which meant she had a 1420 on the standard sections. Perhaps the difference would have been irrelevant to some schools, but not to Georgetown. Georgetown had announced that admissions officers would look at the math and the verbal sections of the SAT out of 1600 and then count the essay separately. According to one college book, the average SAT score for students accepted to Georgetown was a 1468; according to TCCi, the average for Whitman students was a 1480. Audrey's work wasn't done.

Within five minutes after Audrey came back inside, she determined how she could improve when she retook the SAT in the fall, and which classes would make the most sense for her over the summer. She knew she could push herself harder.

C.J., JUNIOR | PERCEIVED AS: THE FLIRT

When C.J. got to school, she remembered: Today was the day that Whitman students both dreaded and anticipated with glee. Today, as C.J. phrased it, was The Apocalypse.

During second period, a classmate came bounding into French, exclaiming, "I just got my SAT scores!"

C.J. hadn't realized she would be able to check her scores online. "Oh, I want to know!" she said. She zoomed out of French, persuading the classmate to come along to show her how to navigate the College Board website. Even after the classmate helped her to log in, C.J. couldn't figure out where to click. All nerves, she shouted, "I don't see it! Where is it? Are we on the wrong website?"

The classmate, whom C.J. didn't know well, laughed. "You're freaking out. Calm down," she said, and pointed to a large link in the middle of the page.

"Okay, close your eyes," C.J. said. When the other girl turned away, C.J. looked.

Because students were checking their scores in the computer lab, classrooms, and library throughout the day, SAT scores were all that juniors were talking about. To C.J., it appeared that her peers were satisfied with their scores—until they asked someone or someone asked how they had done. Then, suddenly, their own numbers weren't good enough. By the middle of the day, C.J.'s opinion of her peers soured.

She divided her classmates, whom she now referred to as "Score Weasels," into the following taxonomy (descriptions verbatim):

1. **The Polite Score Weasel,** who asks, "How did you do?" The Polite Score Weasel hopes for a number but will not ask directly. She/he will, however, ask follow-up questions like "What were your PSATs?" However, if the questions are continually answered in vague terms, the Polite Score Weasel will go on to talk about his/her scores—usually not offering a solid number (after all, what if you did better?).

2. **The Filthy Score Weasel,** who asks specific questions. If you give the answer, she/he will dig deeper: "So you got a 2300. What did you get on math?" These types are hard to avoid because they stop at nothing. Should you shoot them down, they often begin to talk about themselves. See Complaining Score Weasel.

3. **The Complaining Score Weasel,** who asks you your scores and then quickly tells you his/hers, followed by "It's so bad, I'm miserable," etc. The Complaining Score Weasel is actually fishing for compliments or confirmation that you—and everyone else—did worse. He/she will not shut up until you say that he/she is amazing.

There was little attempt at small talk; students walked up to each other and, skipping greetings, launched right into "What'd you get?" C.J. successfully dodged the barrage of questions until she got to physics class, when a Filthy Score Weasel confronted her. It was her Slinky, the smart boy she tried to flirt with to make physics go by more quickly. She was walking down the aisle to her desk when he turned to her and asked, "What'd you get?" She told him. His face crumpled. "You're lying," he said.

"See, I'm not that dumb just because I'm bad in physics!" C.J. said, but thought, *He was 100 percent positive I had the intelligence of a monkey.* Like the rest of their classmates, Slinky would have been shocked to know that C.J.'s family dinner conversations covered ground such as Civil War generals, the necessary characteristics of modern nations to develop large armies, Nietzsche, and whether Ivan the Terrible was literate. She was well versed in Alaskan whaling rights issues before many of her classmates knew that Alaska was a state.

Later, another junior IMed C.J.:

junior: I got my SAT scores today
C.J.: oh good. were you happy with your score?
junior: yes. [Unprompted, she told C.J. her score.]
C.J.: wow thats really good
junior: thank you. what'd you get again?
C.J.: we're in the same range
junior: and the score was . . . . . . are you gonna tell me what you actually got?
C.J.: nope :-)
junior: okay fine be secretive about it. see what i care
C.J.: sorry i just feel weird sharing
junior: no its cool i understand
junior: . . . loser

As soon as C.J.'s mother saw her that day, she asked how C.J. had scored. C.J. told her, with a self-deprecating shrug. "Why is that bad? That's good!" her mother said in her usual chipper tone.

"I did okay," C.J. said. "Worse than my PSATs, but I'm not unhappy."

The next day, when C.J.'s mother came home, she mentioned that she had spoken with the mother of one of C.J.'s closest friends. "Your scores are fine," she reassured C.J. "[Your friend] only got a bit better. Her mom was so proud she stopped to tell me that [her daughter] scored higher than a 700 on all sections! It's the best she's ever done!"

C.J.'s dark eyes blazed. "Mom, why are you telling me this?"

"Well, we were just comparing your SAT scores, and you all got similar ones."

"You told them my SAT scores?! Mom, those are *my* scores!"

"I just told her, and she's not going to tell anyone. Why does it matter? You all got similar scores."

"What do you mean, she's not going to tell anyone? She'll tell her daughter, just like you're telling me, and now [my friends] and I will all know each other's scores without having shared them in the first place!"

C.J.'s mother promised she wouldn't share the scores again, but C.J.

was still upset, even though she knew her mother's only intent was to express how proud she was of her daughter. Usually, C.J. loved to be the focus of her mother's pride, but this case was different. C.J. worked hard to avoid sharing her SAT scores, grades, and college plans with other students. She didn't want her friends to know her scores, and she didn't want to know her friends' scores for fear they would make her feel inadequate (as did learning through her mother that her friend scored better than she had). But there went her mother, telling her scores to other parents, who were probably telling their children. It felt like the mothers all had their own high school–like network where they felt compelled to compare their children in what C.J. called "my-kid-is-better-than-yours playground gossip."

C.J. knew her mother hadn't meant to hurt her feelings; the two had a good relationship, and C.J. greatly admired her as a parent and as a person. But as C.J. pointed out, even the least offensive parents can get caught up in the comparison games of playground politics just as much as their children do, sometimes to an even greater extent. "My-kid-is-better-than-yours playground gossip" can start in the park about preschools when the children are still in strollers; it comes to a head during the college admissions process, when applications and results are discussed among adults at school functions, cocktail parties, and chance supermarket encounters. That's when, for some families, the college admissions process can morph from a hunt to find the most appropriate campus to a battle to avoid bumper-sticker envy. (A San Francisco Bay area mother said, "You're thinking you're at the supermarket to pick up dinner for your family and leave, but you end up feeling like you've just destroyed your child because you haven't prepared her properly for college.")

For some parents, the admissions process boils down to the college sticker they can proudly slap onto their car window beside MY KID MADE THE HONOR ROLL AT . . . "The way people talk about kids and college, the reaction to where everyone gets in and where they think people really should have gotten in or not is depressing," said Erika, a senior in northern California. "My teacher once said someone else's success is not your failure. I wish more kids realized that, because a lot of nasty things have been said about kids and their schools."

We live in the Age of Comparison. Too often, we deem our own achievements worthless if they fall short of others' standards. Our best isn't good enough if it's not as good as someone else's best. The Age of Comparison is a result of societal emphases on competition and judgment. Shiv, an Indian senior in Florida, said that Asian parents in his community play the equivalent of "kiddie poker," comparing their children's achievements until one parent emerges with a "royal flush."

Students fall into a similar trap. C.J. might have been happy with her SAT score if she didn't know how others fared. Alicia Shepard's American University student might not have complained about his A-minus had he not talked to other students about their grades. Some of Stealth's English classmates wouldn't have been so relieved with their hard-won 85s if they knew the apparent goof-off in the back of the room had nailed a 97.

On my visit to New Trier High School, I showed up when the school was in the midst of discussing ways to alleviate pressure among students. But Jim Conroy, the longtime chair of New Trier's Post–High School Counseling office, said that the biggest problem came from parents who compare. A junior recently said to Conroy, "You can't walk anyplace around here without parents saying, 'And where are you applying?' You want to put a name tag on yourself saying, 'These are my reaches, these are my safeties, these are my middles, now can't I just walk into a friend's house without talking about it?'" As he recounted this, Conroy pounded his knee with his palm in frustration. "This talking about it takes a whole year, which takes up so much more time than deciding where you're going to go in May, then graduating in June. It's become the parent report card. Is your kid going to an A school or a B school? That's the part that is so sad."

After meeting with Conroy, I sat down with four of New Trier's most successful students, who, without prompting, affirmed precisely what their counselor described. They mentioned parents who spent hours on New Trier's TCCi website, comparing their children's scores to applicants' at various colleges. The students talked about an atmosphere in which even their friends' parents would ask them out of the blue not only their list of colleges but also their GPA. "People here ask, 'Where did your parents go?'" Thomas said. "It's surprising how many parents are trying to live through their kids. Parents say, 'Where are you applying? What's your GPA again? Oh, okay, Charlie's is X.'"

"I've done this three million times," muttered Matt, a droll senior. "I go through a list of twelve schools pounded into my head that I can list in a second and in the exact same order." He took a breath. "Princetonharvardyaledukestanforddartmouthpennbrownwilliamsnotamherstmichiganbrowncornell. Oh, and people always want to know what your safety is. They measure you by that."

The students made clear that parents weren't the only comparison perpetrators. They said their high-achieving classmates knew everything about one another, from lists of activities to number of AP classes. One student said the only reason she knew she was number one in her class was because other students had told her after they calculated classmates' GPAs. "I had people come up to me I'd never seen before who said, 'Oh, your GPA's such-and-such,'" she said.

The students were confident that a wider-angled juxtaposition was what drove these comparisons, that when admissions officers compared them to other applicants, they expected more from New Trier students. "I love how they say, 'We're not comparing you to other students at your school, we're just comparing you to your school'; but if you're not taking all the highest classes at New Trier, you're underachieving," said Thomas.

Given the current educational atmosphere, how can it be surprising that families are perpetually looking over their shoulders to gauge the competition? In the spring, many high school newspapers publish a list of students and the colleges, if any, that they will attend. One small New England school makes schoolwide announcements when any of its seniors are accepted into college, while a school in Dallas sends out press releases each spring featuring the seniors who were accepted into first-class colleges. Score Weasels are ubiquitous, and not just during SAT season. Class rank is based not on GPA but on how that GPA stacks up against other students'. In Texas, students are guaranteed admission to the public college or university of their choice if they graduate in the top 10 percent of their high school class. Educators perplexed by the ferocity of the cheating epidemic need look no further than grade curves. In order for someone to succeed in the Age of Comparison, someone else has to fail.

Even standardized testing companies are caught up in the notion that self-worth is defined by how one measures up to a rival. In 2005 College Board spokeswoman Chiara Coletti bragged to *The New York Times* that the SAT was more powerful than the ACT. "We're the dominant test, we're the most researched test, and we're racing for the top by requiring writing," she said, as if the essay requirement were less about improving students' writing than about abasing the ACT.

"Racing for the top" in the twenty-first century is based on the idea that merit and value are relative, not self-contained. This idea isn't limited to schools. It's not enough today to be merely an A-list actress when other A-list actresses also have their own clothing labels, perfumes, and singing careers. It's not enough to be a superstar if someone else is a megastar. In 1995 economists Robert H. Frank and Philip J. Cook published the book *The Winner-Take-All Society,* which detailed the calamity of winner-take-all markets, in which ever more people compete for increasingly fewer and larger prizes. In the same way, only a handful of schools are deemed elite, and only a handful of students can attend them. Harvard, the wealthiest university in the world, can boast a $25.9 billion endowment, as it reported in late 2005, while the second–highest endowed school is a full $10 billion behind.

Nor is this just a U.S. phenomenon. As mentioned in Chapter One, overachiever culture can arguably be traced back to the 1983 report *A Nation at Risk,* which was based on U.S. students' standardized test scores compared to those of students in other countries. It is as if class rank has been expanded to a global scale. In 2004 Lawrence Summers, then the president of Harvard, echoed the cry against "mediocrity" at the College Board Forum, an annual conference. He lamented that in the mid-1990s, Europe surpassed the United States in terms of the number of scientific papers produced, and, like *A Nation at Risk,* suggested that U.S. education needed to improve "if the United States is to be a major player in the new global world." Less than two months later, a top Japanese newspaper reported, "The results of two international surveys eventually forced the Education, Science, and Technology Ministry to acknowledge for the first time that Japanese students were no longer world leaders in academic ability."

So what? So what if a continent produces more scientific papers than the United States? So what if a country isn't ranked number one going into the next educational season? Students shouldn't be governmental pawns in a race for global superiority. Why can't a country be good at what it's good at and not panic if it's not the best at everything? Why should education be a competition?

"We can all agree that no child should be left behind, but let us also agree that every child can get ahead," Summers said at the College Board Forum. The question is, ahead of whom?

FRANK, COLLEGE FRESHMAN | PERCEIVED AS: THE WORKHORSE

On a Tuesday in mid-April, Frank was still recovering from a hectic weekend and a Monday that had included chemistry and biology exams. In the past, he would have spent the entire weekend studying for a single exam. This weekend, however, he went to the movies, attended a Tufts friend's choral concert, enjoyed the sunny weather, and played intramural basketball. On Sunday, while he and Mike were studying for the biology exam, they got so punchy by 3:30 A.M. that they ended up entertaining themselves by making up words, singing them in foreign accents, and prancing around Harvard Yard.

Frank recognized the contrast in his studying habits from high school. At Whitman, he worked himself up about getting an A, studied nonstop throughout the weekend, overprepared, and did fine on the exam. At Harvard, he made time for fun, hung out with friends, studied a reasonable amount, and did fine on the exam. He much preferred his college strategy. Gradually over the year, Frank had lost his sense of pressure and urgency. He rarely heard from his mother, and when he called home to check in, he certainly didn't mention that he had opted to major in environmental science and public policy and to spend his summer as a camp counselor instead of at NIH. He could wait a couple of years before telling her that he wasn't going to be pre-law or pre-med, but he was already petrified of the day in June when he would have to tell her that he was going to camp.

Frank was lounging in his room, checking Facebook and listening to music when the first call came. "Frank."

"What?"

"What you doing?"

"Studying."

"Frank."

"What?"

"I never broke your thumb. Why your father saying I did?"

Frank sat up abruptly, his anger flaring. "Uh, he's saying you did because *you did*. Why are you calling me about this?"

"No. That's crazy. Your father lying to lawyer and telling crazy stories. I never broke your thumb. I do not think that is right."

"Uh, yeah, you did."

The calls kept coming.

During marital counseling, his father had apparently brought up what Frank called "the thumb and knee incidents." His mother, who claimed not to recall them, was now phoning Frank repeatedly to interrogate him on details and try to persuade him that the incidents didn't happen.

It had been a long time since Frank thought about those episodes. In fifth grade, during a tetherball game, Frank hurt his thumb so badly it turned purple. The next day, he and his mother were arguing about homework when she grabbed his hand and forced his thumb hard against his desk. Frank howled in pain. His father drove him to the hospital, where they learned his thumb was broken. When Frank was in eighth grade, his mother was upset with him for not making the top fifteen out of 200 in a math team competition. In her rage, she struck him on the knee with the wooden handle of a toilet plunger. The plunger broke on impact, and Frank had a nine-inch-square bruise that lasted for weeks.

"Mom, I have to go do my *work*. I have better things to do than argue about the crap you did to me years ago!" Frank hung up the phone and called his father at the office. They spoke for an hour, their longest phone conversation since Frank's arrival at Harvard. His father told him that he planned to leave Frank's mother in June, and that after camp, Frank could come live with him.

When Frank hung up, he was flooded with an intense feeling of relief. Perhaps his home life would improve after all.

TAYLOR, SENIOR | PERCEIVED AS: THE POPULAR GIRL

Less than a week before Taylor had to decide officially where she wanted to go to college, she was stuck. In the days after she received her letters, she managed to narrow down the list: Georgetown was too close to home, Rice was too small, the University of Michigan was too big, and the University of North Carolina's engineering program wasn't strong enough. This week she crossed the University of Virginia off her list because the school had too much of a party scene.

"Too much partying for *you?*" a friend asked her.

"Well, I don't want to be the only one working if everyone else is having fun," Taylor answered. "Especially because by junior year, the engineers don't have much time to go out."

It came down to Duke and the University of Pennsylvania. Although Taylor knew this was a fortunate dilemma, she still obsessed over its implications. The school she chose would affect the rest of her life: her studies, her friends, her career. Thinking about the weight of the decision, which she couldn't help doing every minute of every day, exhausted her. It didn't help that her mother was a Duke alum, her father had gone to Penn, and both were pulling for their schools. (The only adult she allowed to voice an opinion was her stepfather.)

She visited both universities again in April, but by the time she came home, she still couldn't persuade herself in one direction or the other. Each school had appealing aspects that the other didn't. As she told a friend, "I wish I could breed them and go to their baby school." She loved Philadelphia, for instance, and the idea of going to college in a vibrant city, whereas Durham seemed to be a quiet college town. But Duke seemed like a healthier, more outdoorsy campus, a quality she also prized. She thought she would do better academically at Penn, because Duke's biomedical engineering program was ranked so highly, and she didn't want "to go from being an A student to fighting for a B."

Her popular friends lobbied for Duke. "You're Duke-ish," they told her. "Duke's so much more fun!" She wondered how many of their sentiments were motivated by the fact that five of them planned to go to college in North Carolina. Those friends didn't know much about Duke or Penn—they were just talking—but as much as she didn't want them to influence her, she was sure they did.

While every one of Taylor's popular friends voted for Duke, among those whom she considered her smart friends, the reaction was mixed. Many of them told her to go to Penn because it was an Ivy. She talked to Derek about how to make a decision, because he was in a similar situation with Harvard and Stanford.

In the midst of her indecision, a guidance counselor asked her to sit on a panel with Sam, two other seniors, and a few college admissions officers at a Whitman presentation to juniors and their parents about the college application and decision-making process. Appreciating the irony, Taylor hoped that telling her story would help her make a choice.

After the admissions officers spoke, Taylor was the first student to share her story. "I'm Taylor. I applied to Stanford early and got deferred, and I freaked out and added more schools to my list. I don't recommend that, because writing eleven applications takes a long time." The audience laughed. She talked about how helpful it had been to apply to Michigan, a school with rolling admissions, because of the sense of security it provided. She listed her college results, her acceptances and rejections. "So now I'm deciding between Duke and Penn. Yeah, thanks!" she said to the Penn admissions officer, and gave him a little wave. The audience laughed again.

"I'm not sure how I'm going to make my decision. I really like both schools. I went alone to visit Penn, which I really recommend because I got a better feel for the school. Otherwise, with your parents, there's a lot of reminiscing instead of seeing the school for yourself for the first time. I didn't have high expectations of Penn because of my last visit with my dad." The admissions officer tilted his head. Taylor waited for the laughter to subside before she continued. "But I was wrong!" she said. "Anyway, I guess I'm just going to have to sit down and decide right before I mail my letter."

RYLAND, JUNIOR | PERCEIVED AS: THE SLACKER

After a week on Ritalin, Ryland was feeling more confident about school. He hadn't skipped class since he made his fourth-quarter promise to himself, he was catching up on his work, and he was able to pay attention.

He was half asleep one morning before school when his mother came barreling into his room. "You have to go to school!" she yelled. "You can't miss any more class! You're going to fail your classes. You're going to fail physics."

Ryland was too knocked out to tell her that he had a high A in physics and had gotten As on every physics test this semester. The teacher was relaxed about due dates; as long as Ryland got the work done, the teacher would grade it without marking down for tardiness. Ryland was so tired he could barely think, but he could hear his mother shouting through his fog. "And you're not going to get into college," she continued, "and you're going to go to Montgomery College, and you can't live here if you go to Montgomery College, and you'll have no place to stay."

"I went back on Ritalin again," Ryland murmured, and then realized what he had revealed.

His mother grew livid. "You don't have ADD!" she shouted. "You always want to take a pill for all of your problems, and it doesn't make sense. Your doctor just gives you pills for everything, and you don't need them! It's because you're lazy!" She stormed into the bathroom, swiped all of Ryland's Ritalin, and took it with her to work. Too tired to feel any emotions, Ryland fell back asleep. By the time he awakened, he had given up on Ritalin and on classes. He didn't arrive at Whitman until fourth period, when he skipped class to work on the latest issue of the *Black & White*.

About a week later, Ryland received his third-quarter report card. As he sadly looked down the line of grades, he heard in his head the voice of his mother, who had told him throughout the quarter that if he got another incomplete on a report card, he would be "in a whole lot of trouble." There it was, an incomplete in math. He took the report card to Kinko's, copied it, and cut and pasted until he had listed the grades he thought he could earn once he was able to turn in all of his missing work. By the time he left the store, he had an authentic-looking facsimile of his report card, showing a B in math, a C in Modern World instead of his actual E, and a B in history rather than the C that had first appeared. While he was at it, he changed his absence numbers, which were in the teens, to fewer than ten for each class. The doctored report card was the one he handed to his parents.

Chapter 15

April 26–May 17

YOUNG "ADULTS"

In many cases it begins at conception, when couples put their unborn children on waiting lists for academy-like preschools. They spend much of the pregnancy collecting anything that might give their child an edge over others. Parents can speak to the developing fetus with special microphones, or hook on a maternity support belt that presses "fetal speakers" to the stomach to play CDs purporting to enhance fetal brain activity. Companies prey on future parents' fear that losing any opportunity to bolster their children's intelligence could lower their SAT scores. BabyPlus crows about its Prenatal Education System, "You're never too young to learn. (In fact, you don't even have to be born!)" Bébé Sounds hypes its Prenatal Teacher by pitching, "The stimulation of your unborn baby has the potential to: Increase your child's IQ, Improve the development of your unborn baby's brain, Speed up your baby's motor development, Help your child learn more easily and interact better." And many parents believe. In 2004, *The Wall Street Journal Online* mentioned a woman who had asked an anthropologist how to "maximize" her child's time in the womb.

A California obstetrician has developed courses to further the intellectual skills of his students. The students? All fetuses. The name of the school is, I kid you not, Prenatal University. Perhaps it's natural that today's young students are obsessed with college admissions in a country that boasts a Prenatal University. And yet, as I write this, I know there are parents who will read this paragraph, wonder why they weren't previously aware of Prenatal University, put this book down, and enroll.

A thriving market of stimulating gadgets exists for the budding infant prodigy. With product names like Brainy Baby, Baby Galileo, and IQ Baby peddled by websites such as HarvardBaby.com and GeniusBabies.com, parents are lured by the possibility of nudging their children ahead of the pack even before the age of one. Hoping to make their children smarter, they whiz through newborn flash cards. They plop their Mozart-infused infants in front of Baby Einstein videos, the *Brainy Baby Left Brain* DVD, Genius Products' "IQ Builder," which "will give you the opportunity to make a real difference in your baby's education right now," or "sophisticated CD-ROM" games that supposedly teach baby eight different languages at once. All the while, parents mark their children's progress against books detailing when certain mental and physical stages should be achieved.

Toddler education, too, can begin early. Thousands of parents bring their tots to Junior Kumon, a tutoring program modeled after Japanese cram schools, launched in the United States in 2003 and designed for children as young as two. Some parents write syllabi for their child's playtime. Additionally, in the twenty-first century, the brain development niche has become one of the toy industry's strongest sectors. What good is a stuffed animal unless it is accompanied by multiple educational lessons?

Elementary school students are shuttled from piano lessons to soccer practices, dance rehearsals to karate training, all of which leaves an occasional appointment slot open for an organized playdate penciled into the day planner, after schooldays spent lugging backpacks that are so heavy they're on wheels. Meanwhile, their nights are spent doing homework. In 1981 six-to-eight-year-olds did an average of forty-four minutes of homework a week. In 1997 that figure had nearly tripled to more than two hours. During the same period, the amount of free time for children ages three to twelve decreased by twelve hours per week.

On top of that, both the school day and the academic year lengthened. In some states, even kindergartners are expected to reach certain math and reading levels; the emphasis on academics has forced some teachers to cut out music, finger painting, playtime, and naps. "That's what No Child Left Behind has done," a teacher told the *Ventura County Star*. "The focus . . . is 'Now what do we have to do to get them to pass the test.' It starts in preschool. We don't have the luxury of a developmental kindergarten anymore." Nationally, 65 percent of kindergartners attend full-day kindergarten.

Middle and high school students are overscheduled to an even more intense level. Their class days are whirlwinds of work, meetings, and events; their weekends are filled with travel-team games or tournaments, religious classes and activities, music recitals or competitions, dance or drama performances, language lessons, SAT and other test-prep classes, and whatever extra travails their individual schools or peer groups have devised, such as Whitman's *Black & White,* which held five-hour "work sessions" nearly every other Sunday, in addition to the twice-biweekly eight-hour flat nights. Students at some high schools have six to eight hours of homework a night.

Summer vacation is meant to be just that—a vacation, a welcome opportunity for kids to relax, a respite from the jam-packed academic year. It's supposed to be a period of rejuvenation to refresh kids in time for the back-to-school season. And maybe it is, but not by much. Summer doesn't necessarily translate to free time anymore. Children are bused off to summer classes or goal-oriented camps: computer camp, soccer camp, art camp, debate camp, tennis camp, academic camp, college essay–writing camp.

Naturally, in an era in which it is often necessary for both parents to work, there are limited options for summer care. But the cycle continues even once children are old enough to be left at home alone. Honors classes at some schools assign homework over the summer. High school students take summer courses or standardized-test classes. Some teen tours take advantage of downtime on bus rides by drilling SAT vocabulary words. Summer college preparatory programs have long waiting lists. The more prestigious the desired college, "the more important the summers are," a college counselor told *The Wall Street Journal* in 2005, a notion that college admissions officers dismiss. The counselor said he instructs students to spend the summers after freshman and sophomore years "putting the polish on your extracurricular profile," and tells rising seniors to do "something intellectual. This isn't another break, this is it."

Another break? Between the prenatal and the high school classrooms, it's difficult to find one break to begin with. This generation has spent the majority of its life in structured activities, compared with an estimated twelve minutes a day of vigorous physical activity. Consider "The Organization Kid," an article that David Brooks wrote for *The Atlantic* in 2001 that discussed Princeton University students. He characterized the college students' schedules as "a session of Future Workaholics of America: crew practice at dawn, classes in the morning, resident-advisor duty, lunch, study groups, classes in the afternoon, tutoring disadvantaged kids in Trenton, a cappella practice, dinner, study, science lab, prayer session, hit the StairMaster, study a few hours more."

After a year's worth of high school research for this book, when I reread Brooks's passage, my first thought was at least the college students, unlike my high school sources, had time for lunch. With childhoods structured sometimes to the minute, young people have no time to develop their individual identity, to discover their likes and dislikes. They aren't allotted enough hours to have fun for the sake of fun. Downtime is minimal. Leisure is dead.

In our first meeting, Frank spoke wistfully about a children's-book character from the 1950s. "He went to school and then went biking or fishing. His mother would *tell* him to go out and play," he said, almost incredulous. That doesn't happen enough anymore. That never happened to Frank. Leisure is gone, but the issue is about more than letting children be carefree. Somewhere along the way to losing leisure and dismissing summer, this country lost childhood, too. As *Time* magazine eloquently phrased it in 2001, "The marvelously anarchic institution of childhood has been slowly turning into little more than an apprentice adulthood. . . . Kids who once had childhoods now have curriculums; kids who ought to move with the lunatic energy of youth now move with the high purpose of the worker bee."

Students are overstressed in part because they have been overprogrammed since the womb; they aren't told to set aside time for relaxation, and they don't always recognize the importance of doing so. What's worse, parents' efforts to perfect their children could do more harm than good. Piping music near the ears of a fetus may damage its hearing. Excessively flipping flash cards at a toddler can make him anxious because he'll sense a parent's urgency. Leaving children in front of DVDs or CD-ROMs for extended periods of time can stunt learning because children learn best through in-person interaction. Emphasizing achievement to a grade-schooler can cause stress and set him up to fail. The kicker, as *Time* reported, is that "the type and amount of stimulation needed for proper childhood development is already built into the normal life of an average baby. No whizbang tricks are necessary."

FRANK, COLLEGE FRESHMAN | PERCEIVED AS: THE WORKHORSE

When a cute Wellesley girl agreed to go to an end-of-the-year formal with Frank, his dormmates were so optimistic about his chances that a few days before the dance, Isabel gave him a "First Kiss Seminar." "So you're going to kiss her, Frank?" Isabel asked. "And when are you going to do this?"

"Erm, I dunno. When it seems like a good idea, I guess. Is on the dance floor a good idea?" he asked.

Isabel inhaled sharply and stepped backward. "No!" she shouted, much to Kristen's and Andrew's amusement. "Don't go in like a sleazeball! You can do better than that, Frank. Go in at the end, when you're saying goodbye and you each had a great time."

"But isn't that just ridiculously predictable?"

"That's the whole *point,*" Isabel said. "There's a formula to it. There's a pattern that you follow. Here. Are you left- or right-handed?"

"Uh, right."

"So do you know which way you tilt your head?" she asked. Frank stared at her blankly. "If you're right-handed," she continued, "you tilt your head to the left." Frank tilted his head to the left. It seemed uncomfortable. He had always assumed he would tilt his head to the right.

"Okay. So first you have the goodbye hug—here, come here. What do you normally do, arms around high or low around the waist?"

"Uh . . . low, I guess."

"Okay, good, good. Because that way—here—" She put his arms around her waist. Kristen and Andrew laughed. "You do the goodbye hug, and then you push away slightly and look into each other's eyes and you tell each other what a great time you had, and you *hold* eye contact."

"For how long?" Frank asked, thinking, *Crap, this is getting to be a lot to remember.*

"At *least* three or four seconds. And you hold her hands—" She took his hands. *I really hope my hands aren't going to be sweaty when I do this,* Frank thought. "And you squeeze her hands, and she'll squeeze back—here, squeeze my hands, dammit—and then you lean in, slowly." *Slowly,* Frank thought. *Gotta remember that. Slowly, slowly, slowly.*

"No jerking of the head—that'll just freak a girl out. And don't go all the way. Go 90 percent. And for cryin' out loud, don't go in too fast. I had a guy who went all the way too forcefully, and our teeth clinked, and I thought, 'This is the worst kisser ever.' " *Teeth-clinking = very bad,* Frank thought. *Remember. Very bad. Avoid.* "But I have faith in you, Frank, so just remember what I said here, and you'll be fine."

Kristen was laughing. Isabel gestured to her. "Here, Frank, why don't you practice on her?" Kristen stopped laughing, blushed, and looked at her feet.

"Uh, weird," Frank said, and slipped out of the room.

After the formal, Frank and Andrew, who also had a Wellesley date, walked the girls to the subway. Frank's inner monologue chattered at him incessantly: *Should I link arms with her? No, not the right vibes. I wonder how I'm going to pull this off, with Andrew's date here. Andrew said he's going to try to give me some room. Oh, they're going back to the room to get Andrew's date's shoes. Maybe now we can separate! . . . Maybe not, follow Cute Wellesley Girl upstairs.*

At the subway stop, Frank said to her, "Thanks for coming with me."

"Oh, thanks so much!" she said, and reached for a hug. *Oh, the hug,* Frank thought. *Remember, slowly, go in 90 percent, hold her hands, what else, am I forgetting something? Hrm, neither low or high—it's diagonal . . . This isn't going to work. Dammit.*

" 'Bye, guys!"

After the girls disappeared, Andrew turned to Frank. "Sorry, Frank. I tried to get her away. I wanted you to break off—"

"Not your fault, Drew. I couldn't have done anything. Didn't feel right."

"Ah. You have a good time?"

"Yeah, it was fun." Frank decided he was done chasing girls.

TAYLOR, SENIOR | PERCEIVED AS: THE POPULAR GIRL

One hour before the post office closed on the Saturday by which her responses had to be postmarked, Taylor was still wavering between Duke and Penn. She couldn't help thinking that she wished she hadn't gotten into both of them, so the decision would be made for her. She knew she could be happy at either school; the drawback was that if she chose one, she would miss out on the other. She felt like she was "supposed" to go to Duke, because she believed it meshed with her personality and appreciation of the outdoors. But earlier this month, when she visited Penn, she fell in love with it.

Taylor looked through Webshots of her friends at Penn. Most of the photos were taken indoors, which bothered her. She guessed her core dilemma was whether to go to the school with the better weather or the school with the city that would give her access to anything she wanted to do. Taylor's parents were trying to stay out of it, but they were dropping hints. Taylor called her older brother when she was at the post office, thirty minutes before it closed, with the reply forms in her hand. "Just do what you want," he advised her. "Forget Mom and Dad." He read her the Princeton Review summaries of both colleges, while, in the background, his friends played rock-paper-scissors, one friend representing Duke, the other, Penn. Duke won.

I'll like Duke, Taylor thought, and ten minutes before the post office closed, she gave the postal worker the Duke acceptance to send certified mail. Antsy, she asked to reopen the envelope so she could make sure she had checked the right box, she mailed her regrets to Penn, and then it was done. She drove away. Ninety seconds later, with images of Penn flashing through her mind, she turned around.

Back at the post office, Taylor asked the postal worker if she could have her letter back. The woman looked at her like she was crazy. "We can't give your letter back once you put it in the mail," she said. "We wouldn't be able to find it anyways." Even-keeled Taylor, who almost never cried, burst into tears. "Are you all right?" the woman asked.

"Yeah." Taylor sniffled and went back to her car, where she cried hysterically. She thought about the things at Penn she would be passing up on: the city, Perelman Quad, the new bioengineering building, a nice professor she had met, Houston Hall, northeastern culture . . . After a few minutes, Taylor went back inside the post office, but the woman was gone. Taylor found her outside. "I think I made the wrong decision about college," Taylor told her. There was nothing the woman could do.

That night Taylor was almost sure she had chosen the wrong school. She wanted to go to Penn. She berated herself for listening to her popular friends. She knew if she concluded she would rather be at Penn, then she could probably find a way to persuade the admissions office to let her change her response. The problem was, she didn't know if she was absolutely sure. If she had sent in an acceptance to Penn, it was possible that she would be crying just as hysterically because of the things she would miss out on at Duke. It was imperative that she should *know*.

When she woke up the next morning, Taylor still wasn't positive about what she wanted to do. *How will I be better able to make a decision today than yesterday?* she thought. She resolved to skip school and lacrosse practice on Monday to drive with her mother to Penn, where she would try as hard as she could to know for sure.

When Taylor got to Penn, she was immediately captivated. She showed her mother around campus, but as she walked around, her excitement waned. "You really know your way around here very well," her mother remarked.

"Yeah," said Taylor, "but it's not right." She loved the school but sensed the city was too much for her. She believed she would be healthier at Duke, with its college town and, as she described to her mother, its "more laid-back, less in-your-face lifestyle." She came to a decision. "I'm going to Duke," she said.

"Well, let's walk around a little more," her mom suggested.

Taylor humored her mother, then repeated several minutes later, "Yeah, we can go home. I think I'm going to go to Duke."

"Why don't you show me the fitness center?" her mother said. They continued to tour the campus.

Two and a half hours after they had arrived, Taylor said, "Yeah, Mom, I'm going to Duke."

"Okay, that was the third time," her mother said. "Now we can go."

On the car ride home, Taylor felt a little shaken. She had just confirmed a life-changing decision. What would college bring? She thought about how she was breaking a three-generation legacy at

Penn: her father, grandfather, and great-grandfather were alums. She was relieved to have made her college decision, although she still regretted that in choosing Duke, she would have to abandon Penn. "I know, Mom!" she said. "I'm going here for grad school."

RYLAND, JUNIOR | PERCEIVED AS: THE SLACKER

With his grades continuing to drop, Ryland sought out his Whitman guidance counselor. He told him he was far behind in classes, he couldn't manage his work because he was hurting for time, and he was having problems at home. He explained that his parents wouldn't leave him alone; he couldn't get his work done when they were constantly looking over his shoulder, with his mother repeatedly badgering him about his college options. Weeping, Ryland told his counselor his parents weren't getting along, his house was always tense, and he couldn't escape soon enough.

"Is there anything that could be said to your parents? Is there a way to back your mother down?"

"That would only make it worse," Ryland said.

"Would talking to your father help?"

"Then he would feel obligated to tell my mom, and if he didn't and she found out, she would be really angry." Ryland suggested that the counselor request a meeting with him and his teachers without his parents' knowledge.

Ryland was the first one in his counselor's office after school for the meeting. One by one, his physics, journalism, and history teachers sat down around a table in the room. While they waited for the other teachers, Ryland, who was slouched in a chair next to his counselor's desk, sat silently for several minutes, his foot shaking.

"I guess we'll start, and if anyone else comes, we'll fill them in," the counselor said. "As you are aware, Ryland is struggling. We set up this meeting not to make excuses but to tell his teachers what's going on. He has the impression that he is stuck. He is trying to catch up, but he feels overwhelmed and doesn't know where to go from here. Ryland, do you want to explain what's been going on?"

Ryland didn't. "Well . . . can you start off? Because I don't really know what to say." He disliked the idea of sounding as if he were looking for pity, which was one of the reasons he hadn't approached most of the teachers on his own.

The counselor told the three teachers about Ryland's home life, his squabbling parents, and his sick grandmother. "I hate being at home," Ryland added. "I do whatever I can to not be at home." He started to cry.

"He's dealing with a lot of things," the counselor said to the teachers, "so could we go around and talk about how he's doing in each of his individual classes?"

The physics teacher began. "Despite all this, he's doing pretty well in my class. He was doing quite well until the last test. Despite that and a bunch of work he hasn't turned in yet, which I will accept late, he has a low B." Ryland wasn't happy to hear that. He had gotten As on all of his physics tests that semester except the last one, which took place after his mother confiscated his Ritalin.

The room turned to the history teacher, who seemed to be offended that Ryland was doing better in physics than in her class. "Ryland, as you know, you're not doing that well in my class. You have an E because of incomplete work." She faced the counselor. "Ryland seems very attentive in class. When he's in class, he's one of the people who are a hundred percent there." She said that Ryland participated often and made valuable contributions. "But when he's not in class, I lose him, because he's not doing the work."

The journalism teacher broke in because she had to leave for another meeting. "Ryland is very important to the newspaper," she said. Another student had "fallen down on the job, and Ryland stepped in and did what needed to be done. He is really committed, and I have a lot of confidence in him," she said on her way out the door.

"Now I want to know what you think we should do about this," the counselor said to the two remaining teachers.

"He knows I'll take any of the late work, and that will help his grade. He's doing fine anyway," the physics teacher said.

The history teacher told Ryland she would accept the homework that he hadn't yet turned in, but she didn't want him turning in future work late. "I want us to talk about where you can do the homework if you don't feel you can do it at home," she added. "You can come in during lunch or after school. My room is always open."

"I'll try whenever I can, but I'm usually doing extracurriculars at lunch and after school. I already work at lunch in the library or in the *Black & White* office doing stuff for other classes or for the *Black & White*," Ryland said.

"You need to start putting the commitment you give to the newspaper to your other classes," the teacher said. "I really want you to commit to my class." Ryland agreed. He enjoyed her class.

The adults discussed other ways Ryland could get his work done outside of his home. His counselor suggested going to the Whitman or public libraries after school. "I try to, but I don't really have a computer at the public library because you can only use it a half hour at a time and a total of an hour a day," Ryland said. "The school library closes at three, the public library closes at nine, and oftentimes I'm doing other things until eight."

The teachers repeated that they were available for help. After they left, Ryland's ceramics teacher came in, and they rehashed the meeting. The teacher recognized that Ryland was trying. "I really like Ryland and want to help him, but he has to meet me halfway and do the work," the teacher said. She turned to Ryland. "You can come in at lunch or after school. I want you to commit to my class. I sympathize with you, I really do, but you really have to figure out a way."

I wish I could, Ryland thought.

AUDREY, JUNIOR | PERCEIVED AS: THE PERFECTIONIST

The day that *Black & White* staff appointments were to be announced in the chorus room after school, Audrey was a mess. The position she received would either validate the months she had spent sacrificing time and grades for the newspaper, or dismiss them. Throughout the school day, Audrey tried her best not to think about the paper.

Audrey left her eighth-period class early and was the first newspaper student in the chorus room, the traditional location for *Black & White* staff announcements. She stood fidgeting while the chorus finished practice for the day. As the room emptied, Audrey took a seat in the second row of the risers and waited for the journalism students to file in. While the top editors gave sentimental speeches, some of them shedding tears as they spoke, Audrey, overcome with the tension and weight of more than a year's worth of effort, also started to cry. She tried to keep her sobs quiet, but she happened to be congested that day, so when she unintentionally sniffled, it honked so loudly that she knew everyone heard her. She could feel the sophomores' eyes on her as they wondered what was wrong with the blubbering junior. So much for commanding respect.

The top editors of the *Black & White* and its supplement, *The Spectator,* read the names of the following year's staff, from the bottom of the masthead to the top. Audrey temporarily forgot her anxiety as she listened intently to the other positions for surprises, like a football-player-type guy who had somehow secured co–managing editor of *The Spectator.* When the editors got to the *Black & White,* it was obvious that some of the other hardworking students were getting lesser positions than they thought they deserved, and were perceptibly unhappy about it. Audrey hoped that wouldn't happen to her.

As they neared the highest positions, Audrey's heart pounded in her ears. And then: "Online managing editor . . ." an editor called out. "Audrey." Audrey nodded and smiled in acknowledgment and hid her face in her hands because she didn't want the disappointed students around her to see her beaming with excitement.

When the announcements were over, the students milled around the room congratulating one another, and Audrey broke into tears again. Because many of her classmates assumed she had applied to be editor in chief, they approached her cautiously, asking if she was all right. "I'm so happy," Audrey tried to explain. "That's what I wanted!" When the room emptied out, Audrey was still sitting there, relieved and tear-streaked, slightly overwhelmed at the work she would have to do to prove herself worthy of the position, but overjoyed that she had been given the opportunity.

SAM, SENIOR | PERCEIVED AS: THE TEACHER'S PET

For Sam, the spring passed quickly, a blur of tennis victories, upper-class parties, and an unexpected straight-A third-quarter report card, thanks to an 89.6 in math. The *Black & White* torch had been passed to the next shift of willing diehards, in Sam's opinion, correctly so. When he filled out the evaluation forms for his newswriters, he had thought carefully about what to do for Audrey. She was a hard worker and an excellent journalist, but, remembering the night she had lost her article drafts, Sam worried about how she would cope with the stress of running the paper. If it were two A.M. on deadline night and an issue wasn't finished, would she crumple in tears? Sam had enthusiastically recommended her for online managing editor because he believed she deserved to be one of the paper's top editors, though without the deadline stress of the print issues.

Before he knew it, prom day had arrived. "Be polite," his father said before dispensing advice that his own father had given him prior to prom: "There are three things you shouldn't lose: your tux, your car keys, and your date."

When Julie greeted him at her house, Sam was bowled over by how stunning she looked. As usual, she had managed to distinguish herself from other Whitman girls by dressing in a way that was both funky and fashionable. She wore a strapless black dress with tiny white polka dots and turquoise heels and carried a small turquoise purse. Strewn among her ringlets were tiny, quirky braids. And her eyes—Sam was convinced she could be a supermodel, although he was under no illusion that the night would be anything but platonic. They exchanged the corsage and boutonniere and posed for various photos for Julie's parents. "Now let's take a goofy one!" Julie said, and posed, her arms askew. Sam stood next to her, somewhat wooden. "Sam, be goofy!" she said.

"I can't be goofy," he said. "I'm trying to be mature." Maybe it was just the suit that left him stiff, but it was also difficult to be goofy when all he could think about was reminding himself not to do anything stupid.

Julie and Sam drove to Glen Echo Park, a National Park site not far from Whitman, where the sixty people in their prom group were gathering for pictures and for the two rental buses that would take them to a hotel for dinner. Sam chatted with Derek and C.J. when Julie went to greet her River Falls girls, but otherwise he stayed close to Julie. A local newspaper's sports reporter who had interviewed Sam and Julie many times approached the two of them. After chatting about the upcoming county championships in tennis and track, the reporter asked, "Would you mind my asking why you're going to prom together?"

Sam was amused. If only the reporter knew all that they had gone through. "We've been really close friends for a while," he said. "I don't know what she thinks, but I thought prom would be a great thing to spend with a close friend."

The reporter turned to Julie. "I agree! Prom is sort of a culmination of high school," she said. "It's awesome to spend it with someone who means a lot to you." Sam melted.

Sam stuck by Julie's side for much of prom, relaxed because he didn't have to worry about his status with his date. For the most part they danced together, except when a few other guys asked to cut in. Yet prom didn't turn out to be what Sam had expected. He had envisioned it as a night when he would hang out with a bunch of seniors he hadn't talked to before. He had assumed it would constitute the momentous occasion that would unite the senior class, provide closure with Julie, and distract him for one night so he could relish senior year. But it didn't. He hung out with the same groups as always. He still felt nervous, still a little bit stressed because the seniors were almost done with high school, and yet they continued to talk about homework, AP exams, and college. "I still wasn't living yet," he told a friend later. "I was surviving."

JULIE, SENIOR | PERCEIVED AS: THE SUPERSTAR

Julie kept waiting for the other shoe to drop. Her life was going so smoothly that she was scared something bad would happen. Her school stress had disappeared, and she had pared down her track practices. At the county championships, she set a new personal record in the two-mile with a time of 11:48. Socially, instead of spending an occasional weekend with friends, she was now bonding with them most weeknights, on top of weekends planned to the hour. For the upcoming weekend, Julie was planning on hosting a barbecue, going to a concert festival, and baking cookies for friends.

At yoga class one evening in May, a woman whom Julie had never met asked where she was going to college. Julie told her but thought about the exchange for the rest of the night. What if she hadn't answered with an Ivy League school? What if she had answered that she was taking a year off? Would the woman have judged her a failure? This was partly why deferring from Dartmouth for a year could be no more than a pipe dream. Julie had been thinking about it for the last couple of weeks, ever since a fellow senior told her that he was going to defer. At first she was mystified—*Why would such a non-rebellious kid do something like that?* she thought. But the more she considered it, the more she was drawn to the concept. He showed her a catalog of activities he was considering for the year, such as community service in New Zealand and yoga in India.

Julie liked the idea of doing something different from everyone else. She was so burned out from school that she thought some time off might rejuvenate her. Most of all, she was thinking about deferring because, as much as she tried, she wasn't energized about going to Dartmouth. She believed she had applied early because it seemed like the right thing to do. In hindsight, she wondered how much she had let other people's opinions sway her. Her father had rooted for Dartmouth and had proudly told people when she got in. Her ex-boyfriend had liked Dartmouth. Strangers like the yoga lady were impressed with Dartmouth . . .

Julie stopped her train of thought. What was she thinking? Dartmouth would be perfect for her: outdoorsy campus; smart, athletic students; and a dining hall with health food. Besides, she could hear her father's voice in her head, even though she hadn't told him she was considering deferral. Deferring would not be a "linear progression." Julie had a different mind-set; she subscribed to the theory that life moved too quickly and she didn't want to be in a rush. She convinced herself that it would be best to continue on to Dartmouth in the fall, as planned.

Saturday was supposed to kick off Julie's busiest social weekend of the year, but before the concert, the high she had been on all week abruptly crashed. There was too much whirling around in her head, too many activities to think about. If her weekend was packed with social outings, how would she have time to run, bike, and do yoga? She didn't know why, but she felt she needed to protect herself from being too social or having too much fun. She was afraid of losing control over her life. Julie canceled the barbecue, backed out of the concert, and reduced her baking to a batch of cookies for one friend. She spent Saturday night alone at home, musing over the duality with which she constantly struggled: She liked to be with people, but her lifestyle tore her away from them. She wondered how that duality would play out at college.

$\wp$

Recess. The word conjures up images of kickball, hopscotch, basketball, jungle gyms, foursquare, football, or tag and the notion of the unstructured leisure time that Julie craved. On grass or blacktop, children filled cherished minutes building forts, chatting with classmates, or trading the fad of the era, be it stickers, bracelets, or cards. They explored the natural elements surrounding them, tasting honeysuckle, chinning buttercups, following ants, or eating dirt. They devised creative new games, often involving spontaneously altered rules and red rubber balls. They made friends. They ran free.

Millions of them don't anymore. In a jarring example of the United States stripping leisure time away from children, at least 40 percent of elementary schools have eliminated recess. The years from 1998 to 2003 alone saw nearly a 20 percent drop. In some districts, officials in charge of building new schools aren't including playgrounds. Many young students don't even know what recess is.

Why has recess become expendable? Officials try to bury their reason among a list of inarguables: a litigious society that could take advantage of recess injuries, fewer open spaces, concern over strangers' access to children, playground equipment that doesn't conform to Americans with Disabilities Act standards. But the most disturbing rationale for terminating recess is this: Politicians and school officials say they need that time to prepare students for standardized tests. When schools are faced with the No Child Left Behind Act's threats to reduce funding because of students' reading and math scores, children's physical activity is one of the first things to go. Even at schools that haven't eliminated recess, some principals link its survival to test scores. An Oklahoma elementary school principal, for example, vowed to keep recess "as long as our test scores stay up," as if physical activity were a carrot to dangle as a reward or yank away as a punishment.

Thus, each elementary school day—with many students not allowed to stand or raise their voices in lunchrooms—officials are asking millions of young children to sit still for six hours straight. In the adult world, courts have recess. Office workers have lunch hours and coffee breaks. But five-to-eleven-year-olds—an age group that decompresses by running around—are stuck inside and immobile for the sake of a state test score.

Experts call this irrational. Each year this country is inundated with studies showing that children's increasingly sedentary lifestyle is dangerous. Recent research revealed that 40 percent of young children have significant cardiac risk factors, including obesity, high blood pressure, high cholesterol, and an inactive lifestyle. In 2003 Judith C. Young, then the executive director for the National Association for Sport and Physical Education, stated that "Parents need to know that the elimination of recess and physical education may be detrimental to their children's overall health and learning." Or, as some mothers like to say, recess is crucial for kids because they need to "get the wiggles out."

The push for early academic achievement appears to trump these concerns. "Many parents still don't quite get it. They'll ask, 'So when are we getting a new playground?' and I'll say, 'There's not going to be a new playground,'" Benjamin O. Canada, then the superintendent of schools in Atlanta, told *The New York Times* in 1998. "We are intent on improving academic performance. You don't do that by having kids hanging on the monkey bars."

Actually, you do. Several recent studies have found that recess and other physical activities *increase* academic achievement. The California School Boards Association reported that test scores rose for students whose classtime was reduced in favor of additional physical activity. The CSBA also reported that "children in daily physical activity have shown superior academic performance and better attitudes toward school." Georgia State University child development professor Olga Jarrett found that "children were significantly less fidgety and more on task after having recess." A 2002 California Department of Education study reported that higher achievement on a state standardized test was associated with higher levels of fitness.

What's more, recess encourages children's physical and cognitive development. It also furthers their social development by giving them a chance to interact with peers outside of the classroom. It teaches them self-direction, self-discipline, respect for rules, sharing, cooperation, and conflict resolution without adult intervention, in an era when children are relying increasingly on adults to settle arguments. Emotionally, recess is an important outlet for reducing stress and anxiety. And by observing children's behavior, decisions, and interactions during free time, teachers can better understand their students.

In several school districts, officials claim to compensate for the elimination of recess by holding regular physical education classes (which are also on the decline). But recess and P.E. are not the same beast. Recess is free play, a break from instruction, while P.E. is a structured class with specific goals. In many cases, P.E. doesn't involve as much opportunity for physical activity as recess does; children might spend most of a class waiting for their turn, or most of a baseball game standing still. During her study on the effects of recess on classroom behavior, Olga Jarrett interviewed fourth-graders about how they viewed recess versus P.E. The distinction was sharp: In P.E., they were "told what to play and who to play with [and] received grades for cooperation, which usually included not talking with their friends." Or, as one child offered, "Well, when we don't have recess, I feel like screaming. When we do have recess, I do scream!" The Council on Physical Education for Children issued this statement in 2001: "Recess should not replace physical education. Recess is unstructured playtime where children have choices, develop rules for play, and release energy and stress."

Angry parents aware of the research persuaded Virginia and Michigan to mandate daily recess. But the conflicting messages from states and studies leave many principals stumped. The government judges them by test scores, not by the well-being and physical activity of their students, and there is no reward or punishment based on their students' health. Yet abolishing recess to make time for standardized-test preparation seems cruel.

It may also be inhumane. The United Nations' Convention on the Rights of the Child is a non-negotiable international human rights treaty that has been ratified by all but two countries in the world. It lays out fifty-four articles proclaiming basic human rights that should be afforded to children globally, such as freedom of religion and protection from violence, abuse, and sexual exploitation. Article 31 of the convention, which was adopted in 1989, affirms, "1. States Parties recognize the right of the child to rest and leisure, to engage in play and recreational activities appropriate to the age of the child and to participate freely in cultural life and the arts. 2. States Parties shall respect and promote the right of the child to participate fully in cultural and artistic life and shall encourage the provision of appropriate and equal opportunities for cultural, artistic, recreational and leisure activity." Even educationally rigorous countries like Japan and Taiwan authorize recess, sometimes multiple recesses, as part of their daily school schedule. Why would our own country be unconcerned by a recreation and leisure provision backed by the weight of an international human rights treaty? Because other than Somalia, the only country that hasn't ratified the treaty is the United States.

TAYLOR, SENIOR | PERCEIVED AS: THE POPULAR GIRL

Taylor was running around backstage at the Mr. Whitman pageant as students and parents filed into the Whitman auditorium. A techie poked her head into the changing room. "We want to start in five," she said.

Taylor had been preparing for this night for two and a half months. She had distributed nomination forms, sorted nominations on a spreadsheet, and chosen a diverse group of fifteen boys. She had supervised dance practices and four-hour rehearsals, filmed the wacky video that would air during the show, placed advertising, met with the lighting, set, and sound technicians, sold tickets, and worked with the business management club on programs and concessions. The week leading up to the pageant, Taylor didn't have time to eat lunch.

By the time the talent portion of the pageant commenced, Taylor sat in the auditorium with the crowd, in the front row closest to the backstage door. Everyone knew their places. They had their props set and their acts ready. The show was practically running itself. The only part left for her to do was to relay the vote count at the end to the on-stage hosts. She could tell the pageant was a success because the crowd was interacting with the contestants, laughing and cheering. Friends in the rows behind her whispered to her how great they thought

Mr. Whitman was this year. By the end of the night, the pageant had raised $9,000 for the Muscular Dystrophy Association.

Taylor was relieved the show had gone well, and she was pleased with her involvement. But she was most proud of how the pageant candidates and the staff running the show, a mix of popular and smart students, had come together. During her time at Whitman, Taylor had a theory that the reason that the smart kids and the popular kids didn't mesh was that they thought they didn't have anything to talk about. The students involved with Mr. Whitman had learned they could create a common ground. "I hadn't talked to any of those more popular kids before Mr. Whitman," a smart senior said to Taylor at the post-pageant barbecue. "I wish I'd met them sooner. I was really surprised." Taylor wasn't. Mr. Whitman was less about the winner than it was about fifteen boys from fifteen different circles who came together to put on a show and, by curtain's close, had become tight friends. Taylor was convinced that the smart and popular students could have been friends throughout their time at Whitman, long before senior year—if only they had thought to give one another the chance.

RYLAND, JUNIOR | PERCEIVED AS: THE SLACKER

Ryland resumed attending classes regularly. He began coming in to his history classroom at lunch to catch up on work. As usual, rather than submitting assignments as he completed them, Ryland envisioned a moment when he could proudly turn in the whole stack of completed homework, to be caught up in class, the months-long burden lifted from his shoulders in one swift move. He had made good starts on several different assignments. When his history teacher asked him whether he had any work for her, he handed her the few items he had finished, for which he received partial credit. He didn't tell her that he had made progress on many other tasks. Bit by bit, he began to catch up.

The history teacher assigned a major project and gave her students two class periods to work on it, in addition to the effort they were expected to put in outside of class. Ryland was able to finish most of it in school. Because he knew he couldn't get work done at home, he stopped paying attention in his other classes to work on the history project. When he got to a section for which he had to write about images clipped from magazines, he stopped. He didn't own any magazines because he usually didn't agree with their messages, and he didn't have the spending money to buy them. Not wanting to turn in the project incomplete, Ryland hung on to it past its deadline. A month past the due date, after borrowing old magazines from his teacher's stash, Ryland tried to give his teacher the project with the other late work he had finished during lunch periods. She reminded him that at the counselor's conference, he had agreed to do his work and hand it in on time. She wouldn't accept the project.

She showed Ryland his grade sheet. He had a 17 percent. When Ryland tried to tell her he had done most of the work, she brushed him off. "I don't want to talk about it now. Come to me after class." After class, he brought her his stack of assignments. "I'm not accepting that," she said again. "You know we have two projects coming up. You need to do those instead of getting the old stuff done."

"I've already done it—that's what I'm trying to tell you. I have it here!" Ryland said, holding out the papers.

"No, it's too late. I'm not accepting it," the teacher said.

Ryland couldn't stop the tears from pooling in his eyes. *I've done the work,* he thought. *How can she say I passed the deadline for late work when she never set any deadline? She's just standing there, watching me fail.* His teacher watched him cry. Humiliated, Ryland gave up and walked out of the room, tears streaming down his face.

Ryland was supposed to perform a scene from *Macbeth* in his next-period class, on a stage in a building adjacent to Whitman. He was still crying when he walked toward his car to retrieve his props and drive them to the other building. A security guard yelled after him, demanding to know where he was going. "I have an abbreviated schedule," Ryland lied, hoping the guard would leave him alone before he saw Ryland's face. Ryland got into his car and sat there sobbing, thinking that all he wanted to do was get away someplace where he could lie down, fall asleep, and forget about anything related to school. The guard didn't pursue him.

There had been darker times than this in Ryland's life. Back in ninth grade, when the pressure on him to perform in school was leading to his breaking point, sometimes he would hurt himself. Alone in his room, he would take a razor or a safety pin and cut his arm until it bled. Twice he used matches to burn circles on his flesh, once a circle on his palm, and once a splotch on his forearm. As he did it, he knew the physical pain wouldn't help, and he immediately tried to think of excuses to explain the marks away. But his parents never noticed. He cut himself only about a half-dozen times, preferring to walk out of his house to the nearby community center to climb to the roof that was his refuge. Sometimes, while he stood there on the roof, he peered over the edge and thought about jumping off.

If Ryland couldn't leave the house, he retreated to another secret place. A small cabinet, about three feet high, spanned a shelf above the closet in his bedroom. He stood on the side of his sofa, hoisted himself into the cabinet, and lay there, where it was dark and safe. When his parents looked for him, they never thought to glance in the cabinet. Sometimes Ryland took a Sharpie and wrote about his feelings on the cabinet ceiling. He had since stopped climbing into the cabinet because it was too difficult to get back down, but, like the shiny round scars on his arm, the words he memorialized on the ceiling endured.

The *Macbeth* performance was a group project, and Ryland didn't want to get the rest of the group in trouble. He drove to the neighboring building, got his props out of the car, and walked inside. He apologized to his English teacher for his tardiness. "Are you ready?" she asked.

"No, I need a couple more minutes," Ryland said, still shaky. After he collected himself to the best of his ability, he met up with his group and performed the scene.

SAM, SENIOR | PERCEIVED AS: THE TEACHER'S PET

Sam was sitting at home alone on a Saturday night, enraged. He had gone through his entire cell phone directory and called all of his friends, who had said they were either staying home that night or if they went out, they would call him. Now, a few hours later, Sam could see from their IM away messages that many of those friends had lied. Brad really was staying home, and Julie was spending time with her parents, but it seemed like everyone else deliberately made plans without him.

"I seriously feel like killing myself right now," Sam text-messaged a friend who was out of town. "i dont have one friend."

Sam's friend: **Why would you think that?**
Sam: **Because they all take me for granted so much that when i need it the most none of them care.**
Sam's friend: **Are you okay? why do you need it the most now?**
Sam: **Because i realize how little ive meant to them and that while i would give my life for them . . . they wouldnt do shit for me.**
Sam's friend: **Where are you now—home?**
Sam: **Alone and afraid home.**
Sam's friend: **Seriously? or just pissed off?**
Sam: **Like i have never been more in need of a friend than now . . . i dont have anything to hope for now that i know my friends are lies.**
Sam's friend: **B.S. youre three months from college and new friends.**
Sam: **Then why do i feel like jumping out the window?**

Sam was the type of person to openly tell friends how important they were to him, so he was furious that, in his view, they didn't come close to reciprocating. He had tried chatting online with students he had met on a Middlebury message board for incoming freshmen, but that, too, had left him disheartened. Many of them had asked Sam what his SAT scores were, as if that were a normal topic of casual, get-to-know-you conversation.

The week didn't get better for Sam. One morning he was walking across the Whitman driveway when a parent drove up to the main doors and rolled right into Sam. As soon as the car hit him, he hopped up onto the hood, stunned. Though uninjured, Sam was as surprised as the driver (whose child was obviously mortified). "What the fuck are you doing?!" Sam yelled. "You're an idiot!"

"You have to get out of my way when I drive my kid to school," the mother hissed.

"You know what, I'm going to find out who your kid is, I'm going to find out who you are, and you're going to be hearing from me very, very soon," Sam said.

"Fuck you," the mother said.

Sam was unglued for the rest of the day. While sitting in the journalism room, he called out to two friends walking by in the hall. They said nothing. He slammed his fist into the table. "They probably didn't hear you," said Audrey, the only other person in the room. She looked at him compassionately and asked, "Why aren't you happy?"

Sam could think of several reasons. His friendships seemed hopeless. The rest of the seniors were coupling off. He was anxious about Middlebury. He didn't feel like he even deserved to go there anymore, not when he recalled all the corners he believed he had cut: inventing Raheem, scraping As with 89.6s and 89.7s, giving his college essays to his parents to edit before submitting them. Why wasn't he happy? He wasn't happy because he was frustrated with the present and scared about the future. But he wasn't going to tell anyone that.

✧

Sam later admitted that he hadn't really been suicidal. "I guess it was more for attention than anything else," he told me. "I just needed someone to talk to." Despite his occasional doubts, Sam had a strong support network and close family who helped ensure he could handle the pressure.

But many students can't. Although it is estimated that every hundred minutes a teenager in the United States commits suicide, the American Psychiatric Association places the true number at two to three times higher. Thousands of students try to kill themselves every day; it's said that for every suicide death, there are between eight and twenty-five attempts. In 2003, 16.5 percent of high school students made a suicide plan, and nearly 9 percent attempted to follow through with it. Among college students, one study found that one in four has considered suicide.

A variety of factors contribute to student suicides, but there is no doubt that overachiever culture also plays a significant role. All of the issues discussed in previous chapters—school stress, the college admissions process, high-stakes testing, cutthroat competition, the emphasis on stardom rather than on enjoyment of activities, sleep deprivation, parental pressure, the push for perfectionism, the need for escapism, the Age of Comparison, the loss of leisure and childhood—can weigh on students until, like a fragile Physics Olympics bridge beneath heavy bricks, they reach their breaking point.

As Gail Griffith, the mother of a teenager who attempted suicide, wrote in an article, "How often have we seen media reports of the 'star athlete' or 'president of the student council' or the kid voted 'most likely to succeed'—the teenager with everything going for him—who comes home on a Saturday night, loads a gun and shoots himself? . . . This type of kid typically closets emotions while aiming at goals and self-imposed standards that are impossibly high or prompted by perceived expectations of their parents. They are loath to disappoint family and friends."

A 2005 article in the journal *Adolescence* cited several studies linking overachiever-type school pressures to suicide attempts. "Serious suicide attempts seem to be higher among students who experience considerable academic success," the authors wrote. "Academically successful students experience greater amounts of stress than do their less successful peers because more successful students feel more pressure to maintain their level of performance. This pressure may cause them to increase the lethality of their suicidal intent." A 1999 survey of high-achieving high school students found that almost a quarter of them had considered killing themselves, and 42 percent knew someone their age who had attempted suicide. Behind only general depression, the second most popular reason for these top students to consider suicide was school pressures.

Depression is also on the rise among the student population; while depression rates traditionally increase with age, they are climbing most quickly among younger and younger children. Anxiety is the most common cause of childhood psychological distress in North America; even nine-year-olds are experiencing anxiety attacks. Among teens, studies have shown a strong link between stress and depression, often based on the pressure to succeed and to perform well in the college admissions process. An Illinois teen told me that because of school anxiety, she had a breakdown approximately every two weeks of her junior year and first semester senior year.

In 2004 Harvard's student newspaper, *The Crimson,* reported that 80 percent of its undergraduates had felt depressed in the past year, leading to "a pervasive mental health crisis" at Harvard, that supposed bastion of student perfection. From 1995 to 2000, MIT's mental health services saw a 69 percent jump in the number of undergraduates who needed hospitalization for mental health problems. At least those students sought help. A Maryland International Baccalaureate student who frequented tanning beds to battle times of depression said to me, "If you get pulled in to a shrink, that is valuable time you are losing from doing other things that need to get done."

A 2004 survey of almost 50,000 college students found that 45 percent of students had felt so depressed it was difficult to function, and 63 percent had felt hopeless at times. In 1996 anxiety surpassed relationship problems as the issue most often mentioned by college students who visited campus mental health services. In one of the largest studies of its kind, mental health officials at Kansas State University found that from 1989 to 2001, the number of students with depression doubled, the number of suicidal students tripled, and the number of students taking psychiatric drugs rose from 10 to 25 percent. Mental health professionals also report an increase in student self-injury cases, including cutting— Ryland's mode of self-mutilation—or cigarette burning. Experts call the behavior a coping mechanism that can be caused by intense pressure.

But stories are more important than statistics. In 2000 seventeen-year-old Lancy Chui's suicide note reportedly included an apology to her parents because she had been rejected from Harvard. A California student killed herself, allegedly afraid to tell her parents she didn't achieve a 4.0. A senior in 2000 took her life after learning she was accepted only into a state school. A high-achieving Massachusetts senior told me she slit her wrists because of "the feeling that I wasn't perfect. If I wasn't good enough to be perfect, I wasn't good enough to be alive." Alan Berman, executive director of the American Association of Suicidology, was careful to point out that these types of issues are not necessarily direct causes but, rather, the "final straw that broke the camel's back" on an already vulnerable camel. When I asked him for similar cases, he said, "When I hear about them, they go in one ear and out the other, because these are not uncommon stories."

And then there was Frank. In the spring of sophomore year and the beginning of his junior year at Whitman, Frank was sagging under the weight of his mother's expectations. "Terrified" of his seven-AP course load, Frank became depressed. He had what he called a "feeling of utter helplessness. You see what's wrong with your life, but you can't do anything to change it. You are utterly at the will of that older generation who is 'so much wiser' than you."

I asked him to describe what he felt like at his darkest point. "Imagine being trapped inside a glass box," Frank said. "You can see everyone outside, and people can see you, but they can't touch you, and you can't touch them, and you can't really move around. You can see all those people moving about, unhindered, talking to each other, touching each other, but you can't really take part in that. And you think sometimes, *What if this were an empty glass box? Would anyone really know the difference?*" During the second week of junior year, Frank was sitting at his bedroom desk when he found himself in "a bizarre state of mind," afraid to go to the bathroom because there were sharp scissors there and he was scared of what he might do with them. Frank froze in his room, forcing himself to sit still as stone until he wasn't afraid anymore.

Colleges have noticed that by the time students arrive on campus for their freshman year, some are already burned out from the years of stress it took to get there. MIT, which admitted that its students can be socially and emotionally inexperienced, altered all of the windows in a dormitory after a student leaped from the fourteenth floor in 2000. At NYU, where six students allegedly jumped to their death in a thirteen-month span during 2003 and 2004, therapists now come to students' dorms for individual counseling sessions.

At Harvard, I visited the office of Richard Kadison, the easygoing chief of the university's mental health services. Harvard, too, has stepped up efforts to combat its undergraduate depression rate. Kadison told me that it is evident at Harvard, as at other colleges, that students are coming to campus with more serious mental health problems than in the past. He blamed the trend partly on students' lack of "life-coping skills," missing because helicopter parents take over.

Kadison said students also come to campus with a fixed set of expectations about their prospective careers—medicine and law among the most popular—but once they begin college, they are shocked and disappointed to find they aren't actually interested in those or their parents' preconceived ideas for their future. "Another big adjustment is students who come to Harvard are used to being the best at everything, and then they come to a place where everyone is the best at everything," he added. "There are almost an infinite number of opportunities, clubs, and extracurriculars that exist here, and for people to find ones that feel right to them takes some time." I thought about Frank, who brooded over whether to drop Ultimate Frisbee in order to concentrate on wushu.

"Does the trend of students being hell-bent on perfectionism lead them to be more stressed once they're here?" I asked Kadison.

"Yes, it's certainly a factor; more students are that way. Being obsessive-compulsive, being devoted to your work, is what gets you into a place like Harvard, but it also gets out of balance and becomes overwhelming," Kadison replied. "The typical vicious cycle is they get here, and their baseline is 'I should be getting straight As, and if I don't, I'm a complete failure.' They get a little behind in their work, they say, 'I'll just stay up later and study,' they don't get enough sleep. Students get sleep-deprived, they start functioning less efficiently, and their response is to work even harder, so they stay up later. When people are sleep-deprived, there is a much higher frequency of depression. The numbers are very scary. Very often people get here and they sort of melt down during first semester." Then Kadison made a point that I found telling: "We're also lousy role models, as the faculty, frankly. People here work all the time. There isn't much balance. It's about academic super-rigorous perfection."

In 2000 Harvard dean of admissions and financial aid Bill Fitzsimmons wrote a widely publicized essay in which he encouraged today's "young fast-track generation" to take a "time out" from school, to "step back and reflect, to gain perspective on personal values and goals, or to gain needed life experience in a setting separate from and independent of one's accustomed pressures and expectations." In particular, he advocated exactly the notion that Julie briefly considered: taking a year off between high school and college.

A fifth of Harvard students take a time-out at some point before graduation, while most travel along the "linear progression," as Julie put it, that never seems to end. Fitzsimmons wrote that one student said the majority of her friends would spend eight consecutive semesters at Harvard, and she "wondered if they ever get the chance to catch their breath." Fitzsimmons continued, "The fact remains that there is something very different about growing up today. Some students and families are suffering from the frenetic pace, while others may be coping but are enjoying their lives less than they would like. Even those who are doing extraordinarily well, the 'happy warriors' of today's ultra-competitive landscape, are in danger of emerging perhaps a bit less human as they try to keep up with what may be increasingly unrealistic expectations."

Meanwhile, some top colleges are rejecting students they think might qualify as "teacups," administrator-speak for carefully crafted but easily shattered. "If we think someone will crumble the first time they do poorly on a test, we're not going to admit them. So many kids are coming in, feeling the need to be perfect . . . If you need a lot of pharmaceutical support to get through the day, you're not a good match for a place like MIT," MIT dean of admissions Marilee Jones told *Newsweek* in 2004. "Our culture has become insane—we're making people sick."

FRANK, COLLEGE FRESHMAN | PERCEIVED AS: THE WORKHORSE

On the penultimate weekend of the school year, Frank had a final paper for his Forestry seminar due Friday night and a biology paper to finish by Monday, but there were more important things at hand, such as the culmination of a year's worth of effort, of wrangling, of mud, blood, sweat, heart, and gumption: the Yard Bucket. Frank turned in the Forestry paper a day late—the first time in his entire academic career he had missed a paper deadline—and opted not to proofread the biology paper. The Massachusetts Hall Silencers were in a close fight for first place with their rivals at Hollis, the dorm that had beaten them in the fall Frisbee championship. Frank vowed to play in every intramural game, in every sport, until Mass Hall's season was over.

A year's worth of intramural battles came down to one sport: dodgeball. The Silencers faced Hollis in the quarterfinals for a best-of-five set. Frank recognized one of Hollis's top athletes on the other side of the line, a Frisbee player who had a tremendous vertical leap. But Frank was on fire. Ahead two games to none, Silencers were eliminated one by one in the third game until only Frank and a fellow Silencer remained on one side, and two Hollis men, including the top athlete, on the other.

For a while Frank and the athlete traded fakes, approaching the line, keeping an eye on each other. Frank had two of the balls; the athlete had one. Suddenly, Frank sprinted up to the line and hurled a puffy yellow ball at the athlete. The athlete bent out of the way and rocketed a shot toward Frank. Frank dropped toward the ground as the ball narrowly sailed over his left calf. As Frank fell, he aimed and launched his last ball just before he hit the floor. The athlete jumped and twisted, but Frank's shot smacked him on the shoulder. The Mass Hall sidelines erupted, and the Silencers went on to win the game.

Frank and the rest of Mass Hall didn't have to wait until the intramural office tallied the points. They had already calculated that they would take home the Yard Bucket—a feat that no Mass Hall class had accomplished in recent memory. Frank was proud of his underdog teammates' effort and persistence. The year in intramurals had been at times taxing, as he, Mike, and Andrew made sure the dorm never forfeited a single game, showing up to play even if they had no experience in the sport. Intramurals had supplied bonding opportunities for Frank, especially with B31. He was also proud of his competitive effort—think the House Cup in the *Harry Potter* series—which was, unlike his other accomplishments, in a non-academic arena.

As other Mass Hall freshmen paired off before summer, Frank was feeling down about his luck with girls when, a few days before vacation, Isabel walked into Frank's room and flopped on his bed. "Frank, are you over Lydia?" she asked.

He collected his thoughts before answering. "I'm over liking her, but not over being hurt by her. I don't want to date her, but her presence can upset me a lot sometimes."

"Frank, you can't ask who it is, but I just wanted you to know that someone likes you. She likes you not just because you're a great guy but for your quirks, too. I just wanted you to know that someone legitimately likes you, so you can feel better about that."

Frank perked up and mentally ran through a list of Isabel's friends, beginning with her suitemates. Then he said, "Only Kristen would be concerned about that. She's *very* in tune to my feelings about Lydia because I talked a lot about that with her." Isabel said nothing. *So it's Kristen,* Frank thought. *Interesting.*

Chapter 16

May 27–July 2

CHANGES

SAM, SENIOR | PERCEIVED AS: THE TEACHER'S PET

W ell after midnight, Sam was leaving a party when he decided he didn't want to go home. He pulled from his pocket a Chinese fortune he had gotten the night before: "You will be reunited with old friends." *Why the hell not,* San thought, and called Ellie, the artist who was supposedly behind the lipstick-smacked love note Sam received in February. Throughout the semester, they had continued to take tentative steps toward resuming their friendship.

"Hey, what are you up to?" she asked him.

"I'm going home, but I don't want to."

"Want to go do something?"

Given what Sam had been through this month, he thought it would be nice to have another friend. He picked up Ellie at her house and took her to an overlook off the George Washington Memorial Parkway in Virginia, where they sat in his car talking for two hours about everything and nothing. "What was the worst day you had recently?" she asked. Sam told her about the Saturday night when he was home alone, thinking that his friends had turned on him. Many of his friends had since apologized. Ellie cocked her head. "I was sitting at home that night, too," she said. "You should have called me."

The next night, when Sam hosted a small party, he invited Ellie. After the other friends went home, Ellie stayed until four in the morning talking to Sam and Brad. She wasn't the girl Sam had assumed she was from their brief date nearly a year ago. He realized she was relaxed, friendly, smart, and constantly laughing. When Sam drove Brad home that night, Brad said, "Sam, Ellie's *cool.*" Emboldened by his friend's stamp of approval, Sam asked Ellie out the next day.

He took her to dinner and a show at the Improv but didn't plan their date beyond that stop; the other girls he had tried to date hadn't appreciated his creativity. Instead, on the way home, it was Ellie who said, "Let's do something."

"Okay, what?" Sam asked.

"Well, there are no clouds outside. Let's go stargazing."

Sam drove down one of Bethesda's major roads until it ended in farmland. They pulled over to the side, hopped a fence to get into a field, lay on the grass, and looked up at the stars. Ellie rested her head on his stomach as they chatted. An hour later, Sam was talking when Ellie said, "Shh, be quiet for a second." For five minutes, they lay there in silence, staring at the dotted sky. Then she tilted her head upward, reached for Sam, and kissed him. And while he didn't know during those next fifteen minutes of kissing that he would continue to date Ellie in college, he did know that, for once, he liked a girl who liked him back, that she would become someone he could count on, and that they were creating what would become a high school memory—one of his last, and one he would remember always.

JULIE, SENIOR | PERCEIVED AS: THE SUPERSTAR

Accompanied by the strains of "Pomp and Circumstance," Julie and the rest of the senior class marched into Washington's Constitution Hall to a standing ovation. Julie looked up at the stage, where the senior class officers and student speakers stood. *I could have been up there, too,* she thought, regretting not running for senior class officer or auditioning to be student speaker. It seemed strange that she had worked so hard but was now sitting below the stage with the rest of her class instead of playing an important role in the ceremony.

That morning Julie had woken up feeling as if she had already graduated. Classes had ended a week before, and many of her classmates had thrown graduation parties over the weekend. Julie spent the morning running alone through the thick Maryland humidity. It dawned on her how much she loved being on a team. Her heart lightened among teammates like C.J., to whom she had grown close throughout seasons of competitions against each other that masked personal battles within themselves. She realized that she loved running because of its raw emotions, from the nerves beforehand to the pain during a race to the exhilaration or anguish afterward. Running made her feel alive.

As she thought about the teammates she would never race with again, it struck her that even though she would officially begin her Dartmouth preseason training schedule in two weeks, belonging to a team was an ephemeral experience. *You can be so into something,* she mused. *That was my life—track and those people and daily track dramas—and then it was just done.* Julie realized she was the only constant in her life, while the people she met, the activities she experienced, and the places she went, including schools, would always be in flux. While everything around her continually changed, she needed to learn to be satisfied with herself.

While the graduation speakers waxed on about a class whose formative years were influenced by the September 11, 2001, tragedy, an autumn of sniper shootings that canceled sports seasons, and the tsunami in Southeast Asia, Julie looked around at her classmates. On one side of her sat a student she barely knew, and on the other side was a Nasty she didn't want to know. As she gazed down row after row of seniors, Julie realized how many people there were in her grade whom she hadn't bothered to befriend. Sure, she was swamped throughout high school with homework, practices, club meetings, and test prep, and they were probably nearly as busy tailoring their own résumés. But now that she was leaving Whitman, Julie regretted not getting to know its inhabitants better. She resolved to reprioritize at Dartmouth. She was ready for it now. Every piece of mail she received—about housing, classes, an outdoor activities club—increased her excitement about college.

The principal was at the podium, congratulating the class on its achievements: state championships in girls' soccer, wrestling, and boys' tennis; choral and instrumental groups that garnered perfect scores in state competitions; 30,000 combined hours of community service; and "one academic index that truly reflects the achievements of this class": breaking the county public school record for the highest average SAT score in history, with a mean of 1256.

Then the rows of students were standing, 457 names were called out, Julie was on the stage then off again, filing out of the hall with the rest of the seniors, through the building, and back outside, returning to the thick hug of humidity with her high school life behind her.

C.J., JUNIOR | PERCEIVED AS: THE FLIRT

Several months after C.J.'s vodka-shot night, her mother found out about it. She first expressed her displeasure at C.J.'s lying to her, then explained, "It's absolutely stupid. You can kill yourself drinking vodka. From now on, you have to wake me up when you come in. You need to tell me where you're going, and you can't lie to me."

C.J. accepted this but kept her inner monologue to herself. She wanted to tell her mother how much it bothered her that many Whitman parents had such high expectations for their children—get good grades, do well in extracurriculars, get a job, and be *good*—that it was as if kids weren't allowed to make mistakes anymore. She later wondered, "Why am I expected to be perfect? Because I get good grades and I study for the SATs without a knife to my back. Because I get a job and I go to work. Because I buy my clothes and gas and I can cook my own meals. So I'm expected to be the perfect super-teen with a straight-A report card and a Saturday night of movie marathons at the old folks' home. Yet everything is about numbers, what *number* GPA do I need to get into this school, what *number* SAT. Look at the numbers and know that almost every kid out there who got that coveted 2380 had a shot every weekend."

C.J. admitted to herself that she was the one being unreasonable. She knew her mother was doing what she was supposed to be doing: parenting. She was supposed to be angry when C.J. drank. She was supposed to be concerned about her daughter. In fact, C.J. secretly appreciated the way her mother dealt with her: Rather than punishing her, she talked through the issues, which made C.J. want to do a better job of earning her mother's respect. C.J. knew that she was the one who saw herself as C.J. the Super-Teen, the one who thought that because she did so much without her parents' help, she didn't need them. Her mother's new set of rules were wise. C.J. was scared enough to give up vodka until college.

That same day, C.J. and her mother met with C.J.'s guidance counselor about college application plans. C.J. tried to answer the counselor's questions, but she was having a hard time sounding enthusiastic. Her attention to college planning had slacked off slightly because the track season had lasted until State Championships, in which her relay team had placed second, and she had spent a lot of time with Derek. But she was still getting her homework done because she was regularly working until one in the morning, losing sleep in order to keep her promise to herself to do better in school.

C.J.'s guidance counselor went through her list of colleges. She knew where she wanted to apply early decision: a small southern school that she loved and about which she had a good gut feeling. She was also certain that her second-choice school was Connecticut College, where she was impressed with the campus, gym, classrooms, dining hall, and cross-country coach. The apparent problem was that Connecticut College also happened to be one of C.J.'s safety schools. It didn't go over well with the guidance counselor that her second-choice college was a safety. He urged her to visit other schools.

"I refuse to go on any more college visits," C.J. said. She didn't mean to sound so emphatic. But between touring colleges for herself and for her older siblings, C.J. had visited twenty-one colleges in three years. That was twenty-one information sessions, twenty-one crowded cafeterias, twenty-one libraries, and twenty-one tours with incoherent guides. She had scrutinized college websites and books and come up with her first and second choices and a list that included reaches, realistic schools, and other safeties. Now she was burned out on college planning; she had enough of college visits, meetings, talks, and books. She had made her decisions. Why second-guess? The entire college process had become a bore. When the counselor asked her what she scored on the math section of the SAT, she couldn't remember. When the counselor asked why C.J. wanted to apply to Wake Forest, C.J. couldn't come up with a reason. *I can't explain that to me, college is like a chore,* C.J. thought, *and every step I take toward it, I throw out like dirty laundry when I'm done.*

C.J. got the impression that her counselor wanted her to consider schools that were more prestigious, even though her parents weren't obsessed with the college process like other Whitman parents C.J. knew.

C.J. thought she could get into schools that were more impressive-sounding than Connecticut College, but that didn't mean she wanted to attend them.

"Unfortunately for you, your grades don't reflect your intellectual caliber," C.J.'s counselor said. "If you wind up going to Connecticut College, you might not be as academically challenged as you would at a more prestigious school." C.J. wasn't sure about that. She didn't consider herself *that* smart. She wondered if she cared.

C.J. had never kept a diary, but during that week, she typed out her emotions in what ended up being a twenty-page document.

> I think sometimes I care. I think sometimes I waver between caring and not caring. But when I care, when I tell myself I have to do this, I catch my breath and realize that I don't know why I care. Do I want to be happy or do I want to be successful? But wondering why and wondering if are worse than not wondering at all, so I throw that out too.
>
> And now I've sunken into a summer haze: aware of the future, afraid of the future and yet so indifferent that the future doesn't seem to exist at all. Sometimes I think that my life is so complete right now there can't possibly be another chapter to it. That's what college is, the end of a book. Not a book in the sense that your life is over, but it's the epilogue of high school and [rec] soccer games on Saturday mornings. You know it's there, you want to know what's in it, you want to know what happens. But you don't want the book to end.

Two weeks later, C.J. got her report card. For the first time since sixth grade, she landed a perfect set of straight As.

FRANK, COLLEGE FRESHMAN | PERCEIVED AS: THE WORKHORSE

When Frank came home from Harvard at the end of May, his house seemed empty without his brother around. He spent as much time as he could out of the house, catching up with Bethesda friends and playing Frisbee. He wanted to be excited about leaving for camp, but looming over him was the dread of telling his mother about his plans, a conversation he put off for as long as he could. He and his father spoke candidly whenever she was out of earshot; these days Frank felt he could talk to his father about anything. Frank's father told him he planned to leave Mrs. AP Frank on June 19, the day Frank left for camp. It was only later that Frank realized that June 19 also happened to be Father's Day.

During his first few days back, Frank's mother relentlessly nagged him to call his boss at NIH to ask when his job would start. On June 1, she insisted he call his employer. Defeated, Frank made the call. His mother watched him intently. On the other end of the line, the phone rang three times, clicked, then was silent. Frank hesitated. *Should I call back?* he thought. Then, *No! Damn the torpedoes!* "Hey, this is Frank," he said to the silence. "Can you give me a call back or send me an email about working at NIH this summer? Thanks, see you later." Frank hung up. His mother looked satisfied.

Two days before he was to leave for camp, Frank decided he needed to tell his mother he would be gone for eight weeks. But when he came home that night after seeing friends, his father was asleep. Too afraid to tell his mother without his father awake as a buffer, Frank chose to wait one more day.

When Frank woke up the next morning, he nervously went downstairs for breakfast. The pit in his stomach seemed to rise with every spoonful of Cheerios. "Frank," his mother said, "I want you to drive Richard to NIH on the twentieth for his job." Even though his brother was still in foster care despite their parents' efforts to get him back through the court system, a mediator kept them in the loop about logistics.

It's go time, Frank thought. He took a breath. "I'm not going to be here on the twentieth."

"What are you talking about?"

"I'm going to camp . . . tomorrow," he said.

She turned to him in a fury. "Are you crazy?" she sputtered. She dove into a diatribe about how Frank must have forged parental signatures, about how useless he was.

"Mom, I'm old enough to make my own decisions," Frank said.

"I'm coming home with a 3.76 GPA"—he had gotten two As, a B-plus, and a pass in his second-semester classes. "I know how to handle myself on my own."

"Just because you make good decisions at college doesn't mean you make bad decisions at home. You go to Harvard, so all your friends working at laboratories, getting internships, working in Congress, and you going to be stupid camp counselor! You can't put it on résumé at all. It's junk! Junk job! Junk!"

She still thinks she can control me, Frank thought. *I have to show her that she can't*. He went down to the basement, emptied out three of his college duffel bags, and began to pack. He hoped that if she saw he was packing for camp no matter what, she would have to accept that he was his own person now. He was already surprised that she hadn't thrown anything at him. Her reaction wasn't as explosive as he had expected.

For the next two hours, Frank didn't hear from his mother. When he looked down his camp checklist, he realized he needed to pack fifteen pairs of underwear. He went to his bedroom, opened his drawer, and saw that his underwear was gone. "Mom," he called, "where's my underwear?"

"Underwear for good kids!" she called back.

"Mom, I need my underwear."

"Underwear for college. Only for good kids!"

"Mom, this is ridiculous." Frank was laughing now. He was certain his mother wouldn't do something so preposterous if she hadn't begrudgingly accepted the fact that he was leaving. "Mom, give me my underwear."

"No!" She appeared in his doorway and put a thick packet of papers down on his desk. Frank recognized the papers as lab homework questions that NIH requested high school interns complete in time for the first day on the job. "Richard has problems for job at NIH. Do problems!"

"This is absolute bullshit, Mom. No one did this kind of crap for *me* when I was going through my internship!"

"No underwear!"

As she left, Frank snatched up the packet she had left on his desk. He did three of the problems before telling his mom he was going out.

Frank returned home at midnight after spending several hours saying goodbye to friends. When he entered the living room, he saw that on top of his duffels, his underwear was piled in neatly folded stacks beside shampoo containers and a pair of sandals he thought he had lost.

The next morning, as Frank walked out the door with the friend who was driving him to camp, his mother held out her arms expectantly. Frank reluctantly received the hug as she told him, "Okay, because letting you go camp, you have to go medical school or law school or become law school professor and maybe dean of law school."

Yes! I've won! I triumph! I am king! Frank thought, and grinned as he stepped into the sunshine.

RYLAND, JUNIOR | PERCEIVED AS: THE SLACKER

After two weeks away on a summer trip to build houses for impoverished families, Ryland returned to reality. The day after he came home, he was eating at the kitchen table when his mother sat down across from him. He kept eating. "You're stalling," his mother said, and moved his bag of Goldfish crackers out of reach. She stared at Ryland with a strange look on her face. In her fist, a pen shook almost spastically, tapping out forceful uneven rhythms—*rat-t-tat, rat-t-t-t-tat*—on the table. *She's really freaking me out,* Ryland thought. His father came into the kitchen and sat down next to him. Ryland's mother handed him his third-quarter report card. "Take a look at that," she said.

"You're acting as if I'm on trial," Ryland said.

"Well, you sort of are," she said.

He looked at his third-quarter report card, or, rather, the altered report card he had copied at Kinko's. "Okay," he said.

"Now look at this," she said, and handed him his semester report card, which listed his real third-quarter grades. *Rat-t-tat-t-tat, rat-t-t-tat.*

Ryland already knew what some of his grades were. He had spent May and June in a mad scramble, trying to catch up in all of his classes, but new work piled up on top of the old. When exam week arrived— the one week when no new work was assigned—Ryland, determined to catch up, fell into a pattern: Take the exam, come home and do catch-up work, sleep a few hours if he could. The routine didn't leave time for studying for the tests. He turned in enough work to keep a B in physics for the fourth quarter, but because he unexpectedly failed the exam, he received a C for the final semester grade. He missed the Modern World exam because he was trying to set up a charity fund-raiser.

The Ritalin that Ryland's mother had finally given back to him sat untouched in a bag in his room.

Ryland looked at his report card for a moment before handing it back to his mother, who was still angrily tapping her pen. He saw an A in journalism and multiple Cs and Ds.

"What, did you lie, did you cook this?!" his mother asked.

"Yeah."

"Why?"

Ryland started to cry. "Because I was afraid of what you guys would do."

"If you were doing so bad, why didn't you come to us for help?"

"Because I was behind. I was stuck. I didn't know what to do. I couldn't go to you because whenever I tell you things, it never helps."

"I don't know what you're talking about," his mother said. Ryland reminded her about a meeting they had with his psychiatrist when he was a sophomore. The psychiatrist had told his mother to back off of him, to give him space by letting him go into his room and close the door. She had agreed at the meeting, but when they got home, she told Ryland, "I think that's wrong. I don't think it would help." Not only did she ignore the doctor's reminder but, worse, she bothered him more because she knew he wasn't getting work done.

"I tried to talk to you, Dad," Ryland said now. "After I had that meeting with my teachers and they were helping me catch up, I told you I was struggling, that I couldn't work at home, and that I worked better when no one was home. You didn't understand. I told you it made me miserable to live here, and you said just to deal with it and hang in there. I told you I couldn't deal with it anymore." His father looked as if he were going to cry.

"I don't understand why you can't do things at home," his mother said. "I don't even get home until late, and your dad doesn't bother you."

"The fact that I'm at home, and everything it reminds me of, makes me miserable," Ryland said.

"What are you talking about?" his mother asked.

"The fact that you guys don't have a relationship, Dad is depressed,

Grandma is sick, and that I do everything I can to avoid going home at all costs."

"Maybe we can get you a laptop," his father said. "You're going to have to get a laptop for college—" He stopped himself. "Never mind."

"It's not the end of the world," Ryland said, desperately hoping he could shape up as a senior, but petrified that the catch-up cycle would renew in the fall. "Even if I don't get in to college, and I'm sure there's some college that will accept me, I could go to Montgomery College for two years and then transfer."

"How could you lie?" his mother said, returning to the issue of the report card. "How could you not tell us?"

"We said we weren't going to talk about that," Ryland's father snapped. "What's done is done. He already told us why he couldn't get things done. We need to concentrate on what to do next year."

Ryland's parents argued back and forth, their shouts getting increasingly louder. Ryland's sobs grew hysterical.

∽

The topic of overachieverism is intensely personal to me. I can relate to Audrey's perfectionism, Julie's self-doubt, Taylor's tug-of-war between a social life and a studious one, and Sam and C.J.'s feeling that as successful as they were, there were always Whitman students who were bigger overachievers. For me, like most of the Whitman students in this book, the pressure was entirely self-driven; none of the adults in my life pushed me to be what I was. I was my own harshest critic. A relentless workaholic. Certain that if I didn't distinguish myself, then I would be a failure. This did not end in high school.

In the years since, I've talked to thousands of twentysomethings about why they felt so lost after leaving the school setting, supposedly on their way to becoming independent adults. Many of them blamed their struggles on issues that could be traced directly to overachiever culture. For example, a common problem that perplexes older adults is that twentysomethings don't know what they want to do with their lives after school—and worse, they don't know who they are. Because of the stark difference between this generation and previous ones, there is now a field of study devoted to what researchers refer to as an extended adolescence. Sociologists puzzle over why young adults can't seem to make decisions for themselves, why they are so directionless, afraid of failure, depressed, and unable to solve their own problems.

But these issues aren't surprising if one considers that members of this generation rarely had to make their own decisions. Throughout many of these young people's formative years, parents chose their activities, college counselors or administrators dictated their courses, and *U.S. News* prioritized their university choices. Ferried incessantly from lessons to practices, activities to classes, they spent their childhood zooming toward college admissions, always rushing, always looking to the next step, always trying to stay ahead or at least keep up with the competition. They didn't have the time to pause and reflect on not only what they were doing but why. There was no period of exploration, of development, of self-analysis. Problems were solved swiftly and tidily by helicopter parents. Failure was not an option—and for overachievers, "failure" referred to anything short of unparalleled excellence. To quote columnist David Brooks, today's young adults "are the most honed and supervised generation in human history. If they are group-oriented, deferential to authority, and achievement-obsessed, it is because we achievement-besotted adults have trained them to be."

How can that scenario possibly translate to an easy transition to adulthood? Of course young adults have an inferiority complex and panic that they peaked in school. A twenty-five-year-old from a rural farm town in Ohio overachieved her way into Georgetown University and now obsesses about how to replicate that success. "How does my overachieving history affect me now? I still have a lot of the old messages swimming around in my head. I still feel, whether it's a report card full of As or a particularly positive review from a supervisor, that these are markers that somehow determine my self-worth. To do well is such a part of my self-esteem and identity that failure threatens to erode who I am," she said. "A shocking reality became apparent after school: that to be 'the best' at something is exponentially more difficult on a national scale, and that one's identity has to be drastically redefined in order to survive with just doing the best that one can do (which, in the warped reality of an overachiever, is only 'mediocre')."

Pressure from parents, however well intentioned, can backfire once their offspring reach young adulthood. Even the most diligent, disciplined, obedient child can self-destruct when faced with the reality that he does not know who he is because he let adults' expectations direct his life. Frank could see this coming. As he said to his father before he first left for Harvard, "Before I know it, I'll be in med school, pushing myself to be a doctor when I don't want to be one." Some young people spend their lives trying to please parents, teachers, coaches, and professors, then implode when they realize they don't know how to make themselves happy.

For this reason, Mark, twenty-seven, at the time of this writing was in therapy. Pushed by his parents to become a successful gymnast, he believed the relentless pressure to excel as a child damaged his chances at happiness as an adult. "I feel like I can't measure up to the success I had in school. There are parts of my psyche that haven't developed because I never had one damn moment to stop and think about things. I have terrible anxiety now, low self-esteem, and poor interpersonal skills. I have a strong drive to succeed, but lots of times, I don't even know what I'm striving for."

Post-graduation, overachievers often continue to strive for tangible successes at the expense of more valuable intangibles. Rachel Simmons, the acclaimed young author of the bestseller *Odd Girl Out,* was such a Vassar standout that she was featured in the school's brochures. A straight-A student with the exception of a B-plus in psychology, which she loved but dropped because of the grade, Simmons snagged a prestigious Urban Fellowship in New York City after graduation. She quickly became a star in Mayor Rudy Giuliani's office and was recruited to work for Senator Charles Schumer [D-NY]. When she won a Rhodes Scholarship, Giuliani held a press conference for her in City Hall. Schumer introduced her to then-President Clinton as his Rhodes Scholar. Determined to be "the best Rhodes Scholar that ever lived," Simmons was on top of the world.

When she got to Oxford, she crashed. "It was like the needle on the record just came to this horrible screeching halt. I fought desperately not to hate it. It couldn't be possible that I didn't like being a Rhodes Scholar. It had to mean something was wrong with me, because who could possibly not embrace this once-in-a-lifetime opportunity? It was the first time in my life I was ever depressed," Simmons told me, her hands steady on her coffee cup. "Leaving was not on the table until there was no choice, and by no choice I mean that no matter how much medication I took, and I took a lot, I couldn't stop crying. And I couldn't be happy."

After nine months, Simmons did what she thought was the unthinkable: She walked away from the most prestigious scholarship—the highest pinnacle of academic overachieverism—that the United States had to offer. "I realized I had been living an inauthentic life and I had lost touch with what I truly loved. I didn't know anymore who I was, what I cared about, and what I really wanted. I had no identity. My identity was my self-esteem, my self-esteem was all about achievements, and when I couldn't achieve something, when I couldn't be a good Rhodes Scholar, my identity shattered. That's why I fell apart."

To heal from her breakdown, she learned to keep her overachieverism in check. "It's about keeping your eye on the ball and not looking at where you're going to hit it."

It is a tricky thing to struggle with, to appear as if you have everything but to feel like you are nothing, to know that no matter the number of accolades, there lurks within you an ambitious thirst that cannot be quenched. As I watched the students I followed torment themselves over how their choices would affect others' impressions of them, I remembered promises I made to myself as a teen that I had broken as an adult. I realized that all of the identity issues that haunted me as a twentysomething stemmed directly from the overachieverism that consumed me as a child.

When talking with the students, I tried to walk the fine line between serving as a sounding board and giving them advice (more than one of them happily referred to our interactions as "free therapy"). I wanted to tell them that they—and many of the other students I met across the country—were stuck in a cycle in which they lived their lives according to other people's perceptions, expectations, or labels, even though those labels were often wrong. I wanted to explain how dangerous it was to get caught up in the Age of Comparison, because when comparing themselves to others, they could not truly know—especially in high school—what those other lives were like behind the labels. The Superstar might feel lost and identityless, the Workhorse might not be that way of his own volition, the Slacker might be anything but, the

Flirt might have much more to her than peers realize, the Author might be ashamed she has not been able to curb the workaholism that plagued her in high school.

Certainly, there will be critics who scoff at the notion of straight-A students and superstar athletes as tortured souls. But there is no doubt that the perfectionist tendencies pushed by our overachiever culture can chip away at overachievers' sense of enjoyment well after they march out of what can be hollowed ivy halls.

Chapter 17

August 3-December 9

BACK TO SCHOOL

AUDREY, JUNIOR | PERCEIVED AS: THE PERFECTIONIST

According to plan, Audrey's first stop of the summer was an international relations program at Georgetown, which she thought of as a dress rehearsal—a blueprint—for the college experience she coveted. There, Audrey was in her element. She was already familiar with the topics taught in the program lectures, and she met students, most of whom also planned to apply early to Georgetown, who had the drive, stress, and perfectionist streak that reminded her of Whitman. They talked incessantly about their scores and college lists, just like Audrey's Bethesda classmates. *I found my people,* she thought. They even looked like her; as her parents dropped her off, they laughed at the sea of students wearing Lacoste polos, Abercrombie jeans, and Rainbow flip-flops— because Audrey was wearing those, too.

When the summer program ended in late July, Audrey was even more convinced that Georgetown was the perfect place for her. On paper, it satisfied every need on her dream school checklist: a strong international relations program, a close-knit campus in a city where she wouldn't get bored, a medium-size undergraduate population of students similar to her, grade and score acceptance requirements that challenged her but were just within her reach, and opportunities for internships in her field.

The day that Audrey came home from Georgetown, she had two hours to unpack and pack again for a weeklong college tour in New England with her father. They checked out a few schools in Boston because parts of the city reminded Audrey of Georgetown. Then they stopped at a few other nearby schools, like Dartmouth, a school that didn't interest her in the least. She had steered her high school career toward a Georgetown acceptance, and she wasn't the type of person to change her mind—doing so would mean hopping off a track she had been dead set on for as long as she could remember. Dartmouth was on the way from Boston to other college stops, and its student population was the right size, but it seemed to be the opposite of the kind of school she wanted. Hanover was too remote, and she didn't see how the school could provide her with the international relations program and internship opportunities she sought.

The minute Audrey stepped onto the Dartmouth Green, her world turned upside down.

The beauty of the Green took her breath away. She and her father sat by a tree and took in the lush grass and the centuries-old buildings. Students were playing Frisbee across the lawn, as was true at many of the schools Audrey had seen, but somehow they seemed happier at this school, on this green. This scene didn't have the bustling, vibrant, fast-paced aura of Georgetown. It seemed calmer, nurturing, idyllic. Even the Dartmouth academic year was, as Audrey put it, "out of the box"; rather than two semesters of four or five classes, students had four ten-week sessions of three classes apiece, so while the work was more concentrated, there were fewer subjects and professors to manage at a time.

Audrey decided her initial assumption was correct: Dartmouth was the exact opposite of what she had previously sought in a college—it represented a slower, more flexible atmosphere with students who weren't exactly like her. Far outside of her comfort zone, Dartmouth was also perhaps the opposite of Audrey herself. It scared her that she could suddenly like Dartmouth so much when it had never once figured into her plans. If she changed her mind about school, how was she to know if she would major in international relations, go to graduate school in journalism, and end up working on Capitol Hill, like she had always known she would? Dartmouth wasn't perfect, but it represented a divergence from her pre-formulated path, a place that would, as she later phrased it, "pull me out of my element." Which was precisely why Audrey, uncharacteristically relaxed enough to linger in a moment of self-awareness, gazed at the peaceful campus before her and resolutely decided to apply there early instead.

THE STEALTH OVERACHIEVER, JUNIOR | PERCEIVED AS: ?

Thoughts whirling, Stealth stared at the computer in shock. When Stealth's grandmother had died in July, dejection was tempered by acceptance of the inevitable—she had been sick for some time. Two days after the funeral, Stealth was startled when a local newspaper reported that a former friend was gunned down, but that death, too, had a cause and effect; the boy was buying drugs when he was shot. This one, however, was different.

Over the summer, an internship at an international development company had helped earn money so that Stealth's parents would no longer have to pay for participation on Whitman's debate team. Stealth felt horrible about the cost of being on the debate team, estimating that each debate season, including plane tickets for tournaments, probably cost more than $2,000, in addition to debate camp every summer. Stealth never took their contributions for granted. While teammates signed up for tournaments on whims, Stealth chose trips carefully by price and prestige, competing in only enough to try to secure a bid for the national tournament. Stealth's parents were never told about the more expensive tournaments.

At the end of July, Stealth had reunited with friends at debate camp in California and spent the bulk of the session with Geoffrey, the much-admired debater who was many campers' favorite debate buddy. They worked together on cases, took a field trip to a mall where they dueled with water guns until a security guard stopped them, and visited Master Psychic, a psychic cat who worked the streets of Santa Monica. And now, back home just two weeks later, Stealth was staring at an instant message from a friend: "Geoffrey killed himself last night." For the first time in life, Stealth was completely devastated. Stealth cried in bed before going to sleep.

Throughout the next few weeks, Stealth alternated between guilt— *I should have known, I should have done something*—and denial. After Geoffrey's death, when his IM screen name signed on with a profile that still quoted a funny line Stealth had said, Stealth desperately tried to believe that the suicide was a bad dream or one of Geoffrey's jokes. But Geoffrey's computer probably logged on automatically.

By the time school started, Stealth knew more about Geoffrey than when he was alive. Stealth had known that Geoffrey was bright, hilarious, entertaining, down-to-earth, a star debater, and an excellent storyteller, but after he died, Stealth looked him up on the Internet and learned more. At age thirteen, Geoffrey petitioned his city council to pass an ordinance allowing electric scooters on the roads. In college, he formed a nonprofit foundation to raise money for students who couldn't afford to travel to debate tournaments. In only nineteen years, Stealth realized, Geoffrey had made an impact on people. He had contributed to society. Stealth resolved to stop "living in a straight line" and to start thinking about how to contribute, too. *Geoffrey was the last person who should have died,* Stealth thought. *Of all people, why did it have to be him?*

JULIE, COLLEGE FRESHMAN | PERCEIVED AS: THE SUPERSTAR

When the starter's gun sounded, Julie took off with the rest of her team. She kept telling herself how cool it was to be decked out in her green Dartmouth gear, running in her first college meet, but her nerves shook her into apathy. *You don't need to be here,* a voice in her head whispered. *What if you don't keep up? What if you finish last on the team?* Ever since she had arrived on campus, she couldn't stop thinking about the fact that she was the only unrecruited freshman on the team, and therefore, the slowest. It was an entirely new role for her.

Julie had shown up at Dartmouth for cross-country preseason ten days before the rest of the freshmen arrived on campus. She liked her dorm, which was close to the track, and her roommate, who was busy with her own varsity athletic schedule, but she couldn't help feeling homesick. She missed her parents, being surrounded by people who loved her, the comforts of her home, and even her Whitman cross-country teammates. Julie knew that Dartmouth felt empty because the year hadn't officially begun, but her loneliness was unsettling.

Less than a minute into the race, Julie knew something was wrong. Her legs went lactic, an acid buildup that gave her a deadweight, burning sensation. She tried to stay with the two teammates her coach had assigned as her race group, but they were running at a faster pace than she preferred, and runners from Brown and Boston College separated them. When she rounded the corner of the first mile loop, the team manager yelled, "6:07," which was seven seconds slower than the time her race group had agreed on prior to the meet. *You should be able to go faster,* she berated herself. *What's wrong with you? Now everyone else will know you're the worst.*

A hundred meters ahead, Julie spotted her parents, who had come to campus to bring some of her things. *I shouldn't be here,* Julie thought, and for the first time in her life, she dropped out of a race.

Her parents stopped cheering, looking confused. "Keep going, Julie! You're doing well!" her mother said.

Julie wiped tears from her eyes. "I don't want to do this. I don't want to be here," she said. "I'm done. Let's go home." She was too far out of her comfort zone, in this strange environment with unfamiliar people.

"Do you really want to go home?" her mother asked.

"Yeah," Julie said. She could go back to work at the retail store that had hired her for the summer and transfer to a local university. *I wasn't ready to leave home,* she thought.

Then Julie's team surprised her. As she stood with her parents, awkwardly watching her teammates finish the race, an injured teammate who wasn't running gave her a hug and said, "It's okay, don't worry about it. It's not a big meet at all." As the Dartmouth girls finished, they came over to Julie and, one by one, took her aside and empathized. "It's a huge transition from high school to college, so I understand what you're going through," a sophomore said. A senior added, "I was a walk-on, too, and felt the same way. It was really overwhelming to run here."

"I don't know if I want to run in college," Julie said.

"At least let us have you until the next meet," the senior said. Julie agreed to give running, and Dartmouth, a little more time.

FRANK, COLLEGE SOPHOMORE | PERCEIVED AS: THE WORKHORSE

After a summer at camp, where Frank whiled away lazy hours thinking about Kristen, he returned home to a world again changed. His father had left, his younger brother now lived with his father, and his mother seemed the slightest bit subdued. "Gimme hug," she said as he walked in the door, following him with her arms out, Dr. Evil–style. Frank obliged, then gave her $500 of the money he had earned. He decided to try living with her until he left for college.

Over the next several days, Frank's mother made a few feeble attempts to remind him of his law or medical destiny. She showed him a newspaper article about the Chief Justice and said, "Roberts said real men study law! You have to study law!" Another day she started in with "Rehnquist died. Maybe someday you be Supreme Court Justice, too!" Still, when Frank informed her that he was going to visit Isabel at her Georgia lake house a few weeks before going back to Harvard, she didn't protest. Frank was surprised to sense that there had been a power shift. By leaving the house on his own terms, and then coming back, Frank at last had set boundaries around his mother's control.

Isabel had been in on it since the beginning. She lured Kristen to her lake house, then invited Frank to surprise her. Now Frank was with Isabel, staring at a closed door behind which Kristen slept. "Should I go in?" Frank asked, fiddling with the Coke bottle in his hand.

"Yeah!" Isabel replied.

Frank hesitated. "Should I knock?"

"No, don't knock; go in!"

Frank looked at the doorknob for a moment before stepping into the room. Kristen was napping on a couch, her long black hair, still wet from a shower, drawn up into a bun. The jolt of seeing her after a summer of anticipation caused the speech he had rehearsed to vaporize. "Uh." Frank cleared his throat. "Yo."

Kristen turned around, bleary-eyed, then did a double take. "Oh! You're here!" she exclaimed.

Trying to be cool, Frank took a swig of Coke. "What's up," he said. "Yeah."

The next night Isabel told Frank and Kristen to go out on the roof. A nearly full moon filtered through the surrounding pine trees. Frank and Kristen leaned on the railing, separated only by lightly misting drizzle. *Here we go,* Frank thought, nervous. Their few moments of chatter were chased away by a heavier silence. *Move now, Frank. You gotta do something. Do it now!*

"So now what?" Kristen asked, her small face upturned.

"Yeah, well, I was going to say something about existential thought and philosophy and stuff because I hate the silence and want to fill it, but now I think I'm just going to go with this," he said. He put his arm around Kristen, mentally recapping Isabel's first-kiss seminar. *Slowly,* he thought. *Ninety percent . . .* They leaned toward each other at the same time. When their lips met, the only thought left in Frank's head was *This is how it's supposed to be.* His first kiss lasted two and a half hours.

Back at Harvard, when Frank reunited with Andrew and Mike in their sophomore triple, their friendship picked up where it had left off. Excited about the upcoming year with them, which surely would be full of absurdity, video games, and long conversations about his first girlfriend, Frank left his mother unpacking in his room to buy cold drinks for everyone from a nearby CVS. When he returned, his mother was sitting motionless on his bed. He handed her a drink and rummaged through a bag.

"I know you are doing environmental science," she said, her voice soft.

Frank continued going through his things, careful not to make eye contact. "What? What are you talking about?" he said. "Don't be silly."

"I met with environmental science professor and asked him and he said you were."

Frank suspected she was lying. He later learned that Mike had inadvertently given him away during a conversation while Frank was on his errand. For now Frank was stunned to discover that his mother seemed less angry than resigned. "Oh, bah," he snorted. "So what?"

Frank's mother took on a fake-huffy voice. "You crazy kid! You lied to me!"

"Oh, whatever."

"Well . . ." She paused. "As long as you go to medical school or law school, is okay."

That day, as Frank walked through Harvard Square, noting the easy familiarity of each passing landmark—the same small man playing a one-string fiddle outside the Harvard Coop, the same stores, the same bustle of parents moving a new set of freshmen into Harvard Yard—he thought, *I'm home,* and he couldn't stop smiling.

THE STEALTH OVERACHIEVER, SENIOR | PERCEIVED AS: ?

Stealth sat quietly in the corner of the guidance office while a counselor handed out forms and Whitman coffee mugs to the sixteen National

Merit semifinalists present and talked about the scholarship process. An administrator who used to be a counselor strutted into the room. "I was a National Merit semifinalist, too," he announced. "Are any of my counselees in here?" His eyes canvassed the students, settling on Frank's brother, Richard. "I know you," the administrator said. When Stealth also gave a nod, the administrator's eyes widened. "Oh, *you?*"

A few days later, Stealth was in Spanish class when a guidance aide delivered notes to the five semifinalists in the room. As the teacher wove her way to Stealth's desk, several pairs of eyes tracked her. Stealth noticed an overachiever staring, jaw dropped, eyes narrowed. Stealth ignored him and opened the letter, which offered National Merit Semifinalists a full scholarship to Arizona State University should they choose to attend.

The money was tempting, but Stealth already had settled on a list of colleges to apply to, a mix of state and elite schools. Ultimately, Stealth wasn't worried about college. A rejection letter would not crush Stealth's self-esteem. "The only thing I hate," Stealth explained to a friend, "is when people judge others based on where they go to college. Like at Whitman, when people ask where you're going to college, you say some name that's not Ivy-caliber, and they give you that 'Oh.'" But Stealth had never gotten caught up in the college frenzy, believing prestige to be arbitrary, a false construct. As Stealth's mom once said, "The person makes the school, not vice versa." Stealth expected to have the same opportunities at any college to be successful.

When the bell rang, the overachiever followed Stealth out of Spanish. He stepped in front of Stealth, stopped, turned around, and said, "*You* got National Merit?"

"Yeah," Stealth replied.

The overachiever gaped as he stared up at the guy who was supposed to be a meathead. But Pete, the Stealth Overachiever, had turned away and was walking down the hall, his mind already on more interesting things.

∞

A month after he graduated, I checked in with Charles, the student from Portales, New Mexico, who seemed to have it all. He was smart, talented, ambitious, and had the accolades to match; in addition to his work as district student government president and other leadership roles, his six-page résumé listed several lines of awards for drama, dance, choir (he was all-state), and debate. In the nine months since I met Charles, I chatted and corresponded with him several times, so I knew the efforts it took him to appear so stellar on paper. On a typical school day, he woke up at 7:15, did extracurricular activities after school until six (weekend dance rehearsals could last for eight hours), worked as a McDonald's manager until midnight, finished the homework he hadn't completed during lunch or classes, and finally, at 2:30 A.M., went to bed.

I knew that in October of his senior year, he got his first B, in an AP Calculus class, which devastated him even though he had skipped precalculus; his ACT proctor announced before administering the test that the ACT "will determine the rest of your life"; he worried incessantly about financial aid; and he took a muscle relaxer to help him sleep. I knew that he eventually left the McDonald's job because he needed more time for schoolwork, and that he was elected to run a major school service committee (his school needed two bathrooms restored, which required getting funding from the board of education, securing contractors, ordering supplies, etc.). I also knew that he was overwhelmed. "Man, the pressure comes at you from every direction," he told me. "My parents make me feel like a B isn't good enough. Teachers make me feel like homework could have been better. Competition in speech and debate make me feel like if I didn't get first place, then I didn't try hard enough. Theater and chorale make me feel that my talent isn't great unless the audience thinks so. All of it is overpowering."

I didn't know, until he admitted to me the summer after he graduated, that for much of that time Charles was clinically depressed—diagnosed by a psychiatrist who attributed the depression directly to the pressure placed on him to succeed.

For how long will overachiever culture continue to spiral out of control? Some say that the college admissions frenzy will subside by 2010, when the number of applicants will plateau. Others see only a temporary hiatus before those numbers climb again. But I believe that a comprehensive, nationwide effort by students, parents, schools, counselors, administrators, and admissions officers can reverse the trend. All of those parties agree that there is a major problem; the first step toward solving it is to accept that overachieverism is at its root.

Overachieverism can be an addiction, and our society is its enabler. Several students I interviewed were petrified that the admissions rat race wouldn't end after high school. They feared they would then overextend themselves in college to get into a good graduate school, and in graduate school to get a good job, and again in the working world in order to continue to achieve recognizable success. They were afraid that overachieving has become the norm, and one that is impossible to sustain; after all, nearly 50 percent of college students report that they had an A average in high school. As Thomas, one of the New Trier seniors, explained to me, overachieving isn't considered overachieving anymore. "It's just achieving," he said. "It's expected."

This is not to say that all overachieving is negative; strides in countless fields would be lost had certain individuals not been impelled to sacrifice aspects of their identities to their vision of a greater glory. But there are differences between healthy overachievers (like Stealth/Pete, who balanced Russian lessons, piano lessons, sports, a job at a Russian school, and debate, while pulling excellent grades and test scores and serving as co–managing editor of *The Spectator* as a senior) and those who are sucked into the vortex of overachiever culture.

Overachiever culture accelerates the normal process of setting goals and the all-out crusade to reach them. It allows that crusade to dictate how people live their lives. If a healthy overachiever accomplishes goals mostly for the pleasure of the process, an unhealthy overachiever collects (or is pushed to collect) the goals mostly for the sake of collecting. It is the difference between love and notches on a bedpost. It is a combination of perfectionism, workaholism, and competitiveness. When a person is convinced that time spent not being "productive" is a waste, that every activity must be toward some larger, noteworthy purpose, that any failure to exceed expectations is shameful, then overachieverism has become a problem.

Let me be clear: This is not a call for mediocrity. It is a call for perspective. What good is a nation with the highest test scores in the world if many of its youngest citizens are so miserable they kill themselves? Experts like to cite with astonishment the high teen suicide rates in Asian countries—and yet the rate in the United States is the same as or worse than that of South Korea. Those who wish to live their lives by following rankings, by pitting students, schools, and countries against one another, might try ranking the accompanying numbers of teens who are depressed.

If parenting has become product development, students are helplessly caught up in the commodities trade. As a concerned Bill Fitzsimmons, Harvard's dean of admissions and financial aid, told me during an interview at his office, "Today it seems as though everyone is engaged in marketing. It's not simply marketing one for a position at the very difficult preschool, high school, college, and grad school, and for various employment opportunities. It comes down almost to marketing one's soul, which gets to undermining the meaning of one's entire life." Many administrators and politicians are so dazzled by numbers that they neglect to consider the child behind the digits, just as many families are so blinded by prestige that they don't pay enough attention to the school behind the name.

Or the generation gap. High school today is not the high school of the current parents' generation. It is not even the high school that I attended only ten years before beginning this research. Students must deal with all of the elements that faced teens of the past, though with an added variable: They believe they can't get by with merely running on the hamster wheel—they have to floor it, fast and furious, and can never step off.

The driving force behind much of the frenzy is the belief that a person must attend a top-ranked university in order to succeed in life. Thus, the most important messages we can send students and parents are that: 1) this myth has been debunked; 2) the prestige of a school's name is no longer commensurate with the quality of its education; and 3) there are hundreds of excellent schools to which the majority of applicants can gain admission. Indeed, the growth in student numbers isn't as dire as it seems. The National Association for College Admission Counseling reported in 2005 that since 1974, the growth in post–secondary school enrollment has grown by 50 percent, which is nearly matched by the 40 percent growth in the number of accredited postsecondary institutions eligible for federal financial aid.

There are more than 2,000 four-year undergraduate programs in the United States, in addition to highly respected universities in other countries. Only about 225 of those U.S. colleges practice any form of selective admission; most of the rest would fall over backward to accept good students. Many families, however, are so paralyzed by choice—or unaware of the options—that they narrow their focus to twenty or thirty highly selective schools. They set themselves up for failure when they tunnel toward a school like Yale, which in 2006 accepted only 8.6 percent of applicants. As Audrey, who still has her rock puppy, learned, the idea of a "perfect" university is not set in stone. Students not only have choices; they can select from dozens of schools where they could be happy.

But no student should have to wait for college to find happiness. I worry about the lingering effects overachiever culture will have on the students I followed. Overachieverism is not easily outgrown; many of these students will continue to have issues caused by living their formative years in such a success-centric bubble. I worry that when they are again confronted with the pressure to attain a certain goal, the pursuit will overtake their lives, much like Julie couldn't focus on her health and personal needs until after she was acceped to college. I worry that they will be judged by brand names. I worry that after so many years, overachieving has become an ingrained habit that will lead them to continue to live their lives following a linear progression, treating stages of life like rungs on a ladder. I worry that they will not be free to discover the selves behind the statistics. I worry that they will never learn to stop and catch their breath. I worry that, like me, they will worry too much.

High school, especially, has become a game of *Survivor,* a hypercompetition that swirls around the precepts "Outwit, Outplay, Outlast." It doesn't have to be that way. Here are some suggestions for steps that students, parents, schools, and counselors can take to battle the destructive influence of overachiever culture on our educational system.

What Schools Can Do
Delay High School Start Times
Most high schools across the country have early start times that are directly at odds with adolescents' natural sleep cycles. By delaying high school start times, school districts can save teens from the sometimes disastrous health effects caused by sleep deprivation.

Drop Class Rank
Class rank encourages cutthroat competition, cheating, and choosing classes based on GPA weight rather than on interest, not to mention directly pitting students against one another. Abolishing class rank sends

the message that schools are interested in students as individuals rather than as compared to their classmates. In any case, for more than ten years, the importance of class rank has been diminishing in the eyes of college admissions officers.

Deemphasize Testing

Student success should not be determined or evaluated by how well kids can bubble in answer sheets. By following the lead of schools that shun No Child Left Behind tactics, educators can demonstrate that a love of learning is more important than test-taking skills. An alternative method of evaluating students is "performance assessment," which appraises students on items such as portfolios, projects, and writing samples. Students will be more prone to "deep-approach" learning rather than superficial, temporary memorization of facts, and teachers will have the chance to spend semesters actually teaching rather than reviewing for an exam. Decreasing focus on standardized tests also leaves more resources for more important areas like guidance counseling, which suffers when schools must allot high portions of their budget toward testing.

Provide Less-Competitive Alternatives

For students who may not want the commitment or competition of a varsity sport, full-length theater production, or regularly published newspaper, a school could offer non-competitive, less time-consuming alternatives, such as intramural/recreational sports leagues, a one-act play troupe, and a magazine. These options would give more students a chance to participate and could shift the focus in those activities from competition and commitment to enjoyment of the activity itself.

Assign—and Enforce—Coordinated Departmental Project and Test Days

No student should have to contend with four tests in a day, but that happened to many students I spoke with nationwide. If department heads coordinate testing days and due dates for major projects—English one day, math another, etc.—students can better manage their workload and will be less likely to be overwhelmed (and to resort to cheating). This step also addresses the larger issue of reminding teachers that students have many classes to juggle. Thomas at New Trier pointed out,

"We take more than one class. That's a big thing. Teachers think their class is the only class we should care about." At that, his classmate Carolyn added, "If you ask to go to bathroom during class, they say, 'Can't you go during someone else's class?'" The key to this measure is that administrators must be willing to enforce it, or else teachers, like Sam's during Senior Stress Week, might feel they are exempt. A written policy distributed to students, teachers, and parents can ensure that all parties know what is expected. And yes, quizzes count as tests.

Increase Awareness

Many parents and teachers don't realize what students are going through, and students don't realize their stress can be alleviated. The year I began researching this book, a group of devoted Whitman parents and administrators formed a committee called Stressbusters for those reasons. Stressbusters found that there are a variety of speakers and activities schools can bring in to increase awareness, from someone to lead a lunchtime session on yoga, meditation, or time management to a moderator of a student–parent forum.

Limit APs

If students are bound within certain limits, they won't feel the need to outdo their classmates, because they won't be allowed to. Schools can limit the number of AP classes taken in a semester, thereby taking the pressure off students who worry that each term they must take five or more AP courses for the label and the GPA points. AP classes are supposed to be college-level courses; no high school student should feel the push to take a full load of college-level courses while in high school, especially when decreasing numbers of colleges accept AP credits. Schools that limit APs can describe this policy in their school profile, which accompanies the transcript in every student's college application, so that admissions officers are aware of it.

Reinstitute Recess

Sacrificing children's leisure time in favor of test scores can stunt rather than further their development. Reinstituting children's free-play period can improve their attitude, character, and fitness in and out of the classroom.

What Colleges Can Do

Boycott the Rankings

Precise objective ordering of colleges is a sham. Not only does it fail to inform students which school would be the best match for them, but it is also a dangerous marketing tool that fuels the craze over selective institutions. It is silly to assume that a school ranked twenty-sixth offers a less valuable education because it is not in the top twenty-five. By any appropriate measure, there are probably several dozen schools that could fairly lay claim to "top twenty-five" status. The rankings make too much out of small, often insignificant subjective differences. When I asked admissions officers why their schools didn't boycott the rankings, the most common answer was "fear"; if, like Reed College, they drop in the rankings because they don't provide information, they worry that they will lose applicants and prestige. But when I asked the officers whether they would boycott the rankings if several institutions did so together, they agreed that it was a good idea. (Meanwhile, Reed reports that the number and quality of its applicants has risen since it stopped cooperating with *U.S. News.*)

As some admissions officers remarked to me, the single upside to rankings is that they provide information about schools to people who might not otherwise have access to it. To address this valid point, colleges should boycott only those publications that put schools in ranked order. Instead, colleges can disseminate information to the public through guidebooks and other periodicals that share facts about schools without ranking them. Even if ranking publications try to ascertain statistics via other means, if families know that schools do not support the rankings, they will be less likely to believe those publications carry weight.

Schools would then be able to focus on areas that will improve the educational experience for their students rather than on numbers that might shoot them up a ridiculously overhyped list. A boycott would also take the pressure off college administrators, not to mention students. This would send the right message to families—the message that admissions officers, counselors, teachers, and administrators concede is the most important goal of the college admissions process: Students should focus on finding the best matches, not the "best" schools.

Scrap the SAT

In 2001, when Richard Atkinson recommended that his schools stop requiring SAT scores, he said, "While there is widespread agreement that overemphasis on the SAT harms American education, there is no consensus on what to do or where to start. In many ways, we are caught up in the educational equivalent of a nuclear arms race. We know that this overemphasis on test scores hurts all involved, especially students. But we also know that anyone or any institution opting out of the competition does so at considerable risk." While Atkinson may have been appeased by the changes resulting in the new SAT, the situation he described has not changed. Several schools have already scrapped the test with success. More colleges should muster the courage to opt out of the arms race by eliminating the requirement that students submit SAT or ACT scores with their applications.

Eliminate Early Decision

Critics of early decision call it a ploy for colleges to get students to commit in the fall of their senior year in order to artificially increase their yield. (Until 2003, a school's yield factored into its *U.S. News* ranking.) Unlike early-action programs, under early decision, students who are admitted to a college cannot apply elsewhere. This practice puts lower-income students at a disadvantage because early decision doesn't give them the chance to compare financial aid packages.

Also, early decision puts immense pressure on students to choose one school at the beginning of their senior year, as Julie discovered, as if students had only one ideal match. It's a damned-if-you-do, damned-if-you-don't situation: If students rush to make a choice and apply early, they could get stuck going to a school that isn't a good fit; if they take their time and wait to apply with the regular pool, they will miss out on the higher admission rates of the early-decision period.

Prioritize Mental Health

While 85 percent of directors of college and university counseling centers saw a rise in the number of students with severe psychological problems, 63 percent of those directors reported that their schools either maintained the same level of resources or reduced them. Schools must consider the health of their students above all else and should configure their budgets to reflect that prioritization.

Some schools supplement mental health services with creative ways to help students; Harvard holds workshops for staff so that professors, dining hall checkers, financial aid employees, and maintenance workers are trained to watch for signs of distressed students and to report them to residential deans. The University of Maryland at College Park provides for-credit courses to teach freshmen how to manage their time and stress. These types of programs are laudable supplementary measures.

Send a Message
When Duke changed its application by deleting some of the lines allotted for students to list their extracurricular activities, it replaced those lines with space for students to describe what their activities meant to them. MIT and Bowdoin are among the schools that ask applicants to describe what they do for pleasure.

Not only should other schools follow their lead to send a similar message to students, but also, schools should stop the selfish practice of marketing to unqualified students simply to increase their applicant pool.

What Counselors Can Do
Focus on the Student, Not on the Schools
The single most important thing a college counselor (whether private or school-based) can do for students is to focus on college search rather than on college prep. Rather than helping students devise a list of schools that might suit them, many counselors are strategizing how to rewrite a résumé, or reengineer a life, to suit a school. The Independent Educational Consultants Association clearly states that a major advantage to hiring a counselor is the professional's familiarity with a wide range of schools. Counselors do a disservice to their clients and to their profession when they ignore that benefit.

What Parents Can Do
Limit Young Children's Activities
Hoping to give their children every available opportunity, parents often schedule them by the hour into programs for dance, music, sports,

and languages, among others. But unstructured playtime can be just as valuable to children's development. By enrolling children in no more than one or two after-school activities per season, parents can help to instill a lifelong habit of balancing productive time and downtime.

Get a Life

Parents and their children would benefit from heeding the plea of the child mentioned in Chapter Nine who said, "I wish my parents had some hobby other than me." If parents focus on their own interests and friendships, they will be less likely to overinvest themselves in their children's achievements, thereby reducing parental pressure.

Schedule Family Time

Whether during meals, vacations, or occasional activities, family time—which should not involve discussions of parental expectations for children—is as important to students as it should be to parents. It's a way for families to open lines of communication and to reinforce a mutual support network. A bonus: A recent University of Michigan study found that when families eat together, children are more likely to be high achievers and less likely to have disciplinary problems.

Place Character Above Performance

Perhaps parents shouldn't be surprised if children cheat, given that many parents are doing the same thing. What does it say when a parent drugs a healthy child for better test scores, has a healthy child diagnosed with a bogus disorder to get untimed tests, or hires someone to write a student's college essays? One of the most appalling facts I learned is that some students believe their parents would rather they cheat than get a poor grade. Statistical success doesn't automatically translate to a happy teen—Frank can attest to that—just as a high-powered career doesn't guarantee an adult a happy life.

What Students and Parents Can Do

Stop the Guilt

Parents often feel guilty if they aren't making sure their children, from preschool on, have access to every opportunity possible to get an edge in admissions; students often feel guilty if they don't follow through.

Frantic attempts to pile on the opportunities, however, can backfire by causing burnout, anxiety, or worse. It's easier said than done, to be sure, but parents and students should take care not to feel guilty about not getting caught up in the competition.

Adjust the Superstar Mentality

Too often overachievers exhaust themselves because they—or their parents—believe they need to reach the pinnacle of every activity to which they commit; that if they aren't the captain, high scorer, president, editor in chief, or first-place winner, or if they don't obtain the A-plus or perfect test score, then their efforts and involvement were worthless. These students must learn to find enjoyment even when they can't experience superstardom. Note that fewer than half of all Major League Baseball players have ever hit a home run.

Carve an Individual Path

Just because some students take on certain responsibilities or apply to particular colleges doesn't mean those tracks are ideal for every student. Ultimately, success will hinge more on whether a student is free to pursue passions than whether he goes to a top-ranked school. Further, traditional four-year colleges aren't for every student, even for overachievers. Students who wish to become musicians, chefs, mechanics, carpenters, or cosmetologists, for example, shouldn't necessarily be diverted to a liberal arts school because it's a more familiar path. Half of all students who attend college do not graduate, perhaps in part because students aren't going to schools that are right for them.

Ignore the Peanut Gallery

Name-brand fever often comes down to a look—from parent to parent, from adult to student, from student to student. Much of the frenzy about colleges is geared toward that single moment after another person asks, "So where are you/where is your child going to school?" Too many students told me they changed their college application plans because they were worried about those looks, or "that 'Oh,'" as Stealth put it. It's sad that students are so influenced by looks they might get between the time they receive regular-decision college letters and the time they graduate. That's a couple of months of feeling uncomfortable from a look of judgment versus years of education at what could be an ideally matched school. Looks fade. Choices don't.

Accept That Name Does Not Reflect Ability

Here is another way to view the relative nature of the college admissions process. If Stealth or Richard decided to go to the University of Maryland because of a scholarship, would that make them less of a student than Taylor, who opted for Duke? In Hawaii, students don't have Ivy fever and are much more likely to attend state schools than more prestigious East Coast private colleges. Does that indicate that an overachiever in Hawaii is not as intellectual, talented, or predestined for success as an Ivy League student? People make judgments about students based on where they go to college, but the name rarely tells the whole story. Consider this anecdote: In one survey, respondents listed Princeton as one of the country's top ten law schools. The problem? Princeton doesn't have a law school.

What Students Can Do

Pare Down Activities

It is understandable that students want to try out various experiences in order to discover their true interests. But participating in time-consuming activities merely to add lines to a résumé isn't worth the energy, doesn't impress colleges, and keeps students from pursuing their actual interests. Admissions officers would rather see high school students commit to one or two passions. Some students, like Audrey, Ryland, and Charles, told me they couldn't fathom dropping any of their activities because they loved all of them. In that case, students at least could lessen their roles in some of those activities—be a member of a club, for example, rather than an officer—so they can participate without overcommitting.

Take a Year Off

Taking a time-out from school, either after high school or during college, is a good way to combat the frenetic pace of student life. That period can also help students to redefine their academic and career goals as they become better in tune with the identity behind the achievements. This "gap year" is such an important concept that more than one tenth of all British students take one. Some U.S. universities also encourage students to defer admission for a year in order to heal mental health issues often caused by excessive stress.

Try an "Unrewarding" Activity
If students get involved in an activity they like but aren't good at, they can learn to enjoy something for the sake of enjoyment rather than potential reward or recognition.

Reclaim Summer
After months spent racing at breakneck speeds through papers, tests, and activities toward the last day of school, a structured, overscheduled summer won't give students the chance to unwind. Admissions officers I spoke with weren't swayed by swanky summer academic programs or sports camps. They understood the necessity of a non-academic job or some time off. So should families.

Accept That Admissions Aren't Personal
The day that admissions offices release their results is not Judgment Day. Students applying to selective universities must remember that the numbers of competing students work against them. Sometimes the difference between an acceptance and a rejection is as simple as the fact that the school orchestra needs a trombone player. Admissions decisions do not reflect a student's character or future and should not be viewed as personal commentary.

Take Charge
Tackling the issues in this book may seem like an impossible task for many of today's teens. But the same students who win science contests, organize dances, or write articles can also direct their efforts toward lobbying schools to implement any of the measures listed above. No one should underestimate what students can accomplish.

Ultimately, all of these are smaller, prescriptive actions that can begin to add up to the broader measure that is necessary to save young people from the twisted values of an educational system gone wrong. What is needed is a massive shift in societal attitude. We live in an achievement-oriented, workaholic culture that can no longer distinguish between striving for excellence and demanding perfection. It is time to stop prioritizing how children look on paper 'over their health, happiness, and well-being. By now the message should be clear: Ease up, calm down, and back off. If students are free to follow paths toward their personal joys and interests, then it is worth trusting that everything will be all right in the end.

JULIE, COLLEGE FRESHMAN | PERCEIVED AS: THE SUPERSTAR

When Julie arrived at the Turkey Chase, the annual Bethesda Thanksgiving Day 10K, she saw several people she knew, like her Whitman coaches, C.J., and other former cross-country teammates. She was surprised at how natural it felt to reconnect with them, even after so many months had passed without contact, which reminded her of how, at Dartmouth, she was afraid that she had forgotten how to drive. When she came home, as she backed out of the driveway for the first time in months, she yelled, "HERE GOES NOTHING!" figuring she would embarrass herself. But after a minute she was again comfortable behind the wheel.

Julie distributed hugs and chatted briefly. She noticed that most of the Whitman cross-country girls were dressed similarly in Whitman running gear, while Julie wore a brown shirt and bright purple spandex. It was good to see her friends, but Julie didn't feel the need to be attached to them. She walked away, content to warm up on her own.

Over the past few months, Julie had begun to grasp that she didn't have to depend on other people to dictate what she did with her time. Worrying about what friends were doing on a weekend night, and how she fit into that picture, seemed so positively high school now. Julie had learned that she enjoyed herself more when she did what she truly wanted to do, not what she thought she *should* do.

This revelation was timely, because Julie didn't know what she should be doing with her college life, let alone on a free night. She still vacillated over her feelings for Dartmouth. Sometimes she loved it: She had close relationships with two of her three professors, she was involved in a fascinating pre-med program in which she shadowed a pediatric immunologist (she was even thinking about specializing in hormone research), and the campus was beautiful. But it was also isolated, with few restaurants and no movie theaters. Social options in Hanover were limited to the point where it was considered a date if a guy asked a girl to be his beer pong partner. Julie didn't have time for many outdoor activities because she was so busy training. Sometimes she thought about transferring to a school in a city, and closer to home.

But for Julie, indecision no longer translated to insecurity. With nothing left to prove and no one she needed to impress, Julie stopped agonizing about other people's reactions. Sometimes she walked around campus still wearing her hair in the sloppy bun she had slept in the night before. If she felt like socializing, she created opportunities, organizing study sessions with teammates, or emailing a group about going out to lunch. "You seem really 'real' to me," a classmate told her one day. He couldn't have chosen a better compliment. As she lost her cares about other people's expectations and judgments, Julie gradually became more at ease with herself. The Queen of Awkward was dead.

At the start of the race, Julie found herself in the front row of 5,000 racers. Spotting some of the middle-aged men from a group she ran with during the summers, she tapped one on the arm and said hello. "What time are you going for, thirty-six minutes?" one of them asked.

"No, I really just want to have fun, so I'm not too worried about my time," she replied.

"Set . . . go!" the starter shouted. When the gun sounded, Julie took off with the rest of the leaders. She was the first woman to pass the mile mark.

At Dartmouth, Julie's teammates had encouraged her to stick with cross country. Before meets, the varsity and second varsity teams got together and stated their individual goals in front of the team. For her second college meet, Julie's goal was only to finish the race, which she did. Midseason, Julie began to regain her running confidence but kept her goals simple: Finish the races, think positive thoughts, and enjoy herself. By the regional meet in November, Julie realized that when she focused on having fun and feeling comfortable instead of worrying about her numbers, the times fell into place. She emailed her Whitman coach, "I don't know how long I will stick with running because there are so many things I want to try here, but I will give it my best for a while.

The team is so fun and I realized I don't have to be the best to have fun. I can just run hard and enjoy myself. It isn't like people aren't going to like me if I am not the fastest." In the last race of the season, Julie beat all of her second varsity teammates.

At the Turkey Chase, Julie was losing ground. A Whitman coach and a man from her summer running group ran by her, but she didn't try to match their speed. Soon other women were passing her. Unfazed, Julie didn't bother to keep up with them. Instead, she relaxed and focused on enjoying the run at her own pace. She didn't need to be certain about her place—in meets, with friends, at school—in order to get to know and appreciate herself. It didn't matter that she couldn't see the finish line or the challengers along the way. Julie kept going.

RYLAND, SENIOR | PERCEIVED AS: THE SLACKER

During the second week of December, to the delight of students, the county closed schools because of snow. On this first snow day of the year, Ryland woke up, did some work, and drove to Whitman. The building was open but empty, except for a janitor who gave him a quizzical look. Ryland peeked into the main office. No one was there. Having arrived late to school so many times as a junior, Ryland was accustomed to walking through quiet halls. But this was the first time that he had been the only student in the building. There was something he needed to do.

Ryland was in a much better place than he had been during the summer. Part of that had to do with the community service trip he helped organize in August. Fifteen Whitman students raised enough funds to spend a week at a Native American reservation in North Dakota, where they painted buildings, cleared weeds and bushes from an area where a playground could be built, and spent time with local high school students. There, Ryland was struck by the differences of a world that he doubted most of his classmates knew existed. The Native American teens at the reservation's high school were extremely poor and were surrounded by drugs and alcohol. Many of their peers had dropped out of school or lacked the drive to find a career.

One afternoon a teacher came by to talk to the Whitman students, who were living in tepees on the football field, which hadn't been used in decades because too many students dropped out for the school to recruit enough players for a football team. The teacher explained that while Whitman teens were worrying about college plans, college didn't even cross the minds of her students, who assumed they were too poor or untalented to attend. During one lecture, the teacher was discussing a current event involving Yale when she learned that her students didn't know what Yale was and had never heard of the Ivy League. It was a struggle, the teacher said, to keep students in class. When they skipped, if the school called their parents, many didn't care because they were alcoholics or drug addicts or had dropped out of school themselves.

Hearing this, Ryland felt numb. At Whitman, he and his classmates complained about a good education, took their wide variety of available classes for granted, were supported by their school, families, and community, and had plenty of opportunities after high school. The Native American students didn't believe they had a chance.

Ryland spent much of his time with Timmy, a Native and Mexican-American high school dropout who constantly joked around. During the spring, Timmy was kicked out of school for fighting, and though he had been invited back to repeat his senior year, thus far he had declined. Ryland couldn't fathom dropping out of high school. What would come next?

In front of other students, Ryland tried to joke with Timmy about the importance of school. "You know," Ryland would say, "outside of the reservation, girls don't go for guys who didn't finish high school." When the two were alone, they had long conversations about how they didn't get along with their parents. During those times, when Timmy opened up so seriously, Ryland tried to get across the importance of graduating.

"If you're not going to be in school, what will you do? Do you have a job?" Ryland asked him once.

"I don't know, I don't really have anything to do. Maybe I'll help out at the hospital, but it's really far away," Timmy said.

"Well, if you want to do something like that, you have to at least finish high school," Ryland said. As usual, Timmy smiled, shook his head, and changed the subject, appearing not to listen. After he returned home to Bethesda, Ryland repeatedly emailed Timmy reminders that he should go back to school, but for weeks he received no reply.

Soon after the trip, Ryland and his mother met with his guidance counselor to discuss his senior-year schedule and college applications. When Ryland insisted that he shouldn't take a first-period class (too early) or a math class (too many tests), his counselor helped persuade his mother that Ryland's instincts were right. When Ryland's mother said that he should make up for the first-period void by taking a class during lunch, the counselor convinced her to back off. Once they determined the schedule, Ryland's mother listed the schools he was interested in, all of which were well-respected institutions with strong environmental programs. "Those are some schools he was thinking about," she said, "but I don't think he can get in."

"Actually, he can get into all of those places," the counselor responded. Ryland's mother looked shocked.

A few weeks later, Ryland got an email from Timmy. "I'm sorry I didn't get back to you," Timmy wrote. "I started school this year." Ryland was elated. Timmy had listened after all. *I can't believe I made a difference in this person's life,* he thought.

Now, two weeks before winter break, Ryland was able to discern a difference in his own life. Last year he couldn't pull himself out of his hole because he was already in so much trouble that he was ashamed to go to class. This semester he had skipped only two classes—far below the typical senior tally of skipped days, let alone classes—and his first-quarter grades included four As. Ryland attributed his turnaround to a number of changes. Without a first-period class, he was able to get enough sleep so he wasn't late for school. When his three alarms still didn't rouse him in time, he brought his toothbrush and toothpaste to Whitman and brushed his teeth in the bathroom after second period. Students looked at him strangely, but the looks were worth it if he made it to class before the bell.

Getting decent sleep also left him plenty of energy to expand the scope of the environmental and service organizations that he led. The joy of those activities—and the sense of purpose they provided, the sense of doing something good—gave him a buoyancy that carried him through his schoolwork. Most important, for the first time in his academic career, Ryland chose his own classes, without his parents' help and according to subjects that piqued his interest, rather than courses that he thought he was expected to take as a Whitman student. Fascinated by all of his classes, he paid attention, did his work, and was prepared for tests. He didn't experience test anxiety anymore because he knew the material and he wasn't being tested on math or a math-based science.

Ryland's transformation wasn't flawless. Multiple-choice tests still stymied him—somehow he would get overwhelmed and confused—and since his mother had returned his Ritalin, he still refused to take it. He had Cs in two classes because of low test scores. But he didn't regret taking those classes, because he cared less about the grades than about learning material he enjoyed.

In early December, Ryland began organizing a toy drive for the kids on the reservation, most of whose families didn't have the money to buy gifts for the holidays. He left tall boxes at Whitman and at local stores and oversaw a committee of student volunteers. Now, unfathomably at school on a snow day, Ryland was touched as he surveyed the boxes and bags that lined the hall beside Whitman's main office. An entire room in his house was already full of toys. Over the weekend he and his committee would start packing them in boxes bound for North Dakota.

Ryland happily carried the last of the toy bags to his car, which was crammed to the roof with hundreds of gifts that people had donated because he asked them to. Next year he would miss this ability to take charge of an organization. As a freshman, he would have to work his way up to that level of responsibility. But he wasn't worried. He knew that no matter where he ended up, he would get into a college—a good college—where he would get a solid education, learn subjects relevant to his interests, make close friends, try new experiences, and get involved in activities he was passionate about. As Ryland drove away through snow melting in the bright December sun, he was certain that he was going to be just fine.

For updates on the students or to schedule a lecture, seminar,
or moderated discussion with Alexandra Robbins, please visit
www.alexandrarobbins.com.

Endnotes

CHAPTER 1

3 *perfect 1600*: My research began before the debut of the new SAT, for which a perfect score is 2400. In 2005, the College Board reported the average national SAT score was 520 math and 508 verbal.

4 *journal entry*: I encouraged Julie to keep a journal of her feelings about moments she felt were significant to her high school experience.

13 *"such a smart class"*: Interviews with Jerome Marco, Frank, and Whitman Resource Counselor Fran Landau. I attempted to find a video of the ceremony to confirm the exact wording, but Whitman staff and students could not locate a copy.

14 *"smartest city"*: Chinni, Dante. "PhDs, Planning, and Pet Bakeries." *Christian Science Monitor*, September 18, 2002.

14 *in 1975 . . . 86 percent attend today*: Couric, Katie. *Today*, May 19, 2004.

15 *16.7 million . . . 2.1 million by 2013*: Kronholz, June. "Cram Sessions: For High Schoolers, Summer Is Time to Polish Résumés." *Wall Street Journal*, April 21, 2005.

15 *114 percent spike*: The important article by Stepp, Laura Sessions. "Perfect Problems." *Washington Post*, May 5, 2002.

CHAPTER 2

35 *"an almost fanatical belief"*: Beech, Hannah. "School Daze." *Time International*, April 15, 2002.

35 *In 2001 in Hong Kong*: Ibid.

35 *"Four in, five out"*: Ly, Phuong. "A Wrenching Choice." *Washington Post*, January 9, 2005.

35 *Three-year-olds*: Bert, Alison. "Ready for Carnegie." *Journal News*, June 1, 2004.

35 *students work straight through*: Lee, B. J. "A New College-Admissions System Is Fueling Stress." *Newsweek*, July 4, 2005.

35 *some students steal*: Ibid.

35 *college tiers*: Sang-hun, Choe. "In South Korea, students push back; Protest mourns

suicides and calls for less pressure to succeed." *International Herald Tribune*, May 9, 2005.

35 *mothers pray . . . running late*: Hyun-sung, Khang. "College Exams Put Nation to the Test." *South China Morning Post*, November 17, 2004.

35 *More than eight*: Sang-hun, Choe.

35 *South Korea . . . every test*: Lee, B. J.

35 *two-month period . . . grades*: "School Stress Forces Korean Students to Commit Suicide." *Channel NewsAsia*, May 24, 2005.

36 *"Schools are driving us"*: Sang-hun, Choe.

36 *In China . . . "shame to family"*: Interview by the author.

36 *China and Taiwan . . . in school*: Cody, Edward. "For Some Chinese, a Dark Side of Change." *Washington Post*, March 28, 2004; "NTU Sophomore Student Commits Suicide in Ilan." Asia Africa Intelligence Wire, March 22, 2005.

36 *Indian officials . . . avoid a test*: Chengappa, Raj. "Killer Exams." *India Today*, March 28, 2005.

36 *In Japan . . . vocational school*: Some details confirmed with Brian McVeigh, Adjunct Instructor, East Asian Studies, University of Arizona; Beech, Hannah; Lord, Lewis J. and Horn, Miriam. "The Brain Battle." *U.S. News & World Report*, January 19, 1987.

36–37 *Japanese mother . . . teacher's lessons*: An interesting article on Japan's education system: Mack-Cozzo, Jane Barnes. "If You Think We Have Problems . . ." *American Enterprise*, September 1, 2002; Lord, Lewis J. and Horn, Miriam. "The Brain Battle." *U.S. News & World Report*, January 19, 1987; Ito, Masami. "Are They the Problem or Are We?" *Japan Times*, May 5, 2002. Quoted veteran child psychiatrist Hiroshi Kawai as calling kyoiku mama actions "a form of abuse."

36 *Mitsuko Yamada . . . "exam fever"*: Watts, Jonathan. "Girl, 2, Strangled by Exam Rival's Mother." *Guardian*, November 27, 1999.

36 *Until 2002 . . . creatively*: Beech, Hannah; Lord, Lewis J.; Elliott, Dorinda. "Learning to Think." *Newsweek*, September 6, 1999.

37 *minister of education . . . only on entrance exams*: Beech, Hannah.

37 *international surveys . . . Saturday classes*: "2004 a Year of Worries for Japan's Educators." *Daily Yomiuri*, December 28, 2004. Some details confirmed with Brian McVeigh. Thanks also to Andrew Moore, whose 2005 paper "Looking at Japanese Education Reform: Mediating Achievement and Welfare" was helpful.

37 *Asian-American students*: Interviews with students. Also, thanks to Razelle Buenavista, Youth Services Coordinator for the Asian American Recovery Services in Santa Clara.

37 *kirogi*: Ly, Phuong. "A Wrenching Choice."

37 *Korean student*: Interview with the student.

37–38 *In 1983 . . . superpower*: Colvin, Richard Lee. "What's Wrong with Our Schools?" National Conference of State Legislatures, September 1, 2003; Bracey, Gerald W. "April Foolishness: The 20th Anniversary of A Nation at Risk." *Phi Delta Kappan*, April 1, 2003; Jehlen, Alain. "A Nation at Risk?" *NEA Today*, January 1, 2001.

38 *"The members of the"*: Bracey, Gerald W. A 2003 follow-up report announced there had been "little improvement" in the K–12 education system. Despeignes, Peronet. "Mediocre School System 'Threat to US Future.'" *Financial Times*, February 26, 2003.

38 *response . . . school day*: Colvin, Richard Lee; Bracey, Gerald W. "April Foolishness."

38 *Department of Education report*: Lord, Lewis J.

38   *137: Daily Yomiuri.*

38   *country that government officials:* Bracey, Gerald W.

41   *Webshots:* www.webshots.com.

46   *"goody-goodies":* Frank said he got this impression from *The Unofficial Guide to Life at Harvard.* HAS Publications.

46   *TCCi:* Thank you to Steve Smith, president of Naviance, which operates TCCi, for confirming details about the product.

47   *Princeton Review:* Franek, Robert, et al. *The Best 351 Colleges, 2004 Edition.* New York: Random House, 2003.

48   *magazine: Washingtonian,* October 2004.

49   *Portales High School:* Thank you to the administration, staff, and especially the students at Portales High School. Thanks also to Will Kayatin, Shannon Fresquez, and Shannon Osborne for their help with setting up this group interview.

56   *IMed:* In the students' IMs and text messages, I have edited their punctuation and capitalization when necessary to avoid distraction.

CHAPTER 3

63   *Morehead Scholarship:* See moreheadfoundation.org.

66   *Mediamark survey . . . siblings:* Mediamark Research Inc. Also, in 2005, the Metlife Survey of the American Teacher found that taking tests caused students "the most worry or stress," followed by homework and doing well in class. Markow, Dana and Martin, Suzanne, Harris Interactive, Inc.

66   *teen newsmagazine:* Brenna, Susan. "Stressed Out!" *New York Times Upfront,* January 3, 2000.

66   *Three quarters:* Gallup Youth Survey, June 1, 2004.

66   *student stress levels:* Interview with National Institute of Mental Health academic child psychiatrist Daniel Pine.

66   *overachiever stress:* Interviews with several doctors. Special thanks to Bruce McEwen, author of *The End of Stress as We Know It.*

66   *stress boosts levels:* Interviews with doctors. Special thanks to Carnegie-Mellon University psychology professor Sheldon Cohen.

66   *can cause changes:* Interviews with doctors; Goode, Erica. "The Heavy Cost of Chronic Stress." *New York Times,* December 17, 2002.

66   *stress-induced problems:* Interviews with doctors. Special thanks to University of Utah child and adolescent psychiatry training director Douglas Gray.

67   *Colorado junior:* Interview with the student.

67   *Caitlin:* Interview with Caitlin.

67   *students are perfectionists:* Interviews with Douglas Gray and Dina Zeckhausen, an Atlanta psychologist specializing in eating disorders.

67   *"The girls with anorexia":* Interview with Douglas Gray.

67   *Alyssa:* Interviews with Alyssa.

72   *$30,000:* "Costs Related to College Admission Continue to Climb," CNBC's *Early Today,* November 18, 2002; Steele, Margaret Farley. "The New College Try." *Connecticut Magazine,* February 3, 2004.

73   *national nonprofit:* "Serving the Profession to Better Serve Families." Independent Educational Consultants Association (IECA).

73   *"best college 'fit' ":* "Finding the Right College for You." IECA.

73 *"By learning"*: Ibid.

73 *"Educational consultants are first"*: "Educational Consultants: Advising Families on Educational Options." IECA.

73 *"Last year"*: This quote could be found at Ivysuccess.com in 2005.

74 *like a business*: In 2000, I interviewed then-Stanford dean of admissions Robert Kinnally, who offered this sentiment for an op-ed I wrote for *USA Today*. The article was "Is High School Life Just College Prep?" April 6, 2000.

74 *middle school*: Sodders, Lisa M. "Consultants Help Parents, Kids Find Best Paths to College." *Daily News of Los Angeles*, October 31, 2004.

74 *New Jersey . . . MIT*: Mathews, Jay. "Learning to Stand Out Among the Standouts." *Washington Post*, March 22, 2005.

74 *younger ages*: Interviews with several college counselors; Francis, Ric, Associated Press. "Students Gear Up for Essays on College Admissions Exams." *USA Today*, February 23, 2004.

74 *"We're trying"*: Mary Mansfield, IECA Fall Conference. New Orleans, LA, November 11, 2004.

75 *up to $33,000*: Steele, Margaret Farley. "The New College Try." *Connecticut Magazine*, February 3, 2004.

75 *"I might"*: Kronholz, June.

75 *IvySuccess . . . "STRATEGISTS"*: At the time of this writing, these quotes could be found at ivysuccess.com.

75 *Some companies*: Gose, Ben. "Summer Camp for the College-Bound." *Boston Globe*, November 28, 2004.

75 *write the essays themselves*: Steele, Margaret Farley.

75 *EssayEdge*: essayedge.com; Kronholz, June. "Perfect College Essay Often Takes Extra Help." *Wall Street Journal Online*, July 12, 2005.

75 *"Our 200+"*: At the time of this writing, this quote could be found at essayedge.com.

75 *Admissions officers detest*: Interviews with undergraduate admissions officers.

75 *"fantastically packaged"*: Chan, Daisy. "Ten Things the College-Prep Industry Won't Tell You." *Smart Money*, April 1, 2000.

76 *Swarthmore*: Interview with Jim Bock.

76 *IECA doesn't . . . "from the beginning"*: Interview with Mark Sklarow.

76 *ten years . . . essays*: Interview with Mark Sklarow; Kahlenberg, Rebecca R. "Easing Admission, or at Least Anxiety." *Washington Post*, September 28, 2004; Samuels, Rebecca. "Private Counselors Help College-Bound Find a Calling." CBS MarketWatch, October 18, 2002.

76 *test prep services*: Kronholz, June. "Perfect College Essay Often Takes Extra Help."

76 *Several parents*: Chan, Daisy.

76 *free services*: Berdik, Chris. "Admissions Help for Any Budget." *Boston Globe*, September 26, 2004; Jaschik, Scott. "Not-so-fringe Benefit." *Boston Globe*, November 17, 2004.

76–77 *IBM . . . benefit*: Jaschik, Scott.

77 *In 2000 . . . experienced guidance counselors*: Vaishnav, Anand. "Winthrop Privatizes Its College Counseling." *Boston Globe*, December 11, 2000.

77 *American School Counselor Association . . . every 500*: National Center for Education Statistics, 2002; *Insight*, IECA October/November 2004; Aarons, Dakaraii. "Counselors Lost in Cutbacks." *Dallas Morning News*, August 6, 2005.

77 *one to a thousand*: Interview with Bill Fitzsimmons, Harvard's dean of admissions and financial aid; Samuels, Rebecca. "Private Counselors Help College-Bound Find a Calling."

77 *Earle Hotta*: Interviews with Earle and Carol Hotta. Thank you to the Hottas for their kind hospitality.

77–78 *IECA's fall conference . . . "education"*: IECA Fall Conference session entitled "Selective College Admissions: 2005 Outlook."

CHAPTER 4

85 *Some schools require*: Weil, Jennifer. "Local Schools Among the Best." *Journal News*, May 30, 2003; Christmas, Sakura. "CHHS Students Upset to Discover that AP Exams Mandatory." *Herald-Sun*, March 10, 2003.

85 *many elite*: Chaker, Ann Marie. "Elite High Schools Drop AP Courses," *Wall Street Journal*, November 23, 2004.

85 *students haven't*: Mathews, Jay and Welsh, Patrick. "Is AP Good for Everybody? It's Debatable." *Washington Post*, April 10, 2005.

85 *AP teachers automatically*: Interviews with students and guidance counselors.

85 *incentive programs*: Lewin, Tamar. "The Two Faces of A.P." *New York Times*, January 8, 2006.

85 *a 2002 survey*: *AP and Higher Education*. A booklet published in 2004 by the College Entrance Examination Board, which cites Morgan, Karen Christman. *The Use of AP Examination Grades by Students in College*. New York: RoperASW 2002.

85 *"We're turning"*: de Vise, Daniel. "Enrollment in Advanced Courses Surging at High Schools." *Washington Post*, December 12, 2004

85 *"controlling for other"*: Geiser, Saul; Santelices, Veronica. "The Role of Advanced Placement and Honors Courses in College Admissions." Center for Studies in Higher Education, 2004.

85–86 *2002 . . . eighth grades*: Friel, Brian. "The Bush Record." *National Journal*, March 20, 2004.

86 *at least once*: Associated Press. "Spellings: Testing to Remain at Core of School Reform." February 2, 2005; and the Department of Education web site, ed.gov.

86 *Schools that don't*: Cochran-Smith, Marilyn. "No Child Left Behind: Three Years and Counting." *Journal of Teacher Education*, March 1, 2005; Schrag, Peter. "Bush's Education Fraud." *American Prospect*, February 2004.

86 *Beginning in 2008*: Janofsky, Michael. "Reports Say States Aim Low in Science Classes." *New York Times*, December 8, 2005.

86 *2013–2014*: Friel, Brian.

86 *reauthorization in 2007*: Goldberg, Mark. "Local Discontent with 'No Child Left Behind' Grows." *Christian Science Monitor*, August 19, 2005.

86 *schools that don't release*: Cave, Damian. "Growing Problem for Military Recruiters: Parents." *New York Times*, June 30, 2005.

86 *vomit*: Hardy, Lawrence. "Overburdened, Overwhelmed." *American School Board Journal*, April 2003.

86 *In Florida*: Allison, Sue. "Testimony for the Ehrlich Commission on Quality Education." May 18, 2005.

86 *Psychological Science study*: Carey, Benedict. "When Pressure Is On, Good Students Suffer." *New York Times*, December 21, 2004.

86 *subjects not covered . . . in the spring*: Winerip, Michael. "Making Leaps, but Still Labeled as Failing." *New York Times,* April 28, 2004; Sadker, David and Zittleman, Karen. "Text Anxiety: Are Students Failing Tests—or Are Tests Failing Students?" *Phi Delta Kappan,* June 2004.

86 *Teachers spend classroom*: In one study, 79 percent of teachers surveyed admitted they spent time teaching students test-taking skills. Sadker, David.

86 *In 2003*: Pedulla, Jospeh J. et al. "Perceived Effects of State-Mandated Testing Programs on Teaching and Learning: Findings from a National Survey of Teachers." National Board on Educational Testing and Public Policy, March 2003. Even before NCLB, 79 percent of teachers admitted they spend class time teaching students test-taking skills and 85 percent said their school de-emphasizes subjects that aren't on state tests.

86 *Almost 70 percent*: Sadker, David. In a national poll of more than 1,000 public school teachers, two-thirds believed their states were too focused on state tests.

86 *School counselors*: Interview with Kevin D. Quinn, American School Counselor Association Secondary Level Vice President. See also NACAC's "State of College Admission" 2005.

87 *"makes sense"*: Bush said this during a speech at J.E.B. Stuart High School, in Falls Church, Virginia, on January 12, 2005. Transcript available through the FDCH Federal Department and Agency Documents, Regulatory Intelligence Data.

87 *they are numbers*: Some schools have required students to wear radio frequency identification badges so that officials know where each student—tracked by an ID number—is at all times. Associated Press. "Company Pulls Out of Contract to Track Students," February 17, 2005.

87 *"rebellion" . . . mandates*: "NCLB Left Behind." NCLBgrassroots.org, August 17, 2005.

87 *In August 2005 . . . help its students*: Dillon, Sam. "U.S. Is Sued by Connecticut over Mandates on School Tests." *New York Times,* August 23, 2005.

87 *The same year . . . score students*: Associated Press. "NEA, Three States Sue over No Child Left Behind." MSNBC.com, April 20, 2005; Groves, Dave. "Pontiac Joins Lawsuit over No Child Funding." *Daily Oakland Press,* April 21, 2005.

87 *In response . . . "terrorist organization"*: Associated Press. "NEA, Three States Sue over No Child Left Behind."

87–88 *2000 campaign . . . education secretary*: "The 'Texas Miracle.'" *60 Minutes II,* August 25, 2004. A transcript can be found at www.cbsnews.com.

88 *While Houston reported . . . assessment test*: This doesn't seem to be an extreme rarity; Goldberg, Mark.

88 *Teachers and local officials*: Marks, Alexandra. "Local Discontent with 'No Child Left Behind' Grows." *Christian Science Monitor,* August 19, 2005.

88 *Washington State*: Sadker, David.

88 *created and scored*: Goldberg, Mark. "Test Mess 2: Are We Doing Better a Year Later?" *Phi Delta Kappan,* January 1, 2005.

88 *120,000*: Archer, Jeff. "Connecticut Tests Delayed by Scoring Glitches." *Education Week,* February 11, 2004.

88 *In Massachusetts . . . Michigan and Washington*: Sadker, David.

88 *"It's just really"*: Goldberg, Mark.

89 *At some schools*: Hetzner, Amy. "Schools See Some Scores Dip." *Milwaukee Journal Sentinel*, May 30, 2004.

89 *In 2003 . . . only a point*: Tavis Smiley. National Public Radio, May 27, 2003; Schouten, Fredereka. "Exit Exams Promise 'Meaningless' Graduation for Some Students." *Gannett News Service*, May 20, 2003; Allison, Sue. "Like a Bad Dream Come True." Marylanders Against High-Stakes Testing.

89 *special education students . . . could not attend*: Rothstein, Kevin. "Disabled Aspiring Cape Chef Burned by State MCAS Rule." *Boston Herald*, January 15, 2004; Allison, Sue.

89 *special-needs . . . "Behind"*: Gelzinis, Peter. "MCAS Fails to Recognize Courage." *Boston Herald*, May 13, 2005.

89 *siphoning money*: Neill, Monty; Adler, Margot. "Growth Spurt: The Rise of Tutoring in America." June 6, 2005.

89 *companies that create*: Goldberg, Mark.

89 *"No Child Left"*: Sadker, David.

96 *Carnegie Foundation reported*: Stephens, Jason. "Justice or Just Us? What to Do about Cheating." The Carnegie Foundation for the Advancement of Teaching.

96 *Josephson Institute of Ethics survey*: 2004 Report Card: Press Release and Data Summary: "The Ethics of American Youth." Josephson Institute of Ethics, 2004.

96 *1998 survey*: Conradson, Stacey and Pedro Hernández-Ramos. "Computers, the Internet, and Cheating among Secondary School Students: Some Implications for Educators." *Practical Assessment, Research & Evaluation*, 2004.

96 *looking at . . . bathroom*: Interviews with students; Giacobbe, Alyssa. "The perfect score." *Teen Vogue*, October 2004.

96 *condensed onto . . . shoes*: Interviews with students.

96 *skin . . . unlikely to see*: Interviews with students; Giacobbe, Alyssa.

96 *students signal*: Ho, Rodney. "SAT Perfectionism Can Tempt Students to Cheat Their Way to 1600." *Atlanta Journal-Constitution*, February 2, 2004.

96 *clear cover*: Interviews with students.

96 *peel labels*: An illuminating article: Gross, Jane. "Exposing the Cheat Sheet, with the Students' Aid." *New York Times*, November 26, 2003.

96 *West Coast*: Ho, Rodney.

96 *store-the-formulas*: Interviews with students.

96 *Students plug notes . . . during exams*: Interviews with students; ABC News. "A Cheating Crisis in America's Schools." September 30, 2004.

96 *In wireless schools*: ABC News.

96 *Mathnerds.com*: Thanks to *PC Magazine*'s Sebastian Rupley for providing this information.

97 *paper mills*: Hansen, Suzy. "Dear Plagiarists: You Get What You Pay For." *New York Times*, August 22, 2004.

97 *"Cybercheating"*: Interviews with students; Conradson, Stacey.

97 *group interview in Kentucky*: Interview with the students.

97 *University of Maryland*: Associated Press. "Students Called on SMS Cheating." Wired.com, January 30, 2003.

98 *UC Santa Barbara*: La, Jason. "Altered Grades Lead to Student's Arrest." *Daily Nexus*, March 30, 2005. She also reportedly improved her roommate's grades.

98   *Turnitin founder . . . "significant levels of plagiarism":* ABC News.
98   *Salem High:* Heyman, J.D. "Psssst . . . What's the Answer?" *People*, January 24, 2005.
98   *Glenbard North High School:* Kimberly, James. "Accused Glenbard Student Expelled." *Chicago Tribune*, March 17, 2004.
98   *in 2004 . . . stole a test:* Gaura, Maria Alicia; Gathright, Alan. "Saratoga High Cheating Scandal Gets Uglier." *San Francisco Chronicle*, February 5, 2004.
98   *a third of students:* Ibid.
98   *led to debates . . . "parents are disappointed":* Ibid.
98–99   *Staples High School . . . "you find another way":* Gross, Jane.
99   *sophomore honors student . . . "kind of do it":* Stephens, Jason. "Justice or Just Us? What to Do about Cheating."

CHAPTER 5
107   *waiting list:* "School at home." *Salt Lake Tribune*, December 17, 2004; Graham, Deneshia. "How to Find the Right Preschool." *Post and Courier*, February 15, 2005; Hammack, Laurence. "Fifty Years of Learning Added to Playing." *Roanoke Times*, October 20, 2003.
107   *Some couples take off:* Buchholz, Barbara Ballinger. "A New Kind of Early Admission: Angst." *Chicago Tribune*, March 2, 2003.
107   *hire a team:* Goldman, Victoria. "The Baby Ivies." *New York Times*, January 12, 2003; della Cava, Marco R. "Parents and Preschool: Schmooze or Lose." *USA Today*, August 28, 2002.
107   *In other cities:* della Cava, Marco R; González, Jennifer. "To Do: Pass Out Cigars, Call Preschool." *Plain Dealer*, January 27, 2005; Foster, Margaret. "It's Survival of the Fittest." *Washington Life*, September 2001.
108   *Detroit Test of Learning Aptitude:* Henderson, Nancy. "Getting In." *Washingtonian*, November 2000.
108   *Wechsler Preschool and Primary Scale of Intelligence:* Gardner, Ralph Jr. "Failing at Four." *New York Magazine*, November 15, 1999.
108   *Parents, too, are interviewed:* Buchholz, Barbara Ballinger.
108   *One preschool director:* Interview with the director.
108   *nearly $16,000:* González, Jennifer; Goldman, Victoria.
108   *parting donation:* Walder, Deborah. "Picture Me as a Preschool Consultant." *News & Record*, May 27, 2003.
108   *$26,000:* Willen, Liz. "Manhattan Preschools Become Harder to Get Into than Harvard." *Bloomberg*, March 14, 2005.
109   *One nursery school . . . . " 'on your forehead' ":* Hymowitz, Kay S. "Survivor: The Manhattan Kindergarten." *City Journal*, Spring 2001, a fascinating article about preschool admissions.
109   *donate:* della Cava, Marco R.
109   *one preschool director . . . his child:* Interviews with preschool directors.
109   *join houses of worship:* Buchholz, Barbara Ballinger.
109   *Delray Beach:* della Cava, Marco R.
109   *Jack Grubman . . . $1 million:* Gasparino, Charles. "Blood on the Street" excerpt. *Newsweek*, January 17, 2005; Sorkin, Andrew Ross and McGeehan, Patrick. "Changing the Guard: The Overview." *New York Times*, July 17, 2003; Mulligan,

Thomas S. "Admission Impossible." *Los Angeles Times*, November 20, 2002; Goldman, Victoria; Willen, Liz.

109 *There are coaches . . . accompanying essays*: Interviews with preschool and lower school directors; della Cava, Marco R.; Gardner, Ralph Jr.

109–110 *The preschool . . . "fears and worries"*: Interviews with Peggy Marble and other preschool and lower school administrators.

110 *"The tests don't" . . . additional run-throughs*: Gardner, Ralph Jr.

110 *parents tend*: Hymowitz, Kay S.

110 *"Kids are truthful"*: Interview, Marlene Barron. Other preschool and lower school administrators shared similar sentiments.

110 *The Educational Records Bureau*: erbtest.org.

110 *child's ERB performance*: Gardner, Ralph Jr. "Failing at Four"; Interviews with preschool directors.

110 *some preschools try to return*: Interviews with preschool directors.

110 *Manhattan nursery director . . . "'admissions at Collegiate'"*: Hymowitz, Kay S.

110 *"There's a hype"*: Interview with Marlene Barron.

111 *résumés . . . violin lessons*: Interviews with preschool directors; Goldman, Victoria.

111 *"gourmet cooking" . . . child's anxiety*: Interviews with preschool directors.

111 *"When parents start"*: Interview with Jean Mandelbaum, Director, All Souls School.

111 *All Souls*: Ibid.

111 *Ohio preschools*: González, Jennifer.

111 *New York City preschool*: Goldman, Victoria.

111 *socioeconomic reasons*: Gardner, Ralph Jr.; Willen, Liz.

111 *Census Bureau*: Census Bureau Reports. "One-in-Four in Classrooms: School Enrollment Surpasses 1970 Baby-Boom Crest." June 1, 2005.

111 *Of about 100,000*: della Cava, Marco R.

112 *largest preschool population*: Willen, Liz.

112 *applications to private kindergarten*: Ibid.

112 *Many of these*: Interviews with preschool and lower-school directors.

112 *free public school*: Willen, Liz.

112 *In 2000*: Interviews with preschool directors.

112 *A nursery school director . . . "get in nowhere"*: Hymowitz, Kay S.

112 *average of fifteen*: Willen, Liz.

112 *only eleven students*: Ibid.

133 *midwestern junior*: Interview with student.

133 *"scratched and clawed"*: Perrotta, Tom. *Election*. New York: G.P. Putnam's Sons, 1998.

133 *southern senior*: Interview with student.

133 *Kentucky students*: Interviews with the students.

133 *In 1968*: McGinn, Daniel. "Making the Grade." *Boston Globe Magazine*, January 9, 2005.

134 *Tenafly High School*: Brody, Leslie and Rimbach, Jean. "Grade Inflation; Many See A's as Just Average." *Record*, April 12, 2005.

134 *Between 1997 and 2002*: Davis, Anne. "Elite Math Classes Show Increase." *Milwaukee Journal Sentinel*, October 7, 2003.

134 *81 percent of public high schools*: Borg, Linda. "For Some, Class Rankings Rankle." *Providence Journal*, June 8, 2004.

134 *Since 2001*: Kranz, Cindy.

134 *Brian Delekta*: Talbot, Margaret. "Best in Class." *New Yorker*, June 8, 2005; Associated Press. "Student Sues to Get A+, not A." CNN.com, February 6, 2003.

134 *Plano West Senior High School*: Talbot, Margaret; Breen, Kim. "For Three Dedicated Teens, It's a Race to the Top." *Dallas Morning News*, May 23, 2004.

134 *Blair Hornstine*: Talbot, Margaret; Green, Laura. "From the Classroom to the Courtroom." *Sarasota Herald-Tribune*, May 17, 2004; Kaukas, Dick. "Schools Assess Best Way to Honor Seniors' Grades." *The Courier-Journal*, July 21, 2003; Green, Elizabeth W. and Russell, J. Hale. "Harvard Takes Back Hornstine Admission Offer." *Harvard Crimson*, July 11, 2003.

135 *Indiana county school board member*: Kaukas, Dick.

135 *Haresh*: Interview with Haresh.

135 *Josephson Institute . . . "who do not"*: See 2004 Report Card: Press Release and Data Summary. "The Ethics of American Youth." Josephson Institute of Ethics, 2004.

135 *A student at a top . . . "get by"*: ABC News.

135 *"lie to get a good job"*: "Report Card on the Ethics of American Youth"; Josephson Institute of Ethics, 2002. Frost, Joe L. "Bridging the Gaps: Children in a Changing Society." *Childhood Education*, September 22, 2003.

135 *college admissions officers*: Interviews with admissions officers. I interviewed several admissions officers in person, over the phone, and at the 2004 National Association for College Admission Counseling Conference in Milwaukee; Marklein, Mary Beth. "Is There Any Truth to Today's Résumés?" *USA Today*, February 4, 2003.

135 *Grinnell College*: Interview with Jim Sumner.

136 *some universities have modified*: Marklein, Mary Beth.

136 *91 percent . . . correct a child's homework*: Editor's Advisory. "Exclusive Poll: Cheaters Win." *U.S. News & World Report*, November 13, 1999.

136 *Duke University*: Marklein, Mary Beth.

136 *Half the students*: Slobogin, Kathy. "Survey: Many Students Say Cheating's OK." CNN.com, April 5, 2002. Similar results were reported in: Editor's Advisory. "Exclusive Poll: Cheaters Win." *U.S. News & World Report*, November 13, 1999. Thanks to Don McCabe, founder of the Center for Academic Integrity (CAI), for clarifying the statistics.

136 *82 percent*: Stephens, Jason.

136 *77 percent*: This survey was conducted by Don McCabe as part of CAI's Assessment Project, released in June 2005.

136 *elementary school*: Conradson, Stacey.

136 *Field Day*: Interview with a parent.

136 *prefer they cheat*: "The Ethics of American Youth."

136 *95 percent*: Toppo, Gregg. Associated Press. "Cheating Is Everywhere—Honest." *Deseret News*, March 28, 2002.

136 *More than half*: "ETS Leads an Anti-Cheating Ad Campaign Aimed at 10-to-14-year-olds." *The Chronicle of Higher Education*, September 17, 1999.

136 *"The better grades you have"*: Slobogin, Kathy.

CHAPTER 6

137 *Trinity School*: Thank you to the staff, faculty, and administration at Trinity—particularly June Hilton, Ann Fusco, Jen Levine, and Hank Moses—for allowing me to observe them at the school.

137 *Trinity was founded . . . "Trinity competes with"*: Interview with Hank Moses.

137 *Trinity's own promotional booklets*: Trinity School promotional booklet sent by the Lower School admissions office; also, *Trinity School 1709*. Trinity School, 2005.

137 *"passionately admired"*: Interview with Hank Moses.

138 *"The parents take nothing"*: All quotes from June Hilton are from in-person or telephone interviews, or while I observed her at Trinity.

139 *"interview" four-year-olds*: In the fall of 2004 and the winter of 2005, I observed a total of five children's interviews.

142 *Everything Ann asked*: Interviews with Ann Fusco.

153 *Ohio student*: Interview with the student.

153 *Team parents might handle*: Burnett, James. "The Secret Lives of Soccer Moms." *Boston Magazine*, March 2004.

154 *sacrifice family vacations*: Smith, Mary Lynn. "A Timeout on Youth Sports." *Minneapolis Star Tribune*, December 5, 2004.

154 *many coaches pressure*: Interviews with students.

154 *Extreme training . . . private leagues*: Roquemore, Bobbi. "All for One." *Milwaukee Journal Sentinel*, July 10, 2005.

154 *"specialization"*: Ibid.

154 *demise of the multisport athlete*: Ibid; Emmons, Mark. "Scholarship Pressure Changes Youth Sports." *Mercury News*, April 10, 2005.

154 *Baltimore reading specialist*: Interview with the specialist.

154–155 *Doctors blame . . . same body parts*: Roquemore, Bobbi.

155 *Stress fractures*: Cary, Peter; Dotinga, Randy; Comarow, Avery. "Fixing Kids' Sports." *U.S. News & World Report*, June 7, 2004.

155 *Jeret Adair*: Relin, David Oliver. "Who's Killing Kids' Sports?" *Parade*, August 7, 2005.

155 *"Oreo cookie"*: Cary, Peter.

155 *In Rhode Island*: Pennington, Bill. "Doctors See a Big Rise in Injuries as Young Athletes Train Nonstop." *New York Times*, February 22, 2005.

155 *"epidemic"*: Ibid. The orthopedist is Atlanta doctor James Andrews.

155 *informal survey*: Cary, Peter.

155 *often irreparable*: Pennington, Bill; See also Koutures, Chris. "An Overview of Overuse Injuries." *Contemporary Pediatrics*, November 1, 2001.

155 *Philadelphia orthopedist*: Pennington, Bill. The source is Dr. Angela Smith, an orthopedic surgeon at the Children's Hospital of Philadelphia.

155 *forty-one million*: Jeffrey, Nancy Ann. "Trophy Overload." *Wall Street Journal*, March 11, 2005. The source is the National Council of Youth Sports.

155 *70 percent*: Emmons, Mark. "Scholarship Pressure Changes Youth Sports." *Mercury News*, April 10, 2005.

155 *Colorado dance teacher*: Interview with the teacher.

156 *Wanda Holloway*: Koidin, Michelle. " 'Cheerleader Mom' Freed after Serving Six Months." Associated Press, March 1, 1997; Steptoe, Sonja. "The Pom-Pom Chronicles." *Sports Illustrated*, December 30, 1991/January 6, 1992.

156 *"sports rage"*: Stillman, Dale Frost. "Can Good Sportsmanship Be Legislated?" New Jersey State Bar Foundation, Spring 2004.

156 *In 1995 . . . signs of abating*: Nack, William and Munson, Lester. "Out of Control." *Sports Illustrated*, July 24, 2000. Their source is Fred Engh, president of the National Alliance for Youth Sports.

156 *more than 84 percent*: Dawson, Linda and Colwell, Brad. "Off the Court, It's YOUR Call." *Illinois School Board Journal*, September/October 2005. The survey was conducted by *SportingKids Magazine*.

156 *"assault protection" coverage*: At the time of this writing, information on this insurance coverage could be found at naso.org.

156 *ten-year-old boys' hockey practice*: Nack, William.

156 *head of a Florida*: Robinson, Bryan. "Will Death Deter Bad Sports Parents?" ABC News, January 14, 2002; Bayles, Fred and Sharp, Deborah. "Parental Behavior under Scrutiny." *USA Today*, January 13, 2002.

156 *Little League secretary*: Docheff, Dennis M. and Conn, James H. "It's No Longer a Spectator Sport." *Parks & Recreation*, March, 2004; Relin, David Oliver.

156 *About thirty parents*: Robinson, Bryan.

156 *Ohio father*: Nack, William.

156 *In Connecticut*: Harris, Stephen. "Parents Behaving Badly." *Boston Herald*, June 7, 2005; "Parents, Coaches Can Learn from Incident that Could Have Been Tragic." *Connecticut Post*, May 20, 2005.

156 *Pittsburgh-area T-ball coach*: Associated Press. "Coach Accused of Keeping Disabled Boy Off Field." ESPN.com, July 15, 2005; Associated Press. "Coach Faces Trial in Disabled Boy Attack." MSNBC.com, July 29, 2005.

157 *"The coach was very competitive"*: "Coach Accused of Keeping Disabled Boy Off Field."

157 *Toronto father*: Docheff, Dennis M.

157 *45.3 percent*: National Summit on Raising Community Standards in Children's Sports. *Recommendations for Communities*. The poll was conducted by the Minnesota Amateur Sports Commission.

157 *David Elkind*: Elkind, David. "Superkids and Super Problems." *Psychology Today*, May 1987.

157 *forming their own travel team*: Obert, Richard. "Athletes Torn between Clubs, High Schools." *Arizona Republic*, November 15, 2004.

157 *$3,000*: Harris, Stephen.

157 *$35,000*: "Parents Out of Control." *Oprah*, aired on June 1, 2005.

157 *Fewer than 3 percent*: Keough, Diana. "The Parent Trap." *Plain Dealer*, January 18, 2004.

157 *one in 13,000*: Relin, David Oliver.

157 *Out of 6.9 million*: Emmons, Mark.

158 *perhaps 15,000 . . . for ice hockey*: Harris, Stephen.

158 *soccer scholarships*: Keough, Diana.

158 *two-year-olds*: Macpherson, Karen. "Squeeze Play." *Pittsburgh Post-Gazette*, October 1, 2002.

158 *three-year-olds*: Cary, Peter.

158 *twenty-month-olds*: Stout, Hilary. "Bicycles for the Toddler Set." *Wall Street Journal*, April 14, 2005.

158 *five A.M.*: Hymowitz, Kay S.

158 *Elite wrestling*: Obert, Richard. "Torn Between Teams." *Arizona Republic*, November 15, 2004.

158 *"committed, experienced"*: Bowen, Fred. "Youth Sports Is No Longer Kid Stuff." *Washington Post*, April 16, 2004.

158 *Virginia father complained . . . "an arms race"*: Cary, Peter.

158 *under-eleven*: Burnett, James.

158 *national championships . . . baseball teams*: Prisbell, Eric. "Basketball Rankings Coming Out Earlier." *Washington Post*, July 3, 2004.

158 *Elementary school-age . . . future NBA players*: Prisbell, Eric.

158 *children's athletic skills . . . was a junior*: Harris, Stephen.

159 *Trenton*: Bravo's "Sports Kids Moms & Dads," summer 2005; "Parents Out of Control."

CHAPTER 7

169 *"likely letters"*: Mitchell, John. "Dartmouth Sends 'Likely Letters' to Relieve College-Decision Tensions." *Dartmouth*, February 24, 2005; Smith, Jennifer C. "NYU a Player in Fierce Admissions Competition." *Washington Square News*, December 2, 2003.

174 *Time magazine*: Wallis, Claudia. "How Smart Is AP?" *Time*, November 8, 2004.

177 *87 percent*: Carskadon, Mary. *Adolescent Sleep Patterns: Biological, Social, and Psychological Influences*. Cambridge: Cambridge University Press, 2002.

177 *schedule is roughly comparable*: Krueger, Starry. "Students Can't Excel If They're Not Awake." *Hartford Courant*, June 11, 2005. The source is Minnesota Regional Sleep Disorders Center medical director Mark Mahowald.

177 *As teenagers go through puberty*: Ibid.; interview with Bruce McEwen.

177 *natural bedtime is after eleven P.M.*: National Sleep Foundation Report. "Adolescent Sleep Needs and Patterns." 2000.

177–178 *change in circadian rhythms*: Mayo Clinic staff. "Perpetually tired teens."

178 *9.25 hours*: Jennings, Peter. "Teenagers and Sleep: More Sleep Recommended." *World News Tonight*, March 29, 2005.

178 *figure that supports*: A 1998 poll found that 26 percent of high school students routinely slept less than 6.5 hours on school nights, and only 15 percent got 8.5 or more hours. Wolfson, Amy R. and Carskadon, Mary. "Sleep Schedules and Daytime Functioning in Adolescents." *Child Development*, August 1998.

178 *top-ranked student*: Interview with the student.

178 *Mary Carskadon*: Interview with Mary Carskadon, Director, E.P. Bradley Hospital Sleep and Chronobiology Research Lab.

178 *Pediatrics study*: See Hansen, Martha, et al. "The Impact of School Daily Schedule on Adolescent Sleep." *Pediatrics*, June 6, 2005.

178 *20 percent*: Center for Applied Research and Educational Improvement. "School Start Time Study," 1998.

178 *one in ten*: Mayo Clinic staff. "Perpetually tired teens."

178 *Jill*: Interview with Jill.

179 *Research has linked*: Carpenter, Siri. "Sleep Deprivation May Be Undermining Teen Health." *Monitor on Psychology*. October 2001.

179 *National Sleep Foundation reported*: National Sleep Foundation, "2005 Sleep in America Poll." March 2005.

179 *"heavily involved in school"*: "Adolescent Sleep Needs and Patterns."

179 *North Carolina study*: Ibid.

179 *safest teenage driver*: Wickham, Shawne K. "America Is Dying to Get Some Sleep." *Union Leader*, May 30, 1993.

179 *Mary Carskadon calls school start times*: Interview with Mary Carskadon.

179 *"abusive"*: Carpenter, Siri. Stanford University sleep expert William Dement has also called the start times "abusive"; see, for example, Diconsiglio, John. "Let Me Sleep!" *New York Times Upfront*, February 11, 2002.

179 *Illinois researchers . . . back by two hours*: Adding bright light to a classroom in the morning didn't improve the students' performance. Hansen, Martha.

180 *In 1996*: Dragseth, Kenneth. "A Minneapolis Suburb Reaps Early Benefits from a Late Start." *School Administrator*, March 1999.

180 *University of Minnesota researchers*: Center for Applied Research and Educational Improvement. "School Start Time Study," Technical Report, Volume II: Analysis of Student Survey Data, 1998.

180 *compared to students . . . dropouts decreased*: All of these details were confirmed with Edina Public Schools Superintendent Kenneth Dragseth. Also see "School Start Time"; Fincher, Leta Hong. "Most Americans Suffer from Sleep Deprivation." *Voice of America*, March 31, 2005; "Adolescent Sleep Needs and Patterns."

180 *easier to live with*: Fincher, Leta Hong.

180 *Students felt*: Hopkins, Gary. "Alternative School Calendars: Smart Idea or Senseless Experiment?" *Education World*, November 16, 2004; "Adolescent Sleep Needs and Patterns."

180 *Some schools reported*: "Adolescent Sleep Needs and Patterns."

180 *Congresswoman Zoe Lofgren*: Interview with Congresswoman Zoe Lofgren.

180 *June 30, 2005*: H. Con. Res. 200, 109th Congress, 1st session. June 30, 2005. The resolution was referred to the Committee on Education and the Workforce.

180 *"It's never been"*: Interview with Congresswoman Zoe Lofgren.

181 *Minnesota found*: "Adolescent Sleep Needs and Patterns"; Wahlstrom, Kyla. "Changing Times: Findings from the First Longitudinal Study of Later High School Start Times." *NASSP Bulletin*, December 2002.

181 *In 2004 Connecticut*: "Witkos Introduces School Testing Legislation." February 2, 2004, and "Heagney, Witkos & Williams Introduce School Testing Amendment," February 23, 2004. Government press releases.

181 *"Districts that have"*: Interview with Mary Carskadon.

181 *school districts' decisions*: Jennings, Peter; Lawton, Millicent. "For Whom the School Bell Tolls." *The School Administrator*, March 1999.

181 *Kenneth Dragseth*: Interview with Kenneth Dragseth.

CHAPTER 8

185 *Overachievers across the country*: Interviews with students.

185 *Nebraska junior*: Interview with the student

185 *Vermont Commons School*: Interview with Sarah Soule, the director of admissions and college counseling. Thank you to Soule and to Robert Skiff, the head of school, for helping to arrange the group interview with students.

187 *In 1999*: Krueger, Alan B. and Dale, Stacy Berg. "Estimating the Payoff to Attending a More Selective College: An Application of Selection on Observables and Unobservables." Princeton University, December 1998, revised July 1999. See also the important article by Gregg Easterbrook, "Who Needs Harvard?" *Atlantic Monthly*, October 2004.

187 *By 2005 . . . to 90*: Interview with a Spencer Stuart spokesperson.

187 *from 84 percent:* Jones, Del. "Wanted: CEO, No Ivy Required." *USA Today,* April 7, 2005.

187 *University of Wisconsin:* Interview with a Spencer Stuart spokesperson.

187 *In 2004 and 2005:* Jones, Del.

187 *just as good:* Easterbrook, Gregg.

188 *in fall 2005:* Smetanka, Mary Jane. "College Ratings Are All the Rage." *Star Tribune,* August 29, 2005.

188 *since 1988 . . . millions of people:* Interview with a *U.S. News* spokesman.

188 *began in 1983 . . . other schools:* Thompson, Nicholas. "Playing with Numbers: How U.S. News Mismeasures Higher Education and What We Can Do about It." *Washington Monthly,* September 2000, an eye-opening article about the *U.S. News* rankings.

188 *criteria that include . . . "peer assessment":* Confirmed with a *U.S News* spokesman.

188 *Counselors at a Virginia:* Interview with Mark Sklarow.

189 *former U.S. News staff writer:* Thompson, Nicholas.

189 *first rankings algorithm . . . "until 1999":* Ibid.

189 *Reed College:* Diver, Colin. "Is There Life after Rankings?" *Atlantic Monthly,* November 2005, an article written by the president of Reed College.

189 *faculty resources:* Confirmed with a *U.S. News* spokesman.

189 *the more famous . . . at other schools:* Confessore, Nicholas. "What Makes a College Good?" *Atlantic Monthly,* November 2003. The head of UCLA's Higher Education Research Institute is Alexander Astin.

189 *Students at colleges:* Thompson, Nicholas.

190 *At Harvard:* Thernstrom, Melanie. *Halfway Heaven.* New York: Doubleday, 1997.

190 *"peer assessment":* Confirmed with a *U.S. News* spokesman.

190 *U.S. News asks:* Confessore, Nicholas; Diver, Colin.

190 *Washington Monthly reported:* Thompson, Nicholas.

190 *Over the last decade:* Pascarella, Ernest T. "Identifying Excellence in Undergraduate Education." *Change,* May 1, 2001.

190 *"the weights used":* National Opinion Research Center. "A Review of the Methodology for the *U.S. News & World Report*'s Rankings of Undergraduate Colleges and Universities." Review obtained by Nicholas Thompson for *Washington Monthly.*

190 *Schools might determine . . . financial aid packages:* Keynote speaker Michael McPherson, former president of Macalaster College. NACAC 60th National Conference. Milwaukee, September 30, 2004. See also Bollinger, Lee. "Debate over the SAT Masks Perilous Trends in College Admissions." *Chronicle of Higher Education,* July 12, 2002. Bollinger is the president of Columbia University.

190 *decrease need-based aid:* Confessore, Nicholas.

191 *Most college officials:* Fallows, James and Ganeshananthan, V.V. "The Big Picture." *Atlantic Monthly,* October 2004.

191 *flat-out lying:* Law schools, too, manipulate data for the rankings. Some schools drive up graduate employment rates by hiring students for brief temporary research positions themselves; or they raise student selectivity by admitting more part-time and transfer students, rather than full-time students, because it isn't mandatory to report part-time and transfer student data. As Diver pointed out, "At least one creative law school reportedly inflated its 'expenditures per student' by using an inputed 'fair market value,' rather than the actual rate, to calculate the cost of computerized research

services . . . The 'fair market value' (which a law firm would have paid) differed from what the law school actually paid (at the providers' educational rate) by a factor of eighty!"

191 *Wall Street Journal . . . "marketing strategy"*: Stecklow, Steve. "Cheat Sheets: Colleges Inflate SATs and Graduation Rates in Popular Guidebooks." *Wall Street Journal,* April 5, 1995.

191 *Northeastern . . . state-sponsored program*: Ibid.

191 *Other schools didn't count*: Gladstone, John J. "Are Colleges Right to Fudge?" *Plain Dealer,* April 20, 1995.

191 *Monmouth University . . . 1385*: Stecklow, Steve.

191 *schools fudged enrollment*: "Who Goes Where?" *Pennsylvania Gazette,* May/June 2005.

191 *acceptance numbers . . . reported them as rejections*: Stecklow, Steve.

192 *one West Coast college*: Thompson, Nicholas.

192 *Colby College's . . . "right-looking numbers"*: Stecklow, Steve.

192 *ranked potential spouses*: This line of thinking was inspired by a quote in Nick Thompson's article, in which Princeton Review president John Katzman said, "It's the equivalent of simply giving every woman a rating of 1–10 and saying we don't have to date. Just marry the one with the best score."

192–193 *internal Harvard memo . . . "atmosphere on campus"*: Bombardieri, Marcella. "Student Life at Harvard Lags Peer Schools, Poll Finds." *Boston Globe,* March 29, 2005.

193 *"It is genuinely"*: Easterbrook, Gregg.

200–201 *When I first . . . in mid-December*: Interviews with Matt Lawrence. In 2006, Stanford began reviewing applications online instead of in folders.

202 *applications are read*: Interviews with admissions officers. For a fascinating look at the inner workings of the admissions process at one university (Wesleyan), I recommend the following book: Steinberg, Jacques. *The Gatekeepers: Inside the Admissions Process of a Premier College.* New York: Penguin Books, 2002.

202 *"One of the myths"*: Interview with James Miller.

202 *7.5 percent*: NACAC's "State of College Admission 2005"; See also Kelly, Maura. "Stop the Madness." *Salon,* December 15, 2000, an interesting roundup of various admissions officers' opinions.

202 *"We're not looking"*: Interview with Matt Lawrence.

202 *"misconception" . . . "but about substance."*: Interview with Bill Fitzsimmons.

202 *"the Whys"*: Interview with Jim Bock.

203 *"Think of doing"*: Interview with Jim Sumner.

203 *At the 2004 NACAC annual conference*: "College Admission: Urban Myths Exposed." National Association for College Admission Counseling. 60th National Conference. Milwaukee, October 1, 2004.

203 *During recruiting trips*: Interview with Bill Fitzsimmons.

203 *Grinnell admissions interviewers*: Interview with Jim Sumner.

203 *Swarthmore is close*: Interview with Jim Bock.

203 *In 2003 MIT revised*: Marklein, Mary Beth.

203 *In 2005 Bowdoin*: Interview with James Miller.

204 *Stanford even changed*: Interviews with Matt Lawrence.

204 *"People assume"*: Interview with Bill Shain.

204 *the catchphrase was "intellectual vitality"*: Interviews with Matt Lawrence.

204 *Students don't necessarily*: Interviews with admissions officers.

204 *"If there are that many"*: Interview with James Miller.

204 *"We're not looking . . . whatever has happened to you"*: Interview with Matt Lawrence.

211–212 *Twice in December . . . about to come*: Ibid.

212 *long hours . . . angry parents*: Interviews with admissions officers.

212 *a gun pulled*: Interview with a former Harvard admissions officer.

212 *A student wait-listed*: Interview with Swarthmore dean of admissions Jim Bock.

212 *"There's high anxiety"*: Michael McPherson, NACAC.

213 *panel discussion on anxiety*: "A Bundle of Nerves: Anxieties in the College Admission Process." NACAC. 60th National Conference. Milwaukee, October 1, 2004.

213 *In the early-admission season . . . closure they want*: Interview with Matt Lawrence.

213 *"We make choices"*: Interview with Jim Miller.

CHAPTER 9

216 *Iowa high school counselor . . . work at home*: Gibbs, Nancy. "Parents Behaving Badly." *Time*, February 21, 2005.

216 *A study of academically talented*: Johns Hopkins University Center for Talented Youth. "Parents' Values and Children's Perceived Pressure." Ablard, Hoffhines, and Mills (1996). Cited in *Topical Research Series* #4, 2002.

216 *Detroit tutor*: Interview with the tutor.

216 *"product development"*: Hymowitz, Kay S. The source is University of Minnesota sociologist William Doherty.

216 *Principals say*: Talbot, Margaret.

216 *hold their children back*: Hymowitz, Kay S.

216 *labeled "gifted"*: Zimmerman, Eilene. "Bragging Rights: The 'Gifted' Label May Mean Too Much to Parents." *Psychology Today*, January–February 2004.

216 *Others visit psychologist . . . tests untimed*: Marano, Hara Estroff. "A Nation of Wimps." *Psychology Today*, November 1, 2004. This article is a must-read for parents concerned about the problems in this section.

217 *parents are overinvolved*: Jacobson, Jennifer. "Help Not Wanted." *Chronicle of Higher Education*, July 18, 2003. Several other sources, including a Duke alumna interviewer, also told me about the rise in overinvolved parents.

217 *parents fax . . . "twice a week"*: Jones, Marilee. "Parents Get Too Aggressive on Admissions." *USA Today*, January 6, 2003.

217 *Increasing numbers of parents*: Shellenbarger, Sue. "Colleges Ward Off Overinvolved Parents." *Wall Street Journal Online*, July 29, 2005; Associated Press. "Colleges Try to Contend with Hovering Parents." August 29, 2005.

217 *lack interpersonal skills*: Ibid; Williams, Matt. "Freshmen Arrive at U. Colorado with Parents in Tow." *Colorado Daily*, August 19, 2005; Marano, Hara Estroff.

217 *Northeastern University*: Schweitzer, Sarah. "Case of the Hovering Parents." *Boston Globe*, August 20, 2005.

217 *email college papers*: Rosenberg, Merri. "When Homework Takes Over." *New York Times*, April 18, 2004.

217 *tutors whom parents hired*: Lombardi, Kate Stone. "Tutoring for the Already Brainy." *New York Times*, May 23, 2004.

217 *Multiple students*: Gibbs, Nancy.

217 *in the middle of classes . . . "umbilical cord"*: Shellenbarger, Sue.
There is an apocryphal story of a University of Pennsylvania law school professor

who received a call at his office from a man who said, "Hi, I'm the father of _____, a student in your class. You just failed him so I want to talk to you about it."
  The professor responded, "Do you have a pen? Take down this number."
  The father wrote the number and asked, "Okay, whose number is that?"
  The professor replied, "My father's. You can discuss it with him."

218 *competitive sport*: Interview with child psychiatrist Alvin Rosenfeld.

218 *"Our children are experiencing"*: Keough, Diana.

218 *it costs much more*: Elkind, David. These factors were confirmed by more recent news articles and interviews.

218 *Approximately 70 percent . . . the home*: National Center for Policy Analysis. "Women and Taxes."

218 *working hours generally*: McGrath, Charles. "No Rest for the Weary." *New York Times Magazine*, July 3, 2005.

218 *"Many of these kids"*: Interview with Jean Mandelbaum.

219 *"We baby-boomer parents"*: Herman, Hank. "Applying Themselves." *Pennsylvania Gazette*, May/June 2005.

219 *Some parents have taken*: Zernike, Kate. "Ease Up, Top Colleges Tell Stressed Applicants." *New York Times*, December 7, 2000.

219 *Robert Evans*: Davis, Susan E. "It's the Parents, Stupid." *Diablo*, September 2004.

219 *children can lose self-esteem*: Marano, Hara Estroff.

219 *Colorado junior*: Interview with the student.

220 *aforementioned study*: Johns Hopkins.

220 *Jerome Kagan*: Marano, Hara Estroff; Shea, Christopher. "The Temperamentalist." *Boston Globe*, August 29, 2004.

220 *"Children need"*: Marano, Hara Estroff.

220 *Massachusetts junior*: Interview with the student.

221 *"Parents themselves"*: Marano, Hara Estroff. (The latter part of the quote is from the article subhead.)

221 *parents have sued schools*: Gibbs, Nancy.

221 *YMCA survey*: Keough, Diana.

221 *children's structured sports time . . . family discussions*: Veciana-Suarez, Ana. "Gather Round the Dinner Table." *Miami Herald*, December 7, 2004.

221 *dinners and vacations*: Mattox Jr., William R. "A Diet on Activities." *USA Today*, January 4, 2005.

221 *"warning signs"*: Shellenbarger, Sue. "The Emotional Toll of Being Too Involved in Your Kid's Life." *Wall Street Journal*, April 14, 2005.

222 *"The problem, I'm sure"*: Kelly, Maura.

222 *USA Today op-ed*: Jones, Marilee.

222 *child once said*: Marano, Hara Estroff.

222 *a fifth of parents*: Shellenbarger, Sue.

222 *"much more likely"*: Schweitzer, Sarah.

222 *parents' well-being . . . "feel bad about themselves"*: Shellenbarger, Sue. "The Emotional Toll of Being Too Involved in Your Kid's Life." The source is Missa Murry Eaton of Pennsylvania State University.

222 *City Journal reporter*: Hymowitz, Kay S.

222–223 *parents of a senior*: Yusko, Dennis. "Student Says 2nd Place Rank Unfair." *Times Union*, May 21, 2005.

CHAPTER 10

238 *Alicia Shepard*: Shepard, Alicia C. "A's for Everyone!" *Washington Post Magazine*, June 5, 2005.

239 *When parents complain*: Gibbs, Nancy.

239 *At the college level*: Simon, Anna. "Professors Feel Good-Grade Pressures." *Greenville News*, May 26, 2004.

239 *educational organization in Georgia*: Ghezzi, Patti; MacDonald, Mary. "Pressure to Change Grades Is Common, Teachers Say." *Atlanta Journal-Constitution*, May 8, 2005.

239 *parents threaten*: Gross, Jane.

239 *Emory College*: Interview with Emory dean of admissions Daniel Walls; Marklein, Mary Beth.

239 *the number of teachers*: Gibbs, Nancy. The source is Forest T. Jones, Inc. Also, in a 2004–2005 survey, nearly a third of new teachers said their biggest challenge in schools was communicating with parents; almost three-quarters agreed that too many parents treat teachers as adversaries. *The Metlife Survey of the American Teacher*. 2004–2005.

240 *High school guidance counselors*: Fallows, James.

240 *high school art teacher*: Interview with the teacher.

240 *Ohio private school teacher*: Interview with the teacher.

240 *teacher in Silicon Valley*: Interview with the teacher.

240 *Maine senior*: Interview with the student.

241 *manipulating grading policies*: Marklein, Mary Beth. One interesting phenomenon is that some administrators have been accused of holding students back a year before a major test "in order to make themselves look a bit better." Goldberg, Mark. "Local Discontent with 'No Child Left Behind' Grows." *Christian Science Monitor*, August 19, 2005.

241 *North Carolina . . . their scores*: I first learned of this practice in: Klimek, Brian. "Making a Difference: Cunningham Had Impact." *Southern Pines Pilot*, January 1, 2005. All details were confirmed with (and expounded upon by) Bruce Cunningham, a member of the Moore County Board of Education.

241 *In all, twenty-two . . . school's average*: Interview with Bruce Cunningham.

241 *Bethlehem, Pennsylvania*: Zaroda, Megan. "Battle to Go to Head of the Class a Testy Subject for Area Districts." *Express-Times*, June 26, 2005, which quotes Liberty High School assistant principal Joann Durante.

241 *Bs, teachers say*: Brody, Leslie; Rimbach, Jean. "Grade Inflation: Many See A's as Just Average." *Record*, April 12, 2005.

241 *an increase of .15 points*: Rojstaczer, Stuart. "Where All Grades Are Above Average." *Washington Post*, January 28, 2003.

241 *Harvard's average . . . in 2001*: gradeinflation.com, a Web site maintained by Stuart Rojstaczer.

241 *In the 1990s*: Rojstaczer, Stuart. Also, according to the 2004 National Survey of Student Engagement, approximately two-fifths of college students said they earned mostly A grades, while just 3 percent said they earned mostly Cs or lower.

241 *Princeton . . . A range*: Rojstaczer, Stuart; Arenson, Karen. "Is It Grade Inflation, or Are Students Just Smarter?" *New York Times*, April 18, 2004.

241 *Boston Globe investigation*: McGinn, Daniel.

242 *several factors*: Shepard, Alicia C.

242 *"If I sprinkle"*: Rojstaczer, Stuart.

242 *A 2004 paper*: Nichols, Sharon L. and Berliner, David C. "The Inevitable Corruption of Indicators and Educators Through High-Stakes Testing." Education Policy Studies Laboratory, March 2005.

242 *In Dallas*: Benton, Joshua. "State to Dissolve W-H School Board." *Dallas Morning News*, March 22, 2005.

242 *In Tennessee*: Edmondson, Aimee. "Exams Test Educator Integrity." *Commercial Appeal*, September 21, 2003.

243 *teacher in Nevada*: Nichols, Sharon L.

243 *In California*: Grow, Brian. "A Spate of Cheating—By Teachers." *Business Week*, July 5, 2004.

243 *Staten Island*: Campanile, Carl. "Teachers Cheat: Inflating Regents Scores to Pass Kids." *New York Post*, January 26, 2004.

243 *fourth-grade teacher*: Grow, Brian.

243 *financial incentives*: Gore, Linda. "Do Incentives Cause Teachers to Cheat?" National Bureau for Economic Research, July 2003.

243 *a motivator more powerful*: Goldberg, Mark. "Test Mess 2 . . . ," which cites: Miller, Judy. "ABC News on AOL.com," May 21, 2004, transcribed by Mark Goldberg. "Miller said that many of the 75 teachers involved in a cheating scandal cited pressure as the reason for their behavior."

243 *New York fourth-grade teacher*: Gormley, Michael. "Disturbing New Trend: Teachers Who Cheat." Associated Press, cited in *Buffalo News*, October 28, 2003.

CHAPTER 11

258 *Facebook*: facebook.com.

260 *A 2005 survey*: High School Survey of Student Engagement, 2005. "What We Can Learn From High School Students."

260 *During graduation season*: Borg, Linda.

260 *Montgomery County*: Mathews, Jay. "Deadline Nears for Some to Drop Grades from Middle School." *Washington Post*, April 7, 2005; also see Davis, Ann. "Elite Math Classes Show Increase." *Milwaukee Journal-Sentinel*, October 7, 2003, which reports, "Just as college courses are now in high schools, what are usually thought of as high school courses are turning up more and more in middle schools."

260 *group interview*: Interview with the students. Thanks to Bethany Chamberlin for arranging the Henry Clay group interview.

261 *New Trier*: Thanks to Jim Conroy and staff for arranging the New Trier group interview.

262 *In 1997 . . . was a competitor*: Talbot, Margaret.

262 *senior in Virginia*: Interview with the student.

263 *Caitlin*: Interview with Caitlin.

263 *Haresh*: Interview with Haresh.

263 *Matt*: Interview with Matt.

264 *New England student*: Interview with the student.

264 *A Connecticut junior*: Interview with the student.

264 *a $5 billion business*: Lombardi, Kate Stone; "Some Parents Opt for Prekindergarten Tutoring." *CBS News*, February 21, 2005.

264 *expected to grow*: Hwang, Suein. "Pre-K Prep: How Young Is Too Young for Tutoring?" *Wall Street Journal*, October 13, 2004.

264 *Michigan tutor*: Interview with the tutor.

264 *"normal perfectionist" . . . "neurotic perfectionists"*: Anshel, Mark H. and Mansouri, Hossein. "Influence of Perfectionism on Motor Performance, Affect, and Causal Attributions in Response to Critical Information Feedback." *Journal of Sport Behavior*, June 1, 2005.

264 *so-called middle achievers*: McGinn, Daniel. "Stuck in the Middle." *Boston Globe*, August 28, 2005.

264 *"Every kid"*: Shellenbarger, Sue. "Colleges Ward Off Overinvolved Parents."

265 *"I often feel"*: Interview with Lindsay.

265 *International Baccalaureate student*: Interview with the student.

265 *"I see what's missing"*: Stepp, Laura Sessions.

CHAPTER 12

283 *almost 80 percent*: National Institute on Alcohol Abuse and Alcoholism. "Youth Drinking Trends Stabilize, Consumption Remains High." September 14, 2004.

283 *nearly a third . . . been drunk*: National Institute on Alcohol Abuse and Alcoholism. "Underage Drinking: A Major Public Health Challenge." No. 59, April 2003.

283 *campuses report . . . "go crazy"*: Marano, Hara Estroff.

283 *on the decline*: National Institute on Drug Abuse. "Teen Drug Use Declines 2003–2004." (A release about the 2004 annual Monitoring the Future Survey.) December 21, 2004.

283 *Massachusetts junior*: Interview with the student.

283 *California senior*: Interview with the student.

284 *More than 60 percent*: Morbidity and Mortality Weekly Report (CDC). "Youth Risk Behavior Surveillance." May 21, 2004.

284 *middle schoolers . . . at parties*: Elizabeth, Jane; Carpenter, Mackenzie. "More Kids Are Having Sex, and They're Having It Younger." *Pittsburgh Post-Gazette*, September 14, 2003.

284 *midwestern Latina student*: Interview with the student.

CHAPTER 13

290 *as young as twelve . . . 1993*: Kenney, Edward. "Why Wait? Parents Prod Middle-Schoolers to Take SATs." *News Journal*, May 10, 2004.

290 *Columbia University president*: Bollinger, Lee. "Debate Over the SAT Masks Perilous Trends in College Admissions." *Chronicle of Higher Education*, July 12, 2002.

290 *New York SAT tutor*: Interview with the tutor.

290 *Until 1994*: The landmark go-to book on the SAT: Lemann, Nicholas. *The Big Test: The Secret History of the American Meritocracy*. New York: Farrar, Straus and Giroux, 1999.

290 *"aptitude" . . . students' SAT scores*: Sacks, Peter. "Standardized Testing: Meritocracy's Crooked Yardstick." *Change*, March 13, 1997, which cites a 1991 study by Mark Fetler, California Community College chancellor's office.

290 *in March 2006 . . . scholarship applications*: Arenson, Karen W. "Colleges Say SAT Mistakes May Affect Scholarships." *New York Times*, March 26, 2006; Arenson, Karen

W. "Technical Problems Cause Errors in SAT Test Scores." *New York Times*, March 8, 2006.

290–291 *Students were categorized . . . to use the deep approach*: Ibid. The study was conducted by the National Association of School Psychologists and presented in 1994.

291 *predict students' grades*: Ibid.

291 *Beyond freshman year*: Sacks, Peter. For more information, see Gladwell, Malcolm. "Examined Life: What Stanley H. Kaplan Taught Us About the S.A.T." *New Yorker*, December 17, 2001.

291 *twenty-year study*: Hiss, William C. and Neupane, Prem R. "20 Years of Optional SATs at Bates." Presented to the Trotter Group and the Nieman Foundation, November 8, 2004. See also "20-Year Bates College Study of Optional SATs Finds No Differences." Bates Office of Communications and Media Relations, October 1, 2004.

291 *"Testing is not necessary"*: "SAT Study: 20 Years of Optional Testing," adopted from a Bates College Office of Communications and Media Relations Press Release, October 1, 2004.

291 *William Hiss*: Interview with William Hiss, Bates' Vice President for External Affairs.

291 *In 2000 . . . "test-taking skills"*: Atkinson, Richard. "Does the SAT Level the Playing Field or Unfairly Create a Meritocracy?" *Milwaukee Journal-Sentinel*, April 29, 2001, an excerpt of remarks he made to the College Board in February 2001. Details confirmed in an interview with Richard Atkinson.

291 *struck by . . . analogies*: Barnes, Julian A. "The SAT Revolution." *U.S. News & World Report*, November 11, 2002. Details were confirmed with Richard Atkinson's office.

291–292 *In February 2001 . . . "poorly on the SAT"*: Atkinson, Richard C. "College Admissions and the SAT: A Personal Perspective." Invited address, annual meeting of the American Educational Research Association, San Diego, April 14, 2004.

292 *76,000*: McGrath, Charles. "Writing to the Test." *New York Times*, November 7, 2004.

292 *$28.50*: Gross, Jane. "Sarah Lawrence College Drops SAT Requirement, Saying a New Writing Test Misses the Point." *New York Times*, November 13, 2003.

296 *The exam time*: Dobbs, Michael. "Expensive Coaching Debated as Students Prepare for Revised Exam." *Washington Post*, March 7, 2005.

296 *Analogies . . . Algebra II skills*: Postal, Leslie. "Debut of SAT Essay Has Test Takers Stressed." *Orlando Sentinel*, March 12, 2005.

296 *new SAT . . . sentences and paragraphs*: Ibid; Lewin, Tamar. "SAT Essay Scores Are In, But Will They Be Used?" *New York Times*, May 15, 2005.

296 *Arguably not*: Schaeffer, Bob. "Tossing the Test." *Press-Enterprise*, September 4, 2005.

296–297 *gap between black students and white students*: This thorough and insightful article: Cloud, John. "Inside the New SAT." *Time*, October 27, 2003.

297 *widened in some states*: Chang, Alice L. "Higher Scores, Larger Gaps." *Milwaukee Journal-Sentinel*, August 31, 2005; Vaishnav, Anand. "Mass. SAT Scores Up Again But Racial Disparities Persist." *Boston Globe*, August 31, 2005.

297 *Kaplan Test Prep . . . breaks between sections*: Reimer, Susan. "Longer SAT Just Adds to Takers' Stress." *Baltimore Sun*, March 22, 2005.

297 *National Council of Teachers of English*: Tresaugue, Matthew. "SAT Essays Throw Colleges a Curve." *Houston Chronicle*, May 23, 2005.

297 *Nearly half of 374 schools*: Forelle, Charles. "Many Colleges Ignore New SAT Writing Test." *Wall Street Journal*, December 7, 2005.

297 *MIT . . . length and score*: Ibid; Tresaugue, Matthew.
297 *In 2003 . . . three points*: Cloud, John.
297 *hires thousands of readers*: Katzman, John, Lutz, Andy, and Olson, Eric. "Would Shakespeare Get into Swarthmore?" *Atlantic Monthly*, March 1, 2004.
297 *2.3 million*: Interview with College Board spokeswoman Caren Scoropanos, who gave this figure for 2005.
297 *minute or two per essay*: Katzman, John.
297 *"The pressure to read fast"*: Cloud, John.
297–298 *"To receive a high score . . . Unabomber"*: Katzman, John.
298 *Take the ACT . . . traditionally took the SAT*: Lewin, Tamar. "Strivers Sharpen Their No. 2's for a Different Test for College." *New York Times*, March 4, 2005.
298 *Among 2005 graduates*: Marklein, Mary Beth. "Many Incoming Freshmen Aren't Prepared for College." *USA Today*, August 17, 2005.
298 *22 percent*: Lewin, Tamar.
298 *Richard Atkinson*: Interview with Richard Atkinson.
298 *more than 700*: Schaeffer, Bob.
298–299 *In the months . . . " 'to be part of it:' "* Lewin, Tamar. "SAT Scores Are In, But Will They Be Used?" *New York Times*, May 15, 2005.
299 *"well north" of 20 percent*: Postal, Leslie.
299 *For years the College Board*: Schaeffer, Bob.
299 *Chiara Coletti*: Reimer, Susan; Hoover, Eric. "A Test of Endurance." *Chronicle of Higher Education*, March 25, 2005.
299 *"This new book"*: College Board. *The Official SAT Study Guide: For the New SAT*. Henry Holt, 2004.
299 *$30 million*: Marcus, Jon. "Business Cashes In on SAT Relaunch." *Times Higher Education Supplement*, March 18, 2005.
299 *$9*: Interview with Caren Scoropanos.
299 *"a not-for-profit"*: Collegeboard.com.
299 *In 2006*: Guthrie, Doug. "Easy College Prep Classes Get the Boot." *Detroit News*, August 8, 2005.
300 *College Board's mission*: Cloud, John.
300 *In 2003 some school districts*: Ibid. Also, in an interview, Caren Scoropanos said that the College Board has heard from schools that have changed their curriculum because of the New SAT.
300 *single private group . . . from the general public*: Cloud, John.
300 *"America's overemphasis"*: Atkinson, Richard. "Does the SAT Level the Playing Field or Unfairly Create a Meritocracy?"
300 *In 1994*: Lemann, Nicholas.

CHAPTER 14

315 *universal enhancers*: Deardorff, Julie. "Revving Up the Brain." *Chicago Tribune*, March 7, 2004.
315 *"It won't make"*: Interview with Lawrence Diller.
315 *Doctors report*: Interviews with doctors. When we spoke, Bill Frankenberger was working on a study that he believed would show that the percentage of non-ADD students using these drugs escalated at elite schools.

315 *"It was simple"*: Shoshan, Gabrielle and Briganti, Jessica. "Students Abuse Adderall to Improve Concentration." *Daily Targum*, April 28, 2005.

316 *Several recent studies . . . each finals period*: Interview with Eric Heiligenstein.

316 *"We heard repeatedly"*: Interview with Bill Frankenberger.

316 *2005 study*: Hall, Kristina, et al. "Illicit Use of Prescribed Stimulant Medication Among College Students." *Journal of American College Health*, January/February 2005.

316 *Between 1992 and 2003*: National Center on Addiction and Substance Abuse. "More Than 15 Million Americans Abuse Opioids, Depressants, Stimulants; Teen Abuse Triples in 10 Years." July 7, 2005.

316 *In 2005*: Partnership for a Drug-Free America. "Generation Rx: National Study Reveals New Category of Substance Abuse Emerging: Teens Abusing Rx and OTC Medications Intentionally to Get High." April 21, 2005.

316 *"kiddie coke"*: Weber, Rebecca L. "A Drug Kids Take in Search of Better Grades." *Christian Science Monitor*, November 30, 2004.

316 *Tucson*: Sterba, Jennifer. "ADD Drug Adderall Finds Black Market on School Campuses." *Arizona Daily Star*. November 7, 2004.

316 *Pittsburgh*: Conte, Andrew. "More Students Abusing Hyperactivity Drugs." *Pittsburgh Tribune*, October 25, 2004.

316 *Boulder*: Weber, Rebecca L.

316 *Palm Beach*: Heyman, Steven. "This Prescription Drug for ADD Is Now Being Used by Driven Students Who Want an A." *Palm Beach Post*, June 28, 2004.

316 *$2 to $5*: Interviews with students; Heyman, Steven.

316 *A southern high school senior*: Interview with the student.

317 *Whitman administrators*: Kazzaz, Zak. "Illegal Use of Ritalin, Adderall on the Rise." *Black & White*, October 8, 2004.

317 *"academic steroid"*: Conte, Andrew.

317 *equating non-ADD students*: Deardorff, Julie.

317 *"The drugs enhance"*: Interview with Eric Heiligenstein.

317 *"even though they"*: Interview with the junior.

317 *Ava Kaufman*: Interview with Ava Kaufman.

325 *San Francisco Bay area mother*: Interview with the parent.

325 *Erika*: Interview with Erika.

326 *Shiv*: Interview with Shiv.

326 *"You can't walk"*: Interview with Jim Conroy.

326 *four of New Trier's*: Group interview with the students.

327 *small New England*: Interview with the college counselor at that school.

327 *school in Dallas*: Interview with a recent graduate.

327 *top 10 percent*: Wertheimer, Linda K. "The New College Try." *Dallas Morning News*, May 12, 2003.

328 *Chiara Coletti*: Lewin, Tamar. "Strivers Sharpen Their No. 2's for a Different Test for College."

328 *economists*: Frank, Robert H. and Cook, Philip J. *The Winner-Take-All Society*. New York: The Free Press, 1995.

328 *$25.9 billion*: Associated Press. "Harvard Endowment Cracks $25 Billion." Cited on CNN.com, September 30, 2005.

328 *Lawrence Summers*: Summers, Lawrence H. "Every Child Getting Ahead: The Role of Education." College Board Forum. Chicago, November 1, 2004.

328 *Less than two months later:* Daily Yomiuri.
329 *"We can all agree":* Summers, Lawrence H.

CHAPTER 15

334 *couples put:* "School at Home." Hammack, Lawrence. "50 Years of Learning Added to Playing." *Roanoke Times,* October 20, 2003; Hawkins, Christy. "Fulfilling a Vision for Muslims." *Dallas Morning News,* July 23, 1997; Bogoslavsky, Becky. "Hurry Up and Wait." *Arkansas Democrat-Gazette,* August 15, 2001.

334 *"fetal speakers":* Bébé Sounds' Prenatal Teacher product information.

334 *"You're never too young":* BabyPlus "advertorial."

334 *"The stimulation":* Bébé Sounds' Prenatal Teacher product information.

334 *"maximize":* Zaslow, Jeffrey. "Moving On: Really Early Education." *Wall Street Journal,* April 29, 2004.

334 *Prenatal University:* Ibid.

335 *Genius Products' "IQ Builder":* Macdonald, G. Jeffrey. "Smarter Toys, Smarter Tots?" *Christian Science Monitor,* August 20, 2003.

335 *"sophisticated CD-ROM" games:* One such product, "Dada DaVinci," is advertised on GeniusBabies.com as part of the "Baby CEO" package. Enough said.

335 *Junior Kumon:* Hwang, Suein. "Pre-K Prep." *Wall Street Journal,* October 13, 2004.

335 *syllabi for . . . playtime:* Lombardi, Kate Stone.

335 *brain development niche:* Macdonald, G. Jeffrey.

335 *In 1981 . . . two hours:* Winerip, Michael. "Homework Bound." *New York Times,* January 3, 1999, which cites the Institute for Social Research at the University of Michigan.

335 *twelve hours per week:* Fuller, Laurie. "Make Time for Childhood." *Orlando Sentinel,* August 1, 2004.

335 *school day:* This widely respected article: Brooks, David. "The Organization Kid." *Atlantic Monthly,* April 2001.

336–337 *even kindergartners . . . "developmental kindergarten anymore":* Hutkin, Erinn. "More Time to Learn." *Ventura County Star,* October 4, 2004.

336 *65 percent:* Associated Press. "More Kindergartners in for a Full Day." Cited on CNN.com, August 31, 2005.

336 *six to eight hours of homework:* Interviews with students; Rocha, Alexandria. "Students Scramble to Get into Brand-Name Colleges." *Palo Alto Online Weekly,* February 9, 2005.

336 *summer classes:* Kronholz, June. "Cram Sessions."

336 *Some teen tours:* Keys, Lisa. "High (School) Anxiety: The Latest Gift of the Jews." *Forward,* August 9, 2002.

336 *waiting lists:* Perlstein, Linda. "For Teens with Means, Camp Isn't a Cabin—It's the Caribbean." *Washington Post,* July 6, 2004.

336 *"the more important":* Kronholz, June. "Cram Sessions."

337 *twelve minutes a day:* Kolata, Gina. "While Children Grow Fatter, Experts Search for Solutions." *New York Times,* October 19, 2000.

337 *"a session of Future Workaholics":* Brooks, David.

337 *"The marvelously anarchic institution":* Kluger, Jeffrey.

337 *Piping music:* Brody, Jane E. "Science Watch." *New York Times,* March 31, 1993.

337 *Excessively flipping flash cards:* Kluger, Jeffrey.

337 *Leaving children in front of DVDs*: Macdonald, G. Jeffrey.

338 *"the type and amount of stimulation"*: Kluger, Jeffrey.

349 *40 percent of elementary schools*: Schindehette, Susan, et al. "Learning to Chill." *People*, September 23, 2002.

349 *20 percent drop*: Tyre, Peg. "Reading, Writing, Recess." *Newsweek*, November 3, 2003.

349 *Many young students*: deGregory, Lane. "Out of Play." *St. Petersburg Times*, March 29, 2005.

349 *Officials*: U.S. Fed News. "Sen. Harkin Addresses Healthy Schools Summit in Washington." September 27, 2005; Deam, Jenny. "A plea for play." *Denver Post*, March 22, 2005.

349 *litigious society*: Johnson, Dirk. "Many Schools Putting an End to Child's Play." *New York Times*, April 7, 1998.

349 *playground equipment*: deGregory, Lane.

349 *children's physical activity*: Deam, Jenny.

349 *Oklahoma elementary school principal*: Pemberton, Tricia. " 'Tag, You're It' Still a Favorite." *Daily Oklahoman*, November 5, 2003.

350 *Recent research revealed*: National Association of Early Childhood Specialists in State Departments of Education. "Recess and the Importance of Play." A position statement.

350 *Judith C. Young*: National Association for Sport and Physical Education. "NASPE Tells Parents & Elementary School Officials 'Recess Is a Must!' " July 23, 2003.

350 *"Many parents still don't quite get it"*: Johnson, Dirk.

350 *The California School Boards Association*: CSBA, "Linkages Between Student Health and Academic Achievement," which cites Symons, Cynthia Wolford. "Bringing Student Health Risks and Academic Achievement through Comprehensive School Health Programs." *Journal of School Health*, August 1997.

350 *Georgia State University*: Jarrett, Olga S. and Maxwell, Darlene M. "Physical Education and Recess: Are Both Necessary?" *IPA/USA* (International Play Association), Spring 1999.

350 *California Department of Education study*: "State Study Proves Physically Fit Kids Perform Better Academically." California Department of Education, December 2002.

351 *furthers their social development . . . anxiety*: Council on Physical Education for Children. "Recess in Elementary Schools." A NASPE position paper. July 2001.

351 *by observing children's behavior*: Jarrett, Olga S. "Recess in Elementary School: What Does the Research Say?" *ERIC Digest*, July 2002.

351 *claim to compensate*: Collins, Quincy C. "Time for Recess?" *Corpus Christi Caller-Times*, October 5, 2003.

351 *During her study . . . "I do scream!"*: Jarrett, Olga S. "Physical Education and Recess."

351 *"Recess should not"*: Jarrett, Olga S. "Recess in Elementary School."

351 *Angry parents*: Meiser, Rebecca. "Rise Up for Recess." *New Times*, September 18, 2003.

351 *conflicting messages*: Ferrandino, Vincent L. and Tirozzi, Gerald N. "Healthy Students Are Better Students." *Education Week*, October 9, 2002.

351 *United Nations' Convention*: unicef.org/crc.

352 *Article 31*: United Nations. "Convention on the Rights of the Child."

352 *Japan and Taiwan*: Jarrett, Olga S., et al. "Impact of Recess on Classroom Behavior."

A revision of a paper presented to the American Educational Research Association, April 1998.

352 *other than Somalia*: Child Rights Information Network. "Convention on the Rights of the Child." Thanks to Audrey Skrupskelis, President of the American Association for the Child's Right to Play, for confirming details and discussing the issues.

357 *two to three times higher*: Wilburn, Victor R. and Smith, Delores E. "Stress, Self-Esteem, and Suicidal Ideation in Late Adolescents." *Adolescence*, Spring 2005.

357 *between eight and twenty-five*: National Institute of Mental Health, "In Harm's Way." 2003.

357 *16.5 percent*: Centers for Disease Control and Prevention. "Youth Risk Behavior Survey 2003."

357 *one in four*: Swanson, Stevenson. "Student Suicides Spur Action on Campus." *Chicago Tribune*, October 12, 2004. Suicide is the second-leading cause of death among college students. Gately, Gary. "Colleges Target Mental Health." *Boston Globe*, April 17, 2005.

358 *Gail Griffith*: Griffith, Gail. "The Choice of Life." *Washington Post*, May 17, 2005.

358 *A 2005 article*: Wilburn, Victor R.

358 *1999 survey*: "Who's Who Among American High School Students Annual Survey of High Achievers," 1999.

358 *climbing most quickly*: Marano, Hara Estroff.

358 *Anxiety is the most common*: Ferguson, Sue. "Stressed Out!" *MacLean's*, November 22, 2004.

358 *nine-year-olds*: Keough, Diana.

358 *strong link*: Ferguson, Sue; Elias, Marilyn. "Childhood Depression." *USA Today*, August 13, 1998.

358 *Illinois teen*: Interview with the student.

358 *The Crimson*: Kaplan, Katharine A. "College Faces Mental Health Crisis." *Harvard Crimson*, January 12, 2004.

358 *69 percent jump*: Atwood, Sally. "Someone to Watch Over Me." *Technology Review*, March 2003; Sontag, Deborah. "Who Was Responsible for Elizabeth Shin?" *New York Times*, April 28, 2002.

359 *A Maryland International Baccalaureate student*: Interview with the student.

359 *A 2004 survey*: Kadison, Richard. "The Mental Health Crisis." *Chronicle of Higher Education*, December 10, 2004.

359 *In 1996 . . . problems*: Marano, Hara Estroff.

359 *Kansas State University . . . 25 percent*: Young, Jeffrey. "Prozac Campus." *Chronicle of Higher Education*, February 14, 2003.

359 *self-injury cases*: Gallagher, Robert P.

359 *including cutting*: Marano, Hara Estroff.

359 *Experts call*: Interviews with Armando Favazza, author of *Bodies Under Siege*, and Karen Conterio, coauthor of *Bodily Harm*; kidshealth.org, a Nemours Foundation Web site.

359 *Lancy Chui*: Ames, Mark. "Capturing the Saratogans." *Metroactive*, February 19, 2004.

359 *California student*: Sevilla, Joannie. "Counseling Program Targets Teen Drug Use, Gang Involvement." *San Jose Mercury News*, May 8, 2003. Also, thanks to Razelle Buenavista.

359 *senior in 2000*: Mai-Cutler, Kim. "The Meaning of Success." *WireTap*, October 23, 2001.

359 *Massachusetts senior:* Interview with the student.

359 *Alan Berman:* Interview with Alan Berman.

360 *MIT:* Healy, Patrick. "Death at MIT." *The Boston Globe,* February 5, 2001; Saulnier, Beth and Tregaskis, Sharon. "A Sympathetic Ear." *Cornell Magazine,* November 2000.

360 *At NYU:* McGinn, Daniel and Depasquale, Ron. "Dealing With Depression." *Newsweek,* August 23, 2004; Swanson, Stevenson.

360 *Harvard, too, has stepped up efforts:* Interview with Richard Kadison.

361–362 *In 2000 . . . "unrealistic expectations":* Fitzsimmons, William, et al. "Time Out or Burn Out for the Next Generation." *New York Times,* December 6, 2000.

362 *"teacups":* Phrase used in: Shellenbarger, Sue. "What to Do When You Are Worried That Your Child Has a Bad Teacher." *Wall Street Journal,* September 29, 2005.

362 *"If we think":* McGinn, Daniel and Depasquale, Ron.

CHAPTER 16

374 *thousands of twentysomethings:* I have interviewed twentysomethings about this subject over the last six years.

375 *"are the most honed":* Brooks, David.

375 *twenty-five-year-old:* Interview with the woman.

376 *Mark:* Interview with Mark.

376 *Rachel Simmons:* Interview with Rachel Simmons.

CHAPTER 17

386 *A month after:* Interviews with Charles.

387 *2010:* NACAC's "State of College Admission" 2005.

388 *nearly 50 percent:* McGinn, Daniel. "Making the Grade." *Boston Globe Magazine,* January 9, 2005.

388 *"It's just achieving":* Interview with Thomas.

388 *high teen suicide rates:* In South Korea, more than eight out of every 100,000 students aged fifteen to nineteen committed suicide in 2003. Sang-hun, Choe. In the United States, the National Institute of Mental Health reports that the suicide rate for the same age group was 8.2 deaths per 100,000 teenagers, and 10.4 of every 100,000 fifteen- to twenty-four-year-olds. "In Harm's Way."

389 *"Today it seems":* Interview with Bill Fitzsimmons.

389 *since 1974:* "State of College Admission" 2005.

389 *2,000:* Samuels, Rebecca. "Private Counselors Help College-Bound Find a Calling." *CBS Marketwatch,* October 18, 2002.

389 *225:* Smolkin, Rachel. "Top Colleges Are Getting Tougher on Admissions as Applications Soar." *Plain Dealer,* September 19, 1999.

390 *8.6 percent:* Okwu, Michael. "Many High School Students Not Getting Into Colleges They Want." *Today,* April 7, 2006.

391 *more than ten years:* Borg, Linda.

391 *"performance assessment":* Sacks, Peter.

391–392 *Thomas at New Trier . . . " 'someone else's class?' ":* Interviews with Thomas and Carolyn.

392 *Stressbusters:* I observed several Stressbusters meetings. Some of the ideas in this section originally were Stressbusters suggestions.

393 *When I asked admissions officers*: Interviews with admissions officers.

393 *Reed reports*: Diver, Colin.

393 *single upside*: Interviews with admissions officers.

394 *In 2001*: Atkinson, Richard. "Does the SAT Level the Playing Field or Unfairly Create a Meritocracy?"

394 *Until 2003*: NACAC's "State of College Admission" 2005.

394 *85 percent*: Gallagher, Robert P. "National Survey of Counseling Center Directors." The International Association of Counseling Services, 2004; Atwood, Sally.

395 *Harvard holds workshops*: Interview with Richard Kadison.

395 *University of Maryland*: Gately, Gary.

395 *Duke changed its application*: Zernike, Kate.

395 *MIT and Bowdoin*: Interview with James Miller; Marklein, Mary Beth. "Is There Any Truth to Today's Résumés?"

396 *University of Michigan*: Ferguson, Sue.

397 *fewer than half*: Capuzzo, Michael. "Who Hit That Home Run?" *Parade*, August 21, 2005.

398 *In Hawaii*: Interviews with Earl Hotta and a Kauai high school vice principal.

398 *respondents listed Princeton*: Frank, Robert H., who cites Kingston, Paul W., and Lionel S. Lewis, eds. *The High-Status Track: Studies of Elite Schools and Stratification*. Albany: State University of New York, 1990.

398 *more than one tenth*: "Time Off before College Can Be Worthwhile." CNN.com, July 11, 2005.

399 *"unrewarding"*: This tip comes courtesy of author Rachel Simmons.

Acknowledgments

Attendance

First, I am extraordinarily lucky to have brilliant, kind, loving, generous, and funny parents, whose unwavering support and enthusiasm mean everything to me. Every day of my life I feel deeply fortunate that I am their daughter.

By nature, it's difficult for overachievers to accept that they cannot do everything by themselves. With this book, for the first time in my career, I asked for help. Missy Robbins spent the better part of six weeks holed up with me in my office to do massive amounts of research. I am extremely grateful and humbled by her Herculean efforts, and could not have asked for a more talented and insightful partner. Plus, she invented great snacks.

I am eternally thankful to Dave Robbins. I also would like to acknowledge my brother, Andrew, grandfather Irving, and aunt Ellie for their continuing encouragement and for the joy they bring to my life.

Participation

I could not have asked for more wonderful people to follow for this book. Julie, Audrey, Frank, Taylor, Sam, Pete, C.J., and Ryland not only let me into their lives, but also embraced me as a new part of those lives. The challenge in doing a book about high-achieving students is that they are the very students who have the fewest hours to be involved with another project. Yet these students were incredibly generous with their time and brutally honest about their self-assessments. I will always be grateful to these lovable "sources," many of whom will be my lifelong friends. I hope they are as proud to be a part of this book as I am to have them in it. I also wish to thank their parents, as well as the supporting cast, particularly Richard, Mike, Andrew, Kristen, Isabel, Derek, Cliff, Ellie, Hugh, and Brad.

Thanks also to the hundreds of students across the country who allowed me to interview them, individually or in groups, most notably Charles in Portales.

Extra Credit

In addition to the acknowledgments throughout the Endnotes, I'd like to extend special thanks to the *Black & White* staff and to the Whitman administrators, especially Alan Goodwin, Fran Landau, and Jerry Marco. At Trinity, June Hilton, Hank Moses, Ann Fusco, and Jen Levine were gracious hosts. I was inspired by Whitman's Stressbusters committee, including Terese Bernstein, Anne Hollander, Beth Isen, Suzi Kaplan, Margi Kramer, Leslie Saum, and Bekki Sims. Mary Anne Schwalbe was a terrific guru. I thank Sue Feldman and Erika Lehman for their sourcing help, and Cynthia Loeb and Superintendent Jerry Weast of Montgomery County Public Schools for allowing me access to school grounds.

Homework

I owe a great deal to my manuscript readers, who went above and beyond the call of duty to make *The Overachievers* a better book: my parents; the hilarious Nick Bernstein, who has been my sounding board since we were six; and Sebastian Rupley, a genius whose editorial insights and shrewd observations are invaluable to me.

At Hyperion, I'm honored to have the attention of the wise and wonderful editor in chief, Will Schwalbe, whose great devotion to and excitement about this project since its inception buoyed me through long workdays. I'm grateful for his thoughtful edits, attention to detail, and cheerful willingness to go the extra mile for several aspects of this book. I jumped for joy at the chance to work again with indefatigable super-publicist Beth Dickey, who is not only fantastic at what she does, but also heaps of fun to work with.

Also, my appreciation to Andrea Kirk, Michael Prevett and the gang at Relevant Entertainment, Katie Wainwright, Leslie Wells, Bob Miller, Ellen Archer, Mary Ellen O'Neill, Sarah Lazin, Emily Gould, Beth Thomas, Claire McKean, and Charlie Davidson.

Paula Balzer has been my professional and personal rock for seven years. She is indubitably the "best match" for me. But, then, she also had me at the chocolates.

Non-Test-Based Performance Assessment

Finally, I wish to thank my readers, whose support and feedback I continue to receive and respond to at alexandrarobbins.com.